Asheville-Buncombe
Technical Community College
Learning Resources Center
340 Victoria Road
Asheville, NC 28801

DISCARDED

AUG 4 2025

Teaching Manual for

Jesus of History, Christ of Faith

Teaching Manual for

Jesus of History, Christ of Faith

by
Thomas Zanzig

Revised Edition

Saint Mary's Press
Christian Brothers Publications
Winona, Minnesota

The publishing team for this manual included Julia Ahlers and Barbara Allaire, development editors; Yvette Nelson, test question developer; Susan Baranczyk, copy editor; Gary J. Boisvert, production editor and typesetter; Steve Michaels, illustrator; pre-press, printing, and binding by the graphics division of Saint Mary's Press.

The scriptural quotations in chapters 1–5 are from the New American Bible with Revised New Testament. Copyright © 1986 by the Confraternity of Christian Doctrine, Washington, D.C. All rights reserved.

The scriptural quotations in chapters 6–13 are from the New Revised Standard Version of the Bible. Copyright © 1989 by the Division of Christian Education of the National Council of the Churches of Christ in the United States of America. Used with permission.

The activities "A Dramatic Reading: 'The Samaritan Woman at the Well,'" page 79 and handout 3–A; "A Plan of Action," pages 128–129; "A Short Story: 'The Window,'" pages 141–143; "The Labor Game," pages 143–144; and "'The Sermon of the Mouse,'" page 234 and handout 13–C are adapted from *Creative Learning Experiences,* edited by Wayne Rice, John Roberto, and Mike Yaconelli (Winona, MN: Saint Mary's Press, 1981), pages 104–106, 83, 96–98, 125–126, and 77–80, respectively. Copyright © 1981 by Youth Specialties. Used with permission of Youth Specialties.

The activity "A Service Project: Making a 'Parking Lot Palestine,'" page 89, is taken from *Creative Projects and Worship Experiences,* edited by Wayne Rice, John Roberto, and Mike Yaconelli (Winona, MN: Saint Mary's Press, 1981), pages 27–28. Copyright © 1981 by Youth Specialties. Used with permission of Youth Specialties.

The guided fantasy prayer on page 188 is from *Sadhana: A Way to God,* by Anthony de Mello (New York: Doubleday, 1978), pages 87–88. Copyright © 1978 by Anthony de Mello. Used with permission of the publisher.

The Nicene Creed, used on handout 13–B, "The Nicene Creed Today," is the English translation by the International Consultation on English texts.

Copyright © 1992 by Saint Mary's Press, 702 Terrace Heights, Winona, MN 55987-1320. All rights reserved. Permission is granted to reproduce only those materials intended for distribution to the students. No other part of this manual may be reproduced by any means without the written permission of the publisher.

Printed in the United States of America

Printing: 8 7 6 5 4 3
Year: 2001 00 99 98 97 96

ISBN 0-88489-274-3

Genuine recycled paper with 10% post-consumer waste.
Printed with soy-based ink.

About the Author

Thomas Zanzig has a bachelor's degree in theology and sociology from Marquette University, and a master's degree in pastoral theology from Saint Mary-of-the-Woods College, Indiana. After nearly ten years in parish ministry as a DRE in Wisconsin, Tom joined the staff of Saint Mary's Press as a writer, editor, and consultant.

In addition to *Jesus of History, Christ of Faith*, Tom has authored the popular ninth-grade text, *Understanding Catholic Christianity*. Tom served as general editor of the junior high parish series, Discovering, and was both general editor and contributing author for the recently published Horizons Program for senior high students. He is also the author of the senior high confirmation program, *Confirmed in a Faithful Community*.

Tom has received the National Youth Ministry Award from the National Federation for Catholic Youth Ministry for his more than twenty-five years of service to the church and his contributions to youth ministry as an author. He has also received the LaSallian Distinguished Educator Award from the Christian Brothers. He is a popular workshop and convention presenter throughout the United States and Canada, and has also directed conferences on youth ministry in Germany and Australia.

Tom is married to Kate, and they and their two children, Adam and Barbara, reside in Winona, Minnesota.

Contents

Preface 9

Part 1: Background for Teaching This Course

An Introduction to *Jesus of History, Christ of Faith* 13
Pedagogical Background 27
Lesson Planning 32

Part 2: Teaching Strategies for This Course

1. **The Search for Jesus:**
   Sources in the Christian Testament and Beyond 41
   1–A To Know Another 54

2. **The Gospels:**
   Central Sources for Understanding Jesus 55
   2–A A Reference Guide to the Gospel Story 65

3. **The World of Jesus:**
   History and Politics 67
   3–A The Samaritan Woman at the Well 83

4. **Daily Life in Jesus' Time:**
   Culture and Religion 85
   4–A Searching the Scriptures for the World of Jesus 98

5. **The Mission Begins:**
   Preparing the Way of the Lord 99
   5–A Jesus' Priorities 111

6. **The Kingdom of God:**
   Proclaiming the Dream of Jesus 112
   6–A Who Is Your God? 130
   6–B The Consequences of Moral Decisions 131

7. **Jesus Speaks:**
   Sayings and Stories of the Kingdom 132
   7–A Paraphrasing the Sermon on the Mount: The Beatitudes . . . 146
   7–B Paraphrasing the Sermon on the Mount:
        Being Salt and Light 147
   7–C Paraphrasing the Sermon on the Mount:
        Loving Your Enemy 148
   7–D Paraphrasing the Sermon on the Mount:
        Not Being a Hypocrite 149

    7–E Paraphrasing the Sermon on the Mount:
          How to Pray 150
    7–F Paraphrasing the Sermon on the Mount:
          Not Judging Others 151
    7–G Paraphrasing the Sermon on the Mount:
          Hearing and Acting on the Word of God 152

8. **Jesus Heals:**
   Signs of the Kingdom 153

9. **The Cross:**
   The End or a Beginning? 166

10. **The Resurrection:**
    God Is Victorious! Jesus Is Lord! 179
        10–A The Disciples' Dilemma 193
        10–B The Titles for Jesus 194

11. **Paul:**
    Apostle to the Gentiles 195

12. **The Letters of Paul:**
    Proclaiming Christ Crucified and Risen 204
        12–A The Ideal Church: Romans, Chapter 12 220

13. **Good News from Age to Age:**
    The Church's Understanding of Jesus Christ 221
        13–A Helping the Church of Today and Tomorrow 236
        13–B The Nicene Creed Today 237
        13–C The Sermon of the Mouse 239

Appendices

1. **Sample Test Questions** 243
2. **The Learning Process and This Course** 283
3. **The Teacher as a Witness of Faith** 287
4. **Suggestions for Effective Teaching** 291
5. **An Annotated Bibliography on Christology** 295
6. **A Pretest: "The Good News: Did We Hear It?"** 298

Handout Masters 303

Preface

Our understanding of Jesus is at the heart of our identity as a Catholic Christian community and as persons of faith. Therefore, a thorough, solidly researched, and clear presentation of the life, ministry, message, and meaning of Jesus must be at the center of a complete high school religion curriculum. The revised edition of *Jesus of History, Christ of Faith* provides just such a presentation.

It is important that you, the teacher, recognize the relationship between the student text and the teaching manual for this course. The student text establishes the basic theological content and pedagogical direction of the course. In that sense it provides the "what" of the course, assuring you that the students are given a solid and reliable foundation of information. The teaching manual is designed to provide the "why" and the "how" of the course:
- It provides a thorough explanation of the theology and pedagogy of the course.
- It offers detailed guidance for you as you organize your personal approach to teaching the course.
- It provides numerous practical and creative strategies for effectively communicating the material to the students in the classroom.

The student text and the teaching manual should therefore be seen as complementary and mutually supportive, one relying upon the other. You are encouraged to thoroughly read *both* the student text and the teaching manual before beginning your actual class preparations. Teachers, particularly when teaching a course for the first time, tend to look immediately to "the practical stuff," the "nitty-gritty" ideas and information that can make day-to-day teaching more effective. That kind of material *is* provided in this manual, and you may reasonably want to look ahead to satisfy your curiosity. However, to make the most of all that information, you will need to be fully familiar with the theological and pedagogical foundations of the course.

Two Parts

This teaching manual consists of two parts.

Part 1: Background for Teaching This Course

Part 1 includes three sections of valuable background information for the teacher:
- An "Introduction to *Jesus of History, Christ of Faith,*" which provides material on the theology and content of the course and a brief discussion of the course in light of the characteristics of adolescent faith development
- "Pedagogical Background," which offers a perspective on the learning process and suggests grading procedures
- "Lesson Planning," which describes the teaching tools for the course and a method of planning and scheduling

Part 2: Teaching Strategies for This Course

Part 2 is the heart of this manual—teaching strategies for every major concept in every chapter of the course. In fact, the manual provides so many strategies for classroom teaching that you could not possibly use them all in one course term. You will therefore have to choose from among many optional activities and methods when teaching each concept, at times excluding attractive activities due to a lack of time. (Most likely, though, you will find this preferable to having to create strategies on your own!) The abundance of material suggested in part 2 is the primary reason for including the information on scheduling and lesson planning in part 1. Without a well-planned approach, a teacher may spend too much time on one topic or concept and never complete the student text with his or her class.

And there is more. In addition to all the helpful information in parts 1 and 2, at the end of this manual you will find a series of appendices that may enhance the effectiveness of your teaching:
1. a bank of test questions for each chapter
2. a thorough discussion of the learning process supported by Saint Mary's Press—a process reflected in the content and organization of this course
3. an essay on the role of the teacher as a witness of faith and the implications of that role for your teaching of this course
4. practical suggestions for effective teaching, including guidance on how to use the kind of group exercises frequently recommended in this manual
5. an annotated bibliography on Christology
6. a questionnaire to assess the students' knowledge of Jesus

A Personal Note

I would like to add a final, personal note. The development of the original *Jesus of History, Christ of Faith* course, nearly a decade ago, represented the richest and most exciting period of study, research, and prayerful reflection I had experienced to that point in my life. Since then, I have continued, with the grace of God, to grow in many facets of my life, both personally and professionally. I have had the opportunity and challenge of writing a number of educational resources, of editing many more, of traveling and continuing my studies, and of deepening my spirituality. After all of that, my work on this extensive revision of the original course is my most satisfying and gratifying professional endeavor yet. For everyone involved—the editors, proofreaders, designers, and more—the project has been an act of both faith and love.

My hope and prayer—indeed, my expectation—is that you will find your own faith deeply enlivened and enriched through your teaching of this course. Admittedly, it is a difficult challenge that you face, but it is a marvelous opportunity as well. I have been given a great gift by having the "job" of developing a course such as this. I hope you can enthusiastically accept the chance to teach it as a gift to you as well. That attitude on your part, as much as any other preparation you might commit to, will ensure your success with *Jesus of History, Christ of Faith*.

TOM ZANZIG

Part 1
Background for Teaching This Course

An Introduction to *Jesus of History, Christ of Faith*

This section will introduce you to these aspects of *Jesus of History, Christ of Faith:*
- the theology and content of the course
- considerations about adolescent faith development and consequent implications for teaching the course

The Theology of the Course

The Roman Catholic church's understanding of Jesus, and the means used to approach and achieve that understanding, is at the center of everything Catholic Christians believe, do, and in fact *are* as persons of faith. All of Christian experience—the church's doctrinal understanding of the faith, its communal worship, its moral values and convictions, and more—might be viewed as similar to a calm pool in which believers are nurtured, refreshed, cleansed, and renewed. Whenever a new insight into Jesus and his meaning is discovered, it is as if a pebble were dropped into that pool. Regardless of the pebble's size, it has an impact and a gradually expanding influence upon the entire pool. The effects of the new insight ripple out, in what are often imperceptible waves, to touch and alter the church's doctrinal understanding, prayer, values—virtually every facet of Christian life.

Vatican Council II concerned itself primarily with ecclesiology, that is, with the nature of the church, its mission in the world, the understanding of sacrament, and so on. Almost immediately after the council ended, many claimed the need for the convening of Vatican Council III, a church council that would be committed solely to studying the identity, nature, role, and message of Jesus Christ. There can be no doubt, however, that behind all the dramatic changes brought about by Vatican Council II—changes in liturgy, in practices required of Catholic Christians, in the role of the laity, in the roles and lifestyles of priests and religious—*behind all of that* was a new, enriched (though not necessarily clearly defined) understanding of Jesus, his message, and his meaning for the contemporary world.

In recent decades, that changed understanding of Jesus has been given greater clarity. The number of books on Christology seems to have multiplied geometrically, and these are not just popular books intended to inspire us but also highly academic and scholarly works representing the most intensive and disciplined research. The task that confronts us as educators, I believe, is to make the information in all that material accessible and understandable to the widest possible number of people in the church, in our case particularly to the young people we encounter in religion classes. Our responsibility is to pass on to them an understanding of Jesus that is grounded in truth, the truth as Jesus offered it to us nearly two thousand years ago. Thanks largely to remarkable advances in scriptural study, we today—perhaps more so than Christians at any time in history—are capable of getting in touch with the central meaning of Jesus, a meaning free from many of the historical and cultural embellishments that have often clouded our understanding of him. The intention of *Jesus of History, Christ of Faith* is to present a sound and truthful understanding of Jesus and his message.

An aside: I am aware that many teachers of this course will be familiar with the theological shifts that have taken place in Christology in recent decades. Some students' parents, however, may not be familiar with these shifts and, as a result, may be uncomfortable with the course's approach to Jesus. The information presented here can serve as a helpful resource for teachers trying to explain the approach of the course to such parents.

Where We Have Been: A Christology from Above

Catholics who had their formative religious education before the Second Vatican Council were given an understanding of Jesus quite unlike the one that has been emerging in recent decades. For hundreds of years in the church, beginning as far back as the second century, the church's understanding of Jesus had been highly doctrinal and theological rather than biblical, gradually developing into what scholars call a "high Christology," a "Christology from above," or a "descending Christology." This means that Catholic Christians tended to concentrate relatively little on the historical Jesus who walked the dusty roads of Palestine nearly two thousand years ago. Instead, they focused on the meaning of his life and message as interpreted by theologians and scholars and as officially defined by the church through the centuries.

I would like to summarize here what I feel are the major theological characteristics of a Christology from above, with which many adult Catholics have been raised. Later in this essay, this Christology will be compared with today's Christology.

The Scriptures as God's exact words: The first point to note about a Christology from above is the understanding of the Scriptures that undergirds it. Many of us were raised to view the Gospels, for example, as historical documents almost literally dictated by God to mesmerized authors. Paintings and wood carvings through the centuries often pictured the Evangelists seated at desks with quill in hand, an angel hovering over their shoulders and at times actually touching their hands as they wrote. As will be seen in a moment, a new understanding of the Gospels' development has been a fundamental reason for the change in the understanding of Jesus.

An emphasis on the fall from grace and the need for redemption: The second theological characteristic of a Christology from above is the understanding that the plan of God rests on the alienation of humanity from God through sin (the fall from grace due to original sin) and our consequent need for redemption. This is perhaps most clearly reflected in the great stress that may have been placed on the Adam and Eve story in our education as children.

A distant God: Another characteristic of a high Christology is the concept of God as one who is "out there," removed from humanity—in a sense, beyond us. Jesus is recognized as a kind of intermediary between humanity and a God who is too distant to be accessible to us. One common image from the pre–Vatican Council II era that might reflect this transcendent God is the "eye in a triangle," an image far removed from that of the loving Parent so strongly advocated today.

Jesus as the pre-existent Word: A fourth theological characteristic of this approach to Christology is an emphasis on Jesus as the pre-existent Word of God and the second person of the Blessed Trinity, who was sent by God to be our Savior by ransoming us from our slavery to sin. Please be clear on what I am saying here: I am *not* implying that this doctrinal understanding of Jesus is a false one. But contemporary theologians recognize that when we *begin* our understanding of Jesus with the concept of him as the pre-existent Word, when we *start* with this focus in mind, our total understanding of Jesus' humanity is affected. For instance, with this concept of Jesus as our starting point, it seems only reasonable to believe that Jesus, from birth, would have been fully conscious of his identity as God and fully conscious as well of his role in the plan of God. This has dramatic implications for our understanding of his ministry, his miracles, and the meaning of his death.

The Perfect Sacrifice: Finally, a Christology from above recognizes that Jesus saved us by "dying for our sins," thereby satisfying God with an act of perfect sacrifice, one beyond the reach of people. This death won God's favor, and the gates of heaven were reopened. To put it another way—the way we may well have learned it as children—Jesus died for our sins as a kind of payment to God for Adam and Eve's offense, for which we inherited the guilt.

We can say that a Christology from above emphasizes the following dimensions of Jesus' life and message:
- his divinity as the pre-existent Word of God and the second person of the Trinity
- his incarnation as a man, with his birth recognized as *the* central Christian mystery (leading to an emphasis on Christmas as the central Christian feast)
- his sacrificial and salvific death (leading to an emphasis on the cross as a major Christian symbol and on the sense of the Eucharist as primarily "a re-enactment of Calvary," as "the sacrifice of the Mass")
- salvation of the individual as being accomplished through baptism (which "unites us with Jesus' death") and adherence to the will of God, particularly as it is discerned by the leaders of the Mystical Body, the church

This theological understanding of Jesus has been with the church for hundreds of years. As noted earlier, many adult Catholics were raised with this basic approach for at least a good part of their life, and they may still have it as their underlying theology. This is neither good nor bad perhaps, but it is important to recognize this fact as you prepare to teach this course. The Christology represented by *Jesus of History, Christ of Faith* offers a significantly different approach to understanding Jesus, an approach that in turn results in a large shift in our emphasis when discussing him and his message. Before clarifying the new approach, however, we must pause and ask: Why did things change so much? What caused the shift in the church's perspective on Jesus?

What Happened to Christology from Above?

When trying to identify the causes of the change that has occurred in the church over recent decades, there is an understandable tendency to claim that Vatican Council II was responsible for all of it. But actually the council itself was preceded by, and at least partially the result of, great strides in liturgical renewal and—particularly important for our purposes—a dramatic and renewed openness to biblical scholarship among Catholics.

Two significant documents influenced this development in biblical scholarship:

Divino Afflante Spiritu: The change began in earnest with a 1943 encyclical by Pope Pius XII, titled *Divino Afflante Spiritu* (*On Promoting Biblical*

Studies). That encyclical is often referred to as "the Magna Charta of Catholic biblical scholarship." Essentially, it stated that the time of fear and defensiveness that had characterized Catholic biblical research had passed, and that Catholic scholars could begin to use modern biblical critical methods in their research, the kind of approaches that had been used by Protestant scholars for decades. We began to acknowledge, for instance, that the Scriptures in many cases were not to be taken literally, and we started to take a new look at biblical stories such as those of Adam and Eve, the parting of the "sea of reeds" by Moses, the Creation, and Jonah and the whale. This was an extremely important shift for the church that would affect its understanding of Jesus.

"Instruction on the Historical Truth of the Gospels": The second significant document to note, one having direct implications for the Christology in *Jesus of History, Christ of Faith,* was issued by the Pontifical Biblical Commission in 1964 under the title "Instruction on the Historical Truth of the Gospels." This document officially recognized that *the Gospels were written by believing Christians as post-Resurrection testimonies of faith about their experiences with and beliefs about Jesus.* They were not intended to be *historical* documents in our traditional sense of that term. The commission's document noted that the Gospels actually developed over an extended period of time through three basic stages:

1. Jesus, speaking and acting as a first-century Jewish teacher, shared his message with his disciples as they traveled Palestine with him.
2. After Jesus' death and resurrection—and in light of those events—the disciples recognized Jesus as the Messiah, the Christ, the One who had been promised. But rather than sitting down to write about their experience of Jesus, the disciples began an intensive missionary campaign throughout the Roman Empire to share the Good News with others.
3. After thirty-five to seventy years of this missionary activity, the Gospels as we know them were finally developed by the Evangelists, men who served as editors more so than authors by collecting oral traditions, liturgical prayers developed in community, sayings of Jesus, and so on. Each Evangelist organized this material into accounts that responded to the specific needs of the community for whom he wrote.

The questions arising from the shift in our understanding of the Gospels are extremely important. For instance:

- Who did the disciples think Jesus was *before* they recognized him as the Christ of Faith, the Messiah, the Son of God—a recognition that fully came to them only *after* the Resurrection?
- Was Jesus fully conscious of his identity and role prior to experiencing his resurrection?
- How did the disciples grow in their awareness of Jesus' identity as he lived and taught among them? Is it not possible that contemporary Christians are to discover the Jesus of History as the Christ of Faith in the same way they did? In other words, should not today's Christians also begin with reflection on Jesus' humanity—as the disciples did—rather than begin with reflection on his divinity?

Ultimately, questions like these, and the answers that biblical scholars and theologians have arrived at to this point, have led to the development of what is often called a "Christology from below," a "low Christology," or an "ascending Christology," one that moves from the human to the divine rather than the other way around.

Where We Are: A Christology from Below

I will attempt here to summarize the major theological characteristics of a Christology from below, as I did earlier for a Christology from above. A summary of the comparison between the two positions can be found on page 19.

The human experience as a starting point: In a Christology from below, we begin with the human experience of Sacred Mystery and humanity's search for God in everyday life and in the religious history of humanity. Rather than starting with a fall from grace, for example, we begin with our present human experience of sin and alienation in our relationships with one another, with God, and within ourselves as individuals. The conviction is that if God does not speak to the felt needs and yearnings of people today, then their belief in God can be neither relevant nor influential in their lives.

Jesus as a Jew: Another major theological characteristic of a Christology from below is that Jesus is first recognized as precisely who he was as he walked the roads and hiked the hills of Palestine—a Jewish teacher and prophet. He was thoroughly Jewish in his religious background, his mentality, his social and family relationships, and so on. He was a man whose vision was firmly rooted in the Hebrew Scriptures, and he was a monotheist committed to Yahweh—the God of Abraham, Isaac, and Jacob. He, like all Jews of Palestine, experienced the domination of the Romans, and he, along with his people, thirsted for freedom from oppression.

A universal call to a relationship with the Father: At age thirty or so, Jesus of Nazareth went out among his people, proclaiming his vision of the Kingdom of God, the Reign of God over all creation. During his development Jesus had arrived at a profoundly new sense of the nature of God, so new that he used an unheard of name for Yahweh, calling God "Abba," the equivalent of our word "Daddy." Jesus recognized that God is not "out there" but is closer to us than we are to ourselves. And out of this intense awareness of the closeness and unconditional love of God, Jesus arrived at an awareness that all people are related to one another as brothers and sisters. In other words, "The Kingdom of God is among you!" Jesus came to proclaim not himself but Yahweh, and he lived and died to call all people to a relationship not just with himself but with the Father.

No avoidance of the human condition: A fourth insight into a Christology from below addresses Jesus' consciousness of himself and his role in the world. In this view, Jesus confronted the world and all its evil just as we do, with no consciousness of his divinity. Such knowledge of his divinity might have, on the one hand, made his life easier while, on the other hand, effectively separating him from us rather than uniting us with him. Jesus did not escape the trials and torments of life. He experienced loneliness, frustration, fear, anxiety, hunger, exhaustion—just as we do.

Jesus' death as the consequence of his loving commitment: In a Christology from below, the understanding of Jesus' death also shifts. Rather than beginning with a theological conviction that Jesus died for the sins of humanity in order to ransom people by satisfying God's anger, Jesus' death is seen as a logical consequence of a life lived in total love of God and others. As Jesus gained recognition and a following, he angered and alienated the political and religious powers of his time, and he became a threat to the established authorities, who eventually had to execute him to preserve their own power. As Hans Küng puts it in his book *On Being a Christian* (Garden City, NY: Doubleday and Company, 1976), "Jesus' violent end was the logical conclusion of his proclamation and his behavior. . . . [His] death was the penalty he had to pay for his life" (p. 335).

Yahweh's victory in the Resurrection: Finally, and perhaps most critically of all, a Christology from below emphasizes not the sacrificial death of Jesus but the fact that not even death could conquer this man and his vision. For after three days, God raised Jesus from the dead. Note especially the emphasis here on God's activity. Jesus did not raise himself. In the Resurrection, it is Yahweh who is victorious, and in and through God's victory Jesus is eventually recognized as Lord, that is, as one with God.

This understanding of Jesus, this Christology from below, leads to an emphasis on the following dimensions of Jesus' life and message:
- his humanity as the Nazarene, the carpenter's son, the Jewish teacher and prophet, the One who is one with us in all things except sin
- his resurrection (which logically leads to a renewed emphasis on Easter, rather than Christmas, as the central Christian feast)
- his ongoing presence among us and his call to a new way of living in his Spirit (leading to a concentration on the experience of the Spirit of Jesus in community and to the recognition of the Eucharist as a communal banquet celebrating Christ present, not only as a sacrifice or a re-enactment of Calvary)
- salvation of the individual as being accomplished not only through ritual baptism but also through mature, personal, and free acceptance of Jesus, and through a commitment to live out his message and values in daily life (a concentration, therefore, on lived rather than learned faith, with profound implications both for understanding the church and for understanding the particular tasks of catechists)

The Catechetical Implications of a Christology from Below

It is clear that the church has experienced a dramatic change in its understanding and experience of what it means to be a Christian. I am convinced that the kind of changes brought about by the Second Vatican Council will not be fully understood and accepted, and will not truly affect the community of faith, if they are perceived to be simply modifications in the structures of the church, in the way roles in the church are defined, or in the way the sacraments are celebrated. Rather, individual Christians and the church community as a whole will grow and develop only when—or if—they see these changes as a way to get more deeply in touch with Jesus and his Good News. I believe a Christology from below helps us do precisely that.

The shift in the understanding of Jesus implies a great deal for us as catechists or teachers of religion, and I want to conclude this section with a few reflections on that fact. I see three primary implications of a Christology from below for us as religious educators:

1. Sound scholarship: Our teaching about Jesus must be biblical; that is, it must be rooted in sound, contemporary biblical scholarship rather than in the literal or fundamentalist approaches that are now explicitly denied validity by the church.

2. A sense of the church's development of doctrine: Our teaching about church doctrine must be firmly grounded in church history, but not trapped by it. That is, our teaching must reflect a sound understanding of the church's development of doctrine through the centuries; at the same time, it must remain open to new insights into that doctrine in light of contemporary scholarship.

3. Personal reflection: Finally, our teaching about Jesus must be personal, reflecting not only the church's teaching but also our personal reflection upon that teaching and the experience of the Risen Jesus in our own life. The Good

News, after all, is that God loves us enough to reveal Sacred Mystery not only in Jesus, not only through the church as a whole, but to each of us as persons. The students want to hear *your* story; they want to know why *you* believe in Jesus.

The course *Jesus of History, Christ of Faith* is founded upon and flows from a Christology from below, a theological perspective taking precedence in the church today. The course is also sensitive to the catechetical implications of this Christology in that it is heavily biblical, it respects and integrates the church's historical development of christological doctrine, and—particularly through the strategies offered in this manual—it invites the teacher to share a personal faith in Jesus as well as help the students identify and nurture their own unique relationship with Jesus.

The following is a summary of this discussion on Christology:

Who Is the Jesus We Are Teaching?

Christology from Above

1. Theological foundations:
   a. the Gospels as historical documents dictated by God
   b. humanity's fall from grace and the need for redemption
   c. God as transcendent, "out there"
   d. Jesus as the pre-existent Word of God, the second person of the Trinity, sent by God
   e. Jesus, from birth, as fully conscious of his identity and role
   f. Jesus' saving us by "dying for our sins" in an act of perfect sacrifice, thereby satisfying God and reopening the gates of heaven
   g. salvation through baptism and adherence to the will of God as it is discerned by church authorities

2. Characteristics of Jesus that are emphasized:
   a. his divinity as the second person of the Trinity
   b. his incarnation as a man (leading to an emphasis on Christmas as the central Christian feast)
   c. his sacrificial and salvific death on the cross (leading to an emphasis on the Eucharist as a re-enactment of Calvary)

Christology from Below

1. Theological foundations:
   a. the Gospels as inspired, post-Resurrection testimonies of faith
   b. the lived experience of alienation from self, others, God
   c. God as personal, immanent
   d. Jesus initially perceived as a Jewish prophet and teacher in first-century Palestine
   e. Jesus as gradually growing in his consciousness of his identity and role
   f. Jesus' death on the cross as a direct result of conflicts with Jewish and Roman authorities and as a consequence of his total love
   g. salvation through personal decision and commitment; personal discernment and responsibility within community

2. Characteristics of Jesus that are emphasized:
   a. his humanity as the Nazarene, who experienced life as we do
   b. his resurrection by God (leading to an emphasis on Easter as the central Christian feast)
   c. his ongoing presence and call to life in the Spirit (leading to an emphasis on the Eucharist as a communal banquet)

Guidelines for Teaching About Jesus Today

Our teaching must be all of the following:
1. *biblical:* rooted in sound biblical scholarship
2. *historical:* reflecting doctrinal development
3. *personal:* inviting reflection upon the personal experience of both the teacher and the students

In closing this discussion of the theology of *Jesus of History, Christ of Faith*, it bears emphasizing that the "Christology from below" approach does not negate the truth of the divinity of Jesus. Rather, the approach affirms that truth—but by starting with a thorough realization of Jesus' humanity. Approaching Jesus with a Christology from below is like viewing a tree by looking up from the base, versus looking down from the treetop. The view from below shows you a different perspective of the tree than does the view from above. Whether viewed from below or from above, the tree is still the same reality, but the view from below gives you the perspective from the earth.

The difference between approaching Jesus "from below" versus "from above" is, in a way, the difference between Peter's and Paul's experiences of Jesus. Peter first knew Jesus as the humble and rejected leader of a band of disciples and later came to recognize him as the One exalted by God to sit at God's right hand. Paul, however, first experienced Jesus as the glorious Son of God, who dwelt with the Creator, and later he came to appreciate the reality that the Son of God had taken on our human condition.

Both of these men came to the same conclusion about Jesus, but they came to it by different routes. Peter came to identify his own friend and teacher, Jesus, with "the suffering servant," the Messiah prophesied in Isaiah. Paul came to see the divine Jesus as having taken on humanness, accepting everything about the human condition, even death. Both of these formative leaders of the Christian faith eventually recognized Jesus as human and divine.

In this course, I have chosen to follow the lead of virtually all respected contemporary biblical scholars and theologians in approaching Jesus "from below." In addition to having a solid scholarly foundation, this approach more closely parallels the common human experience than does a Christology from above. Few of us can identify with Paul's mystical encounter with the Risen Jesus when it comes to a starting point for our Christian faith. We are all much more like Peter, whose initial encounter with the historical Jesus only gradually, and with many fits and starts, evolved into an understanding of and commitment to the Messiah and Lord. This course, too, moves from a portrait of the historical Jesus toward the recognition of him as Lord.

In light of this discussion of the theology of *Jesus of History, Christ of Faith*, we can now look more closely at the content of the course.

The Content of the Course

It is helpful to step back and take a bird's-eye view of the course in order to see the inner coherence and flow of the material:
- After grounding itself in a solid understanding of the Christian Scriptures and, more specifically, in the four Gospels (in chapters 1 and 2), the course explores the religious and political world of Jesus (in chapter 3) and the daily life of the Jewish people (in chapter 4). Next, the infancy narratives, the "hidden years" of Jesus' childhood, and the beginning of his public life are explored (in chapter 5). In other words, the entire first part of the course helps the students get in touch with the historical setting of Jesus' life and proclamation. This is a very reasonable orientation, given the commitment to a Christology from below.
- The course then shifts to a thorough discussion of Jesus' message and ministry. The theme around which that material centers is Jesus' proclamation of his "Dream," the Kingdom of God (discussed in chapter 6). Jesus' marvelous sayings, teachings, and stories and his astounding actions are properly presented (in chapters 7 and 8) in the context of his vision of the Kingdom.

- Next, the last days of Jesus, culminating in his tragic death on the cross, are explored to the degree possible within their historical context (in chapter 9). This concludes, in one sense, the course's treatment of the Jesus of History.
- Chapter 10, then, marks a shift in the course toward a discussion of the Christ of Faith, the resurrected Jesus. Because of the pivotal importance of the Resurrection for those who profess belief in Christian faith, it is discussed in considerable detail.
- The next two chapters present the life, ministry and insights of the figure who is second in importance only to Jesus himself in the founding of the Christian church—Paul, "the Apostle to the Gentiles." The student text first provides an overview of Paul's life and ministry (in chapter 11) and then summarizes his profound understanding of the Christ of Faith (in chapter 12).
- Finally, the course concludes with a general review and summary of the church's developing understanding of Jesus through history (in chapter 13). It is here that the students are introduced to the major church doctrines and creedal statements about Jesus the Christ, which are presented within the historical context that gave birth to them. Significantly, a course grounded in a Christology from above would likely *begin* its discussion of Jesus at this point.

The following is a summary of the course by the major concepts in each chapter. These concepts roughly parallel the major section titles within each chapter of the student text. The chapters of this manual are organized according to the same major concepts.

Though I can appreciate the normal tendency of a teacher to either skim over or altogether ignore this kind of outline, I encourage you to read through this one rather slowly and thoughtfully. Ask yourself if you would have organized the material differently, either for the entire course or for individual chapters. In what ways? For what reasons? This exercise will give you a clearer understanding of the theological rationale behind *Jesus of History, Christ of Faith*.

1. **The Search for Jesus:**
   Sources in the Christian Testament and Beyond
- *Preliminary Concerns:* Introductions and icebreakers, grading procedures and student responsibilities
- *"Who Do You Say that I Am?"* The question of who this man Jesus is; an overview of the course
- *How Do We Learn About Jesus?* The major sources, both historical and from the perspective of faith, for information about Jesus
- *The Christian Testament:* The origins, content, and purposes of the Christian Testament

2. **The Gospels:**
   Central Sources for Understanding Jesus
- *Searching for the "Jesus of History" in the Gospels:* The unique nature of the Gospels as sources of religious truth—not necessarily "historical" truth—about Jesus
- *The Development of the Gospels:* The three-stage development of the Gospels
- *The Gospels as Four Portraits of Jesus:* The different characteristics of each of the Gospels

3. **The World of Jesus:**
   History and Politics
- *Jesus the Jew:* The importance of recognizing and understanding Jesus' roots as a Jew of his time
- *A Brief History of the Jewish People:* A broad sweep of the religious history of Jesus' people

- *The Political World of Jesus:* A summary of the Greek and Roman domination of, and consequent influence in, Palestine; the individuals, groups, and regions that come into play in the Gospel story
- *An Oppressed People Dream of a Liberator:* The dream of a Messiah as that dream emerged from the Jewish situation before Jesus' birth

4. **Daily Life in Jesus' Time:**
   Culture and Religion
- *Jesus in a Particular Time and Place:* The need for a sense of Jesus' daily life in first-century Palestine
- *Palestine:* The geography, climate, crops, and animals of first-century Palestine
- *The People and Their Daily Life:* The food and meals, houses, and occupations of the ancient Jewish people
- *The Jewish Family:* Marriage and family life among the ancient Jews; the roles of men and women in that society
- *Social Classes in the World of Jesus:* Various social groupings—rich and poor, in-groups and outcasts—that were the focus of much of Jesus' ministry
- *Major Features of Judaism:* The special places, central religious practices, and key religious-political groups and persons that form the context of the Gospel story

5. **The Mission Begins:**
   Preparing the Way of the Lord
- *The Infancy Narratives:* The literary style and theological significance of the stories surrounding Jesus' birth
- *The Hidden Years of Jesus' Life:* Likely characteristics of Jesus' childhood in Nazareth
- *The Beginnings of Jesus' Public Life:* The significance of the Gospel stories about Jesus' baptism and temptation in the desert
- *Wandering Preacher, Unique Teacher:* Jesus' teaching style and relationship with his disciples compared with that of the rabbis of his day

6. **The Kingdom of God:**
   Proclaiming the Dream of Jesus
- *Dreams:* The idea that all religions present their followers with a particular "Dream," or vision of life
- *The Kingdom of God Proclaimed:* Jesus' notion of the Kingdom of God as his Dream
- *Jesus' Understanding of God:* Jesus' conviction that God is a Father who loves without condition
- *Jesus' Understanding of the Command to Love:* Jesus' unique understanding of the call for people to love one another
- *The Reign of God and "the Reign of Sin":* Jesus' proclamation that the Kingdom is a response to both personal and communal sin and evil
- *Right Now, but Not Yet:* The Kingdom—fully present in Jesus but not yet fully realized

7. **Jesus Speaks:**
   Sayings and Stories of the Kingdom
- *Unlocking Jesus' Words:* The Gospels as a record of Jesus' speaking style
- *Jesus' Sayings and Stories in the Gospels:* Jesus' various styles of speech—direct pronouncements, short sayings, instructions for disciples, and parables
- *A Closer Look at the Parables:* Jesus' special stories and their relationship to his proclamation of the Kingdom

8. **Jesus Heals:**
   Signs of the Kingdom
   - *Jesus' Marvelous Deeds:* The variety of miracles in the Gospels
   - *Why Are the Miracles So Challenging?* The problems that the Gospel miracles present for today's believers
   - *The Jews and Miracles:* The ancient Jewish experience of and understanding of miracles
   - *Understanding Jesus' Miracles Today:* The central meaning of the Gospel miracles for contemporary Christians

9. **The Cross:**
   The End or a Beginning?
   - *The Road to the Cross:* Jesus as a source of conflict; the nature of the Passion accounts
   - *Jesus' Final Days:* The Last Supper and Jesus' eucharistic presence; "the agony in the garden"
   - *Jesus' Final Hours:* Jesus on trial; his scourging and crucifixion
   - *Understanding the Cross:* The multiple meanings of Jesus' death

10. **The Resurrection:**
    God Is Victorious! Jesus Is Lord!
    - *The Resurrection of Jesus:* Gospel accounts of the Resurrection; evidence for accepting the Resurrection
    - *What Does the Resurrection Mean?* Affirmation of claims made by and about Jesus; the paschal mystery
    - *Recognizing the Risen Jesus Today:* Encountering Jesus in the Eucharist, in the community of believers, and in remembering and living out his Dream
    - *The Ascension of Jesus:* What the Scriptures tell us about the Ascension; what the Ascension means
    - *Pentecost:* The gift of the Spirit; the birthday of the church

11. **Paul:**
    Apostle to the Gentiles
    - *A Brief Review:* Understanding Paul, his ministry, and his preaching about Jesus, within the context of the preceding material in the course
    - *Getting to Know Paul:* Sources of information about Paul; his life prior to the Damascus experience
    - *The Damascus Experience:* What happened to Paul on the road to Damascus and what it meant for him; conversion and vocation
    - *Paul's Missionary Work:* Paul's three main missionary journeys and their results; Paul's epistles and their audiences

12. **The Letters of Paul:**
    Proclaiming Christ Crucified and Risen
    - *An Introductory Overview of Paul's Epistles:* The roots of Paul's message in the Damascus event; the main themes of Paul's writing
    - *Salvation Through Christ Crucified:* Salvation and sin; the relationship between salvation, the Law, and love
    - *Salvation and Contemporary Culture:* Making sense of salvation in a world that hides from the need for it; Jesus as "the new Adam"; salvation as a gift from God; faith as more than just "me and God"
    - *The Church as the Body of Christ:* The relationship of the individual Christian to and with the community of believers; Jesus as head of the body of Christ

13. Good News from Age to Age:
The Church's Understanding of Jesus Christ
- *The Church's History:* The question of whether Jesus intended to found a church; the struggle to balance persistent tensions in the church's understanding of Jesus
- *Understanding Jesus in the Early Centuries:* From proclamation to explanation; the Great Christological Heresies and Councils
- *Understanding Jesus in the Middle Ages:* The rise of Scholasticism; a strong reaction by "the common folk"; the Reformation
- *Understanding Jesus in the Modern Age:* The Age of Enlightenment; the contemporary church; from "Jesus from above" to "Jesus from below"
- *The Journey of Faith in Jesus:* Finding an answer to Jesus' question, "Who do you say that I am?" is an intensely personal journey that is best made in the company of a faith community.

Adolescent Faith Development and This Course

It is assumed, based on research, that you are teaching *Jesus of History, Christ of Faith* to students who are sophomores or older. To provide some parameters for the content of this discussion, I must also assume that you are a teacher well-grounded in the developmental characteristics of adolescents—their physical and emotional traits, their cognitive abilities, the influence of peers in their life, and so on. Additionally, it is quite likely that you have a good sense of the faith characteristics common to this age-group, knowledge gained either from your own study or from the personal experience of living and working with young people. Based on these (hopefully accurate) assumptions, I am restricting myself here to a few reflections on the nature of this course vis-à-vis the normal pattern of faith development for the senior-high student.

Styles of Faith

To situate adolescents within the broad sweep of lifelong faith development, the work of Protestant religious educator John Westerhoff III is helpful. He identifies four *styles of faith* (see *Will Our Children Have Faith?* [New York: Seabury Press, 1976], pp. 89–103). He is quick to point out that these are not *stages* of faith in the common sense of that term. He says, rather, that most, if not all, of the four styles of faith can appear at any stage in the life process and that they may not appear in any particular sequential order. Nevertheless, I believe that a natural continuum seems to be reflected in his four styles:

1. Experienced faith: In Westerhoff's theory, experienced faith is seen most commonly during early childhood. At that time, faith is modeled by significant people in the child's life, and he or she imitates and assumes the attitudes, beliefs, behaviors, and religious practices of those people. This is a nonreflective faith, a product more of socialization than of education or personal choice.

2. Affiliative faith: Affiliative faith usually appears for the first time in early adolescence, during the middle-school grades and junior-high years. In this period, the young person's need for a sense of parental and peer acceptance and for participation in a caring community finds expression in a desire to feel included in the religious community in which he or she has been raised. Because of this, learning about the traditions of the faith community and participating in various youth-group activities can be attractive to the early-adolescent age-group.

3. Searching faith: According to Westerhoff, searching faith normally emerges during the mid- to late-adolescent years, that is, from the end of the junior-high years to the post–high school period. This style of faith is characterized by questioning, doubt, and serious reflection upon the faith that the person has inherited from others. The essential question asked at this time is, Do I now want to freely accept as my own the traditions, beliefs, and practices of the community with which I have been affiliated? For some people, the response to this question may be a rather spontaneous assent; for others, deep and even painful reflection may last for years.

4. Owned faith: If the needs of searching faith have been met, the individual is free to expand into an owned style of faith. Owned faith not only comes from within the person, as opposed to being imposed from the outside, but it is also shown by the individual's personal and social *behavior*. Arriving at owned faith often involves some negotiating with or accommodating of the central beliefs and practices of the tradition in which one has been raised. A typical Roman Catholic expression of this, for example, is the adult who professes to be a practicing Catholic yet rejects the church's stand on celibate priesthood, mandatory participation in the liturgy, or birth control. Research has shown this accommodation to be a common characteristic of contemporary adult Roman Catholics. It is important, for our purposes, to recognize that owned faith is generally observed only in a minority of adults; it is not to be expected of adolescents.

Practical Implications of Adolescent Faith Development for Teaching This Course

While recognizing that making generalizations about the faith development of any age-group is somewhat risky, I would suggest that the majority of the students with whom you will share *Jesus of History, Christ of Faith* will be in the process of moving from affiliative into searching faith. And this broad movement will itself be characterized by widely diverse levels of depth and intensity.

Some of your students will be deeply affiliated with the church and its teachings, convinced by their upbringing and experience that the church possesses truth and should not be questioned. Perhaps a larger number will be only culturally affiliated, bound to the church more by socialization than by personal conviction. Some will be facing the emergence of major questions on many levels of their life, perhaps most strongly in the areas of self-esteem and relationships. For them, religion and faith may virtually be nonissues while other concerns dominate their life. (Such young people, it should be noted, often *are* clearly involved in profound issues of faith, yet they would not likely identify the issues as such.) Finally, a minority of your students may well be engaged in a conscious searching faith, raising questions about everything from the existence of God to the right of the church to dictate moral guidelines. Students with strong cultural affiliative faith or intense searching faith—particularly if they are extroverted and vocal—can dominate class discussions and activities, while those "in the middle" will often feign or actually experience disinterest or boredom.

A Nonpresumptuous Stance Toward Students

This course responds creatively to a diversity of student starting points. *Jesus of History, Christ of Faith*, both the student text and this teaching manual, takes what I call "a nonpresumptuous stance" toward the students. This means that the course does not *presume* that the students are already committed Catholic Christians. Throughout the course, the church's beliefs are discussed from the outside, that is, objectively rather than subjectively.

A concrete example will make this point clearer:
- In a presumptuous course, we might find this kind of statement: "As committed Catholics, we are convinced that Mary is the Mother of God, and we honor her as a special model of the faith that each of us strives to achieve in our life."
- In a nonpresumptuous course, the point might be discussed this way: "Roman Catholics hold Mary, the mother of Jesus, in high esteem, calling her 'the Mother of God.' A variety of religious practices and liturgical feasts remind Catholics of her central role in the plan of God. This understanding of the role of Mary has been the source of some tension and misunderstanding between Catholics and Protestants." A brief description of the conflicts might follow.

The first of these two statements *presumes* that the readers are believing, practicing, fully committed Catholics. As a result, readers who do not fit this description—including many of those in the midst of searching faith—will automatically feel excluded from, put off by, or apathetic toward the material. The second statement, however, is nonpresumptuous. It gives the readers permission to reflect on the content without being judged by it. If they agree with the Catholic belief expressed in the second statement, that is fine. But if they doubt or disagree with it, they need not feel threatened or alienated.

The nonpresumptuous stance is particularly freeing and helpful when addressing groups that include both Catholic and Protestant students, a common situation in today's Catholic high schools. The objectivity makes it easier to speak forthrightly of sensitive matters, such as the differences between various religious traditions. We can simply state the facts—for instance, that Catholics believe in Jesus' real presence in the Eucharist and that some Protestants do not—without implying judgment against those who do not hold the Catholic position. Furthermore, this posture avoids the accusation by students—often rightly stated—that religion courses are an attempt by adults to impose their faith on the students.

Finally, a nonpresumptuous stance allows the teaching of religion to assume its rightful place as an academic discipline deserving the same status as other subjects. Because the material is approached objectively, we have less reason to fear that students will view grades in their religion courses as a measure of their personal faith, a point to which I will return in my discussion of grading procedures.

Here is an important clarification: When I state that the course assumes a nonpresumptuous stance, I mean that it does not presume that the *students* are committed Catholic Christians. However, it is often evident in the student text that the *author*—me, Tom Zanzig—*is* a deeply committed Catholic Christian who is writing out of his own convictions. Accordingly, I am surely not suggesting here that you as a teacher are to avoid speaking of your own faith convictions. These may run so deep that you could not hide them even if you chose to. Remember, too, that in the earlier discussion of the theology of this course, I called teachers to share their personal convictions about Jesus. The point is that we can and must speak freely and openly about our own Catholic faith, but we must always do so in a way that does not alienate our students by implicitly or explicitly judging their personal positions. Paradoxically, when we create such a safe and nonthreatening environment for our students, our own faith convictions become all the more appealing, attractive, and worthy of our students' serious reflection. When we try to impose our convictions on them, we only create impenetrable walls of resistance.

Let's turn now to a consideration of the pedagogy of *Jesus of History, Christ of Faith*.

Pedagogical Background

In this section, we will explore the following dimensions of the pedagogy involved in this course:
- the nature of the learning process employed
- a recommended approach to grading students

The Learning Process

Jesus of History, Christ of Faith employs a learning process modeled after one described in Richard Reichert's *A Learning Process for Religious Education* (Dayton, OH: Pflaum Publishing, 1975). It is student-centered, combines a concern for formation with a concern for information, offers students opportunities for self-examination and reflection, and seeks to move them along in their personal faith development. The process is described in full in appendix 2 of this manual, and you are encouraged to read that essay if you are unfamiliar with the process. The following is an abbreviated discussion of Reichert's model, with a comment on its application to this course.

The learning process can be divided into four interrelated moments:
- the starting point
- the significant experience
- reflection
- assimilation

The Starting Point

The *starting point* in any learning process is basically the sum total of all that the learner has learned up to that point. A teacher needs to consider the backgrounds, values, concerns, and life experiences of the students in order to accurately assess their starting point as they engage a particular topic or concept in this course.

The effective teacher must begin as much as possible where the students are and must act as a midwife, helping the students give birth to new insights and perspectives. In organizing and then writing this course, I tried to constantly stay aware of the students' starting point, always asking myself how I might make the content intelligible and engaging for *these* students in *this* setting. That is the question you must ask as well in selecting strategies, assigning homework, leading discussions, and so on.

The Significant Experience

The *significant experience* is an internal or external event that leads to movement beyond the starting point. Something motivates the learner to reflect upon or become uncomfortable with her or his starting point. The event is

called "significant" because it invites a meaningful change in the person. Significant experiences related to this course might be the following:
- receiving new information from the student text or the teacher
- challenging previously held attitudes or positions
- examining a fresh perspective on oneself or one's world
- simulating or trying on new behaviors
- experiencing prayer or a deeper sense of prayer
- developing new relationships; seeing old relationships in a new light

This teaching manual offers numerous strategies—group exercises, games, discussion starters, and more—for helping the students move from one point in their understanding of Jesus to another. All suggested strategies are designed to prompt the students to get in touch with their starting point—where they are, who they are, and what they believe—regarding the concept at hand.

So we see that the first two steps of the learning process call for the teacher to assess the students' starting point in terms of the topic at hand and then to engage the students' interest and focus their attention on the topic by providing a significant learning experience. The teacher can also facilitate the next phase of the process: reflection.

Reflection

When a person asks, What does this experience mean? he or she is engaging in the *reflection* stage of the learning process. This stage often involves solitary thinking, sorting things out in writing, intense discussions with others, even prayer. Reflection activities allow students an opportunity to think through the growth to which they are invited.

Reflection activities for this course include the many activities located at the bottom of the pages of the student text. These can be used as homework assignments, classroom activities or discussion starters, or prompts for private reflection. Also, for each of the significant experiences offered in this manual, various means of reflection are provided.

At some point, either consciously, spontaneously, or intuitively, the learner must respond to this question: Do I want to accept this new information as part of my worldview? Implicit in this question is a more fundamental one: Am I willing to change who I am? Every time we truly learn *anything,* we are going to change. The resolution of these questions directly affects the fourth and final stage of the learning process: assimilation.

Assimilation

Assimilation refers to a change integrated into the life of the student—a changed perspective, understanding, value, or attitude. *Jesus of History, Christ of Faith* offers many opportunities for truly significant change—that is, for real learning—on the part of the students. However, in light of our previous discussion of the nonpresumptuous nature of the course, it is *not* the goal or expectation of this course that the students come to a personal acceptance of and commitment to Jesus and his message. Such a decision is more appropriate at a later age, perhaps during young adulthood. Our prematurely expecting or, worse, attempting to force such a decision would amount to gross manipulation.

The course *is* intended to guide the students to a deliberate and conscious reassessment of their *understanding of and attitudes about* Jesus and the Gospel. This course intends to challenge and, yes, change the common negativity and apathy toward things religious that is normal and even necessary at this stage of human development. Students who successfully complete the course may leave it with a new interest in and openness to further exploration of the Good News that they have inherited from others. This is the stuff of profound learning—and of gratifying teaching.

We turn now to the "more practical" considerations of grading procedures.

Recommended Grading Procedures

Giving grades for courses in religion is a persistent problem. The need for some measure of academic success or failure, such as letter grades, appears evident; most attempts at a pass-fail approach to religion grades have been unsuccessful, many times because of the dissatisfaction of the students themselves. Yet there is a legitimate concern that letter grades given in religion courses are often incorrectly interpreted by students and their parents as a measure of personal faith-life, a misconception we certainly want to avoid.

Space does not permit me to consider the complexity of the grading issue in this teaching manual. It is likely that each school has its policy well established and already functioning. What I offer here is a grading approach that respects the sensitivity of the issues involved in this course while offering some means to measure student performance. This approach uses letter grades (*A, B, C, D, F*), which is the most common practice, and will require some adjustment in schools using numerical grading procedures.

A Combination of Three Factors

Three factors can be evaluated and combined to determine a student's grade for this course:

1. Tests and quizzes: In appendix 1 of this manual, you will find resources for creating a test or quiz for each chapter of the student text. Most of the questions deal objectively with the essential content of *Jesus of History, Christ of Faith,* and students who answer them correctly can be viewed as understanding the major concepts of the course. Some of the suggested essay questions, however, go beyond measuring comprehension to tap into the students' abilities to analyze, reflect upon, and apply the material.

2. Classroom activities: As will become increasingly clear throughout this manual, the classroom activities recommended for the course significantly expand upon and clarify the student text. Because a heavy emphasis is placed on experiential methods—games, group dynamics, discussion, and so on—open minds and good cooperation on the part of the students are essential to the effectiveness of the course. Not only should students be encouraged to enter fully into classroom experiences, but they should be rewarded if they do so. Therefore I recommend that students who become fully involved in the classroom receive a grade that reflects their contributions as well as their success on chapter tests or quizzes.

Note: Two cautions need to be made regarding the evaluation of the students on this point:
- "Full involvement" and "good cooperation" in this course are not defined as "agreement with all that is taught." Students can disagree and can even take the role of devil's advocate in discussions of the course material and still deserve a favorable grade.
- Teachers must be sensitive to students who, because of shyness, find it difficult to participate actively in class. These students should not be penalized

for this personal trait; in fact, a higher grade may help to affirm them and alleviate some of their fear.

3. Special projects: The third factor to consider is the possibility of requiring the students to do a special project if they wish to achieve an *A* for the course. One such project might be an autobiographical essay on a theme related to this course. For instance, you might ask your students to write an essay on the theme "My Changing Understanding of Jesus," in which they review significant moments in their religious development. Another relevant theme would be "The Message of Jesus and the World of Today's Youth." A less personal special assignment would be to have the students rewrite a Gospel parable, or create a contemporary one, to speak to young people today. Again, whatever the project, the students must be allowed to state their positions and opinions without fear of condemnation—or worse in their mind, a lower grade!

I recommend that only students pursuing such a special project be eligible for an *A* for the course. In this way an *A* becomes what it is intended to be—a measure of excellence above and beyond what could be expected of the average student.

I suggest that you establish the relative weights of these three factors in a way that seems appropriate for a particular class of students, recognizing that each class will be different in ability and maturity. For example, in a class of students with high academic potential, you might give a *C* to the student who achieves 90 percent or better on tests but contributes little to classroom discussion and does no additional work. In such a class, high test results plus good classroom participation might warrant a *B*, but an *A* could be achieved only with completion of a special project in addition to high test scores and full participation.

If, however, the class has average academic potential, these standards should be adjusted. In such a case, test results could account for 80 percent or more of the grade, and students performing well on tests alone could achieve a solid *B*. Active class participation could raise that to an *A*, in recognition that average students usually cannot do extra research or writing assignments. The point remains, however, that an *A* should always be a reflection of effort and accomplishment above the norm.

Self-Grading

As an additional means to assure equitable and effective grading for this course, some teachers have found it helpful to institute self-grading by the students. This not only provides a good check on the teacher's sensitivity to the individual student but also opens the possibility of some significant personal dialog between the teacher and the student.

Self-grading generally works as follows:
1. The criteria for the letter grades are explained thoroughly to the students at the start of the course. At grading time (middle and end of semester), both the teacher and the individual student submit the grade that they think the student deserves for the course, given the criteria established.
2. If the same grade is submitted by both the teacher and the student, the grade stands. If different grades are submitted, the teacher and the student meet to discuss the issue and arrive at an agreement on the grade the student will receive. Again, the criteria previously established should be the basis for the decision.
3. Experience has shown that in the vast majority of cases in which self-grading has been employed, the teacher and the student initially agree on the

grade deserved by the student. In those cases in which there is disagreement, commonly the teacher submits a higher grade than the student does. The meeting between the teacher and the student becomes, then, an opportunity for affirmation of the student rather than a situation of conflict.

Finally, it should be emphasized throughout the course that the grades are intended only to reflect academic performance in the course, and they in no way reflect the faith-lives of the students.

Lesson Planning

Every experienced teacher has likely developed an approach to lesson planning that meets her or his needs. The process described here may or may not immediately feel comfortable to you. I am not suggesting that you radically change or discontinue your current practice, particularly if you have found it effective. However, I do encourage you to carefully evaluate the process described here and to imagine ways that it might enhance the approach you now use. At the very least, certain components of the process can quite likely be added to your present approach.

To use the planning process recommended for this course, please note the following:
- *Tools for teaching:* Familiarize yourself with how the material for teaching each chapter is organized. During the brief explanation given here, you may find it helpful to periodically glance at one of the chapters in the manual to see examples of the teaching tools described.
- *A method of planning and scheduling:* All of the teaching tools provided in this manual can be used as you follow the steps of lesson planning and scheduling suggested here.

Tools for Teaching

For each chapter in the student text, you will find a corresponding chapter of teaching material in this manual, organized according to the major concepts in the student text chapter. The major concepts for each chapter offer an important organizing principle for teaching the material. These concepts are concise statements of what can be learned in the chapter, or short summaries of the significant ideas conveyed by the chapter. Also, the major concepts parallel the major sections of each chapter in the student text. The titles of the major concepts are listed as part of the course summary on pages 21–24 of this manual. Typically, a chapter will have about four major concepts.

At the opening of each chapter in this manual, the major concepts for that chapter are listed together. Then each concept is treated in turn: the major concept is repeated, with the relevant student text pages listed, and the following material is provided for the concept:

Review Questions

The review questions that end each section of the student text are repeated, and a suggested answer is provided for each question. The intent of the review questions is only to check whether the students have retained the basic information in a given section. The questions do not require full comprehension or assimilation of the material, as more analytical or reflective kinds of questions would. Students who can accurately answer the review questions demonstrate basic comprehension, and it is hoped that by your using other course methods, the students will go beyond that level to analysis, reflection, and application.

Student Text Activities

Numbered text activities appear in the bottom margin of the student text pages and correspond with the orange numbers in the student text material itself. The activities are repeated for you in this manual. Your students will not be able to do all of the activities in the span of a semester, the time normally allotted for this course, so you will need to select from these activities to fit the needs of your class. Even if you do not assign a given text activity, however, the students' reading the activity along with the regular text material can have the positive effect of helping them see the text material in a new light—perhaps a more personalized light. Encourage the students not to view the text activities as burdensome assignments that must be accomplished to complete a chapter but as intriguing "reflection starters" that may or may not be assigned as class or homework activities.

All of the text activities require the students to respond in writing. This is done intentionally, to avoid having the *teacher* be the one to require written work. You may decide not to require written work for all, or even most, of the activities, telling the students that they can complete the activities in some other way.

Using the activities as written assignments will work most effectively if you combine the writing with some other processing of the students' reflections or findings in class. Here are some ways to use the activities:

1. Paired exchange: Have the students exchange their written reflections with a partner (if you judge that the material generated by the activity is appropriate for the students to share). Direct the partners to read each other's reflections and then to discuss them. Afterward, a whole-class discussion could draw insights from students who volunteer their thoughts from the paired discussions. However, caution the students that they should not bring up what their partner wrote or said unless the partner gives the okay.

2. Quiet collection of thoughts: Ask the students to spend a few quiet moments thinking about the question presented in an activity, rather than writing down their thoughts. Then follow up the quiet time with a discussion in pairs, in small groups, or with the whole class. Giving the students a few moments to collect their thoughts before you ask for class involvement in a discussion often yields a more fruitful discussion than when their thoughts are off the top of their head.

3. Brainstorming: Depending on the nature of the text activity, you may use it to brainstorm with the whole class. For instance, an activity may call for the students to recall times when they have experienced something similar to what is described in the text discussion. Sometimes you can generate examples like this by having the students call them out to you, without discussion, as you write them on the chalkboard. Once the whole list is out, you can go back and ask for elaboration on the examples you think would be most helpful to discuss.

4. Skits and role-plays: Some activities that call for examples from the students' experience can be extended into skits or role-plays. Of course, to pull this off, you must have willing students, who are comfortable letting their experiences be the subject of dramatization.

5. Extra credit: Certain text activities—for instance, those that call for the students to do some research or interview someone—might be assigned to individuals or small task groups for extra credit. The results of their work could then be shared with the whole class in an oral report.

6. Fishbowls: When a text activity calls for reflection on an issue that is likely to generate controversy or at least pro and con sentiment, an effective way to discuss the issue is by way of a "fishbowl." This is a small group of students discussing the issue in a circle, with the rest of the class observing from outside the circle. Try to compose the small group out of students with a variety of viewpoints on the issue, or both viewpoints if there are only two. Leave one chair in the circle empty. Explain that if someone outside the circle wants to make a comment, she or he can occupy that chair briefly, making the comment and then vacating the chair. This can sustain interest in the discussion by enabling participation by potentially everyone in the class, but it also avoids the pitfalls of a large-group controversy, which can get out of hand.

7. Test questions: Text activities often can check for deeper levels of comprehension than typical test questions can. (In many cases, the text activities require personal reflection, analysis, evaluation, application of the material to one's personal life, etc.) Because of this, you may choose to incorporate some of the activities into your quizzes and tests as, for example, essay questions. In doing so, however, remember that these activities generally require subjective responses from the students, responses that cannot be judged for accuracy as easily as can answers to objective test questions. (Sample test questions, both objective and essay, are given in appendix 1 of this manual.)

Additional Activities

For almost every major concept in this manual, following the repeated student text activities, you will find additional activities you can use. These are most often classroom activities that suggest small-group processing. They occasionally require handouts that must be photocopied and then distributed to the students. These handouts appear at the end of the respective chapters in this manual and are also provided as handout masters on perforated pages at the end of the manual.

Be aware of an attractive but potentially frustrating feature of this teaching manual: with rare exceptions, you are provided with more activities than you can reasonably use in your teaching, and you will need to carefully select the strategies that will best meet the needs of your students. The attractiveness of this feature is self-evident. Yet it can be frustrating to pass up intriguing strategies when you know that the limits of time do not permit you to use them. The need to make such decisions is a major reason for presenting here, on pages 35–38, a method of planning and scheduling your teaching of the entire course.

Above I mentioned rare exceptions when a wide variety of teaching strategies is not provided. Some major concepts, though clearly dealing with significant information, are comparatively short, to the point, and treated in only a few pages of the student text. Other major concepts may best be handled by having the students just read the material, briefly checking their comprehension through class discussion (or perhaps by using an activity from the text itself), and then including the concept in a quiz. Additional activities would be counterproductive.

A Method of Planning and Scheduling

This section suggests a method for developing your overall course schedule as well as for planning how you will teach individual major concepts. The process is first explained in summary form; then each step in the process is described in greater detail.

Following this explanation of a method of planning and scheduling, you will find a lesson planning chart that may prove helpful (more on the use of the chart shortly).

An Overview of the Planning and Scheduling Method

The basic approach to lesson planning and scheduling recommended for *Jesus of History, Christ of Faith* includes these five steps:
1. Identify the total number of class periods available for this course.
2. Assess for the entire course the approximate number of class periods needed for each major concept.
3. Divide the course approximately into two-week blocks of time. In advance of each two-week block, make more specific decisions regarding which major concepts to present during that block. Determine how many and which class periods will be devoted to each of those concepts.
4. For each major concept to be taught during a given two-week block, select the teaching strategies that you will use, keeping in mind the number of class periods available for that concept.
5. After each class period, briefly evaluate for future reference your experience with the strategies selected.

The Steps in Greater Detail

1. Identify the total number of class periods available for this course. This discussion is based on the assumption that the course will be taught within a conventional full semester. (Some schools may choose to teach the course over an entire academic year or, less often, in a quarter.) In most school systems, a semester comprises eighteen weeks. Our research shows that most Catholic high schools hold religion classes at least three times per week, with a growing majority holding religion classes every school day. The standard class period is fifty minutes long. Finally, each semester in a school calendar includes vacation or holidays, special school functions, test days, and so on. For purposes of planning, therefore, sixteen of the eighteen weeks in a semester may actually be available for teaching. This would result in a total of about eighty class periods. Naturally, you will have to adjust this estimate in accord with the variables of your school calendar.

2. Assess for the entire course the approximate number of class periods needed for each major concept. To assist you in this step, the major concepts are listed on pages 21–24 of this manual and at the beginning of each chapter of this manual.

It may be immediately apparent that you want to treat some concepts only briefly, perhaps in one class period or less. And you may well find that you prefer not to expand on some concepts in class at all, simply telling the students to read the text and complete an assignment or take a quiz on the material. Other concepts may require two or more class periods. Such preliminary decisions should be made at this stage of planning.

Of course, decisions at this point must be viewed as general and tentative, particularly if you are teaching the course for the first time. The primary objective here is to take a broad view of the course to ensure that you will cover all that you intend to cover. Consciously planning to reduce or eliminate some of the course material is one thing; running out of time is quite another. This step of the planning method should help you avoid such surprises.

3. Divide the course approximately into two-week blocks of time. In advance of each two-week block, make more specific decisions regarding which major concepts to present during that block. Determine how many and which class periods will be devoted to each of those concepts. I suggest working in blocks of two weeks or so because that is generally a sufficient amount of time to teach an entire chapter or more of material. Your teaching of the course, therefore, can be cohesive and integrated as you work with a series of interrelated concepts. On the other hand, a two-week block of class periods is not *too* long. Attempting to look further ahead than that in your selection of specific concepts and teaching strategies would potentially impair the students' learning process by reducing the flexibility that is necessary on your part. *A month from now, you will know what and how to teach the class based only on your students' response to material in the interim.*

4. For each major concept to be taught during a given two-week block, select the teaching strategies that you will use, keeping in mind the number of class periods available for that concept. At this point you may experience both the benefits and frustrations of this manual that were mentioned earlier. You may often encounter a situation in which you have two class periods available for teaching a major concept but enough material and creative strategies in this manual to fill ten periods. How do you decide what to do?

Not surprisingly, the learning process (briefly explained earlier and discussed in full in appendix 2) provides direction for making such decisions. In such cases, always begin by evaluating your students' starting point in terms of the available strategies. What approaches have they responded well to in the past? What kinds of strategies seem ineffective with them? To put this another way, which strategies have the greatest chance of being significant experiences for the students, given their starting point? What about your own starting point as a teacher? What are you comfortable doing in class? Which strategies just feel right to you, and of course, how much time do you have available? How much time is required by each available strategy?

5. After each class period, briefly evaluate for future reference your experience with the strategies selected. Ongoing evaluation may be one of the most talked about and least practiced aspects of effective teaching. We are usually so caught up with preparing for our next task that we do not take the time to look back on classes we have already successfully completed—or maybe only survived! Perhaps the difficulty is that the task of ongoing evaluation can seem so time-consuming, so tedious, that we feel oppressed by it before even attempting it.

In this planning process, I have attempted to make the step of evaluation so simple that it can quickly and consistently be included in your teaching. For the details, see paragraph 6 in the following explanation of a lesson planning chart.

A Lesson Planning Chart

On page 38, you will find a lesson planning chart developed for a hypothetical three days of this course. A blank copy of the chart is provided with the handout masters at the end of this manual for use in your planning.

Here is how to use the chart:

1. In the first column, write the date or number of the class period. That is, you may specify each session by the date on which it will occur, or you may number your class periods for the semester from, say, one to eighty. If you are following the five-step planning process described on pages 35–36 of this manual, you will want to date or number your class periods in blocks of two weeks or so.

You may want to complete the chart in pencil rather than pen, knowing that you will have to make at least minor adjustments, given the students' response to the material, missed class periods, and so on.

2. In the second column, state the major concept to be taught during the class period. Use an abbreviation of the concept title listed in this manual.

3. In the third column, identify the relevant pages of the student text *for the class period*. That is, you may be teaching one concept for two or more class periods, so you will want to identify the specific pages of the text that will be covered in each of those periods. The reason for this may become clearer in step 5, which deals with homework assignments.

Notice that the student text pages for the entirety of each major concept are listed in this manual, directly preceding the teaching strategies for the respective major concept.

4. Now you are ready to specify the teaching strategies, or activities, that you will use during the class. Note that all of the activities in this manual are numbered or titled, for example, "Activity 3" or "A Demonstration on the 'Books' of the Bible." In completing the chart, use these numbers and titles along with page references so that you can easily locate the activities when you need to.

5. In the column titled "Homework Assignment," specify the student text pages to be read (usually the pages that will be covered in the following class), any reflection activities to be completed, or any other task that you want to assign as homework.

6. Finally, after teaching each class, briefly jot down in the last column your evaluation of the class, particularly concentrating on the activities identified in the fourth column. You will likely develop a kind of shorthand of your own for this. Perhaps you might state, "Effective as described in manual; repeat next time." In another case you might write, "Too much material; drop text activity." These statements, brief as they are, may be all you need to refresh your memory when teaching the course in the future.

Lesson Planning Chart

Date, Class	Major Concept	Text Pages	Activities	Homework Assignment	Evaluation
Mon. 9/28	Chap. 1: C Learn About Jesus	13-15	Do Activity 3 and "You Know More" (TM, p. 50) with discussion.	Rd. 15-17, answer review questions on p. 17.	Worked well with talkative class.
Tues. 9/29	Chap. 1: C Learn About Jesus	15-17	Go over review questions done as homework. Do "Truly Knowing Another" (TM, pp. 49-50).	Rd. 18-21, answer review questions on p. 21.	"Truly Knowing Another" didn't work well; try again?
Wed. 9/30	Chap. 1: D Christian Testament	18-21	Do "Demo on Books" (TM, p. 52) and "Oral Review" (TM, p. 53).	Rd. chap. 2, 23-27, and answer review questions on p. 26. Do Activity 2 w/out writing.	Both activities very good; do again.

Part 2
Teaching Strategies for This Course

CHAPTER 1

The Search for Jesus: Sources in the Christian Testament and Beyond

Major Concepts

A. **Preliminary Concerns:** Depending on how well the students know one another and you, time may need to be devoted to introductions and ice-breakers. Other preliminary concerns, such as grading procedures and student responsibilities, should be discussed at this time.

B. **"Who Do You Say that I Am?"** Making a personal decision about Jesus requires in-depth information about him as a historical person and as the Christ of Christian faith. The information in this course is offered to aid young people in answering Jesus' question, "Who do you say that I am?"

C. **How Do We Learn About Jesus?** The Christian Scriptures, and particularly the Gospels, are the primary sources for learning about Jesus. Various nonscriptural sources verify his historical existence but tell us little else about him.

D. **The Christian Testament:** The Christian Testament is composed of twenty-seven separate writings, or books, representing different authors and different types of writing, yet one theme is consistent throughout. All of the books deal in some way with the life and ministry of Jesus and the impact he had on his initial followers and the early Christian community.

Concept A: Preliminary Concerns

Depending on how well the students know one another and you, time may need to be devoted to introductions and icebreakers. Other preliminary concerns, such as grading procedures and student responsibilities, should be discussed at this time.

Activities: Preliminary Concerns

Establishing a Personal Touch

If the students have not met you before, they will likely be interested in "where you're coming from"—what your background is, what kind of teacher you are, and so on. This presents an opportunity to establish the personal touch needed to effectively teach a religion course from a faith perspective. (For more on the topic "The Teacher as a Witness of Faith," see appendix 3 in this manual.) Spend a considerable amount of time (even a half or a full session if you feel comfortable with that) introducing yourself to the students. Possible information to include would be the following:
- how long you have been a teacher and why you chose to be one
- when and where you were born; where you were raised; your family background; whether you are single, married, or a religious and why you have chosen that form of Christian lifestyle
- why you are a teacher of religion and, more specifically, why you feel it is important and challenging to teach a course on Jesus; what you, as a person of faith, hope to accomplish during this course
- your personal philosophy of education—comments about your teaching style and what the students can expect from you as a teacher

You may also want to invite the students to ask any questions they have about you as their teacher. (Let them know that you will be introducing the course itself, discussing grading procedures, etc., later.) After introducing yourself, move directly to student introductions (see "Getting to Know One Another," below).

Getting to Know One Another

The student introductions will be greatly affected by how well the students already know one another, whether it is their first semester in the school, whether this class also serves as their homeroom, and so on.

Option 1: If the students do not know one another well, the simplest approach would be to have them quickly give their name, the name of the grade school or middle school they attended (if this is their first year in the high school), and perhaps a brief comment about themselves (e.g., the number of children in their family and whether they are the oldest or youngest, their favorite pastimes).

Option 2: If the students already know one another somewhat, or if you want to expand option 1, create a fun, nonthreatening get-to-know-you exercise. You might try one of the following:
- *Analogies:* "Select an animal, a mineral, and a historical person and explain how you identify with each of them."

- *Sentence completions:* "I like . . . I hope . . . I fear . . . I get angry when . . ."
- *Questions:* "What is your favorite room in your house and why? What time of day do you like the best and why? What time of day do you like the least and why? Which TV personality would you most like to be and why?"

Divide the class into pairs. Give the students 1 minute to introduce themselves to their partner, sharing their responses to the exercise. (If the students do not know one another well, encourage them to say their partner's name every time they share something with him or her.) Then give each student 30 seconds to introduce his or her partner to the class.

Option 3: To more concretely connect the student introductions to the course itself, ask the students to quickly write down five words that come to mind when they think of Jesus. They should do this without thinking a great deal. After 2 minutes or so, ask them to pair off. The partners should introduce themselves to each other and then share their lists, finding the similarities and differences in the lists.

If you feel that the students would be comfortable doing so, have them introduce one another to the class by giving their partner's name and the three most interesting words on her or his list. Or if that would be too threatening, invite the students to randomly call out words from the lists while you jot the words on the chalkboard.

Close by commenting on the most common responses, the funniest or strangest responses, and so on. Be aware that some of the responses may not be particularly "religious" and avoid reacting negatively if that is the case.

Notes to the Teacher: Preliminary Concerns

Breaking the Ice

At the beginning of a course, there is often a need to break the ice and initiate an attitude of openness. You are encouraged to carefully evaluate the needs of your class in this respect and to take all the time required to create an open attitude early in the course. The time invested in this effort at this point can pay tremendous dividends in terms of long-range teaching effectiveness. The following are recommended sources for icebreakers to use in this course:

Creative Resources for Youth Ministry. Winona, MN: Saint Mary's Press. This series provides many group exercises, all organized under the following titles: *Creative Learning Experiences,* edited by Wayne Rice, John Roberto, and Mike Yaconelli, 1981; *Creative Communication and Discussion Activities, Creative Activities for Small Youth Groups,* and *Creative Crowd-Breakers, Mixers, and Games,* compiled by Wayne Rice and Mike Yaconelli, 1991. These books would be invaluable not only for icebreakers but also for learning activities to be used throughout this course and others you might be teaching. They are available for $8.95 to $12.95 each from Saint Mary's Press, 800-533-8095.

Zanzig, Thomas. *Teaching Manual for Understanding Catholic Christianity.* Winona, MN: Saint Mary's Press, 1989. This teaching manual is part of a survey course for first-year students in Catholic high schools. The author, who also wrote the *Jesus of History, Christ of Faith* course, shares some of the most effective icebreakers and other group exercises that he has found. If your school does not offer the course *Understanding Catholic Christianity,* you can use the suggestions in the manual (particularly those on pp. 49–52) without concern about repeating exercises your students have done. If your school does offer *Understanding Catholic Christianity*, check to see which exercises have already been used with your students. The manual is available for $18.95 from Saint Mary's Press, 800-533-8095.

Student Access to Bibles

During the course *Jesus of History, Christ of Faith*—concentrating as it does on the Scriptures, and especially the Christian Testament—the students will need access to Bibles both in and out of class. A few options for assuring such access follow:

Option 1: Many students may already own a Bible or know of one they can use. As long as the translation is a reasonably recent one and the Bible is of a size and format that could easily be used in class, you could allow its use for the course. The various translations used by the students might result in some minor confusion during class discussions, but this can serve the positive role of introducing the students to a variety of translations and thereby correcting the possible misunderstanding that there is only one acceptable way to translate the Scriptures.

Option 2: You could ask the students to purchase a Bible for the course. This might meet with some resistance, but it has the advantage of giving you control over the translation used. In choosing the translation for the students to purchase, note that all the scriptural quotations in chapters 1–5 of the student text are from the New American Bible. With a few exceptions, all the scriptural quotations in chapters 6–13 are from the New Revised Standard Version. Another translation you might want to consider is the New Jerusalem Bible.

Two attempts to capture the Scriptures in contemporary language have become popular: Good News for Modern Man and the Living Bible (the Way is the illustrated version of the Living Bible). Neither of these is highly respected from a scholarly point of view, and both tend to be too free in their translation of the original scriptural text. During the course, when discussing specific verses, always look to the more respected versions for accurate translations.

Nearly all of the versions mentioned here are available in reasonably priced paperback editions.

Option 3: The school could purchase enough Bibles for all the students in the class. These could then be available for future classes as well, making the Bibles a one-time expense. One drawback to this option is that the school might be reluctant to allow the Bibles to leave the classroom. This presents a problem because the students will need the Bibles while doing homework assignments.

Explaining Grading Procedures and Student Responsibilities

Information on your grading procedures should be given to the students during this orientation to the course. Refer to "Recommended Grading Procedures," on pages 29–31 of this manual, for suggestions, or be prepared to thoroughly explain your alternative approach to grading.

As part of the explanation of grading procedures, you may want to comment on the mutual commitment that is required for the success of this course. You could say something like this:

- In order for our time together to be successful and rewarding, a lot of preparation before class and participation during class is called for on the part of each one of us—both me as your teacher and you as students. I have made a personal commitment to teach you as well as I can, and I hope that you will make a similar commitment to cooperate and share as students.

Concept B: "Who Do You Say that I Am?"

Making a personal decision about Jesus requires in-depth information about him as a historical person and as the Christ of Christian faith. The information in this course is offered to aid young people in answering Jesus' question, "Who do you say that I am?" (Pages 7–12 of the student text)

Review Questions: "Who Do You Say that I Am?"

Question: What sentence is repeated several times throughout pages 7–10? What point is the author trying to make by repeating the sentence?
Answer: The repeated sentence is, "How much we think we know of him; how little we really do." The author is trying to say that we often *take it for granted* that we know a great deal about Jesus, when in fact there are many things about him that we do not know.

Question: Jesus' followers responded to his death differently than people have responded to the deaths of other great leaders throughout history. Why was this so?
Answer: Before Jesus' followers really had time to grieve and talk of "what might have been," the proclamation of Jesus' resurrection rang out. Jesus was still with his followers, but in a different way than before.

Question: What three main questions will be addressed in this course?
Answer:
1. Who was the historical Jesus, the man who lived nearly two thousand years ago in a place called Palestine?
2. Why did this man, Jesus, come to be recognized as the Christ of Faith?
3. And perhaps most important of all, what does it mean to call Jesus by this title, *Christ of Faith?*

A Text Activity: "Who Do You Say that I Am?"

Activity 1

Imagine that right now Jesus confronts you with the question, "Who do you say that I am?" Write your honest response to that question.

1

Additional Activities: "Who Do You Say that I Am?"

How Do Young People React to Jesus?

On page 10 of the student text, the author suggests that people react to Jesus with everything from heroic commitment to total boredom. In this activity, the students assess the author's suggestion as it pertains to themselves and their peers.

    1. On the chalkboard, draw an 8- to 10-foot horizontal line that can serve as a continuum. Label the left end "Totally Bored" and the right end "Totally Committed." Then further divide the line into four or five sections of equal size and label each section with a level of commitment (e.g., "Not Too Concerned," "Fairly Convinced").

    2. Break the class into groups of five or six, and ask the groups each to arrive at a consensus on the percentage of people their age who fit in each category on the continuum. For example, a group might say that 10 percent of people their age are totally bored with any discussion about Jesus, 25 percent accept the Christian faith but really do not think about it much, 55 percent take their faith fairly seriously, and 10 percent are totally committed to it. The group must make sure that its percentages for the entire continuum add up to 100.

After 5 minutes or so of discussion, have the groups report their results. Record these results appropriately on the continuum. If the differences between the groups' estimates are significant, attempt to achieve a class consensus through further discussion. If the groups' estimates are reasonably close, simply average their estimates to determine a final percentage for each category.

    3. Identify the section of the continuum that represents the majority attitude of people the students' age. Help the students determine five reasons that this attitude might prevail. Mention the common perception that of all influences, peer-group attitudes have the strongest effect on the behavior and cultural values of young people. Ask if this might also be true regarding their religion and faith convictions. That is, when it comes to religion and faith, do young people believe and value only what their peer group allows or expects them to believe and value? It is likely that students will have mixed responses to this question, with many claiming that they are not subject to peer pressure in such matters.

Course Goals

Building upon the preceding activity, introduce the goals of this course with a statement such as the following:
- As young people go through their high school years, it is appropriate for them to draw some of their own conclusions about Jesus and the Christian faith. But making a sound personal decision about Jesus and his message requires in-depth information about him as a historical person and as the Christ of Christian faith. The information in this course is offered to help you work toward your own response to Jesus.

Then state the major goals of the course:
- To provide a solid and reasonable foundation of information about Jesus and his message, upon which you can make a free, mature, and personal response to him—or move closer to making such a response

- To provide this information about Jesus and his message in a way that respects your maturity and intelligence—free of preachiness on the one hand, but requiring some serious study, reflection, and discussion on the other
- To present a portrait of Jesus as he is understood by "insiders," or people of faith, but without unfairly presuming that you are already committed Christians (For those of you who already believe, the course will clarify and strengthen your convictions. For those of you who doubt or question your faith at this time, the course will attempt to inform but not convert you.)

An Orientation to the Student Text

After your students have read the section titled "A Look Ahead," on pages 11–12 of their text, thoroughly examine the text with them, as preparation for the course.

1. Look at the basic content and progression of the student text. This can be done by reading through the table of contents with the students, briefly commenting on each chapter. Note how the material unfolds from an early concentration on the Jesus of History (his life as a Jew, his political and social world, etc.) to a detailed discussion of his mission and ministry, his death and resurrection, and the early church's proclamation about him as the Christ of Faith, especially in the letters of Paul.

The course closes with a discussion of three main periods in the church's history, highlighting the development of the church's doctrinal understanding of Jesus as the Christ of Faith. Make particular note that the formal doctrines about Jesus that may be familiar to us (in particular, the Incarnation and the Trinity) are not discussed until late in the course. These teachings gradually evolved out of the church's historical reflection on the meaning and message of Jesus as recorded in the Christian Testament, and they are best understood in that light.

2. Refer the students to the glossary and the index at the end of the student text. A lot of material is going to be covered in the course, and occasionally the students will need to review their understanding of key concepts. The glossary and the index will be helpful in such cases.

3. Note the location and purposes of the "For Review" questions and the numbered text activities. Both may be used as homework assignments or as in-class discussion starters. The review questions are also useful as study guides prior to quizzes and tests. (For more suggestions on how to use the text activities, see "Student Text Activities," on pages 33–34 of this manual.)

4. Point out the other learning and study tools provided throughout the student text, including a number of charts, maps, and shaded feature boxes. For examples, turn to pages 35, 49, and 77 of the text. The students can take full advantage of these aids by referring to them often.

Concept C: How Do We Learn About Jesus?

The Christian Scriptures, and particularly the Gospels, are the primary sources for learning about Jesus. Various nonscriptural sources verify his historical existence but tell us little else about him. (Pages 13–17 of the student text)

Review Questions: How Do We Learn About Jesus?

Question: Provide a one-sentence definition of each of these terms: *Christian Scriptures, Hebrew Scriptures, Christian Testament.*
Answer:
- *Christian Scriptures* refers to the Bible, both the Hebrew Scriptures and the Christian Testament combined.
- *Hebrew Scriptures* is a more sensitive term for what has commonly been called "the Old Testament"—the testament that is central to Jewish faith.
- *Christian Testament* refers to what has been called "the New Testament"—the section of the Christian Scriptures that pertains specifically to Christian faith.

Question: What role do the Gospels play in the church's teaching about Jesus?
Answer: Just about everything the church teaches about Jesus comes through the Gospels. The Gospels, in turn, serve as the scale or test of truth and authenticity for everything the church teaches about Jesus.

Question: Identify each of the following persons and summarize what they, as a group, contribute to a study of Jesus: *Josephus, Tacitus, Pliny the Younger, Suetonius.*
Answer: Josephus was a Jewish historian. Tacitus was a Roman historian. Pliny the Younger was governor of one of the Roman provinces in Asia Minor. Suetonius was a Roman historian and lawyer. All of these men were non-Christians. As a group, through their writings, they support the historical existence of Jesus, and they show Christianity as worthy of at least brief mention.

Text Activities: How Do We Learn About Jesus?

Activity 2

Before reading further, write a brief response to the following question: *How can we be sure that what we are taught about Jesus is true and not just made up?*

Activity 3

Using any complete Bible, compare the size of the Hebrew Scriptures with the size of the Christian Testament. Then locate the Gospels and note what percentage of the entire Bible these readings take up. Write down any insights or questions that come to mind in light of these comparisons.

Additional Activities: How Do We Learn About Jesus?

Truly Knowing Another

A recurring theme throughout *Jesus of History, Christ of Faith* is the need for an integrated, balanced response to Jesus and his message. Such a response involves the whole person, both the heart and the mind. Without an emotional component in our response to Jesus, we Christians run the risk of being nothing more than disembodied intellects. Without an intellectual component of faith, we are little more than irrational beings controlled solely by our emotions. Neither the emotional nor the faith component by itself reflects the totality of a human response, and neither by itself forms the foundation necessary for meeting the challenges Jesus calls people to.

Although this course on Jesus and his meaning necessarily focuses more on the intellectual and cognitive end of faith, an effort has been made (by way of the text activities) to relate the material to the students' own life experiences, so as to lend some degree of balance to the discussion. This activity is intended to introduce the notion that a true faith response to Jesus involves the heart as well as the mind.

1. Begin the activity by pointing out the difference between knowing *about* someone and truly knowing that person. Say something like this:
   - It is possible to know a great many facts about a person but never truly know him or her in the sense of forming a personal relationship. The same can be said about how we know Jesus. We can know *about* him without ever truly knowing him as a person of significance in our life. Knowing Jesus—in the sense of developing a faith relationship with him—requires both an intellectual understanding of him and his message *and* a free response of love for him. That is, faith in Jesus requires both "head knowledge" and "heart knowledge."

handout 1–A

2. Distribute handout 1–A, "To Know Another." Read the instructions to the students. Then have them complete column A individually. Allow 5 to 10 minutes for their work.

3. Direct the students to use column B to identify each item as a "head" or a "heart" item. That is, if the item of information can be discovered simply by accumulating objective facts about a person, the students should write "head" in column B next to the item. If knowledge of the item requires knowing a person in a personal sense, the students should draw a heart. Wait for all of the students to finish.

4. Divide the class into groups of five or six. Ask the groups each to arrive at a consensus on the ten most important items on the list. The group members should use their individual rankings as a starting point for discussion. Obviously, they will have to discuss, compromise, clarify meanings, and so on, in order to accomplish their task. However, they need not argue over small differences of opinion (e.g., whether an item should be ranked fourth or fifth in importance). The goal is to agree on the top ten items in any order. The group members should indicate these top ten items in column C on their handouts.

Give the groups 15 to 20 minutes, longer if you feel that the discussion is fruitful.

5. Call for each group to report its choices, and record these on the board in columns (i.e., under "Group 1," record the numbers of the items selected by that group, etc.).

6. Look across the columns of small-group responses, noting the numbers that appear in all or most of them (but try to avoid noting more than fifteen numbers). In a final column to the right of all the other columns on the board, write these numbers in order of popularity (e.g., all of the groups might have chosen item 23, while only four might have picked item 7). After each item number, include an abbreviated description of the item, to facilitate discussion. For instance, after the number 23, you could write, "Lonely?" Also indicate whether the item is a "head" or a "heart" item.

7. Class discussion of this exercise can revolve around questions such as the following:
- What do you find most striking about the results of this exercise? [It is hoped, for one thing, that all of the items chosen as significant for the development of a deep friendship are "heart" items.]
- What is required in order to gain "heart" information from another person? [Possible responses are trust, openness, honesty, communication, and plenty of time.]
- The goal of this course is to help you know Jesus both "by head" and "by heart." Look at the list of significant items on the board. How can we hope to discover these things about Jesus?

"You Know More than You Think You Do"

This activity can demonstrate to the students that they are already quite familiar with the Gospel story.

1. Ask the class to take out their Bibles and locate the Gospels. Then have them randomly flip through those pages and, without looking, point a finger at a passage.

2. Ask for a volunteer to read the passage that his or her finger has fallen on—that is, to begin reading at the nearest start of a paragraph. If no one volunteers, call on someone who you believe is a confident reader. After the student has read several verses, stop him or her and ask the following questions:
- Can anyone identify the Gospel scene or section from which the passage was taken?
- Can anyone guess what the next few verses will say?

3. After some guesses have been shared, ask the student who read the passage to read another three or four verses, to determine whether any of the guesses were correct.

4. Repeat the exercise several times, with different students reading their random selections.

5. In summary, point out that most of the students are already quite familiar with the Gospel story from hearing it proclaimed at liturgies over the years. This course will build on that basic familiarity and explore more deeply what the Gospel story has to teach us.

Researching Non-Christian Sources

Divide the class into four groups and assign each group one of the four non-Christian sources of information about Jesus that are mentioned in the student text: Josephus, Tacitus, Pliny the Younger, or Suetonius. Give the students the individual homework task of writing a one-page report on their assigned person. They can most easily do this using an encyclopedia as their primary resource. When the reports have been completed, lead a class discussion on the non-Christian sources, asking members of each group to summarize what they discovered.

The chief purpose of this exercise is not to overwhelm the students with historical information about these figures but, rather, to affirm that a belief in the historical Jesus of Nazareth is grounded in fact, not fantasy. Conclude your class discussion with a strong statement to that effect.

Concept D: The Christian Testament

The Christian Testament is composed of twenty-seven separate writings, or books, representing different authors and different types of writing, yet one theme is consistent throughout. All of the books deal in some way with the life and ministry of Jesus and the impact he had on his initial followers and the early Christian community. (Pages 18–21 of the student text)

Review Questions: The Christian Testament

Question: How many books are in the Christian Testament? During what years was the Christian Testament written?
Answer: The Christian Testament is composed of twenty-seven books. It developed from roughly twenty years after the death of Jesus (that is, from about 50 C.E.) to about 100 C.E.

Question: What is the principal theme that unifies the writings of the Christian Testament?
Answer: The writings all deal in some way with the life and ministry of Jesus and the impact he had on the community of those who believed in him—what we now know as the church.

Question: What are the main concerns of the non-Gospel writings of the Christian Testament?
Answer: The happenings within the early community of faith; the meaning of Jesus' life, death, and resurrection for the individual believer; various difficulties encountered by the first Christians as they moved out into the world, and so on.

Question: Provide a one-sentence description of each of the following: *the Gospels, the Acts of the Apostles, the Pauline epistles, the Letter to the Hebrews, the catholic epistles, the Book of Revelation.*
Answer:
- The Gospels include information about the life, works, message, death, and resurrection of Jesus.
- The Acts of the Apostles is Luke's account of the early days of the Christian community and the spread of the Good News throughout the Roman Empire after the death and resurrection of Jesus.
- The Pauline epistles were written, either by Saint Paul or by others, to support and further educate individual Christians or small communities that had been brought to believe in Jesus through the missionary work of Paul and others.

- The Letter to the Hebrews, often attributed to Paul but probably not written by him, is a kind of extended sermon to a group of Christians who are in danger of falling away from their belief in Jesus.
- The catholic epistles, attributed to four different personalities (James, Peter, John, and Jude), are called "catholic" because they are addressed to believing Christians as a general audience rather than to specific individuals or communities.
- The Book of Revelation, filled with highly symbolic and mysterious language, was written to encourage late-first-century Christians to remain faithful to Christ during times of severe persecution.

A Text Activity: The Christian Testament

Activity 4

Write down the titles of any twenty-seven books you find on any bookshelf in a library, in the classroom, or at home. Then look at the collection of books in the Christian Testament (see the list on page 20). Write a short paragraph discussing the different meaning the word *book* has for each collection.

Additional Activities: The Christian Testament

A Demonstration on the "Books" of the Bible

This demonstration is an alternative to having the students do text activity 4.

Gather twenty-seven books from bookshelves in your classroom or borrow that many from the library. Display the books in a stack at the front of the room and, without giving any clues, ask the class what the stack of books might represent. If no one can guess, ask one of the students to count the books and announce the number to the class. Then ask if anyone has a response. Close by making the obvious point that when the term *book* is used in connection with the Bible, it means something different from what we normally imagine.

Locating Scriptural Verses

Before proceeding to chapter 2, make sure that the students understand the organization of each scriptural book into chapters and verses, and that they know how to locate cited verses. Too often teachers presume that their students have picked up this knowledge along the way.

Start by slowly thumbing through the Bible with your students, making note of the following information:
- The Hebrew Scriptures, like the Christian Testament, consist of a number of books rather than one continuous narrative.
- Each book in the Bible is divided into chapters.
- Each chapter is divided into verses. A verse might be only part of a sentence, or it might be more than a sentence.

Have the students locate specific verses that you choose and announce verbally. Then write a scriptural citation on the board and, after explaining what each number stands for, ask the students to locate the verse or verses specified. Be on the alert for students who seem confused, because they will not be able to follow the course well if they do not have this basic skill.

An Oral Review of the Christian Testament Books

This activity is a variation on the last review question in this chapter. In advance, prepare six index cards by writing one of the following phrases on each: *the Gospels, the Acts of the Apostles, the Pauline epistles, the Letter to the Hebrews, the catholic epistles, the Book of Revelation.* Walk through the classroom and randomly hand a card to a student, giving her or him just a few seconds to accurately describe the particular part of the Christian Testament. The description should approximate that given on pages 51–52 of this manual. If the student cannot immediately respond, take back the card and give it to another student. Repeat the exercise until you are convinced most or all of the class can describe each writing or set of writings.

To Know Another

Listed below are twenty-eight items of information that we might be able to discover about another person. In column A, rank the items in terms of how important it would be to discover each of them if you wanted to develop a deep friendship with someone. Use **1** for the most important item to discover, **2** for the second most important, and so on. Then your teacher will tell you what to do with columns B and C.

A	Item	B	C
_____	1. The amount of money they have	_____	_____
_____	2. Their favorite sport	_____	_____
_____	3. How they feel in a large group	_____	_____
_____	4. Their favorite color	_____	_____
_____	5. What they like most about themselves	_____	_____
_____	6. What grade school they attended	_____	_____
_____	7. What makes them cry	_____	_____
_____	8. Where they were born	_____	_____
_____	9. Who their best friend is	_____	_____
_____	10. What makes them feel secure	_____	_____
_____	11. Their favorite subject in school	_____	_____
_____	12. What they are afraid of	_____	_____
_____	13. What they would like to change about themselves	_____	_____
_____	14. Their favorite food	_____	_____
_____	15. How many brothers and sisters they have	_____	_____
_____	16. What makes them angry	_____	_____
_____	17. Whether they like little kids	_____	_____
_____	18. How they get along with their parents	_____	_____
_____	19. Their height, weight, and hair color	_____	_____
_____	20. Whether they believe in God	_____	_____
_____	21. Their birth date	_____	_____
_____	22. What makes them laugh	_____	_____
_____	23. What makes them feel lonely	_____	_____
_____	24. What they value most in life	_____	_____
_____	25. Their favorite time of day	_____	_____
_____	26. What makes them feel loved	_____	_____
_____	27. Their favorite TV program	_____	_____
_____	28. Their favorite hobby	_____	_____

Handout 1–A: Permission to reproduce this handout for classroom use is granted.

CHAPTER 2

The Gospels: Central Sources for Understanding Jesus

Major Concepts

A. **Searching for the "Jesus of History" in the Gospels:** The Gospels are neither biographies of Jesus nor historical records of his words and actions. The concern of the Gospels is religious truth, the deeper meaning that God intends to reveal to people through historical events. The discernment of religious truth is the task of the entire Christian community.

B. **The Development of the Gospels:** Perhaps the best way to understand the Gospels is to look at their development, which took place in three major stages.

C. **The Gospels as Four Portraits of Jesus:** The Gospels differ from one another in terms of author, time of writing, audience, and purpose. While each Gospel is a separate and unique "portrait" of Jesus, no one Gospel tells us everything we need to know about him. To gain a fuller understanding of Jesus, we must consider all four Gospels together.

Concept A:
Searching for the "Jesus of History" in the Gospels

The Gospels are neither biographies of Jesus nor historical records of his words and actions. The concern of the Gospels is religious truth, the deeper meaning that God intends to reveal to people through historical events. The discernment of religious truth is the task of the entire Christian community. (Pages 23–27 of the student text)

Review Questions:
Searching for the "Jesus of History" in the Gospels

Question: Is the record of past events that we call "history" a totally accurate description of the events as they actually happened? Explain your response.

Answer: "History" is not a totally accurate description of past events, because it usually involves an interpretation of those events. The information comes to us through the eyes and perspective of the person doing the recording. And no one's perspective is totally objective, because this would require one to be without a point of view, which is impossible.

Question: What do the origins of the word *gospel* suggest about the purpose of the Gospels?

Answer: The word *gospel* is derived from the very old English word *godspell,* which means "good news" or "glad tidings." That word, in turn, is a translation of the Greek word *evangelion,* meaning "the proclamation or announcement of good news." So from the origins of the word *gospel* we learn that the purpose of the Gospels is to proclaim a message of faith in Jesus. It is not to provide accurate historical accounts of Jesus' day-to-day life.

Question: Briefly explain what is meant by the term *religious truth* and discuss its relationship to the Scriptures.

Answer: Religious truth refers to the deeper meaning that God intends to reveal to people through historical events. It is religious truth that the Scriptures are primarily filled with. The authors of the biblical literature were attempting to reveal reality through the eyes of God. They were far less concerned with the historical facts, or what an event might have appeared to be on the surface.

Question: What can we gain from the Gospels besides some basic information about Jesus and his message?

Answer: The Gospels, together with the rest of the Christian Testament, also offer us an understanding of the meaning and significance of the historical Jesus for the people of his time.

Text Activities:
Searching for the "Jesus of History" in the Gospels

Activity 1

Choose any public figure—for example, an athlete, a musician, or a politician—and list at least ten items of information you would expect to find in a thorough biography of that person. Keep your notion of a biography in mind while reading about the nature of the Gospels.

Activity 2

Pick a photograph of a room or a landscape and briefly describe everything that you can see in it. Next, list the things that you cannot see clearly, or at all, because of the point of view from which the photo was taken. For example, if you can see one side of a tree, you most likely cannot see its other side. What are two ways that you might learn about the things you cannot see?

Activity 3

In a short paper, briefly summarize a favorite story that has been told over and over by one of your relatives. Then respond to the following questions: *To what degree do you think the story has been changed or exaggerated over the years? If the story has been changed, does that lessen or cancel out the value or meaning of the story itself? Why or why not?*

Additional Activities:
Searching for the "Jesus of History" in the Gospels

Getting a Sense of History

To help the students better understand the discussion of history on page 23 of the student text, have the class analyze a current event. Choose a happening of significance to them and instruct them to take in as many reports of the event as possible. For example, in the case of a national political event, the students should be able to review newspaper, magazine, radio, and TV reports. Assign a paper in which the students discuss the different approaches found in the reports and the perspectives of various parties involved in or affected by the event.

To conclude the activity, stress that the coverage of any event, and therefore of all history, consists of more than objective facts and information; it also reflects biases, perspectives, strengths and weaknesses, the intended audience, and so on, of the reporter. Make the connection to the Gospels, saying that each Evangelist worked from a unique perspective and with specific intentions as he developed his own Gospel portrait of Jesus.

It's All a Matter of Perspective

As an alternative to the preceding activity, or in addition to it, have the students analyze a recent school sports event, viewing the event from the perspectives of losers and winners, coaches and players, and so on. You may want the students to take the roles of reporters covering the event, writing short essays with a newspaper flavor to them. Or you may want to arrange for mock TV interviews in class. Conclude the activity along the same lines as the preceding one.

Guest Faculty Speakers

Consider inviting one or more teachers from outside your department to offer their insights into the importance of considering levels of meaning and interpretation when looking at historical or literary sources. For example, a history teacher might speak about what constitutes "history" and illustrate the fact that all of history is subject to the interpretation and biases of the one recording it. An English teacher might explore the fact that all great literature involves multiple layers of meaning and note that the richness of such literature can be experienced only when those deeper layers of meaning are explored.

It would be particularly helpful if the teachers could connect their insights to material the students are actually studying in your school's nonreligion classes. That is, the history teacher could draw illustrations from the material the students are currently covering in their history course, and the English teacher could refer to a story the students have recently read in their English course.

Concept B: The Development of the Gospels

Perhaps the best way to understand the Gospels is to look at their development, which took place in three major stages. (Pages 28–34 of the student text)

Review Questions: The Development of the Gospels

Question: Briefly describe the three major stages in the development of the Gospels.
Answer:
- *Stage 1:* Jesus lived and worked, having a profound effect on his disciples.
- *Stage 2:* After the death and resurrection of Jesus, the disciples and the early church proclaimed the Good News throughout the Roman Empire.
- *Stage 3:* The Gospels were actually written by the Evangelists, who likely served as editors or collectors of material that had gradually developed through the years.

Question: *Christ* is not Jesus' last name. Explain.
Answer: Christ means literally "anointed one." It is based on the Greek word *Christos,* which is itself a translation of the Hebrew word *messiah.* To those Jews who accepted Jesus as the Messiah after his resurrection, he became known as "Jesus the Christ," which in turn became rather quickly shortened to what we now know as a single name: *Jesus Christ.* This clouds to some degree the recognition of the Christian conviction that the Jesus of History is truly the Christ of Faith.

Question: What two major factors explain the transition from an initial oral telling of the Good News to the written form found in the Gospels?
Answer:
- *The passage of time:* It gradually became clear that Jesus would not return as quickly as the Christians had hoped he would. With the realization that the church had a future, it became necessary to find a means for preserving the church's teachings for future generations.
- *The need for continued instruction:* The church needed to continue instructing and inspiring the already existing communities of faith that had been formed throughout the Roman Empire during the previous decades of missionary activity.

A Text Activity: The Development of the Gospels

Activity 4

Fold a piece of paper in half to create two vertical columns. Title the left column "Oral Storytelling" and the right column "Written Storytelling." List at least five benefits and five shortcomings of each type of storytelling. For example, what can be done with an oral story that cannot be done with a written one, and vice versa?

Additional Activities: The Development of the Gospels

Summarizing the Development of the Gospels

Tell the students to close their books. On the chalkboard, draw a timeline using the years from the timeline on page 35 of the student text. Then ask the students to help you summarize the development of the Gospels by placing the stages of that development on your timeline. The students may have difficulty doing this, but the effort will help clarify their understanding of the text discussion. If they are unable to complete the timeline, refer them to page 35 of the student text and discuss the timeline presented there. Go through the timeline with them stage by stage, commenting appropriately.

Becoming Evangelists

This activity is designed to give the students a more in-depth sense of how the Gospels developed. Allow two full sessions for it.

Note: This activity is similar to one in the *Teaching Manual for Understanding Catholic Christianity* (Winona, MN: Saint Mary's Press, 1989), which accompanies Thomas Zanzig's survey course for first-year students in Catholic high schools. The activity in that manual is titled "The Gospel According to Young People" (see pp. 228–230). It is more elaborate than what you will find here, and it involves four handouts. If the course *Understanding Catholic Christianity* is offered in your school, find out whether your students have experienced that activity. If they have not, you may want to use that version instead of this one.

1. Begin this version of the activity by giving an introduction along the following lines:
- A number of years ago, there was a popular movie titled *Oh, God!* It depicted the problems encountered by a young supermarket manager who was visited by God and informed that he had the job of telling the world about God and God's plan for humankind. Though the movie was a clever and entertaining comedy, its success was probably due just as much to its simply stated but profound insights. The supermarket manager's ultimate realization—that all he could really do was say what he believed and hope people would listen—is certainly one of the key lessons each Christian must learn.

    Today's Christians, like all followers of Jesus throughout history, have a profound message to share, one that seems almost too good to be true. Despite the fact that many people will doubt the message and laugh at its apparent absurdity and at those who believe in it—just as people laughed at that supermarket manager in the movie—the message must be passed on. The question is, if you were to pass on the Christian message, which images and stories would you use?

To give you a sense of how difficult this question really is, we are going to do a project now. Most of you have probably been hearing about Jesus since you were young children. You've most likely heard your parents talk about him. Without knowing it, you have probably heard all of the Gospels at least several times by going to Mass throughout your lifetime. You've attended religion classes for years. So you should know quite a bit about Jesus. We're going to find out what things about Jesus stand out the strongest in your memory, mean the most to you, touch you deeply. In effect, you are going to write your own gospels.

Using the movie *Oh, God!* as an example will, of course, be most effective if you have seen the movie and can describe it vividly. If you have not seen the movie, consider not using it as an example.

2. Divide the class into four groups. Give each group some large sheets of newsprint, some felt-tip markers, and the following assignment:
- First, list the miracles of Jesus that you, as a group, would want to share. Your list should include only the miracles that have special significance for you, the ones you remember most vividly.
- Then list the parables, or stories, told by Jesus that you want to include in your gospel—the ones that are particularly meaningful or important to you.
- Next, list brief summaries of the teachings of Jesus that you strongly think others should hear. All that is needed are the general topics.
- Finally, list all the events in the life of Jesus—other than his teaching, miracles, and telling of parables—that you feel are essential for people to know about. For example, you might want to include the stories of his birth, his being lost in the Temple, his confrontations with the Pharisees, and his crucifixion. You do not need to explain your choices. Just list them.

Instruct the groups to record their answers on the large sheets of paper, clearly labeling each list.

Handout 2–A

Handout 2–A, "A Reference Guide to the Gospel Story," is for the students to use during this part of the activity. It lists most of Jesus' miracles and parables as well as Jesus' most significant teachings and many important Gospel events. Distribute the handout when you give the assignment. Make sure that the students also have their Bibles handy.

Variation: You may want the students to first try the assignment relying only on their memory. What stories and information about Jesus are important enough for the students to have remembered them? The handout and the Bibles can then be used as backups.

Tell the groups that they have about 5 minutes to spend on each part of the assignment, or about 20 minutes total. The idea is for them to quickly identify the elements of the Gospel story that they feel are most important. After the 20 minutes has passed, check on the groups and, if necessary, give them another 5 minutes to wrap things up.

3. After the groups have completed the assignment, give them the remainder of the class session to decide how they would like to introduce their gospel. To help them get started, say something like this:
- Luke and Matthew began their Gospels with stories about Jesus' birth and childhood. Mark began his Gospel with the baptism of Jesus, the event that signaled the start of Jesus' public life. And John opened his Gospel with a poetic description of how "the Word became flesh." Decide how

you would like to open your gospel. What will you do—tell a story, share a favorite poem, plunge into your own convictions about Jesus, or approach the opening some other way?

4. At the second class session, invite each group to give the class an overview of its gospel outline and to talk about any difficulties it had with the assignment, any strong reactions or discussions that came up. After each group has made its presentation, ask a group member to post the sheets of newsprint in a place that can be seen by all the students.

5. Wrap up the activity by giving your reactions to the students' gospel outlines, along with a summary of the purpose of the activity. Your summary could be something like this:
- What you have done is a very abbreviated version of what the first Christians had to do after the death and resurrection of Jesus nearly two thousand years ago. Those people loved Jesus, had hope in him, in many cases staked their lives on the belief that he was the Messiah they had long awaited. And then they watched him die. Imagine their grief, their fear, the turmoil their lives were in. But then imagine as well the incredible joy of the Resurrection, the experience that Jesus was no longer dead but alive in their midst! The implications of that reality have been experienced by Christians ever since that day.

  But how have Christians heard the Good News? It has been handed down largely through the efforts of the original followers, who knew Jesus, and those to whom they passed their message. Eventually their recollections of the man Jesus and all he meant were written down. And the writers recorded not just what Jesus meant to them while he walked the earth but, even more so, what he meant to them after his death and resurrection.

  In your group discussions, you just recalled the elements of Jesus' life that mean the most to you, bringing several ideas together into a whole, into something that would make sense at least to people who would believe those images and stories and view them with faith. What you have done is what the Evangelists had to do, and the results of their efforts are the four Gospels.

Concept C: The Gospels as Four Portraits of Jesus

The Gospels differ from one another in terms of author, time of writing, audience, and purpose. While each Gospel is a separate and unique "portrait" of Jesus, no one Gospel tells us everything we need to know about him. To gain a fuller understanding of Jesus, we must consider all four Gospels together. (Pages 35–43 of the student text)

A Review Question:
The Gospels as Four Portraits of Jesus

Question: For each of the four Gospels, summarize the following information: *author, approximate date when written, primary audience, central themes.*
Answer:
- The Gospel of Mark was written by an unknown author (possibly a certain John Mark who is mentioned in the Acts of the Apostles) around 70 C.E. It

was written for the church in Rome and for Gentile readers, and it stresses Jesus' humanity and suffering.
- The Gospel of Luke was written by an unknown author (possibly a Gentile doctor) around 85 C.E. It was written for Gentile Christians and perhaps for well-to-do Christians. Luke's Gospel stresses the mercy and compassion of Jesus and the central role of the Holy Spirit in Jesus' life.
- The Gospel of Matthew was written by an unknown author around 90 C.E. It was written for Jews who were converting to Christianity, and it stresses Jesus as the Messiah whom the Jews had been waiting for.
- The Gospel of John was probably written by followers of the Beloved Disciple around 95 C.E. It was written for the church of that time, which had had many years to reflect on Jesus' true identity. John's Gospel stresses Jesus as the divine Son of God.

A Text Activity: The Gospels as Four Portraits of Jesus

Activity 5

Write a short paragraph describing the differences between a *portrait* and a *picture* of someone. How do these differences relate to the notion of the Gospels as four "portraits" of Jesus?

Additional Activities:
The Gospels as Four Portraits of Jesus

Getting to Know the Gospels Better

Use this exercise to review and expand upon what the student text says about each of the Gospels.

1. On the chalkboard, draw four broad columns and label each with the name of a Gospel. Divide the class into four groups, one for each Gospel. Ask the groups to tell you as much as they can about their assigned Gospel: its author, when it was written, its primary audience, its major themes, and so on. List this information on the board in the appropriate column.

2. Fill out each column with any of the following information. Note that the information provided in boldface type here is not included in the student text discussion and should not be expected to come from the students. These items provide you with the opportunity to expand the students' knowledge of the Gospels. You may want the students to take notes on the additional material.

Mark's Gospel
- possibly written by John Mark, a companion of the Apostle Peter
- written around 70 C.E. (the earliest Gospel)
- written for the church in Rome and for Gentiles
- **often recognized as "the Gospel of action," in which Jesus is always "on the move"**
- stresses the humanity and suffering of Jesus
- **portrays Jesus as the unrecognized Messiah (Jesus' followers seem to take forever to catch on to who Jesus is, and when they finally do, Jesus tells them to keep it a secret.)**

Luke's Gospel
- possibly written by a Gentile doctor
- written around 85 C.E.
- written for Gentile Christians and perhaps for well-to-do Christians
- stresses the universality of the Christian message, particularly by showing women and poor people in important roles
- stresses Jesus' compassion, mercy, and concern for sinners
- **in the miracle stories, emphasizes Jesus' compassion for those who are suffering**
- stresses the central role of the Holy Spirit in Jesus' life
- is the first part of a two-part work, part two being the Acts of the Apostles

Matthew's Gospel
- written around 90 C.E.
- written for Jews who were converting to Christianity
- stresses Jesus as the fulfillment of promises made by God in the Hebrew Scriptures
- demonstrates Jesus' role as a teacher and preacher (**e.g., the Sermon on the Mount, in chapters 5–7**)
- discusses the responsibilities of Jesus' followers (**e.g., chapter 18**)

John's Gospel
- probably written by followers of the Beloved Disciple
- written around 95 C.E.
- reflects theological sophistication and concentration on spiritual realities
- presents Jesus as "the Word of God" and stresses his incarnation
- **emphasizes faith as coming from God and as truly present when the believer is "without sight," that is, without visible evidence of God**
- builds poetic and memorable images of Jesus as "the vine," "the good shepherd," and so on

3. Close this exercise by restating the student text's explanation that the Gospels of Matthew, Mark, and Luke are known as "the synoptics" because of their great similarities, while John offers a unique portrait of Jesus.

A Special Reading Assignment

At this point in the course, you are strongly urged to break from the student text for a few class sessions and have the students actually read at least one of the Gospels from beginning to end. This initial familiarity with the content of a Gospel will be valuable—and perhaps critical—to effective study for the remainder of the course. **All lesson material from this point on will presume that the students have read one complete Gospel.**

1. Divide the class into four groups, assigning one of the Gospels to each group. (The Gospels are not of equal length, with Mark and John being considerably shorter than Matthew and Luke. The students may not notice this, but if they do, just acknowledge the discrepancy and draw lots to determine which group has which Gospel. There appears to be no way to avoid the dissatisfaction of those students who are assigned the longer Gospels.)

The reading of one Gospel may take two or three hours. Assign the reading as homework to be done individually and according to a schedule (e.g., over a five-night period, with each Gospel divided into five reading assignments). You may also choose to allow time for quiet reading during class sessions.

2. Take some time during class to have the students gather in their Gospel groups. They should discuss their reading, with one student in each group recording on paper any terms, events, persons, groups, or incidents that were completely foreign or confusing. For example, a group might note that they did not know who the Sadducees were and that the genealogy of Jesus was confusing. These items should be reported to the class as a whole and listed on the chalkboard under a heading for the appropriate Gospel.

3. When the groups have completed their reading, discussion, and identification of difficult points, collate the items listed on the board, looking for points of interest and recurring questions. Then refer the students to the table of contents in the student text, remarking on how the chapters will clarify many, if not all, of the items listed on the board. Because the students have become familiar with at least one Gospel, they will see how the course is designed to lead them logically through the maze of information toward a clear portrait of Jesus.

A Reference Guide to the Gospel Story

A Partial Listing of Jesus' Miracles

Cleansing a leper (Matthew 8:1–4)

Healing a centurion's servant (Luke 7:1–10)

Calming a storm (Matthew 8:23–27)

Healing a paralytic (Mark 2:1–12)

Restoring life to Jairus's daughter (Luke 8:40–56)

Healing two blind men (Matthew 9:27–31)

Multiplying loaves (Mark 6:30–44)

Walking on water (Mark 6:45–52)

Healing a deaf man (Mark 7:31–37)

Healing the blind man of Bethsaida (Mark 8:22–26)

Healing a boy with a demon (Luke 9:37–42)

Cleansing ten lepers (Luke 17:11–19)

Cursing a barren fig tree (Matthew 21:18–22)

Changing water to wine at Cana (John 2:1–12)

Raising Lazarus (John 11:1–44)

A Partial Listing of Jesus' Parables

The sower (Matthew 13:1–23)

The weeds among the wheat (Matthew 13:24–30)

The wedding banquet (Matthew 22:1–14)

The faithful servant (Matthew 24:45–51)

The ten bridesmaids (Matthew 25:1–13)

The talents, or sums of money (Matthew 25:14–30)

The great feast (Luke 14:15–24)

The wicked tenants (Mark 12:1–12)

The mustard seed (Mark 4:30–32)

The good Samaritan (Luke 10:25–37)

The house built on rock (Matthew 7:24–27)

The rich man and Lazarus (Luke 16:19–31)

The rich fool (Luke 12:16–21)

The lost sheep (Matthew 18:12–14)

The prodigal son (Luke 15:11–32)

The unjust servant (Luke 16:1–13)

The laborers in the vineyard (Matthew 20:1–16)

The Pharisee and the tax collector (Luke 18:9–14)

Some of Jesus' Most Significant Teachings

The Beatitudes (Matthew 5:3–12)

Salt of the earth (Matthew 5:13)

Attitude toward sinners (Luke 15:1–32)

God and money (Matthew 6:19–34)

The vine and the branches (John 15:1–8)

The greatest commandment (Matthew 22:34–40)

The true disciple (Matthew 19:16–22)

Forgiveness of injuries (Matthew 18:21–22)

Finding life by losing it (Matthew 16:24–26)

God revealed in the simplicity of children (Mark 10:13–16)

Not judging others (Luke 7:36–50)

How to pray (Matthew 6:5–13)

The Last Judgment (Matthew 25:31–46)

Trust in God (Luke 12:22–31)

The gift of the Spirit (John 16:5–14)

Some Important Gospel Events

Jesus' birth in Bethlehem (Luke 2:1–20)

The boy Jesus lost in the Temple (Luke 2:41–50)

Jesus' baptism (Matthew 3:13–17)

The temptation in the desert (Luke 4:1–13)

The calling of the Apostles (Matthew 4:18–22)

Picking corn on the Sabbath (Matthew 12:1–8)

Dinner at Simon's house (Luke 7:36–50)

Jesus' conversation with the Samaritan woman at the well (John 4:4–30)

Jesus' conflicts with the Pharisees (Matthew 23:1–39)

The rejection of Jesus at Nazareth (Matthew 13:54–58)

The cleansing of the Temple (John 2:13–17)

Peter's confession of faith (Matthew 16:13–20)

The Transfiguration (Matthew 17:1–9)

The entry into Jerusalem (Mark 11:1–10)

The Last Supper (Luke 22:7–38)

The agony in the garden (Mark 14:32–42)

The arrest and trial of Jesus (Mark 14:43–65; 15:1–15)

The Crucifixion (Matthew 27:32–56)

The Resurrection (Matthew 28:1–10)

The post-Resurrection appearances (Luke 24:13–49)

The Ascension (Luke 24:50–53)

CHAPTER 3

The World of Jesus: History and Politics

Major Concepts

A. **Jesus the Jew:** To properly understand Jesus and his message, we must recognize that Jesus was a first-century Palestinian Jew and that he preached his message in that context.

B. **A Brief History of the Jewish People:** Jewish history began with Abraham, nearly two thousand years before Jesus. God established a series of covenants with Abraham's descendants. Over time, led by Isaac, Jacob, Joseph, and Moses, they became the People of God, or Israel. A succession of conquerors, along with the people's own sinfulness, prevented Israel from settling peacefully in the Promised Land.

C. **The Political World of Jesus:** The world of Jesus' day was politically dominated by the Romans. Even so, the people of Israel continued to be culturally influenced by the Greek rulers of the past. The Christian Testament mentions Jesus' encounters with the Sadducees and the Pharisees, Jewish political factions that had formed during a period of Jewish independence.

D. **An Oppressed People Dream of a Liberator:** Out of the complex religious and political history that preceded Jesus' birth, there emerged within the minds and hearts of the Jews the dream of an "anointed one," the Messiah, who would liberate them from their oppression.

A Note to the Teacher: Chapters 3 and 4

Though chapters 3 and 4 of the student text are relatively long, they may require less class time than the remaining chapters, which deal more directly with Jesus' ministry and message. Keep this in mind as you plan your teaching.

Together, chapters 3 and 4 provide some basic background for understanding all of the material that will follow them:
- Chapter 3 summarizes the religious and political history of the Jewish people, including their domination by the Greeks and the Romans.
- Chapter 4 describes the land, family life, and social characteristics of Jesus' people, and it concludes by summarizing the major features of ancient Judaism—its sacred places, religious practices, and key religious-political groups.

The primary objective in teaching this material is that the students gain a very basic comprehension of the ancient Jews' history and lifestyle. Do not feel pressed to belabor the content of these chapters. Much of this material—especially the straight historical narrative in chapter 3—requires an emphasis on discussion of the student text material along with direct input by you.

This recommendation for a lesser amount of attention certainly does not mean that the material in chapters 3 and 4 is unimportant. On the contrary, it is by knowing about the history and lifestyle of the ancient Jews that we can most readily get in touch with the Jesus of History. And it is only in light of this knowledge that we can fully understand and appreciate his impact as the Christ of Faith.

Concept A: Jesus the Jew

To properly understand Jesus and his message, we must recognize that Jesus was a first-century Palestinian Jew and that he preached his message in that context. (Pages 45–46 of the student text)

A Review Question: Jesus the Jew

Question: Explain why studying Jewish history is important to understanding Jesus and his message.

Answer: Jesus was a faith-filled and profoundly committed Jew of his day. We cannot understand him outside the context of his Jewish heritage.

A Text Activity: Jesus the Jew

Activity 1

In writing, answer the questions in parentheses concerning the story of Jesus in the synagogue. Do the best you can without using a source other than the story itself.

An Additional Activity: Jesus the Jew

Religion: In Every Corner of Our Lives

This activity will help the students realize how pervasive and influential religion is in our lives.

1. Ask the students to imagine that an expedition of travelers from outer space has come to our planet to investigate the role of religion in our lives. The aliens have asked the students to identify all the things related to religion (objects, structures, practices, events, etc.) that affect them in their home, school, and community. Be sure to encourage the students to draw their responses from their own life experiences. For example, they might note the following:
- *For home:* crucifixes, paintings, and other religious symbols on the walls; the Bible and other books; U.S. currency, which bears the motto "In God We Trust"; prayers before meals
- *For school:* architecture, the curriculum, the faculty
- *For community:* all schools, hospitals, and other structures associated with religious institutions; community celebrations, such as Christmas

After the students have exhausted their ideas on this, add some of your own.

2. To sum up the activity, make the connection between the experience of religion in our lives and that in Jesus' life as a faith-filled Jew of his day:
- Just as a great deal of what we think, feel, believe, and experience is rooted in our religious history and traditions, so it was for Jesus in his day.

Concept B: A Brief History of the Jewish People

Jewish history began with Abraham, nearly two thousand years before Jesus. God established a series of covenants with Abraham's descendants. Over time, led by Isaac, Jacob, Joseph, and Moses, they became the People of God, or Israel. A succession of conquerors, along with the people's own sinfulness, prevented Israel from settling peacefully in the Promised Land. (Pages 47–57 of the student text)

Review Questions: A Brief History of the Jewish People

Question: List two major characters in ancient Jewish history that received new names. Give both their original and their new names. Briefly explain the significance of their receiving a new name from God.
Answer: Abram was given the name *Abraham,* and Jacob was given the name *Israel.* Each was given a new name as a sign of the new and unique relationship that God had established with him.

Question: What name did God reveal to Moses, and what does the name mean? Why was God's giving of that name so significant?
Answer: God revealed *Yahweh,* the name of God, to Moses. The name is thought to come from the Hebrew word for the verb "to be," and it can be translated as "I am who am." The name signifies that God is the Creator, the Ruler of nature and history, and the One who is always present.

The significance of God's revealing that name to the Israelite people lies in the fact that for the Israelites, the act of naming anything indicated the power of the namer over the named. By revealing God's name to the people, God claimed sovereignty over the people. Also of significance is the fact that at a time when many gods were believed in, the Israelite people were told who the one true God was.

Question: Briefly explain the origin and meaning of the term *Passover*.
Answer: By sending ten plagues, Yahweh helped free the Israelites from their slavery in Egypt. The tenth plague involved the death of all the firstborn children in Egypt. But Yahweh gave the Israelites a sign that would protect them, and the Israelites' homes were "passed over" by the plague. The event became memorialized in the feast of Passover.

Question: Identify *Saul, David,* and *Solomon* and briefly explain the relationships among the three.
Answer: Saul was the first king of Israel. He was very jealous of one of the leaders of his army, a young man named David. After the death of Saul, two of the twelve tribes of Israel recognized David as their king, and eventually all of the tribes became unified under him. Solomon, the son of David, became king after David's death.

Question: Define the term *Diaspora*.
Answer: When the kingdom of Judah was overrun by the Babylonians, many of the people who were not captured left the country and formed small colonies along the Mediterranean Sea. These people made up a settlement called the Diaspora, from a word meaning "dispersion" or "those who have been dispersed."

Text Activities: A Brief History of the Jewish People

Activity 2

As you read this history of the Jewish people, record and briefly identify the major characters, in the order in which they appear. Use the information as a study guide.

Activity 3

Choosing from among all the characters of Jewish history identified up to and including Solomon, write a brief paragraph on the one you would most like to meet and talk with.

Activity 4

Consult a dictionary and write down the definitions of these words: *prophet, priest, scribe.*

Additional Activities:
A Brief History of the Jewish People

Research and Discussion on Key Persons in Jewish History

This activity is a way of reviewing the material covered in the student text. Allow two class sessions for the activity.

1. As preparation for the activity, print the following names on separate pieces of paper and place them in a bag or box: *Abraham, Isaac, Jacob, Joseph, Moses, Saul, David, Solomon, Isaiah, Jeremiah, Second Isaiah.*

2. Break the class into eleven groups of equal size, or as close to that as possible (e.g., ten groups of three and one of four if you have a class of thirty-four students). Have a representative from each group randomly choose one of the pieces of paper to determine the historical person his or her group will study and report on. Then give the following instructions:
- Your group is to develop an oral report on the selected historical person. The report should be between five and ten minutes long. Each person in the group is responsible for researching and reporting on one of the following points [in small classes, each student may have to assume more than one task]:
  a. who the person was and when he lived
  b. what the person did or experienced that was significant in the history of the Jews
  c. two short but significant scriptural readings about the person
  d. two lessons we might learn from the experience of the person

To ensure that the students understand what they are to do, you may want to include the preceding instructions on each piece of paper placed in the bag or box.

3. Allow the students to work on their projects during class time for at least one session, more than that if you feel it is necessary. They should have access to resources that might help them, including *The New Jerome Biblical Commentary* and John L. McKenzie's *Dictionary of the Bible*.

4. When it is time for the presentations, draw a timeline (about 10 feet from left to right) on the chalkboard and mark it off as follows:

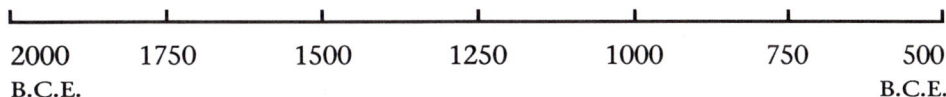

| 2000 B.C.E. | 1750 | 1500 | 1250 | 1000 | 750 | 500 B.C.E. |

Request that the reports be given in this order: Abraham, Isaac, Jacob, Joseph, Moses, Saul, David, Solomon, Isaiah, Jeremiah, Second Isaiah. As each group introduces its report, write the name of the historical person above the appropriate point on the timeline.

History Clues

As an alternative or supplement to the preceding activity, prepare your own brief sketches of the historical persons and events discussed in concept B. Break the class into teams of five or six students. Tell them that there is going to be a contest: You will give clues about certain persons, events, and so on, covered in this section of the chapter. As soon as a team wants to guess who or what you are describing, the team members should raise their hands. If the team guesses correctly, you will record a point for that team on the chalkboard. If the team guesses incorrectly, you will subtract a point from its score. A team can guess as often as it likes on any set of clues, but it can win only one point for a correct answer, and it risks losing a point for every wrong answer. At the end of the contest, the team with the most points will win a prize determined by you (e.g., candy bars or exemption from the next quiz).

This game, or something similar devised by you, can make the review of historical material both helpful *and* enjoyable.

How God Communicates in the Hebrew Scriptures

In the Hebrew Scriptures, God often communicates with people through visions, out of clouds, on mountaintops, and so on. Use this discussion activity to get the students thinking about these scenes and what the scriptural writers were trying to convey through them.

1. Divide the class into small groups of four to six students. Instruct the groups to spend 10 minutes discussing the following questions (you may want to write these on the chalkboard):
   - In the Hebrew Scriptures, God often communicates with people through visions, out of clouds, on mountaintops, and so on. Do you believe that God actually communicated in those ways? Why or why not?
   - Given our earlier discussion of the development of the Gospels, and assuming that the Hebrew Scriptures developed in a similar progression (that is, from historical events, to a period of reflection, to an evolving oral tradition, and eventually to a written form), how might we explain these scenes of God's self-revelation in the Hebrew Scriptures?

2. After the small-group discussion, call everyone together and try to lead the class to a consensus on answers to the questions. Afterward, provide your own insights and concluding comments.

Searching the Scriptures for God's Communication

This exercise is intended to further familiarize the students with God's communication in ancient Jewish history.

1. Divide the class into five groups of about four or five students each. Make each group responsible for reading and discussing one of the following sets of passages from the Hebrew Scriptures. (If your class is much larger than twenty-five, develop ten groups of fewer than four students and assign two groups to each set of passages.)
   - Gen. 12:1–7; 17:1–12,15–19
   - Exod. 3:1–10; 19:16–19; 20:1–17
   - Isa. 1:11–20; 6:1–13
   - Jer. 1:4–10; 31:1–4,31–33
   - Ezek. 1:1–28; 36:24–38

2. Instruct the groups each to prepare a report on their assigned readings, answering the following questions:
   - To whom is God communicating?
   - Is God visually present to the person or persons?
   - What does God promise, if anything?
   - What does God demand, if anything?

3. When the groups report their findings, record the information in an abbreviated fashion on the chalkboard. The groups' findings should be along these lines:

For the readings from Genesis
- God communicates with Abram, whose name is later changed to *Abraham* as a sign of God's choosing him.
- God appears to Abraham, but the Scriptures do not say what form God takes.
- God promises to bless Abraham, to make him great, to give him a land. Abraham will be the father of many nations, he and his wife Sarai (now to be called "Sarah") will have a son named Isaac.
- Abraham's descendants must be faithful to God.

For the readings from Exodus
- God speaks first to Moses and then later addresses all of the Israelites.
- God appears to Moses in a burning bush. God's presence is revealed to the Israelites by thunder, lightning, trumpet blasts, a cloud, and fire.
- God promises to free the people from their slavery in Egypt.
- The people must keep the Ten Commandments.

For the readings from Isaiah
- God communicates with Isaiah.
- God is seated on a throne, guarded by angels.
- God promises that the people will eat good things.
- The people must convert, stop their evil ways, and love and serve others.

For the readings from Jeremiah
- God communicates with Jeremiah.
- The hand of God is probably visible, because it touches Jeremiah's lips and puts God's words into Jeremiah's mouth.
- God promises to rebuild Israel and makes a new covenant with the people.
- The people have to abide by the covenant.

For the readings from Ezekiel
- God speaks to Ezekiel.
- God appears in a whirlwind, a cloud, and fire.
- God promises to deliver the people from their captors, to give them a new spirit, and to let them dwell in their own land.
- The people have to repent of their old ways and keep the Commandments.

4. Discuss with the students the recurring pattern of promises and demands that is found in ancient Jewish history. In the student text's discussion of the Gospel portraits of Jesus, the students will see that the Evangelists pick up on this pattern, expanding it to one of promise and *attainment*.

Concept C: The Political World of Jesus

The world of Jesus' day was politically dominated by the Romans. Even so, the people of Israel continued to be culturally influenced by the Greek rulers of the past. The Christian Testament mentions Jesus' encounters with the Sadducees and the Pharisees, Jewish political factions that had formed during a period of Jewish independence. (Pages 58–67 of the student text)

Review Questions: The Political World of Jesus

Question: Briefly explain how the Greeks—in particular the Syrian Greeks—came to dominate the people of Israel.
Answer: Alexander the Great led the Greeks to a military conquest of much of the Mediterranean world, including Palestine. After Alexander's death, Palestine was divided between two of his generals. These men and their successors dominated Palestine for 150 years. One of the lines of generals was centered in Syria; the other, in Egypt. For about the first one hundred years after Alexander's death, most of the people of Israel were ruled by the Greek power located in Egypt, and that Greek power seldom interfered in the affairs of the Jews. But in 198 B.C.E., all of Palestine came under control of the Syrian Greeks, who taxed the people heavily.

Question: Identify two major Jewish reactions to Greek rule.
Answer:
1. The Jewish leaders, the wealthy landowners, and the priestly class tried to get along with the Greeks, simply because they had the most to lose in any conflicts with them.
2. Another group, called "the Hasidim," meaning "the pious ones," resented the Greek rulers and felt that any compromise with them amounted to a rejection of the Jewish faith.

Question: Identify and define three major political factions within Judaism that developed during the period of Jewish independence.
Answer: The Sadducees were the priestly class that worked out accommodations with the new political leaders.
The Essenes withdrew from Jewish society altogether in order to observe strict religious traditions.
The Pharisees tried at first to find a middle ground between the political accommodations of the Sadducees and the withdrawal of the Essenes. In the end, however, they refused to compromise their religious beliefs. They therefore lost some influence in the higher levels of power but were very much respected among the common people.

Question: Explain the origins of the Jewish hatred for the Samaritans.
Answer: The Samaritans were among the descendants of the old northern tribes of the kingdom of Israel (conquered by the Assyrians in 721 B.C.E.). They had not been sent into Babylon during the Exile, and they had lost touch with their Jewish "cousins" in the south. As a result, many of the Samaritans' religious practices and traditions differed from those of the mainline southern Jews, and when the remnant returned from the Exile, they completely rejected the Samaritans.

A Text Activity: The Political World of Jesus

Activity 5

Imagine yourself as a young Jewish person living during the time of Jewish independence and facing the problem of weak and untrustworthy leaders. Which political faction would you most agree with—the Sadducees, the Essenes, the Pharisees, or none of these? Explain your response in a paragraph.

Additional Activities: The Political World of Jesus

A Study of the Geography of Palestine

For this exercise it is suggested that you order two sets of Bible map transparencies from Abingdon Press, 201 Eighth Avenue South, Nashville, TN 37202; phone 800-251-3320.
- *Set 1, "Palestine—Old Testament," item code number 001633, $33.95:* This set includes a physical map of Palestine and maps of the Exodus, the kingdom of Saul, the empire of David and Solomon, and the kingdom of Israel and Judah.
- *Set 2, "Palestine—New Testament," item code number 001641, $19.95:* This set includes maps of the kingdom of Herod the Great, Palestine in New Testament times, and Jesus' Galilean ministry.

These are beautiful full-color maps developed for use with an overhead projector. They are durable, can be used for years, could be shared with other religion teachers, and therefore are very reasonable. Though just two of the maps are recommended for use here, you will no doubt find use for several of the others as well. This exercise can be adjusted to work without the transparencies (for example, by referring students to maps in the text), but it will not be as easy or as effective.

 1. Begin with the physical map of Palestine, transparency 1A in set 1. This map illustrates a number of the features of the landscape and terrain that figure into the eras of both the Hebrew Scriptures and the Christian Testament. The set of transparencies comes with a helpful guide on how to discuss the maps with your students, so that information for this map is not repeated here. A similar map appears in the student text on page 75, in chapter 4, as "Sizing Up Palestine."

 2. Show the map of Palestine in New Testament times, transparency 2B in set 2. A similar map appears in the student text on page 63 as "Palestine at the Time of Jesus." Again, the guide provided with the transparencies will lead you through a presentation on the material. In this case, much of the presentation relates the division of Herod the Great's kingdom among his sons after his death.

Have the students study the map carefully, telling them that they will be quizzed in a few moments. Suggest that they also look at the map on page 63 of the student text, as this one keys in on the towns and areas most often referred to in the Gospels. Give the students 5 minutes for study, and then turn off the overhead and ask everyone to close their books.

 3. Ask the students to imagine that the entire classroom has been converted into the land of Palestine, with the front of the room being the north, the right-hand wall the east, and so on. To heighten interest in the quiz, you may want to divide the class into competing groups of five or so students,

recording their correct and incorrect responses on the chalkboard. Ask them to identify the following:
- What determines the border to our left, that is, to the west of Palestine? [The Mediterranean Sea]
- Where in this room would we find the Sea of Galilee? [The answer will vary depending on the room.]
- What is the second-largest body of water on the map? [The Dead Sea]
- What connects the Sea of Galilee and the Dead Sea? [The Jordan River]

Continue this line of questioning until you feel that your students have a firm sense of the geography of biblical Palestine.

A Simulation of the Political World of Jesus

This exercise is intended to give the students a concrete sense of the persons, groups, and events discussed in concept B. The simulation suggested here can range from a fairly simple, straightforward presentation by you (using only a few signs and situating the students in certain areas of the room) to a full-blown, highly involved representation of the political world of Jesus (requiring a lot of effort by both you and your students). The exercise can be used for the discussion of this concept alone, or it can be repeated with some modification throughout the entire course.

Preparing the classroom and the students: Organize the room to represent the Palestine of Jesus' day. The diagram below is based on a class of thirty students and conventional room size. You will need to make adjustments for your own situation.

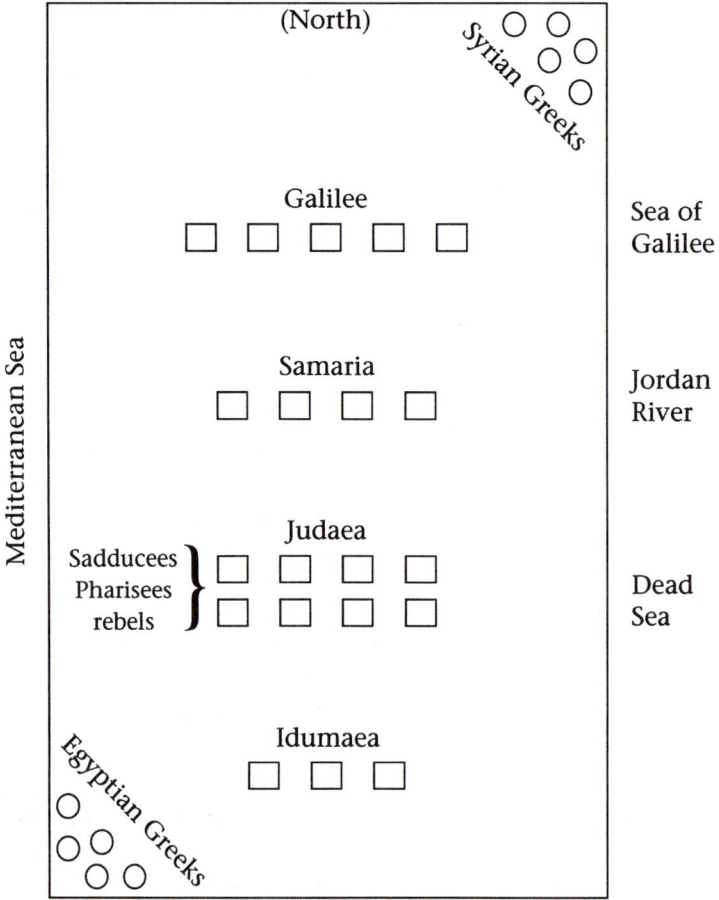

You may want to hang a long sign on the left-hand wall of the room, indicating the Mediterranean Sea, and three signs on the right-hand wall, representing the Sea of Galilee, the Jordan River, and the Dead Sea. Consider asking the students to help create the signs and otherwise decorate for the simulation.

Divide the class as indicated on the diagram, with five students in desks representing Galilee, four representing Samaria, eight representing Judaea, and three representing Idumaea. Designate the eight representatives of Judaea as follows: two are Sadducees, three are Pharisees, and three are rebels. Two groups of five students each should be seated in chairs in the northeast and southwest corners of the room, representing the Syrian Greeks and the Egyptian Greeks, respectively.

You may verbally assign these roles to the students and count on them to remember who is who. However, it would be best to aid the students' memory—and enhance the simulation environment—by hanging a sign over each "region," having each group wear paper hats of a particular color, having the students wear signs around their necks, or implementing some other option of your own creation.

Conducting the simulation: Begin the simulation with a commentary of your own on the history discussed on pages 58–60 of the student text, or assign some students to prepare and present the commentary. In either case, use the students in the various groups to illustrate in some way the historical commentary being delivered. The simplest way to do this would be for the speaker or speakers to just wander around the room while talking, indicating which groups were involved during which historical events. However, if you involve the class more, they will be more likely to retain the material.

The following sample commentary includes bracketed stage directions suggesting one way the groups might be involved. Remember, though, that the simulation is limited only by your own imagination and the amount of time available to you.

- After Alexander the Great died in 323 B.C.E., Palestine came under the control of the Greeks based in Syria, to the northeast of Palestine [the students representing the Syrian Greeks stand and take a bow], and the Greeks centered in Egypt, to the southwest of Palestine [the students representing the Egyptian Greeks stand and take a bow]. For about one hundred years, the leaders in Egypt ruled most of Israel, but they stayed pretty much where they were and allowed Israel its freedom. The leaders in Syria, however, controlled the region of Galilee, and the Jews there were highly influenced by Greek ways [the Galilee students bow their heads and look submissive]. The area therefore became known as "Galilee of the Gentiles." It was there that Jesus would be raised about two hundred years later.
- In 198 B.C.E., the Syrian Greeks took over all of Palestine [the Syrian Greeks move throughout the room with their hands clenched in fists above their heads]. They began to tax all of Israel in order to cover Greek war efforts [the Syrian Greeks act as if they are demanding money from the Palestinians, who at this point comply grudgingly].
- The Jews reacted to the Syrian Greek control in two basic ways: Some tried to get along with the rulers, because they had a lot to lose in any conflict with them [the Sadducees pat the Syrian Greeks on the back]. Others resented the Syrian Greeks [the rest of Judaea scowls and hisses]. These different reactions would eventually evolve into factions within Judaism, primarily the Sadducees and the Pharisees. More on that later.
- Eventually the Syrian Greeks tried to extend their control over an even wider region by assuming control of land that was still held by the

leaders from Egypt [the Syrian Greeks and the Egyptian Greeks yell at one another or in some other way indicate conflict]. The Romans [represented by you], however, were able to deal the Syrian Greeks a serious blow in a naval conflict. Some rebels among the Judaeans [note the three students assigned to this role] were so heartened by the Romans' defeat of the Syrian Greeks that they figured they too could overthrow them [the rebels stand up and act cocky and self-confident]. They guessed wrong, and the Syrian Greeks not only put down the rebels [the rebels fall to floor] but went so far as to build an altar to the Greek god Zeus in the Holy of Holies, in the Temple [the Syrian Greeks pretend to build something]. At this, all of Judaea erupted in rage, and to everyone's surprise, the people overthrew their oppressors [all of the Judaeans, including the rebels, stand up and drive the Syrian Greeks out while everyone cheers]. In 164 B.C.E., the Temple was rededicated, an event remembered to this day with the feast of Hanukkah.

Discussing the simulation: First, allow the students to react to the experience, raising any questions or making any observations. Next, lead a discussion to determine if all of the commentary made sense to the students, and clarify areas of confusion if necessary. Finally, ask the students if this approach helped their comprehension of the text material.

A Debate Between Religious Factions

It is important that the students recognize the Sadducees, the Pharisees, and the Essenes as groups *within* ancient Judaism. All three groups were made up of loyal and committed Jews; they just disagreed on the implications of their faith for their daily lives. Help the students gain a more personal sense of this fact.

First, have the students try to identify parallel groups within Catholicism today, that is, factions within the church that exhibit some of the characteristics of the Sadducees, the Pharisees, and the Essenes. Then ask for volunteers, or assign students, to role-play a debate between these groups, arguing one or more topics of current interest in the church (e.g., whether women should be ordained to the priesthood or how the church should respond to a U.S. military intervention in another country).

Searching the Scriptures for the Sadducees, the Pharisees, and the Samaritans

Use this activity to make certain that the students have become thoroughly familiar with the three Jewish groups who are most involved in the Gospel story: the Sadducees, the Pharisees, and the Samaritans.

1. Write the names of the three groups across the top of the chalkboard, creating three columns. Put a list of scriptural references in each column, as follows:

Sadducees	Pharisees	Samaritans
Matthew 16:1–12	Matthew 9:10–13	Luke 9:51–56
Mark 12:18–27	Matthew 15:1–9	Luke 10:25–37
	Matthew 23:13–32	Luke 17:11–19
	Mark 12:13–17	John 4:1–30
	Luke 14:1–6	

2. Have the students reread the material about the Sadducees and the Pharisees on pages 61–62 of the student text, as well as read the more detailed descriptions of these groups on pages 93–94 (in chapter 4).

3. After the students have finished reading, lead a brainstorming session in which the students identify as many characteristics of the three groups as they can. Jot down these characteristics in their respective columns on the board. (If you care to fill out the character sketches a bit further, see the short articles on these three groups in John L. McKenzie's *Dictionary of the Bible,* under "Sadducees," "Pharisees," and "Samaritans." Use whatever information you feel is pertinent.)

4. Randomly call on students to choose a scriptural reference from the board. Ask them to read the passage out loud. Then lead a class discussion centering on questions such as these:
- What characteristic(s) of the group is (are) reflected in the passage?
- What is the main lesson conveyed by the passage?
- Would the same lesson be taught if a different group or person were referred to?

A Dramatic Reading: "The Samaritan Woman at the Well"

Handout 3–A

The story of the Samaritan woman at the well, in John's Gospel, is revealing in terms of concept C. Handout 3–A, "The Samaritan Woman at the Well," is a script based on the story.

Pass out handout 3–A. Assign the various parts and conduct a dramatic reading of the "play" in class. Then discuss the story, using the following as a guide:
- Discuss the Samaritan woman's growing conception of who Jesus is.
- Compare and contrast Jesus' attitude, the disciples' attitude, and the typical Jewish attitude toward this woman of another race.
- Talk about the imagery in the story: What is the living water of which Jesus speaks? What is the nature of the harvest that he refers to?
- Discuss the lessons in the story: What does Jesus teach the woman about worship? If we took the passage seriously, what specific differences would there be in our lives tomorrow?

Incidentally, preparing other scriptural passages for a dramatic reading in class would be an excellent way of making them come alive. Many sections of the Christian Scriptures can effectively be adapted for such group use.

A Simulation of the Roman Domination of Palestine

If you previously conducted the simulation of the political world of Jesus (see pp. 76–78 of this manual), return to that basic form of simulation when discussing the Romans.

For this simulation, the commentary should be on the persons and events discussed on pages 60–67 of the student text. The arrangement of the room, the basic breakdown of the class, and so on, should remain as outlined earlier. Ask those who previously played the role of the Syrian Greeks to now take the role of the Romans. And ask those who previously took the role of the Egyptian Greeks to now assume the roles of Herod the Great, his three sons, and Pontius Pilate.

Concept D:
An Oppressed People Dream of a Liberator

Out of the complex religious and political history that preceded Jesus' birth, there emerged within the minds and hearts of the Jews the dream of an "anointed one," the Messiah, who would liberate them from their oppression. (Pages 68–69 of the student text)

A Review Question:
An Oppressed People Dream of a Liberator

Question: Briefly explain the origins of the ancient Jews' expectations of the Messiah.
Answer: The expectations of the Messiah were strongly associated with the kingship of David. For generations the Jews had yearned for a "son of David," who would restore them to their place of prominence in the world and bring them into an age of peace and prosperity. Over the many years of waiting, the son of David that the people yearned for took on mythic qualities. By the time the Jews were dominated by the Romans, the Messiah had taken on the image of a mighty warrior-king, a great military leader, who would overthrow the Romans.

Text Activities:
An Oppressed People Dream of a Liberator

Activity 6

List groups of people besides the Jews, either past or present, who have experienced long-term domination and control by another group. Write about what their life might be like.

Activity 7

Imagine what it would be like to yearn for a messiah in today's world. List five or more qualities that such a person would have to possess in order to be recognized as a great leader by people today.

An Additional Activity:
An Oppressed People Dream of a Liberator

Bible Quiz Bowl

As you complete your work with this chapter, you may wish to check the students' comprehension with something other than a conventional chapter test. Playing Bible Quiz Bowl is an enjoyable way to do so. It is a competitive game based loosely on the old TV game show "College Bowl," which has contemporary parallels at the high school level on stations in many parts of the country (e.g., "High School Quiz Bowl"). The idea is to have teams of students compete for points and possibly prizes based on their knowledge of particular subjects—in this case, the subjects covered in this chapter.

1. Divide the class into two teams of equal size and have each team elect four students to represent it in the game. The representatives should be chosen based on their presumed knowledge of the material in this chapter. After the representatives have been elected, separate them from the rest of the class, perhaps allowing them to spend some time reviewing the material.

2. Instruct the remaining members of the two teams to develop at least twenty questions based on this chapter—questions that they will ask of the opposing team's representatives. The questions must be reasonably clear and answerable. That is, the teams can try to develop "trick" questions, but these must be stated in such a way that a correct answer can be given by someone who understands the material well. You may want to break the two large teams into smaller groups, with each small group assigned to develop questions on specific pages of the chapter. This will speed up the process.

3. To make the game more interesting, circulate while the teams are developing their questions and assign each question a value of five, ten, or twenty points or dollars, based on your assessment of the relative difficulty of the question.

4. When all of the questions have been prepared, ask the elected representatives to rejoin the class, taking seats in the front of the room. Choose some fair means, such as flipping a coin, to determine which team will ask a question first. From that point on, have the teams alternate in asking questions. The questions can be read either by one appointed team member or by the students who originally developed the questions, the latter giving more students a chance to participate. Allow a team's representatives 10 seconds or so to consult before answering, but keep the game moving quickly to maintain interest.

If you opted to give the questions different point values, those should be announced by the questioners when they read their questions. Award points for correct answers and withdraw points for incorrect answers, keeping score on the chalkboard. Or if you decided to assign a monetary value to each question, you can use play money for scoring. Prizes (such as candy bars or some other inexpensive treats) for the entire winning team—the four representatives and the students who elected them—will provide a helpful incentive for the students.

Teacher Background: Jesus' Identity as the Messiah

Jesus seldom if ever referred to himself as the Messiah, or Christ. In Mark's Gospel, the first Gospel written, there is only one case when Jesus may vaguely have been doing so (see Mark 9:41).

In the following scriptural passages, Jesus is called the Messiah by others, but not specifically by himself:
- *The cure of the Gerasene demoniac (Mark 5:1–20):* Jesus seems to accept the possessed man's calling him "'Son of the Most High,'" which is equivalent to "Messiah."
- *The cure of a blind man at Jericho (Mark 10:46–52):* Bartimaeus, a blind man, addresses Jesus as "'son of David,'" again the equivalent of "Messiah."
- *Peter's profession of faith (Matt. 16:13–20):* At a pivotal point in the Gospel story, Jesus clearly seems to accept Peter's claim that he is "'the Messiah, the Son of the living God.'" But interestingly, Jesus gives the disciples strict orders not to tell anyone that he is the Messiah.
- *Jesus before the Sanhedrin (Mark 14:53–65):* The high priest explicitly asks Jesus, "'Are you the Messiah, the son of the Blessed One?'" Jesus replies, "'I am.'"

Scholars believe that these and other references in the Gospels illustrate important factors about Jesus' identity as the Messiah:
- Jesus did not refer to himself as the Messiah, because he knew that such a reference would be misinterpreted by his followers and others, given their expectations of the Messiah.
- Jesus only gradually grew to a sense of himself as the Messiah, and perhaps never fully realized his identity as such.
- The Christian community did not recognize Jesus as the Messiah until after much reflection, and it is the later reflection that comes through in the Gospels. When the Evangelists began to write the Gospels, they wanted to make it clear that they truly believed Jesus was the Messiah, and they developed wordings such as those in the passages cited above to illustrate that conviction.

Some scholars speak of the "messianic secret," a literary device perhaps developed by Mark. Repeatedly, Mark has Jesus tell his followers not to reveal his identity to others. The intent of this device, the scholars say, was to explain why Jesus never publicly acknowledged himself as the Messiah.

The Samaritan Woman at the Well

Characters: Narrator, Jesus, Woman, Disciple

Narrator: Jesus was journeying northward from Judaea to Galilee, and he had to pass through Samaria on the way. Samaria was near the village of Sychar on the piece of property that Jacob had given to his son Joseph. Tired from the long walk in the hot sun, Jesus sat down beside a well while his disciples went into the village to buy food. A Samaritan woman came to the well to draw water.

Jesus: Would you give me a drink of water?

Woman: You are a Jew, and I am a Samaritan. How can you ask me for a drink?

Narrator: The Jews usually would not even speak to Samaritans, much less drink from the same cup.

Jesus: If you only knew what wonderful gift God could give you and who I am, you would ask me for some living water.

Woman: But you don't even have a bucket, and this is a deep well. Where would you get living water? Besides, you surely are not greater than our ancestor Jacob. How can you offer better water than this which he and his family and his cattle drank?

Jesus: Everyone who drinks the water from this well will become thirsty again, but whoever drinks the water I will give him will never be thirsty again. For my gift will become a spring within him, which will provide him with living water and give him eternal life.

Woman: Please, sir, give me some of that water! Then I'll never be thirsty again and won't have to make this long trip out here to draw water.

Jesus: Go, get your husband, then come back here.

Woman: But I'm not married.

Jesus: You are telling the truth when you say you are not married. You have been married to five men, and the man you are living with now is not really your husband.

Woman: You must be a prophet, sir! But if I may ask a question, why do you Jews insist that Jerusalem is the only place of worship? We Samaritans, meanwhile, claim that where our ancestors worshiped—here at Mount Gerizim—is a fitting place.

Jesus: Believe me, ma'am, the time is coming when we will no longer be concerned about the *place* to worship the Father! For it's not where we worship that's important but how we worship. Worship must be spiritual and real, for God is Spirit and we must have his Spirit's help to worship as we should. The Father wants this kind of worship. But you Samaritans know so little about him, worshiping with yours eyes shut, so to speak. We Jews know all about him, for salvation comes to mankind through the Jewish race.

Woman: Well, at least I know that the Messiah will come—you know, the one they call the Christ—and when he does, he will make everything plain to us.

Jesus: I am the Messiah!

Narrator: Then the woman left her water pot beside the well, went back to the village, and excitedly told everyone about Jesus. Soon the people came streaming from the village to see him. In the meantime, the disciples had returned to Jesus. They had seen him talking to the Samaritan woman and were astonished, but they did not ask Jesus why nor ask him what he had said to the woman. Instead they urged Jesus to eat.

Disciple: Teacher, eat some of the food we bought.

Jesus: No. I have some food you don't know about.

Disciple [*to other disciples*]: Did someone else bring him food?

Jesus: My nourishment comes from doing the will of God, who sent me, and from finishing his work. Do you think the work of harvesting will not begin until the summer ends—four months from now? Open your eyes and look around you! Fields of human souls are ripening all around us, and they are ready for harvesting. The reaper of the harvest is being paid *now,* and he gathers the crops for eternal life; the planter and the reaper will be glad together, for in this harvest the old saying comes true, "One man plants and another reaps." I have sent you to harvest a crop in a field where you did not labor; others labored there, and you profit from their work.

Narrator: Many of the Samaritans in that town believed in Jesus because the woman had told them of his ability to know all things. So when the Samaritans came to him they begged him to stay with them, and Jesus stayed there two days. Many more believed because of Jesus' own words, and the villagers told the woman: "We believe now, not because of what you said but because we have heard him with our own ears and we know that he is the Savior of the world."

Reprinted from "Jesus Met a Woman (John 4)" in Wayne Rice, John Roberto, and Mike Yaconelli, editors, *Creative Learning Experiences* (Winona, MN: Saint Mary's Press, 1981), pages 104–106

CHAPTER 4

Daily Life in Jesus' Time: Culture and Religion

Major Concepts

A. **Jesus in a Particular Time and Place:** A true understanding of Jesus must include a basic sense of his daily life. Jesus' immersion in the world of first-century Palestine enabled him to speak to his fellow Jews using images they understood.

B. **Palestine:** The land in which Jesus lived and preached was one of great diversity and richness.

C. **The People and Their Daily Life:** The Gospels are filled with references to the daily life of the ancient Jewish people: their food and meals, homes, and occupations.

D. **The Jewish Family:** The ancient Jews recognized the family as the essential basis of society, and the Law upheld the permanence and authority of the family.

E. **Social Classes in the World of Jesus:** Every society develops social classes or groups—the "haves" and the "have-nots," the prestigious and the scorned, the politically powerful and the oppressed. Jesus challenged and even condemned his society because of such divisions.

F. **Major Features of Judaism:** The features of Judaism that play a part in the Gospel stories are the holy city of Jerusalem, the Temple, central religious practices such as feasts, and key religious-political groups and persons, including priests, scribes, Sadducees, Pharisees, Zealots, and tax collectors.

Concept A: Jesus in a Particular Time and Place

A true understanding of Jesus must include a basic sense of his daily life. Jesus' immersion in the world of first-century Palestine enabled him to speak to his fellow Jews using images they understood. (Pages 71–72 of the student text)

A Review Question: Jesus in a Particular Time and Place

Question: Why is a basic sense of Jesus' daily world important to understanding Jesus and his message? Illustrate your response with an example.

Answer: Jesus was a Jew, born in a particular place within a particular culture at a particular time in history. His life experiences are woven into his teachings. Having a sense of Jesus' daily world enables us to read between the lines of the Christian Testament and gain a deeper appreciation for the profound message expressed there. [Any of the examples listed below would be appropriate for illustrating this response.]

- Jesus' reference to forecasting the weather, in Matt. 16:2–3, came out of his culture.
- Discerning the meaning of the scene in Mark 2:16–17, where Jesus eats with tax collectors and sinners, requires an understanding of the tremendous importance of meals in the life of the Jewish people.
- When Jesus called his first disciples, he made his point by referring to a large number of fish that the men caught under his direction (Luke 5:10).
- Jesus was a carpenter, and the vocabulary of his trade found its way into his teaching, as in Matt. 7:3–5.

A Text Activity: Jesus in a Particular Time and Place

Activity 1

Select one of the four examples of Jesus' teachings given above. Keeping in mind the point Jesus was trying to make, rewrite the scene as you imagine it might occur today. For example, what words would Jesus use? Where would the scene take place?

An Additional Activity: Jesus in a Particular Time and Place

Searching the Scriptures for the World of Jesus

On page 71 of the student text, the author notes that the Gospels are filled with images and experiences from the day-to-day lives of first-century Jewish people. This activity can give the students a fuller sense of that fact and its importance in understanding the Gospel portraits of Jesus. It is also a basis for later activities in this chapter: "Questions for a Discussion on Food and Meals, Housing, and Occupations," under concept C, and "Social Classes Then and Now," under concept E.

1. Divide the class into the four groups that were assigned to read a Gospel from beginning to end in "A Special Reading Assignment," on pages 63–64 of this manual. Next, break each of these four groups into five smaller sections. (For example, a class of thirty-two students would be divided into four groups of eight students each, and within each of those groups there would be three subgroups of two students each and two sections of only one student each.)

2. Give a copy of handout 4–A, "Searching the Scriptures for the World of Jesus," to each group. Have someone in each group cut the handout along the dotted lines and randomly distribute the resulting slips among the five sections. These slips contain assignments for the sections. Members of the sections consisting of more than one person are to work as a team on the assignment. You yourself may want to give assistance to the sections consisting of only one person. (If you think that your students may need more than the 40 minutes stated on the assignment slips, consider giving the assignments as homework.)

3. When all of the sections are done, or in the next class period, have them join with the rest of their group to share the results of their search. Each section should first note how many references to their respective topic they found and then quickly run through their list of general descriptions.

4. Ask the sections to each count up the number of *verses* they recorded during their search. Then have someone in each group add all five of the sections' numbers together to get a total verse count for the entire group.

5. Tell each group how many verses make up their entire Gospel:
- *Matthew:* 1,070 verses
- *Mark:* 677 verses
- *Luke:* 1,150 verses
- *John:* 879 verses

Instruct the groups to compute the percentage of their Gospel that deals with or refers to the basic characteristics of Jesus' world. Ask for the results. Comment appropriately on the obvious importance of getting in touch with the human, everyday dimension of the Gospel story and show how this chapter will help the students do so.

You may want to have the students refer to their lists later, so make sure they hold on to them.

Concept B: Palestine

The land in which Jesus lived and preached was one of great diversity and richness. (Pages 73–77 of the student text)

Review Questions: Palestine

Question: What is one explanation for the sense that Jesus and his disciples continually move from place to place in the Gospels?

Answer: The Jews were great walkers, thinking nothing of walking distances we might hesitate to drive.

Question: Explain why the people of Jesus' day had a great concern for water.
Answer: Water was scarce.

Question: What was Jesus telling the people when he described himself as "the bread of life"?
Answer: Bread was the essential food of Jesus' day. When Jesus described himself as "the bread of life," he was saying that he could totally satisfy the deepest hungers of people.

Text Activities: Palestine

Activity 2

Write a paragraph comparing what it means to know a *thing* (such as the land on which you live) by heart with what it means to know a *person* by heart.

Activity 3

List at least ten characteristics of water that make it a symbol or image rich with meaning.

Additional Activities: Palestine

Comparing Jesus' World with Ours

To help the students gain a good sense of the size of Palestine in Jesus' time, have them look carefully at the map "Sizing Up Palestine," on page 75 of the student text. That map relates distances between cities in the United States to distances between cities in ancient Palestine. In this exercise, you will carry the idea one step further.

First, refer the students to the mileage scale on the map and have them estimate the following distances:
- from Jerusalem to Jericho
- from Damascus to Nazareth
- from Jerusalem to Nazareth

Next, show the students a map of your state and have them investigate questions such as the following:
  - If we think of our state capital as comparable to Judaea's capital, Jerusalem, what city or town in our state would be comparable to Nazareth in size, importance, and location?
  - The caption for the map in your textbook says that the Sea of Galilee and the Dead Sea are about sixty-five miles apart. What two cities or towns in our state are that same distance apart?

This will almost literally bring Palestine "home" to your students.

For a more thorough comparison, use the transparency of New Testament Palestine that is required for the chapter 3 activity "A Study of the Geography of Palestine," on pages 75–76 of this manual.

A Service Project: Making a "Parking Lot Palestine"

If your students are expected or encouraged to become involved in service projects during the course of the year, they might be interested in devising a learning experience on Palestine to be offered to the Catholic grade schools in your area.

For example, using the map "Palestine at the Time of Jesus," on page 63 of the student text, as a model, the class could construct a "parking lot Palestine" by painting a large map of Palestine on the parking lot of your school (using water-based paint and assuming good climate!). Or the map could be outlined with tape and labeled with signs on the floor of your school gym. Major cities and geographical features could be indicated, and one student could be assigned to each place to research the events in the life and ministry of Jesus that took place there. If you wanted to make the map more elaborate, you could have the students display photos and other materials at each location (e.g., three crosses at Calvary, in Jerusalem).

The class could offer guided tours to children from the grade schools, giving the children a unique learning experience and giving the guides a better knowledge of the land of Palestine.

(This activity is taken from Wayne Rice, John Roberto, and Mike Yaconelli, eds., *Creative Projects and Worship Experiences,* pp. 27–28.)

Concept C: The People and Their Daily Life

The Gospels are filled with references to the daily life of the ancient Jewish people: their food and meals, homes, and occupations. (Pages 78–82 of the student text)

Review Questions: The People and Their Daily Life

Question: What status did meals have among the Jews of Jesus' day?
Answer: The sharing of a meal was a sacred act. To "break bread" was an outward sign of unity and friendship. Whenever a meal is shared in the Gospels, we can be sure that something significant is happening.

Question: What qualities of fishers might have attracted Jesus to them when he was seeking disciples?
Answer: Fishers were men of courage and patience, and they had hearty spirits. Perhaps most important, they had a basic reliance upon and trust in the goodness of God, who supplied the fish they needed for their livelihood.

Question: What might Jesus have learned about life from his years as a carpenter?
Answer: We can imagine that Jesus' years in that work gave him a real sensitivity to the needs of the people he lived and worked with. His trade would also have put him in touch with the glories of God's creation as he roamed the forests in search of good wood and then struggled to make something out of the varied woods he found there.

Text Activities: The People and Their Daily Life

Activity 4

According to many religious leaders, several of the problems of modern families can be explained by the fact that family members rarely eat meals together. Explain in writing why you agree or disagree with that claim.

Activity 5

Choose any one of the four Gospels and page through it. Jot down the chapter and verse numbers for every instance in which eating a meal is mentioned.

Additional Activities: The People and Their Daily Life

Questions for a Discussion on Food and Meals, Housing, and Occupations

This activity builds on "Searching the Scriptures for the World of Jesus," recommended for concept A. (If you did not use that activity, consider using an abbreviated version of it now to lead into this discussion on food and meals, housing, and occupations.)

1. Ask the students who previously looked for scriptural references to food and meals to review their findings for the class:
   - How often did the theme of food and meals come up?
   - Did you see any pattern to the scenes in which meals were eaten?
   - Your textbook states, "Whenever a meal is shared in the Gospels, you can be sure that something very significant is happening." Did your research bear this out? Explain.

2. Open the discussion to the entire class, using some or all of the following questions as a guide:
   - Bread was the staple food of the ancient Jews. What is it about bread, especially homemade bread, that makes it special even today?
   - Do other foods or drinks have this almost religious quality about them?
   - Sometimes real estate agents suggest that people showing homes to prospective buyers bake bread and, if possible, build a fire in the fireplace before the prospective buyers arrive. Why?
   - Some people fear that in our society the sharing of meals has lost much of its importance and quality. They say that fast-food chains, frozen foods, and so on, have decreased our sense of the sacredness of "breaking bread" with one another. Do you agree? Why or why not?
   - Identify the most memorable meals you have experienced in the past year. Are all of them the same kinds of meals? If so, why? What qualities made those meals so special? [List the qualities on the board and discuss them.]
   - Your textbook stated earlier that Jesus' choice of bread and wine as symbols of himself at the Last Supper made good sense in terms of his culture. Was it also significant that the entire gesture or ritual of sharing a meal with his Apostles was the way he chose to end his time with them?
   - What does the significance of Jesus' sharing a meal at the end of his life say about the nature and purpose of the Eucharist for us today?

3. Invite those who studied housing and occupations in the Gospels to share their insights and observations in light of the student text material for this concept.
- How often did the topics of housing and occupations come up?
- Did you notice any pattern in those Gospel scenes? For instance, were some occupations mentioned more often than others? Did Jesus seem to prefer people from some occupations more than people from others? If so, can you explain why that might have been the case? What kinds of events were most commonly associated with the homes of the people?

4. As with the theme of food and meals, open the discussion of housing and occupations to the entire class, focusing on questions such as the following:
- According to your textbook, the people's homes were commonly only one room shared by both the people and their animals. In contrast, the ideal in our modern homes is for every child to have his or her own bedroom, and our homes usually have many other rooms as well. What might the Jews of Jesus' day have learned from their housing situation that we might never learn from ours? What might we learn from our housing situation that they might never have learned from theirs?
- The kitchen in our homes often becomes the center of family and social life. What was the normal cooking arrangement for the ancient Jews? What might they have learned from that arrangement that we would not likely learn from ours?
- If you have ever gone fishing, what have you learned from the experience that gives you insight into the fishers of Jesus' day?
- Of all the occupations mentioned in the textbook, which would you have wanted to pursue if you had lived in Jesus' time? Why? [Girls need not feel restricted to only those occupations that the ancient Jewish culture viewed as appropriate for women.]

Research Projects on the Occupations

Assign small groups of students to do brief research projects on the various occupations of Jesus' time: farming, shepherding, wine making, fishing, carpentry, tent making, and so on. John L. McKenzie's *Dictionary of the Bible* is a helpful resource on these topics.

Headlines from Palestine

Have the students "publish" newspapers from the time of Jesus.

1. Divide the class into groups of five or six students and explain that each group will design an imaginary newspaper from Jesus' time. Pass out large sheets of poster paper or newsprint, glue, and a pair of scissors to each group and give the following instructions:
- One or two members of your group should do a lead article on a major Jewish celebration, giving particular attention to the preparation of food and the sharing of a meal or banquet for the occasion. (The wedding at Cana would be a good selection.)
- Two other members should pretend to be real estate agents, advertising various homes for sale and listing the characteristics of each.

- A third pair of members should create a section of want ads, listing job opportunities with descriptions of responsibilities.
- You can decide as a group to include some additional items in your newspaper.
- Write your articles and ads on notebook paper in columns of uniform width and then organize these on large sheets of paper in a newspaper format. Also, be sure to come up with a name for your paper, perhaps even designing a masthead (that is, a special lettering of the name with or without an accompanying symbol).

2. When all of the newspapers are finished, set them out on display and invite the students to walk around the room and take a look at them.

Concept D: The Jewish Family

The ancient Jews recognized the family as the essential basis of society, and the Law upheld the permanence and authority of the family. (Pages 83–84 of the student text)

Review Questions: The Jewish Family

Question: Why did Joseph want to quietly divorce Mary when he discovered she was pregnant?
Answer: If he had *publicly* accused her of committing adultery, the Jewish Law would have demanded that she be killed.

Question: What was unusual about Jesus' actions and attitudes regarding women?
Answer: Jesus' actions and attitudes regarding women were contrary to the belief that women were the property of men and were inferior to them. Jesus treated women as equal in dignity to men.

Question: Why were female children in Jesus' day regarded as less desirable than male children?
Answer: Girls married at a young age and then became the property of someone else.

A Text Activity: The Jewish Family

Activity 6

Fold a piece of paper in half to create two vertical columns. In the left column, list the major characteristics of Jewish family life in Jesus' day. In the right column, note how modern family life compares on each point listed in the left column.

Additional Activities: The Jewish Family

The Family Yesterday and Today

The information in concept D should be of high interest to the students and rather easily spark discussion, if not debate. Consider the following options for pursuing such a discussion.

Option 1: Pose these questions to the students:
- Girls in the ancient Jewish society often married right after puberty, that is, at about age thirteen. What would have been the pros and cons of this practice? What did such early marriage imply for the life of a woman?
- What were the rights and responsibilities of children in the Jewish society? Do you think that childhood was an enjoyable time in those days? Explain.
- Should your parents have the right to decide on or greatly influence you regarding what school you attend? who your friends are? who you will marry? How might your responses to these questions be similar to or different from the responses that would have been given by the young people of Jesus' day?
- If Jesus were to come among us today to evaluate the family life of the American people, what do you think his chief concerns and criticisms would be? How would people react to his concerns and criticisms?

Option 2: It has been said that seeing childhood as a specific stage of development is really a relatively recent perspective, dating from the eighteenth century. Assign students to research this and report on it, or provide the information yourself and lead a discussion. See Henri Daniel-Rops's *Daily Life in the Time of Jesus* (New York: Hawthorn Books, 1962) for helpful material.

Option 3: Though it is clear that Jesus offered an alternative view of the role and dignity of women in his society, the Christian community, even to the present, has not always followed his lead. For an interesting discussion—though perhaps extended and tangential—have the class discuss the relative roles of men and women in the church today, determining to what degree the church has responded to or developed Jesus' stance toward women. This is a complex but highly important issue in the church today and one, it is hoped, of interest to the students.

Fiddler on the Roof

If possible, have the class view the movie *Fiddler on the Roof*, or have them listen to the sound track from it. Then discuss the various Jewish customs and practices reflected in the movie or its music: parents arranging marriages, the importance of religion in family life, the roles of women and children, and so on.

Concept E: Social Classes in the World of Jesus

Every society develops social classes or groups—the "haves" and the "have-nots," the prestigious and the scorned, the politically powerful and the oppressed. Jesus challenged and even condemned his society because of such divisions. (Pages 85-86 of the student text)

Review Questions: Social Classes in the World of Jesus

Question: Why did Jesus often speak about the rich and the poor?
Answer: The gap between the two was so great.

Question: Give two reasons that slavery was not practiced as much among the Jews as among the Greeks and the Romans.
Answer: Most Jews could not afford slaves. Also, the Jewish Law demanded that all slaves be freed after seven years of service, and this made a Jewish slave worth much less money than a pagan slave.

Question: Give three examples of how Jesus challenged his society's social structure.
Answer: [The students can choose any three of the following.]
- Making the poor and the weak the center of his message and those to be most honored
- Telling the story of the good Samaritan
- Freely associating with women and accepting them as central participants in his ministry
- Embracing the sick and the "unclean," and attacking the people with wealth and power who refused to share with those in need

A Text Activity: Social Classes in the World of Jesus

Activity 7

List the groups considered outsiders in the religion or the culture you are most familiar with. For each group, provide at least one example of how the members are discriminated against.

Additional Activities: Social Classes in the World of Jesus

Social Classes Then and Now

This activity builds on "Searching the Scriptures for the World of Jesus," recommended for concept A. (If you did not do that activity, consider doing an abbreviated version of it now.)

Ask the students to identify and then describe the various social classes that existed in the world of Jesus. List these on the chalkboard. Ask the students who did the earlier research on social classes in the Gospels to provide any scriptural references they found for each of the groups listed. Have volunteers

read selections related to each of the groups and discuss Jesus' attitude toward and response to the groups in each situation. Then have the students try to identify groups of people in contemporary society who might be comparable to or representative of those listed on the board. Use the following questions as a guide for discussion:
- Based on Jesus' responses in his time, how should Christians respond to the present-day social groups listed on the board?
- Were Jesus' responses reasonable or naive, realistic or too idealistic to be socially acceptable?
- What about the possibility of our living out Jesus' values as they are revealed in the Gospels—is this reasonable or naive, realistic or too idealistic? Explain.

The Haves and the Have-Nots

To give the students a sense of what it means to live in unfair social conditions, try some of the following ideas, keeping your purpose a secret until the students have reacted and discussed their reactions. By combining two or more such ideas in class (think up some of your own too!) you can generate strong feelings, reactions, and discussion.

1. Prepare a large amount of popcorn for the class, but distribute it very unfairly, offering 80 percent of the popcorn to only 20 percent of the class.
2. Tell five students that they can be excused from the next homework assignment, just because you like them.
3. Announce that contrary to prior plans, you have decided that all of the students will get the same grade for the class, regardless of test scores or class participation, except for two students who will get *A*'s because they come from "nice families."
4. Initiate a discussion on a topic related to this section of the student text, but continually call on the same two or three students, disregarding other students who ask to be heard.

After making your point, discuss what Jesus' response might be to both the unfair treatment and the feelings generated by it.

Concept F: Major Features of Judaism

The features of Judaism that play a part in the Gospel stories are the holy city of Jerusalem, the Temple, central religious practices such as feasts, and key religious-political groups and persons, including priests, scribes, Sadducees, Pharisees, Zealots, and tax collectors. (Pages 87–95 of the student text)

Review Questions: Major Features of Judaism

Question: Why did the synagogues become more important for the Jews after the time of Jesus?
Answer: The Temple had been the center of the Jews' religious life, but the Romans destroyed it in 70 C.E.

Question: What was the origin of the Sabbath day, and what was it a sign of?

Answer: The Sabbath day was based on the Creation story from the Book of Genesis, in which God rests after creating the world. It was also linked to the Exodus experience. The Sabbath was recognized as a central and sacred sign of Yahweh's presence with the people and of their covenant relationship with God.

Question: Identify and briefly describe the three major religious feasts of the Jews.

Answer:
- Pentecost is a celebration of Yahweh's giving the Law to Moses.
- The Day of Atonement is a time for the Jews to solemnly repent of their sins.
- Passover celebrates the miraculous liberation of the Israelites from Egypt.

Question: Identify the major characteristics of both the Sadducees and the Pharisees. Why did the Sadducees have greater political power than the Pharisees?

Answer: The Sadducees were mainly the aristocracy of the priestly caste. They were liberal in politics but very conservative in religion. They rejected all attempts to add to or interpret the Law, and they rejected any belief in a resurrection after death.

The Pharisees were conservative in politics but more liberal than the Sadducees in religion. They were open to new developments in Jewish thought. Their commitment to the Law rather than the Temple allowed them to survive beyond the destruction of the Temple.

The Sadducees had greater political power than the Pharisees because they were willing to compromise with the people in power.

Text Activities: Major Features of Judaism

Activity 8

As you read the following section on the major features of Judaism in Jesus' day, make a list of those features. For each one, try to identify a parallel feature in modern Roman Catholicism.

Activity 9

Using an encyclopedia or other sources, write a one-page essay that expands upon any feature of ancient Judaism discussed in this chapter.

Additional Activities: Major Features of Judaism

Searching the Scriptures for Major Features of Judaism

This exercise is intended to demonstrate the importance of Jewish religious tradition and practice to the Gospel story.

1. For chapter 2, this manual recommended "A Special Reading Assignment," with each of four groups assigned to read one of the Gospels from beginning to end. Assuming you did that exercise, form groups of four students now, with each group having one student who read Matthew, one who read

Mark, one who read Luke, and one who read John. (If you did not do the exercise in chapter 2, consider doing it now. See pp. 63–64 of this manual.)

2. Write each of these twelve major features of Judaism on a separate slip of paper: *Jerusalem, the Temple, synagogues, daily prayer, the Sabbath, religious feasts, the Sadducees, the Pharisees, the priestly caste, the Zealots, tax collectors, scribes.* Ask a representative of each group to come forward and randomly select one of the slips of paper out of a container.

3. In class, the students in each group are to individually search through their respective Gospel, noting each time their group's chosen feature appears—in which verses and what the circumstances surrounding the incident are.

You may want to acquaint the students with how to use a concordance, or show them that many translations of the Bible have a topical index to help readers locate specific passages. However, it could be fruitful and worth the time for the students to carefully leaf through the Gospels during this part of the exercise. It would be a good way for them to quickly review the progression of the Gospel material.

4. After the students have completed their individual searches for Gospel references, have them gather in their groups of four to share their notes, discuss similarities and differences in their notes, and arrive at one group listing of Gospel references. They should then prepare to share the results of their work with the class.

5. Close the exercise by having the groups orally summarize what the Gospels have to say about the feature they were assigned to search for, thereby effectively reviewing the material in concept F while at the same time showing how these features of Judaism continually appear in the Gospel narratives.

Jewish Guest Speakers

Arrange for a presentation by a rabbi, or perhaps a panel of Jewish young people, on the major religious practices of contemporary Jews. Request that the presentation center on the family and communal celebrations of major religious feasts.

You may want to provide any guest speakers with a copy of the student text so that they have an idea of what information has already been made available to the students.

A Synagogue Field Trip

Organize a field trip to a synagogue, with a tour and a rabbi's explanation of the synagogue's historical and present role in Jewish religious life.

You may want to provide the tour guide or the rabbi with a copy of the student text so that he or she has some idea of what information has already been made available to the students.

Searching the Scriptures for the World of Jesus

Cut this handout along the dotted lines to form five slips of paper.

Geography and Climate

Go through your assigned Gospel and note all the occasions when the geography or climate of Palestine enters directly into the teachings of Jesus (that is, any time he refers to images of the land and its weather to make a point or teach a lesson). Record the chapter and verse references and brief descriptions of the occasions. You have 40 minutes.

Food and the Sharing of Meals

Go through your assigned Gospel and note all the occasions when Jesus refers to food or the sharing of meals in his teachings, and all the occasions when a meal is actually shared. Record the chapter and verse references and brief descriptions of the occasions. You have 40 minutes.

Family Life and Its Traditions

Go through your assigned Gospel and note all the occasions when Jesus refers to family life and its traditions (for example, marriage, child-rearing) in his teachings. Record the chapter and verse references and brief descriptions of the occasions. You have 40 minutes.

Housing and Occupations

Go through your assigned Gospel and note all the occasions when Jesus refers to the housing and various occupations of his people. Record the chapter and verse references and brief descriptions of the occasions. You have 40 minutes.

Social Classes

Go through your assigned Gospel and note all the occasions when Jesus refers to social classes—rich and poor people, slaves and free people, people in power and people without power—in his teachings. Record the chapter and verse references and brief descriptions of the occasions. You have 40 minutes.

CHAPTER 5

The Mission Begins: Preparing the Way of the Lord

Major Concepts

A. **The Infancy Narratives:** The infancy narratives in Matthew's and Luke's Gospels can be properly understood in light of the Evangelists' intentions, which were to provide faith-filled responses to the early church's interest in Jesus' birth and early life.

B. **The Hidden Years of Jesus' Life:** With some reservations it can be said that the historical Jesus experienced life as a typical Jew of his day. Therefore, a portrait of his childhood and family life can be drawn from the preceding course material on daily life in Jesus' time.

C. **The Beginnings of Jesus' Public Life:** The stories of Jesus' baptism and his temptation in the desert provide us with important insights into his self-understanding.

D. **Wandering Preacher, Unique Teacher:** Jesus' relationship with his disciples, especially the twelve Apostles, was unique in his day, and it signaled a special role for those who would follow him.

A Note to the Teacher:
How to Respond to Special Questions About Jesus

Some areas of discussion in Christology are not examined or touched on at all in the student text for this course: the virginal conception of Jesus, his sinlessness, his human consciousness, and his sexuality. The author believes that these issues are too theologically sophisticated, too potentially confusing, and too controversial for a text intended for high school students. (The course as it is presently constructed is challenging enough, without including issues that give theologians and biblical scholars gray hair!) Nevertheless, because your students may raise these issues on their own, the following suggestions are offered to guide you in your response:

1. Before teaching this chapter, make sure that you are reasonably aware of the church's position on these issues so that you can offer at least an initial response, and perhaps a satisfying response, to student inquiries. You will not find a more concise and clearly stated summary of the church's teaching on these matters than the one in Richard P. McBrien's *Catholicism*, volume 1, chapter 15, "Special Questions in Christology," pages 513–546. Of particular help is the section on criteria for determining whether a given Christology is consistent with the Catholic Tradition (pp. 538–541). McBrien closes his discussion with a helpful reading list for further study (p. 546).

2. Avoid unnecessarily complex theological responses to the students' questions. Generally students find such presentations neither interesting nor persuasive. Begin your discussions, rather, by requesting that the students try to answer their own questions first. Invite them to give their personal convictions and also to attempt to come up with answers based on information they have from this course and other courses. If you perceive strong disagreement among your students, provide a forum for them to exchange views in a constructive way (e.g., a debate, a panel discussion, or a fishbowl discussion).

3. With any discussion of these special topics, make sure that you clearly and directly state the Roman Catholic teaching, preferably as part of a concluding comment. But be careful not to make your statements seem too absolute, too cut-and-dried. The fact is that scholars continue to debate these issues, and to claim otherwise would be misleading and unfair to the students.

4. View the students' questions as opportunities for growth rather than threats. Neither the church nor your students expect you to be a theologian with "all the answers," and you should not try to assume that role. View yourself as being on the journey of faith with your students, and treat these specific issues as interesting but noncritical diversions in your collective search for the truth. Your own openness, honesty, and acceptance of mystery in regard to faith will generate a like attitude in your students.

Concept A: The Infancy Narratives

The infancy narratives in Matthew's and Luke's Gospels can be properly understood in light of the Evangelists' intentions, which were to provide faith-filled responses to the early church's interest in Jesus' birth and early life. (Pages 97–104 of the student text)

Review Questions: The Infancy Narratives

Question: Define *infancy narrative* and name the Gospels that contain an infancy narrative.
Answer: An infancy narrative is a story about Jesus' birth and early life. The Gospels of Matthew and Luke each contain an infancy narrative.

Question: List the major intentions of each writer of the infancy narratives. Give an example of how each intention is reflected in the writer's narrative.
Answer: Matthew wanted to show his Jewish readers that Jesus was the Messiah they had been waiting for, so he provided a genealogy of Jesus to demonstrate that Jesus was from the line of David. Matthew wanted to show his Jewish readers that Gentiles often accepted Jesus as the Messiah even though many Jews rejected him. He did this by including the story of the Magi, who were non-Jewish men. And Matthew wanted to portray Jesus as "the new Moses." In Matthew's Gospel, the Holy Family flees to Egypt and is called out after Herod's death, reflecting the Exodus.

Luke wanted to show that the Good News is for everyone, especially those who are poor and downtrodden. He brought this point out with the shepherds in his story. [Another possible response is that Luke demonstrates the universality of Jesus' message by offering a genealogy of Jesus that goes back to Adam, who is the father of all people, not just the Jews.]

Text Activities: The Infancy Narratives

Activity 1

Make a list of words, phrases, objects, places, and names associated with Christmas—as many as you can think of. While reading about the infancy narratives, put a check mark by the items on your list that seem to have a basis in the Gospels.

Activity 2

Write a brief essay describing the Christmas when you felt most in touch with the true meaning of the season. Explain what made that celebration of Christmas so special.

Additional Activities: The Infancy Narratives

Reading and Discussion Activities

Consider the following options in pursuing discussion of the infancy narratives.

Option 1: In class, read aloud both Matthew's and Luke's narratives, and as you do, comment on the basic organization of each. You can rely on the student text's outline of the accounts as you prepare your comments (see pp. 97, 99–100 of the text) and perhaps consult Richard P. McBrien's *Catholicism* for further information.

Option 2: To illustrate the impact and use of the Hebrew Scriptures in the development of the Gospels, have the students analyze Mary's Magnificat, in Luke 1:46–55. They can do this by tracking down, in the Hebrew Scriptures, the origins of all the verses. Many translations of the Bible include marginal notes that will help in this exercise.

Option 3: Ask the students to read John 1:1–18. Then ask whether the passage might be understood, in any sense, as a kind of infancy narrative. (Like Matthew and Luke, John attempts to deal with the theological implications of Jesus' origins.) Have the students find parts of John's Gospel that seem to have parallels in Matthew's and Luke's Gospels. For example, John says,

> He came to what was his own,
>   but his own people did not accept him.
>
> (1:11)

This might parallel Matthew's use of the Magi to illustrate that Gentiles accepted Jesus even though many Jews rejected him.

Reflection on Favorite Christmas Carols

Have the students, as a class, decide on their five favorite Christmas carols. To help them, take time to actually listen to Christmas carols in class. Doing this out of season will strike some students as "weird," but tell them that doing so is the best way to jog their memory.

After the students have made their selections, assign small groups of students to each of the carols, asking them to do three things:
1. Identify any lyrics that seem to have their origin in one or both of the infancy narratives.
2. Offer some explanation for the lyrics that are not directly tied to the Scriptures. Why, do you think, did the songwriter include them? Do they make any sense in our contemporary world? If not, why do they still touch us deeply—so deeply that the song was selected as a favorite?
3. Discuss how this and other Christmas carols might be understood as "infancy narratives," that is, as artistic creations intended to respond to our real needs, just as Matthew's and Luke's narratives responded to the needs of their respective audiences.

At the end of the small-group work, call everyone together and discuss what the small groups arrived at regarding their respective carols. Then ask the students to name popular Christmas songs that have little or nothing to do with the original meaning of Christmas. Elicit the students' opinions on why these songs are popular.

Concept B: The Hidden Years of Jesus' Life

With some reservations it can be said that the historical Jesus experienced life as a typical Jew of his day. Therefore, a portrait of his childhood and family life can be drawn from the preceding course material on daily life in Jesus' time. (Pages 105–108 of the student text)

Review Questions: The Hidden Years of Jesus' Life

Question: Why must we be careful about the images we have of Jesus during his early life and hidden years?
Answer: Fanciful images of Jesus can make him sound like a freak of sorts, rather than what the church has continually claimed him to be—the Son of God, certainly, but also a person who was one with us in all things but sin.

Question: Identify at least four factors that influenced Jesus while he was growing up.
Answer:
- He was raised in the Galilean village of Nazareth. [The students may mention that it was a community of just a few thousand people or that its location led to contact with the languages and ideas of other cultures.]
- He worked along with his father, who was a carpenter.
- He likely attended school in a room attached to the synagogue, studying the Hebrew Scriptures and the faith and history of his people.
- He had a faith-filled family life.

Text Activities: The Hidden Years of Jesus' Life

Activity 3

Based on what you know of the adult Jesus, write a description of what Jesus might have been like when he was fifteen years old. For example, how would he have related to his parents? Would he have been popular among his peers or a "loner"?

Activity 4

Of all the things that influenced Jesus while he was growing up, which do you think had the greatest impact on him? Explain your opinion in a paragraph.

Additional Activities: The Hidden Years of Jesus' Life

'Shua: The Human Jesus

'Shua: The Human Jesus (ACTA Publications, 1987) is an unusual, intriguing videotape created by Fr. William Burke, a master storyteller. To convey the humanity of Jesus, Burke has invented a boyhood friend of Jesus, who calls Jesus "'Shua." This character, played by Burke in contemporary dress, tells stories of his own childhood, adolescence, and young adulthood with his beloved friend

'Shua in Galilee. He speaks as a person who has heard about Jesus' ministry and crucifixion—not as someone who believes in Jesus as the Messiah but as someone who has been profoundly affected by his friendship.

Though well-grounded in scholarship about the Holy Land and the culture of Jesus' time, the incidents relayed in the video *are* fictional, and viewers must keep that in mind. The stories are quite plausible, and they give marvelous insight into how the Jesus whom we know in the Gospels could have developed and formed his convictions through the experiences of his youth.

'Shua is 60 minutes long. Ordinarily it is not advisable to have high school students watch a video of a talking person for an hour, even if the person in the video moves around. The students' interest usually cannot be sustained for that long. But this video is an exception.

You can purchase the VHS version of *'Shua*, which comes with a sixteen-page discussion guide, for $49.95. An audiocassette and a book version (the latter with artwork by Sr. Mary Southard) can also be purchased, each for $8.95. Order from ACTA Publications, 4848 North Clark Street, Chicago, IL 60640; phone 800-397-2282.

Searching the Scriptures for Information on Mary and Joseph

In your treatment of concept B, you may want to spend some class time discussing Mary and Joseph, the parents of Jesus. Be aware, however, that the Gospel information on them is sketchy, and a discussion about the role of Mary, in particular, might well lead to a discussion of historical theological developments that are beyond the scope of this course. Perhaps simply conduct a brief search of the Scriptures for references to Mary and Joseph, discussing any insights that can be gained into the family life of Jesus. Helpful references and commentary can be found in John L. McKenzie's *Dictionary of the Bible* under "Mary," point 1, and "Joseph," point 3.

Dialog from Jesus' Early Years

Ask the students to individually write a one-page dialog, or to get together and do a short role-play, of one or more of the following situations:
1. *Jesus and Joseph in the carpenter shop when Jesus was seven years old:* What questions and concerns would have been typical of a seven-year-old Jewish boy?
2. *Jesus and Mary in the "kitchen" when Jesus was twelve:* What would a twelve-year-old boy have discussed with his mother in such a situation?
3. *Jesus with Mary and Joseph on the way home from a synagogue service when Jesus was fifteen:* What kind of religious discussion would a fifteen-year-old boy have shared with his parents?
4. *Jesus with a friend his own age when Jesus was seven, twelve, or fifteen:* What would Jewish children likely have talked about?

Suggest that the students refer to earlier chapters in the student text to generate ideas for their dialog or role-play.

TV Interviews with Important People from Jesus' Childhood

Ask the students to imagine that they are in first-century Palestine. Jesus has just been executed, and rumors of his resurrection are sweeping across the country. Television stations are doing special reports on the events, interviewing people who were involved with Jesus throughout his life.

Have the class prepare a 30-minute "Special Report" featuring TV news personalities (anchorpersons, field reporters, commentators, etc.) and centering on an investigation of Jesus' childhood. Students, aided by preparation in small-group discussions, might take the following roles:
- Mary, the mother of Jesus, reflecting on things about him that concerned her even when he was a boy
- Joseph, the father of Jesus, reminiscing about the kind of boy Jesus was and describing what Joseph's hopes and dreams for Jesus were then
- the rabbi who taught the child Jesus in the synagogue
- childhood friends of Jesus who are gathered to discuss what he was like when they knew him and what, if anything, he did then that could have given them a hint about his future

Note: This type of exercise could be useful at other times in this course (e.g., during chapter 9, on Jesus' arrest, trial, and execution, or during chapter 10, on the Resurrection). You could either save the format for a later chapter or repeat it at that time.

Concept C: The Beginnings of Jesus' Public Life

The stories of Jesus' baptism and his temptation in the desert provide us with important insights into his self-understanding. (Pages 109–113 of the student text)

Review Questions: The Beginnings of Jesus' Public Life

Question: Describe the significance of John the Baptist in the story of Jesus. What religious ritual is associated with John the Baptist?
Answer: John's task was to prepare the way for Jesus' ministry by calling people to an awareness of their sin and to repentance. The religious ritual associated with John is baptism.

Question: Why was the early church uncomfortable with Jesus' accepting baptism? How did Matthew respond to the church's concern?
Answer: The early church was uncomfortable with Jesus' accepting baptism because it seemed to suggest on his part a need for repentance of sin. In response, Matthew stated that John was reluctant to baptize Jesus. Then he explained that Jesus accepted baptism "'to fulfill all righteousness'" (3:15). Jesus' acceptance of baptism was not an admission of sin but, rather, an indication of his willingness to completely immerse himself in the life and concerns of his people.

Question: What two chief lessons did Jesus learn from his baptism?
Answer:
1. That he was chosen in a special way to proclaim and begin a new kingdom
2. That he would be given the power to fulfill his role through the Spirit of God

Question: What does the story of the three temptations in the desert tell us about Jesus' understanding of his messiahship?

Answer: Jesus rejected the messiahship expected by his people. He refused to use economic, magical, or political power.

Text Activities: The Beginnings of Jesus' Public Life

Activity 5

Based on recollections by your parents and others, write a short description of your own baptism.

Activity 6

For each of the three temptations Jesus experienced in the desert, write a brief explanation of how a similar temptation might be experienced by a young person in today's society.

Additional Activities: The Beginnings of Jesus' Public Life

Research on Baptism

Assign a short research paper on baptism as a ritual common to various religions throughout history. Recommend that the students use encyclopedias and other library resources. As a conclusion to their paper, they should write one paragraph explaining why, they believe, water baptism has such a universal appeal. Lead a discussion on the results of the students' work.

The Symbolic Power of Water

Water is a rich religious symbol, and it can be explored from a variety of perspectives. Lead a brainstorming activity in which the students call out as many qualities, characteristics, and purposes of water as they can think of. Write these ideas on the chalkboard as the students give them.

When the students have finished brainstorming, check off all the ideas on the board that might be related in any way to faith or religion. Do not discuss the ideas as you check them off. Then, for each item checked, ask the students to tell you what the connection with faith or religion might be. Point out that there are no right or wrong answers in this exercise, because it is up to the students to see the significance for themselves.

To connect this exercise more directly with the student text material, ask the students to suggest, based on the results of their discussion, additional meanings in Jesus' baptism, beyond those discussed in the text.

Jesus' Baptism in Art and Film

Jesus' baptism has been a popular theme of Christian art for over a thousand years. Have the students find, in art history books, paintings that attempt to capture the event. Analyze similarities and differences in the paintings, identify the most unique interpretation, and discuss why the approaches of some renderings (e.g., those picturing the Holy Spirit hovering overhead as a realistic dove) no longer seem popular. Also, randomly choose a few of the paintings and ask the students to assess how scripturally based those interpretations appear to be.

In addition to, or as an option to, the above, find videotapes that portray the baptism of Jesus (e.g., Franco Zeffirelli's *Jesus of Nazareth* or some of the biblical epic films, such as *The Greatest Story Ever Told*). Analyze these interpretations of Jesus' baptism in light of the discussion of the event in the student text. If the students were directing such a film, how would they interpret the event?

Jesus' Priorities

This exercise is to help the students recognize Jesus' real struggle to come to terms with the values that would guide his life.

1. After reminding the class that Jesus was a faith-filled Jew, one steeped in the Hebrew Scriptures, have someone read Psalm 139 slowly and prayerfully. Ask the students to try to imagine Jesus himself praying this psalm, both privately and in community with his Jewish brothers and sisters. Point out that it no doubt was this kind of personal and communal prayer and reflection that prepared Jesus to faithfully respond to situations such as the desert temptations.

Handout 5–A

2. Distribute handout 5–A, "Jesus' Priorities." Read aloud the instructions at the top of the handout. Then give the students time to complete the ranking in the left-hand column.

3. When the students are done, break the class into ten groups of approximately the same size, giving each group the task of looking up one of the passages from Matthew's Gospel given at the bottom of the handout. After reading the passage, the group is to match it with the appropriate value listed in the center column and to determine what the passage indicates about Jesus' real attitude toward that value.

4. Call for the groups to report their findings to the class, reading their assigned passage and indicating what it reveals about Jesus' values. Class response can be invited after each report. Final matches between the scriptural passages and the values listed can be recorded by placing the number of each passage (1 through 10) in the space provided next to the appropriate value. Make sure that at least one passage number is indicated for each value.

5. To conclude the activity, select three students who can read with inflection and emotion, and ask them to do a dramatic reading of Matt. 4:1–11, taking the roles of the narrator, Jesus, and the devil. Follow this reading with a class discussion of the relationship between Jesus' desert temptations and his values as revealed in Matthew's Gospel. Start out the discussion with a question such as this:
- Do the three desert temptations reflect choices that Jesus had to make at other times in his life? In what ways?

Temptation About Priorities

This activity is a takeoff on text activity 6. Introduce this activity by saying something like the following:
- Your textbook states that the temptation story, in addition to relaying information about Jesus' ministry, warns Christians to resist the temptation to find their own meaning and purpose in life through economic security or through personal or political power over others. Right now we are going to look at ways that people today are faced with this type of temptation.

Divide the class into six groups and assign two groups to each of the following discussion questions:
- What are three ways that people today give in to the temptation to find meaning in economic security?
- What are three ways that people today give in to the temptation to control other people's emotions or thoughts for their own benefit?
- What are three ways that people today give in to the temptation to exert political power over other people?

After 10 minutes or so of discussion, have the groups report their responses. List these in three columns on the chalkboard. After each group's report, allow for class reactions, questions, insights, and so on. Close by brainstorming concrete, practical ways that people might be able to resist the temptations.

Concept D: Wandering Preacher, Unique Teacher

Jesus' relationship with his disciples, especially the twelve Apostles, was unique in his day, and it signaled a special role for those who would follow him. (Pages 114–117 of the student text)

Review Questions: Wandering Preacher, Unique Teacher

Question: In what ways was Jesus the teacher both similar to and different from the rabbis of his day?

Answer: Jesus was similar to the rabbis of his day in that he roamed from place to place teaching and was accompanied by a band of disciples. He taught in the synagogues or wherever people were willing to gather to listen to him.

He was different from the rabbis in several ways:
- He proclaimed a truly different notion of the Kingdom of God.
- He claimed for himself a special role as the one who would personally establish the Kingdom and embody it.
- He claimed himself as the sole judge of the truth of what he taught.
- He used parables and performed miracles.

Question: Briefly describe Jesus' relationship with his disciples called the Apostles.

Answer: Jesus' relationship with his disciples differed from the relationship that was common between rabbis and their followers:
- The disciples did not choose Jesus; he called them.
- Jesus did not simply share a body of teachings that his disciples were expected to memorize; he called them into a lasting relationship with him.
- The disciples were not only expected to watch and learn from Jesus; they were actually called to share in his mission.

Question: What connection can be made between the twelve Apostles and the early history of the Jews?

Answer: The Israelites at one time consisted of twelve tribes, each descending from one of the twelve sons of Jacob. The early Christian community recognized exactly twelve Apostles to suggest that the Apostles would be the foundation of a new community of faith, a new Israel, what we recognize today as the Christian church.

A Text Activity: Wandering Preacher, Unique Teacher

Activity 7

According to the Gospels, the Apostles came from ordinary walks of life. Write a brief description of twelve people Jesus might choose as Apostles today. Consider questions such as these: *Would the twelve people all be men? What occupations would they come from? In terms of personality traits, would they be similar to one another or a mix?*

Additional Activities: Wandering Preacher, Unique Teacher

Discussion on the Apostle Peter

Refer the students to the shaded feature box titled "The Apostle Peter," on page 115 of the student text. Have someone read the introductory part, "So Much Like Us," and then break the class into nine groups, assigning each group one of the scriptural passages given in the right-hand column of the feature box. Instruct the students to answer the following questions:
- What does the passage reveal about Peter?
- What does the passage reveal about Jesus?
- What lesson does the passage hold for contemporary Christians?

After 5 to 10 minutes of small-group discussion, begin a whole-class discussion of the passages, in the order they are given in the text. You may want to have these passage cites already listed on the chalkboard and then jot down after each cite the key points raised by the students, thereby developing a brief but fairly thorough portrait of Peter, his relationship with Jesus, and the implications for today's Christians.

Variation: If you are willing or able to give more class time to this activity, allow for further insights by the class at large after each small-group report. If you are short on time, you might need to approach this entire activity as a brainstorming session. The activity can also easily be adapted as a writing assignment.

In your own preparation for leading this activity, consult John L. McKenzie's *Dictionary of the Bible* under "Peter," which offers a thorough discussion of Peter in the Scriptures.

A Different View of Peter

The popular theologian and storyteller John Shea has retold the story of Peter and the large catch of fish (Luke 5:1–11) in a delightfully refreshing way. You could read Shea's story to the class, or three well-prepared students could take the roles of Jesus, Peter, and the narrator. You might also consider adapting the story as a skit, perhaps acted out for extra credit by three student volunteers.

The story originally appeared in the journal *Chicago Studies* (21 [Spring 1982]: 39–41). Then it was reprinted in *Storytelling: Imagination and Faith,* by William J. Bausch (Mystic, CT: Twenty-third Publications, 1984), on pages 123–125. Bausch's book, incidentally, is filled with marvelous stories, many of them reworkings of Gospel stories or tales from other traditions. They could add a spark to any course on Jesus.

Jesus' Priorities

For each value listed below, circle a number to indicate how much priority Jesus gave it in his ministry, from no priority at all to high priority. Your teacher will tell you what to do next.

No Priority — High Priority	Value	Passage
0 1 2 3 4 5 6 7 8 9 10	a. Elimination of all laws	_____
0 1 2 3 4 5 6 7 8 9 10	b. Accumulation of material goods	_____
0 1 2 3 4 5 6 7 8 9 10	c. Public approval of one's faith	_____
0 1 2 3 4 5 6 7 8 9 10	d. Fair punishment for all offenses	_____
0 1 2 3 4 5 6 7 8 9 10	e. Avoidance of bad company	_____
0 1 2 3 4 5 6 7 8 9 10	f. Recognition for good deeds	_____
0 1 2 3 4 5 6 7 8 9 10	g. Speaking openly about one's convictions	_____
0 1 2 3 4 5 6 7 8 9 10	h. Intellectual ability	_____
0 1 2 3 4 5 6 7 8 9 10	i. Self-preservation	_____
0 1 2 3 4 5 6 7 8 9 10	j. Power over others	_____

Scriptural Passages

1. Matthew 5:11–12
2. Matthew 20:25–28
3. Matthew 9:10–13
4. Matthew 6:19–21
5. Matthew 10:26–31
6. Matthew 11:25–26
7. Matthew 16:24–26
8. Matthew 5:17–19
9. Matthew 5:38–42
10. Matthew 6:1–4

Handout 5-A: Permission to reproduce this handout for classroom use is granted.

CHAPTER 6

The Kingdom of God: Proclaiming the Dream of Jesus

Major Concepts

A. **Dreams:** A Dream, either an individual's or a group's, is a guiding force for one's life, a vision of the future that shapes one's thoughts, feelings, and actions in the present. Jesus' Dream was the Kingdom of God.

B. **The Kingdom of God Proclaimed:** The basic notion of the Kingdom of God was part of the worldview with which Jesus was raised. However, Jesus' understanding of the Kingdom went beyond the narrow political and military understanding that had become popular among his people.

C. **Jesus' Understanding of God:** Jesus' Dream of the Kingdom of God was closely tied to his unique understanding of the nature of God, an understanding reflected in his use of the word *Abba* for God. This intimate understanding of God shocked many Jews.

D. **Jesus' Understanding of the Command to Love:** Jesus saw the Kingdom of God as the reign of God's love over the hearts of people and, consequently, as a new social order based on people's unconditional love for one another. The Jews had always had a deep sense of communal love, based on the Law. But over time, nationalism and legalism had developed among the people and conflicted with their following the command to love.

E. **The Reign of God and "the Reign of Sin":** Throughout the Gospels we see Jesus encountering the power of personal and communal sin as well as other forms of evil. The constant message of the Gospels is that God in Jesus ultimately does conquer evil in all its manifestations.

F. **Right Now, but Not Yet:** In the Gospels we encounter a repeated tension between the claim that the Kingdom of God is a present reality and the notion that it is something to be achieved only at the end of time. The Kingdom *is* present in that it was fully revealed in the life and work of Jesus and is made real today in Jesus' risen presence. It will, however, be fully realized only when people choose to live compassionate, forgiving lives.

Concept A: Dreams

A Dream, either an individual's or a group's, is a guiding force for one's life, a vision of the future that shapes one's thoughts, feelings, and actions in the present. Jesus' Dream was the Kingdom of God. (Pages 119–121 of the student text)

Review Questions: Dreams

Question: Define *Dream,* spelled with a capital *D.*
Answer: A vision of the future, perhaps idealized, that can focus our energies, guide our choices, influence our friendships, and even lead us closer to personal happiness

Question: What is the name given to Jesus' Dream?
Answer: The Kingdom of God

A Text Activity: Dreams

Activity 1

Think of a time when you were so committed to achieving a certain goal that you regularly made sacrifices to attain it. As you read the rest of this section, jot down your thoughts on how your experience might be similar to Jesus' commitment to his Dream, the Kingdom of God.

Additional Activities: Dreams

Picture in Your Mind

Create a writing or discussion activity out of page 120 of the student text, the section titled "Everyone Has a Dream." The easiest approach would be to have the students carefully consider their response to the second paragraph and the list below it, which ask them to imagine their week of graduation from high school—friends, class spirit, parties, and so on. Then either ask them to write a short essay summarizing their graduation Dream or guide them in a brainstorming exercise to describe it orally.

Many other variations on the exercise are possible: For example, each of six small groups might be assigned to discuss one of the six details from the list. Or the students' graduation Dreams could be acted out in role-plays.

To Dream or Not to Dream

Contemporary sociologists and psychologists warn that many young people have lost the capacity to look to their future with hope. The young people, in other words, have not been able to find a *Dream* in the sense of that term in this chapter. The suggested causes for the lack of a Dream range from changing economic structures in our society to the threat of nuclear annihilation.

1. After the students have read pages 119–120 of the student text, discuss the idea that many young people do not have a Dream. Use the following questions:
- Is the lack of a Dream common among the young people of our area? If so, why? [Urge the students to be as specific as possible in the reasons they give.]
- If a young person, because of family, culture, or social and economic background, is deprived of a Dream, what can she or he do to overcome that?
- Both historically and in the present, some people who seem to have had no reason to look to the future with hope *have* found a Dream, and it has taken them to great heights in politics, the arts, social activism, or athletics. What has enabled these people to find and follow their Dream?

2. Provide, or elicit from the students, examples of historical or contemporary people who have overcome great odds to find a Dream. If you know of such persons in your area, invite them to tell their story to the class. Also, many films and videotapes deal with this theme—people who have overcome the odds to find and live out their Dream. Check with your diocesan media center or local library for possibilities.

Concept B: The Kingdom of God Proclaimed

The basic notion of the Kingdom of God was part of the worldview with which Jesus was raised. However, Jesus' understanding of the Kingdom went beyond the narrow political and military understanding that had become popular among his people. (Pages 122–123 of the student text)

Review Questions: The Kingdom of God Proclaimed

Question: Briefly explain the Jewish notion of God as a king.
Answer: The Jews recognized God's kingship first in the wonders of creation, which Yahweh ruled. Some rabbis also taught that the Kingdom of God was present in the Law, which was God's instrument for ruling people.

Question: Why did the ancient Jews believe the Messiah would be a great warrior who would establish the Kingdom through military conquest?
Answer: In the centuries following King David's military conquests, the people's expectation of a savior became bound up with the notion of a new national, political kingship. And by the time of Jesus' ministry, after nearly a hundred years of Roman domination, many Jews expected the Kingdom to begin with a military takeover of the country and the expulsion of the Romans. This overthrow was to be led by the Messiah.

Question: What ideas about the Kingdom of God did Jesus clearly reject?
Answer: Jesus clearly rejected any notion of the Kingdom that involved political or military power. He did not have in mind a geographical state or nation. Nor was his concept of the Kingdom simply a new philosophy or a new plan for social reform.

A Text Activity: The Kingdom of God Proclaimed

Activity 2

Respond in writing to the following question: *If you did not know anything about Jesus and Christianity, what might you think the term* Kingdom of God *referred to?*

An Additional Activity: The Kingdom of God Proclaimed

Jesus' Roots and the Kingdom of God

This activity is designed to demonstrate how Jesus' understanding of the Kingdom of God was rooted in his Jewish heritage.

1. Have the students brainstorm as many words as they can think of to express what the Kingdom of God means to them. List these words on the chalkboard.

2. Divide the class into two groups. Assign group 1 the following passages from the Psalms: 93; 95:1–7; 96:10–13. Assign group 2 these passages from the Psalms: 97:1–5; 98:4–9; 99:1–5. Tell the students that the Psalms were originally hymns that the people sang communally as well as prayed or sang privately. To gain a sense of the communal use of the Psalms (without asking your students to sing!), arrange for the groups to read the assigned passages aloud prayerfully, alternating verses from group 1 to group 2 and back again repeatedly. This will amount to a modified chant.

3. As a class, discuss the kingship of God conveyed by the recited psalms. Ask questions such as these:
   - What images were repeatedly mentioned?
   - What titles or descriptions of Yahweh predominated?
   - In what ways was the power or reign of Yahweh shown?

List these images, titles, concepts, and so on, on the board.

4. Ask the students to reread Mark 12:28–34, quoted as the opening reading for chapter 6 of the student text. Pose the following question and record the students' responses on the board.
   - When Jesus says, "'You are not far from the kingdom of God,'" he is referring to the scribe's insight into what is most important to focus on in life. How does that understanding of the Kingdom differ from the imagery and sense of the Kingdom reflected in the psalms we read?

5. Lead a discussion comparing the students' images of the Kingdom (from step 1) with those reflected in the psalms and the passage from Mark's Gospel. Close by noting the centrality of the Kingdom idea to Jesus' life and ministry and the importance of working toward a reasonably clear understanding and appreciation of what he meant by it.

Concept C: Jesus' Understanding of God

Jesus' Dream of the Kingdom of God was closely tied to his unique understanding of the nature of God, an understanding reflected in his use of the word *Abba* for God. This intimate understanding of God shocked many Jews. (Pages 124–126 of the student text)

A Review Question: Jesus' Understanding of God

Question: With what Aramaic word did Jesus address God? Why did this shock the people of Jesus' time?

Answer: Jesus addressed God with the word *Abba*, which meant "Dad" or "Daddy." Many Jews were shocked by this kind of intimacy because they would not even have considered using God's name in prayer.

Text Activities: Jesus' Understanding of God

Activity 3

Slowly say the Lord's Prayer to yourself. Then repeat the prayer, substituting the words "My Daddy" for "Our Father." In a paragraph, describe any feelings or insight you had from this exercise.

Activity 4

Referring to Matthew 6:26–34, as quoted above, select one line that you think would be particularly significant for young people today. Write a short explanation of your choice.

Additional Activities: Jesus' Understanding of God

Getting in Touch with God

It is important that students get in touch with the images and understandings of God that are already a part of their religious identity, attitudes, values, and so on. This exercise will help the students become conscious of what they already know and believe about God.

1. Divide the class into groups of three or four, giving each group three 3-by-5-inch index cards. Ask the groups to imagine that God is going to appear before them in about 15 minutes and that God has indicated a desire to listen to their concerns and questions and respond to them. The groups are to spend 5 minutes brainstorming a list of all the questions they would like God to answer. They should jot these down in rough draft form on a piece of scrap paper.

After the 5 minutes is up, tell the groups that they are now to rank their questions in terms of importance. When they have done that, they are to refine and polish their three most important questions and neatly print one question on each of the index cards.

2. Collect all the cards and shuffle them thoroughly. Remind the students of the following:
- When Jesus said, "The Kingdom of God is among you," he meant that we can get truly in touch with God by looking deeply within ourselves. If we spend time reflecting upon ourselves and our life experiences, we will find the wisdom that we often seek from sources outside ourselves.

To demonstrate what you have said, redistribute the cards, again giving three to each group. The groups are now to imagine that they have been commissioned by God to speak on God's behalf, answering each question as they believe God would answer it.

The students should again write in rough draft form before printing their final responses on the reverse side of the cards they have been given. Encourage the students to be as creative as possible in their "God-responses," perhaps even writing with a biblical or godlike touch.

3. To preserve anonymity and encourage free exchange, collect the cards one more time, shuffle them, and redistribute them—this time, one to each student. After giving the students a moment to look at the question and answer on the card they have received, ask for volunteers to share a question and answer with the class. Allow for reactions and feel free to share your own thoughts. Continue the discussion for as long as you feel it is productive.

4. Close the activity by summing up the qualities and images of God reflected by the responses to the questions. You may wish to do this by brainstorming all the characteristics or images of God that come to the students' minds as a result of their sharing, listing these ideas on the chalkboard. As a final step, you may want to attempt a definition or description of God (in twenty-five words or less) based on the list on the board.

Discussion on the Prayer Life of Jesus

The student text says that Jesus' understanding of the Kingdom of God flowed out of Jewish history, the Hebrew Scriptures, Jewish worship, and his personal prayer and reflection upon all of these. Jesus' personal prayer life as well as his public teaching on prayer is central to the Gospel story and therefore vital to our understanding of him.

1. Divide the class into the four groups that were assigned to read a Gospel from beginning to end in the activity "A Special Reading Assignment," on pages 63–64 of this manual. Divide each of these four groups into two sections. Assign the following tasks to the sections within each group:
- Those of you in section 1 are to scan your assigned Gospel and locate all the times when Jesus publicly says something about prayer. On a piece of paper, record the chapter and verse numbers and briefly summarize the point Jesus is making.
- Those of you in section 2 are to go through your assigned Gospel and locate all the times when Jesus goes off to pray privately or prays directly to his Father in a public way. Record the chapter and verse numbers and briefly summarize the situation, particularly identifying what seems to motivate Jesus to pray.

Give the students as long as they need to complete the assignments.

2. Randomly call on students or ask for volunteers from section 1 of each group, asking them to share what they discovered in their search for Jesus' teachings on prayer. You may want them to actually read their scriptural selections. Then ask the students in section 2 of each group whether they discovered

any times when Jesus actually prayed in the manner he described in his teaching. That is, did Jesus practice what he preached?

3. In general terms, summarize all the occasions when the Jesus of the Gospels seems almost driven to pray (e.g., when he is overworked, making difficult decisions, experiencing either apparent success or painful rejection). Close the discussion with a statement along these lines:
- We too should rely on prayer when confronting such situations, keeping in mind Jesus' teachings on prayer as we do so.

Solo: Experiencing the Presence of God in Nature

The videotape *Solo* (15 min.) is an exhilarating study of one young man's solitary climb and descent of a mountain. The cinematography is spectacular, and the fluctuating tension and euphoria make for a delightful and prayerful viewing experience. In the context of concept C, the primary value of the film is its portrayal of the human experience of awe, wonder, "splendid isolation"—that is, the experience of God's presence in nature. A transition to a discussion of how Jesus dealt with this universal human experience in and through prayer is natural and easy.

Related areas of discussion are the significance of mountains as a common biblical symbol and the relationship, if any, between the experience of mountains and the experience of desert, to which Jesus was often drawn to pray. To relate the film to the Jewish experience of God's presence revealed in the wonders of creation, read aloud Psalm 104. Following a discussion of the film, you may want to close with Ps. 139:1–18, which expresses an awareness of God's powerful presence in our life. The primary purpose of prayer is to help us to do just that—discover the God who lives within us.

Solo is distributed by Mass Media Ministries, 2116 North Charles Street, Baltimore, MD 21218; phone toll free 800-828-8825. One-day rental of the videotape (or 16mm film) is $25. Purchase of the videotape is $95. Also, many diocesan libraries and media centers, as well as public libraries, have the video or film available.

Who Is Your God?

Note: This exercise is included in the teaching manual for the course *Understanding Catholic Christianity* (Winona, MN: Saint Mary's Press, 1989). Make sure the exercise has not been used with your students, should your school offer that course.

1. Introduce the exercise by telling the students that you want them to try to pin down their understanding of who God is, just as Jesus had to struggle with his own understanding of God.

Handout 6–A

2. Distribute handout 6–A, "Who Is Your God?" Read aloud the directions on the handout and give the students about 5 minutes to complete their task. Then tell the students to go back over the understandings of God that they checked on their handout and to decide which three they most agree with. They should indicate their choices by circling the respective check marks.

3. Divide the students into small groups that are to arrive at a consensus understanding of God, based on the items they circled. After discussion, each group should write down an understanding that is not only reasonable but

can be defended by the group members. You may want to limit the groups to a combination of, or variation on, no more than three of the suggested understandings from handout 6–A, both to limit the length of their final response and to promote more intensive discussion.

The groups will need about 20 minutes to work.

4. Have the groups share their consensus understanding of God with the entire class. Challenge the groups to explain their responses. It may be difficult for them to come up with sound reasoning, but the difficulty will only enhance the effectiveness of the next phase of this exercise.

5. After the groups have shared their ideas, offer a comment such as the following:
- It often seems that when we talk about God, we have to go beyond the usual words and concepts of everyday life. God is too big for our simple definitions; that's why it's so hard to find the right words in a discussion like this one. We need to break free from our traditional thinking and imagine God in unusual ways.

Follow with these questions:
- When you think of God, what color do you think of? Why?
- When you think of God, what kind of music do you think of? Why?
- If God had a voice, what would it sound like?
- When do you feel closest to God? Why? [Leave this question and the next one open for those who want to answer, but do not require that everyone respond.]
- When in your life have you most "sensed the sacred"? That is, when have you felt the most "holy," however you define that term?

The answers to these kinds of questions can be illuminating as well as entertaining. They give us more than just a definition of God—they give us a sense of who God is, a feel for God's presence in our life.

Concept D:
Jesus' Understanding of the Command to Love

Jesus saw the Kingdom of God as the reign of God's love over the hearts of people and, consequently, as a new social order based on people's unconditional love for one another. The Jews had always had a deep sense of communal love, based on the Law. But over time, nationalism and legalism had developed among the people and conflicted with their following the command to love. (Pages 127–130 of the student text)

Review Questions:
Jesus' Understanding of the Command to Love

Question: According to Jesus, what is the meaning of the word *conversion*?
Answer: A change of heart, a turning from selfishness to openness to God and the call to love

Question: What does it mean to say that Jesus understood the Kingdom of God as being communal in nature?

Answer: The Kingdom of God proclaimed by Jesus was not simply a "me and God" situation, a one-to-one relationship between God and an individual person. Jesus clearly understood the Kingdom of God as implying a relationship not only between God and individuals but *among* individuals.

Question: Name and briefly describe the two problems that developed among the Jews and conflicted with their following the command to love one another.

Answer:
- *Nationalism:* An excessive sense of separation from all other cultures led some Jews to believe that "love your neighbor" referred to Jewish neighbors only.
- *Legalism:* The Jews' extensive system of religious laws dominated virtually every aspect of life and actually oppressed the people rather than just guiding them.

Question: When will, or does, Jesus' Dream of the Kingdom of God become realized?

Answer: When people conform their lives to God's will

Text Activities:
Jesus' Understanding of the Command to Love

Activity 5

In writing, respond to the following question and support your response with an example. *Do Christians have the same tendency toward legalism that the Jews of Jesus' time had?*

Activity 6

Rewrite the story of the good Samaritan (Luke 10:25–37) as you believe Jesus would tell it today if he were addressing your class or school.

Activity 7

In a paragraph, react to the following statement: *True Christianity can never be understood as a "me and God" religion.*

Additional Activities:
Jesus' Understanding of the Command to Love

Discussion Starters

Consider one or all of the following options to initiate discussion on concept D.

Option 1: Ask the students to call out the Ten Commandments, and list these on the chalkboard. Then have the students identify the commandments that are directly related to the general command to love one another. Lead the class in discussing Saint Paul's contention that the person who loves automatically fulfills the commandments of the Law (Rom. 13:8–10). For example:
- Is it true that one who loves automatically fulfills the commandment not to steal? not to kill? Why or why not?

Option 2: To help the students overcome the common perception of the Jewish Law as totally restrictive and judgmental, have them read Psalm 19 and at least scan Psalm 119 (it is very long). Certainly Jesus did not condemn the profound, almost sensual love for the Law that is expressed in these psalms. Rather, he criticized the *loss* of this attitude and its replacement by rigidity and legalism. Compare the spirit of these psalms, for example, with the attitude of the Pharisee in the parable of the Pharisee and the tax collector, in Luke 18:9–14. Then the almost embarrassing rage of Jesus in Matt. 23:13–32 becomes more understandable (remember, Jesus loved the Law!).

Option 3: Have one student read aloud Matt. 5:44–48 as it is quoted on page 128 of the student text. Then go through the passage, one phrase or verse at a time, asking students to paraphrase the passage in a way that expresses its full meaning for them as young people today. After doing so, discuss the following questions:
- In the everyday world, how realistic is this command to love our enemies?
- How would you change the passage, if at all, to make it more "attractive" to most people in society?
- On page 130 of your textbook, the author states that the experience of God's love for us empowers us and frees us to love one another unconditionally, thus freeing and empowering others. Which kind of love would be more "freeing" and more "empowering"—the kind commanded by Jesus or the kind suggested by your "revised version" of Matthew's passage. Why?

Role-play: The Good Samaritan Today

This exercise applies the lessons of the important parable of the good Samaritan to the students' everyday life. It can be used in place of, or as an extension of, text activity 6.

1. Break the class into groups of seven or eight. Have the groups carefully read and then discuss the parable of the good Samaritan, in Luke 10:25–37. Before they begin their reading, mention that in Jesus' time, the road between Jerusalem and Jericho was notoriously dangerous, frequented by bandits. Also, remind the students of your past discussions on the Samaritans and define the Levite in the parable as a kind of assistant to the priesthood in Jewish society. Instruct the groups to identify on paper what each character in the parable did and what was implied about the characters' values by the way they acted.

2. Have the groups update the story as it might be told by Jesus today, using a situation from their experience to make the same points. To do this, assign one of the following questions to each group:
- How would Jesus tell the story today if the setting were to involve a group of high school students out on a Friday night? For instance, who might be the equivalent of the Samaritan? the man on the road? the Levite?
- How would Jesus tell the story today if the setting were to involve a typical family stranded on a car trip?
- How would Jesus tell the story today if the setting were to be our community?
- How would Jesus tell the story today if the setting were to be our whole society? Which group in our society might be the injured man? Which group might be the Levite? And so on.

The students should take notes on their discussion.

3. Announce that the groups will be asked to do a role-play of their updated parable in the next class session. Each student in each group must take a part as one of the seven or eight characters in the group's version of the parable. The groups have the remainder of this class session to work on their role-play and will have 15 minutes or so at the beginning of the next session to review and briefly rehearse it.

4. In the next class session, ask the groups to perform the role-plays. Discussion questions can include these:
- How well did each group get across the meaning of the original parable?
- Which characters were easy to pick out?
- Did you identify with any of the characters? Which ones?
- Did you find it easy or difficult to "get into your part"? Why?

Love Made "Practical"

The purpose of this activity is to translate the biblical command to love into concrete terms and to apply those terms to specific moral issues. This is the only way that the teaching of Jesus can be recognized for what it clearly is: incredibly practical.

1. Introduce the activity with a comment such as this:
- Jesus' teaching on the law of love and its relationship to the Jewish Law is at the center of Christian moral decision-making. Many people claim that we must continually fall back on the clear-cut dictates of law in our actions because love is too abstract, too undefined, to guide us. Others feel that Jesus' call to love is an ideal to shoot for, but certainly not something to be expected of "average people." The problem with these lines of thought is that they reduce the Gospel message to "nice ideas" but effectively remove it from the "real world." This allows us to pay our religious dues on Sundays but to forget about Christian morality in everyday life.

2. Have the class brainstorm as many "wrong" actions, or sins, as they can think of (e.g., stealing, lying, cheating, murder). Write these on the chalkboard. After the students have come up with a list, lead them in discussing *why* each action or attitude is wrong or sinful, based on their understanding of Christian love.

Variation: To extend and enliven the exercise, take time for the students, in small groups, to actually create moral dilemmas for discussion and resolution by the class, or provide such moral "case studies" yourself.

3. Sum up the discussion with a comment such as this:
- Christians—in fact, mature persons in general—must have reasons for the way they act, values that they have consciously formed and freely live by. This way they can take some control of their life rather than let life control them. In other words, for Christians, taking control of one's life means making our intent to love "practical," making the teachings of Jesus concrete and understandable so that one can live according to those teachings freely, consciously, and with maturity.

Handout 6–B

4. Distribute handout 6–B, "The Consequences of Moral Decisions," and go through the handout point by point with the students.

Comment that this handout is just one attempt to identify what makes an action loving or selfish, right or wrong, moral or immoral. Try to illustrate each point with examples, or ask the students to do so. For instance:
- Is it true that love increases our ability to trust and that selfishness decreases it? Can you think of an example to illustrate that?

5. Go through the list of wrong actions that were listed on the board earlier (or the moral dilemmas created by the students or yourself) and apply the handout to each action or attitude to determine why it is wrong. Here are some examples to offer to get things started:
- Stealing is not wrong solely because we have taken an object that belongs to someone else. It is wrong also because it increases distrust and exploits others and therefore makes love more difficult, if not impossible.
- Using drugs is not wrong solely because a law is violated. In addition, using drugs limits our human potential. It makes us less than we are called to be and can therefore diminish our self-respect.

6. Conclude the discussion by noting the following:
- Christians believe that they are called to be "people for others," just as Jesus, in the words of some, is "the man for others." Christians are people-conscious. They strive for the growth and welfare of all their brothers and sisters by becoming morally loving people themselves. Their faith calls them to a way of life, not just to a code of ethics or to a series of laws. That's why the faith of Christians is, contrary to the opinion of some, totally relevant and practical—at least for those who understand and live it.

The Legalists' Dilemma

This is a discussion exercise and presentation on the relationship between love and law in Christian moral decision-making.

1. Divide the class into groups of six to eight students. Explain that this activity will show how law, conscience, and circumstance can work together. Instruct each group to quickly elect a judge. Then ask those who have been elected to take a seat in a row of chairs at the front of the class. (You may even want to set up some tables for these students to sit behind.)

2. Select as many of the Ten Commandments as you have groups. Then assign each group one of those commandments and tell all the groups that they have 5 minutes to come up with a situation in which they feel they could justly and reasonably break that commandment, while remaining good, conscientious people. Stress that they must support their decision with sound arguments. Each group must appoint one member to be the group's legal counsel, who will present its case to the judges.

3. When the 5 minutes is up, have each legal counsel (one at a time) come before the judges, briefly state his or her group's situation, and present its arguments for breaking its assigned commandment. The judges can accept or reject each group's proposal and must briefly give reasons for their ruling. Each report by legal counsel and the judges' decision that follows it should take no longer than 5 to 6 minutes. Be prepared with a stopwatch to restrict the discussion if necessary. Also, take the role of both sergeant at arms and court reporter, making sure that the discussion is orderly and recording on the board, in capsule form, the arguments used by the "winning" side, whether it be the group or the judges.

4. Following the last judges' decision, comment on the discussion appropriately, perhaps keeping in mind the consequences of moral decisions suggested in the preceding activity, "Love Made 'Practical.'" In other words, try to ascertain whether the groups' and the judges' arguments and decisions could be supported on the basis of general Christian principles. Your comments could lead directly into a mini-lecture on the topic "Making Moral Decisions as a Christian—Love and Law" (see the background on this topic provided below).

Teacher Background:
Making Moral Decisions as a Christian—Love and Law

Though it is risky to summarize something as complex as the process used to decide what is right or wrong in a given situation, doing so at least gives the students a general understanding of what is involved in making moral decisions. Before proceeding, you may want to read to yourself the following general explanation of the Christian approach to moral decision-making:

For the Christian, the foundation of morality is the teachings, actions, attitudes, and values of Jesus. His "definition," if you will, of what it means to be human is the basis of all Christian morality. So the ultimate task of the Christian is to discern the answer to the basic question, What would Jesus himself do, given a certain moral situation?

Jesus' own moral heritage was based on the Jewish Law, particularly as summarized in the Ten Commandments. But as mentioned earlier, if laws are not followed consciously and lovingly, they can end up dehumanizing people. Jesus was aware of this, and though he did not deny the Commandments, he definitely preached a morality that went beyond them (see Matt. 5:17–48).

As the community of faith that professes belief in Jesus and strives to live according to his teachings and values, the church rightly does what all communities do. It reflects on the principles that guide it (in this case, the principles in the message of Jesus), applies those principles to everyday life, and occasionally but rarely makes a ruling regarding a practice that has become customarily accepted or rejected by the community.

A critical distinction needs to be made when talking about church law (and here we are talking specifically about the law of the Roman Catholic church). There are two kinds of laws to be concerned with:
- *Functional laws* of the church involve the church's efforts to direct its internal order and affairs. These are regulations set up by the church to achieve particular goals of order or discipline in the church—for example, regulations regarding reception of the sacraments, the necessity to attend Mass, fasting, and celibacy. These kinds of laws can change or even be dropped. For example, Saturday evening Mass attendance was not always an option, and eating meat used to be forbidden on all Fridays.
- On the other hand, the Roman Catholic church also occasionally makes statements of law regarding issues that go beyond mere functional order in the community. These statements are strictly *moral laws* and are direct interpretations and applications of the law of love as Jesus taught it. Examples are the church's teachings on the issues of abortion and euthanasia.

By the very nature of authentic morality, the law of love cannot be legislated. An action is moral only when it is freely chosen. To pass a law in order to force people to conform to a certain standard might be a way of achieving a particular action, but the action cannot be called moral.

The purpose of moral laws is to provide people with guidelines, with *norms of behavior,* to help them live up to their potential and grow closer to the ideal that is held out to them. If the law is good, the morally good person will choose to follow the law.

In other words, the church realizes that it cannot force people to be good; that is a contradiction in terms. But it can give guidelines, aids, indications arrived at generally by the community at large, about proper moral behavior. Every person who professes belief in Christ and believes that the church is continuing Jesus' mission will see such moral proclamations of the church as important guidelines and will shape her or his actions accordingly.

Therefore, when faced with a moral situation in which he or she cannot make a decision, the Christian will generally evaluate the situation in terms of Jesus' values, attitudes, and teachings as he or she—the individual—sees and understands them. Then he or she will look at the moral teaching of the church regarding the situation, not simply as a statement of law but as a reflection of the collective effort of the community of faith to apply Jesus' principles to the situation.

Obviously, when the preliminary decision of the individual coincides with the teaching of the church, there is no problem. When, however, the individual's decision stands in disagreement with the church's teaching, there are basically two alternatives:

- If the individual remains confused about what to do, it is common sense and mature Christian morality to follow the law of the church as stated. To do otherwise is to deny the collective wisdom of the community of faith.
- But if the individual, after careful, honest, and mature evaluation of the situation, finds himself or herself in disagreement with the church regarding a particular moral issue, he or she has a *duty* as a Christian to follow his or her conscience, even if it means running contrary to church law. (It should be noted that such a situation is highly unusual, not the norm, and that such a decision demands much evaluation, prayer, consultation with others, etc.)

Living out Christian morality is not simple. Those who think they can just follow the laws risk living more as machines than as humans. Those who take the opposite course, disregarding all the laws and doing their own thing, have no sense of Christ's values or of their own worth and the dignity to which they are called. Those who sincerely attempt to "put on Christ" in union with the community of faith will find maturity—and happiness.

Concept E:
The Reign of God and "the Reign of Sin"

Throughout the Gospels we see Jesus encountering the power of personal and communal sin as well as other forms of evil. The constant message of the Gospels is that God in Jesus ultimately does conquer evil in all its manifestations. (Pages 131–132 of the student text)

Review Questions:
The Reign of God and "the Reign of Sin"

Question: Define *sin*, both personal and communal.

Answer: Sin is commonly thought of as personal, freely chosen actions that have negative effects on the sinners as individuals and on their relationships with others. But sin can also be understood as a social evil that affects all people simply because we live in community with one another. That is, we can say that the effects of the sinful actions of individual people accumulate over time into communal sin, which affects all who are born into it.

Question: In what sense are sin and evil different realities? What kind of evil is not caused by sin?

Answer: Sin refers to freely chosen actions that harm others, and the kind of evil associated with and brought about by sin is called moral evil. Another kind of evil finds expression in the suffering, pain, and often untimely deaths brought about by natural but powerfully destructive occurrences (such as hurricanes and earthquakes) and also by sickness and disease.

A Text Activity: The Reign of God and "the Reign of Sin"

Activity 8

Write a brief essay about a time in your life when you struggled to understand an evil situation for which no single person seemed responsible.

Additional Activities: The Reign of God and "the Reign of Sin"

Discussion Starters

Use the following questions to provoke some interesting discussion on concept E.
- What do you think it means when we pray in the Lord's Prayer that God "lead us not into temptation"? Would God *ever* lead us into temptation?
- Do you agree with the author of your textbook when he states that the message of Jesus must say something about both sin and evil if it is to be accepted as Good News? Why?
- Give examples of personal sin and suggest ways in which the Gospel message offers some concrete response to them. Do the same for communal sin.
- Does Jesus' acceptance of the effects of sin and evil—even to the point of accepting death on the cross—make his message more credible, more believable? Or would it be easier to believe in him if he had not endured the troubles of the world? Explain your answer.

Searching the Newspapers for Sin and Evil

This exercise is intended to sensitize the students to the multiple levels of sin and evil in real life, to which the Gospel message must speak if it is to be recognized as relevant.

1. Divide the class into six small groups and give each group a stack of newspapers, scissors, glue, and a sheet of poster paper. Assign two groups to each of the three expressions of sin and evil described in the student text:
- personal, willful acts of selfishness
- communal sin (e.g., war, poverty)
- the destructive forces of nature upon individuals (e.g., sickness, retardation) and in large-scale disaster situations (e.g., floods, earthquakes)

Each group is to look for and cut out articles, photos, and other newspaper items related to its assigned expression of sin or evil, in order to create a collage. Allow 15 minutes, or more if necessary.

2. When the groups have completed the collages, give them the following situation to respond to:
- Imagine that you are looking at your collage with someone who does not believe in God. He or she makes the following statement: "How is it possible for someone to believe in a loving God, and believe the Gospel is 'the Good News,' when they see all that evil in the world? What reasons can a Christian give me to believe that faith is anything more than a fairy tale, a pipe dream of people who are just trying to escape the real world?"

Give the groups up to 15 minutes to discuss and prepare their response.

3. Ask a representative from each group to come to the front of the room to briefly explain the group's collage as well as the group's prepared response to the question of the nonbeliever. At your discretion, either pursue further discussion with the class at large or simply move on to the next group. Encourage applause for each presentation.

4. Close by briefly discussing the following:
- One person has said, "I believe in the sun even when it is not shining. I believe in love even when I am lonely. And I believe in God even when God is silent." How would you characterize that attitude? Is it courageous? ignorant? foolhardy? wise? naive? sensible? Why?

A Biblical Examination of Conscience

This exercise is designed to help the students recognize that sin and evil will be conquered when we both listen to and actually live out the Good News.

1. Introduce the activity with words along these lines:
- A famous author, G. K. Chesterton, once commented that "it is not that Christianity has been tried and failed. It has never been tried." What Chesterton meant was that if each Christian looked into his or her own heart and life, he or she would see that the Gospel has not truly taken root within. Only when it takes root, as Jesus said, can a person hope to "bear good fruit."

    It has been traditional in the Roman Catholic church to use the Ten Commandments as a starting point for examining one's conscience before confession, for evaluating how well one has done in the attempt to live out Christian principles. In this exercise, we will do an examination of conscience, instead using the *Gospel* commandments. But first we have to look at key passages from the Gospels and summarize them as commandments.

2. Divide the class into groups of five, giving each group a large sheet of poster paper and felt-tip markers or crayons. On the chalkboard, list the Gospel references given below. (These are followed by short descriptive phrases here, but the phrases are for your benefit and should not be included on the board.)
- Matthew 16:24–27 [Take up your cross.]
- Matthew 25:14–30 [Use your talents.]
- Matthew 20:20–28 [Seek to serve, not to be served.]
- Mark 10:13–16 [Become like little children.]
- Matthew 5:21–26 [Reconcile before going to the altar.]

- Matthew 6:25–34 [Trust God.]
- Luke 12:13–21 [Do not seek security in material possessions.]
- Matthew 7:1–5 [Do not judge others.]
- Matthew 7:7–11 [Pray with confidence.]
- Mark 12:41–44 [Give generously of what you have.]

3. Instruct each group to develop a set of Gospel commandments as follows:
- Divide the scriptural references on the board among the members of your group. Each member should look up their references and then develop short, positive statements summarizing the implications of the passages for those who would take them seriously. These statements can be written in the form of the traditional wording of the Commandments if you wish. At this point, just write out a rough draft of your statements on a piece of scrap paper.
- When everyone in your group is done, each of you is to share your statements with the group. If necessary, your group should refine and polish the statements to reflect a common group style, such as making all of them a similar length, and so on. Do this refining on a piece of scrap paper too. The final versions of the statements need to be approved by everyone in the group.
- When all ten statements have been approved by the group, have someone carefully print them on the poster paper. This will be your group's version of ten Gospel commandments. You can make it as fancy as you like.

4. Start out the discussion portion of the activity by asking a representative from each group to share the group's commandments with the class. Lengthy comment or discussion is not necessary at this point. Encourage applause for each presentation. When all the presentations are done, discuss the following questions:
- Are the commandments you developed realistic and livable, or are they so idealistic that they would be impossible to live by? Why?
- Have you lived by these commandments?
- Would a person following these commandments automatically fulfill the original Ten Commandments?

If your class did the preceding activity, "Searching the Newspapers for Sin and Evil," discuss ways in which the various expressions of sin and evil in the newspapers would be eliminated if enough people lived by the values reflected in the groups' commandments. Perhaps refer directly to the collages that were created earlier and ask which, if any, of the new commandments address specific evils reflected in the collages.

5. Close the activity with a comment such as the following:
- At the time Jesus was born, a Jewish view of the Kingdom of God stated that the Kingdom would become a reality only when people started to live as if it were already present. Jesus seems to have taken that understanding of the coming of the Kingdom to its ultimate expression, living his life totally as if God reigned over the world. Christians are called to do likewise.

A Plan of Action

It is easy to see problems in the world but to despair of finding solutions to them. To help the students recognize what they as individuals can do about social issues, give the following instructions one at a time, allowing the students enough time to think through each point. Discussion on the exercise can follow.

1. List five social problems in our community.
2. Circle three of those five that the church might be able to have an impact on.
3. Underline one of those three that you might be able to help with.
4. List five concrete things that need to be done to deal with the issue.
5. Circle two of those five that you can do.
6. Underline one of those two that you *will* do.
7. What will hinder you from accomplishing your task?
8. What resources are available to help you accomplish your task?
9. How will you begin?

(This activity is adapted from Wayne Rice, John Roberto, and Mike Yaconelli, eds., *Creative Learning Experiences,* p. 83.)

Concept F: Right Now, but Not Yet

In the Gospels we encounter a repeated tension between the claim that the Kingdom of God is a present reality and the notion that it is something to be achieved only at the end of time. The Kingdom *is* present in that it was fully revealed in the life and work of Jesus and is made real today in Jesus' risen presence. It will, however, be fully realized only when people choose to live compassionate, forgiving lives. (Pages 133–135 of the student text)

A Review Question: Right Now, but Not Yet

Question: What does it mean to say that the Kingdom of God is "right now, but not yet"?

Answer: The Kingdom of God is "right now" in that the power of God was fully present in Jesus and then released to all humanity through Jesus' death, his resurrection, and the gift of the Spirit. All the power we need to overcome sin is available to us. The Kingdom is "not yet" because God has given people freedom, and people have not fulfilled their responsibility of making the Kingdom real by living compassionate and forgiving lives.

A Text Activity: Right Now, but Not Yet

Activity 9

Read the material in the shaded box titled "The Kingdom of God Is Among You." Write a paragraph explaining how the examples in the box illustrate the "right now, but not yet" quality of the Kingdom of God. Add an example or two from your own experience.

Who Is Your God?

Listed below are twenty-four possible understandings of God. Some of them you may have already heard, and some of them may be new to you. Put a check mark in the blank next to each understanding that you agree with. Then your teacher will give you further directions.

___ 1. The only one who loves me for myself

___ 2. The computer that programmed the universe

___ 3. A puppeteer who manipulates people as if they were toys

___ 4. An energy that is hinted at when a baby is born or when we fall in love

___ 5. A "world soul" that we are all a part of

___ 6. A creator who believes that all of creation is good

___ 7. A force that became inert sometime between when the world was created and today

___ 8. A parent who loves his or her children selflessly

___ 9. Someone who forgives my mistakes

___ 10. A being so beyond me that I cannot describe it

___ 11. Someone who loves us enough to die for us

___ 12. An eccentric being who created this world and then forgot all about it

___ 13. Someone who dares to let me be free

___ 14. A being who gave me life

___ 15. A lawgiver whose commands urge me to do right rather than wrong

___ 16. The future, the end of all human striving

___ 17. The type of being that humans will evolve into

___ 18. A ruler whose power is freedom and love rather than force

___ 19. A lover who urges me to come to the heavenly marriage feast

___ 20. An idea created by past generations to explain the world

___ 21. The peace that will reign when all persons are brothers and sisters

___ 22. The perfect one, who says that I am sinful and makes me feel guilty

___ 23. The one who wants me to be me

___ 24. A clown who created laughter by making human beings free

The Consequences of Moral Decisions

Our actions, decisions, and attitudes that are **loving** or **morally right** produce all or some of the following results in us or those we affect:

1. an increased ability to trust others
2. greater honesty in relationships
3. a lessened sense of separation from others; a breaking down of barriers
4. an increased attitude of cooperation
5. greater self-respect; the ability to look in the mirror and feel genuinely happy with oneself
6. a better attitude toward people in general; more confidence in the idea that people are really good
7. a feeling of peace and joy; a sense of doing what one is called to do and making the most of life

Our actions, decisions, and attitudes that are **selfish** or **morally wrong** produce all or some of the following results in us or those we affect:

1. a decreased ability to trust others; suspicion
2. phoniness in relationships; being two-faced
3. a sense of separation from others; a feeling of isolation
4. a decreased attitude of cooperation; trouble getting along with others
5. less self-respect; more guilt or embarrassment
6. difficulty in accepting others; a feeling that people are concerned only about themselves
7. a feeling that life is meaningless or hopeless

Two factors are closely related to the above sets of consequences and affect them in an important way:

First, when we talk about the breaking down of barriers between people (number 3), this means less separation and more unity between individuals. But this is also true of relationships between those individuals and others in the world around them. For example, a boy and a girl can be so "together" that they have no room for anyone else.

Second, in everything we do or decide, we have to be concerned not just with right now but also with what the long-range effects are going to be on ourselves and others. Each of us must ask, How will this affect me and others later on?

CHAPTER 7

Jesus Speaks: Sayings and Stories of the Kingdom

Major Concepts

A. **Unlocking Jesus' Words:** The Gospels do not record the everyday conversations of Jesus but, rather, his most significant thoughts and ideas—expressed through the words of those who heard and believed in him. The Gospels give us *more* than Jesus' words; they also give us the *meaning* his words had for the earliest Christians.

B. **Jesus' Sayings and Stories in the Gospels:** Jesus' teaching and preaching included these four styles of speech: direct pronouncements, short sayings, instructions for disciples, and—perhaps most significant—parables.

C. **A Closer Look at the Parables:** Through parables, Jesus was able to connect his teaching with the everyday experiences of his listeners.

Concept A: Unlocking Jesus' Words

The Gospels do not record the everyday conversations of Jesus but, rather, his most significant thoughts and ideas—expressed through the words of those who heard and believed in him. The Gospels give us *more* than Jesus' words; they also give us the *meaning* his words had for the earliest Christians. (Pages 137–140 of the student text)

Review Questions: Unlocking Jesus' Words

Question: Do the Gospels give us Jesus' actual words? Explain your answer.
Answer: No, we do not find Jesus' everyday, casual conversation in the Gospels. We have, rather, his most significant thoughts and ideas—expressed through the words of those who heard him. What we find in the Gospels is *more* than just some words Jesus said; we also find the *meaning* his words had for his followers.

Question: What two words do scholars agree were uniquely used by Jesus? What was unique about Jesus' use of these words?
Answer:
- *Abba:* The reference to God as "Abba" originated with Jesus.
- *Amen:* Jesus began many statements with *amen*. Used in this way, the word was a confirmation of his own teaching, a manner of giving weight to what he was saying. This use of the word *amen* was unheard of in Jesus' time.

Question: In what ways did Jesus follow the traditional Jewish format of public speaking? Why did he speak in these ways?
Answer: The Jewish manner of speaking was far more poetic than our own, filled with a heavy use of symbolism, figures of speech, exaggeration, and so on. Public presentations were filled with imagery from the Hebrew Scriptures. In all these respects, Jesus followed the traditional Jewish format of public speaking. He did so because he was a Jew speaking to fellow Jews.

A Text Activity: Unlocking Jesus' Words

Activity 1

In a paragraph, react to the following statement: *If we cannot be sure that Jesus actually said the things that the Gospels say he did, we have no reason to trust in any of what the Gospels tell us.*

Additional Activities: Unlocking Jesus' Words

Every Word Was Not "Gospel"

This activity should help the students understand the fact that the sayings and stories of Jesus recorded in the Gospels are really a collection and condensation of his teachings, not a day-to-day record of them.

1. Begin the activity with a comment such as this:
- Based only on what the Gospels give us, it is easy to think of Jesus as always preaching, saying nothing but profound things, and constantly

being surrounded by crowds who strained to hear his every word. Yet such a perception is not accurate. We also know, from what we have learned so far about the nature of the Gospels, that these writings are not day-to-day records of Jesus' life and ministry.

Have the students brainstorm various forms of speech and conversation that "everyone" today uses or hears, and list these on the chalkboard. Some examples are the short exchanges that occur in school hallways between class periods, chitchat at parties, and heart-to-heart talks over the phone or face-to-face with friends.

2. Ask the students to make up scenes in which Jesus likely experienced forms of communication similar to those listed on the board (e.g., Jesus and a few disciples sitting around a campfire the evening after feeding the five thousand, Jesus having a long talk with his parents as his popularity grows, and Jesus enjoying himself at the wedding feast at Cana). You may even want the students to role-play the imaginary conversations.

Doing PR for Jesus

Use this activity to help the students understand that Jesus was a Jew attempting to communicate with fellow Jews. Ask the class to imagine that they have been hired to serve as public relations consultants for Jesus as he begins proclaiming his message to the people of our day and culture. That is, they must find a way for him to speak to us using forms of communication that we are accustomed to. Focus the discussion around this question:

- How would you advise Jesus to "sell" his message to the people?

You can simply pose the question and follow with a class discussion. Or you can expand and elaborate on that, perhaps brainstorming a list of forms of mass communication available today (radio, television, film, newspapers, magazines, even music videos!) and then having small groups develop "sales campaigns" using these media.

Concept B: Jesus' Sayings and Stories in the Gospels

Jesus' teaching and preaching included these four styles of speech: direct pronouncements, short sayings, instructions for disciples, and—perhaps most significant—parables. (Pages 141–147 of the student text)

Review Questions: Jesus' Sayings and Stories in the Gospels

Question: Identify and briefly define the four main styles of speech that Jesus used in his teaching.
Answer:
- *Pronouncement stories:* Stories that acted as a setup for a pronouncement (or "punch line") containing the main lesson Jesus wanted to get across
- *Short sayings:* Short statements that were "words to the wise," offered without any story leading up to them

- *Instructions for disciples:* Instructions for those who would be Jesus' followers (At times, these passages incorporate other forms of teaching, such as short sayings and the pronouncement stories.)
- *Parables:* Stories that usually build from a simile, in which two very different things are compared to one another in order to illustrate a point

Question: Explain Matthew's organization of the Sermon on the Mount.
Answer: Matthew developed a scene in which Jesus instructs his disciples on a hill, offering them a series of short sayings or proverbs. Matthew used this as a method for presenting the short sayings of Jesus. That is, he put them together in a sort of collection.

Text Activities:
Jesus' Sayings and Stories in the Gospels

Activity 2

Create a modern pronouncement story that leads to this "punch line": *People were not made for Sunday Mass; Sunday Mass was made for people.*

Activity 3

Looking at the Book of Proverbs (in the Hebrew Scriptures), pick a chapter from 10 to 20 and then any proverb that catches your attention within that chapter. Copy the proverb onto paper and write down its chapter and verse numbers. Then briefly explain why the proverb caught your attention.

Additional Activities:
Jesus' Sayings and Stories in the Gospels

A Sound Collage

Use this activity in conjunction with the student text material on the pronouncement stories and short sayings.

1. Divide the class into the four groups that were assigned to read a Gospel from beginning to end in "A Special Reading Assignment," on pages 63–64 of this manual. Then divide each of those groups into two smaller sections. Instruct one section in each group to look for pronouncement stories in their assigned Gospel, writing down the chapter and verse numbers and the "punch lines" of these stories. Instruct the other section in each group to look for short sayings in their Gospel and write down the chapter and verse numbers along with the sayings.

2. Have the students in each section choose just three or four of their favorite punch lines or sayings, those that are most meaningful for them as young people. Choose representatives from the sections and instruct them to practice reading their selections with feeling and inflection.

3. While the representatives are rehearsing, set up two tape recorders close to each other at the front of the room. Choose some melodic, instrumental background music to be played on one tape recorder. Adjust the volume on that tape recorder so that the music will be loud enough to be picked

up by the second tape recorder but not so loud that it will interfere with words spoken directly into the second tape recorder's microphone.

After explaining the setup to the class, invite the students who were practicing their readings to come to the front of the room. Start the music and then signal each student to recite his or her selections into the microphone. When you are done, you will have a prayerful collection of sayings that could be used as part of a prayer service.

Option: Many young people are sophisticated in the use of audio equipment. If you find some students' interest piqued by this exercise, discuss the possibility of doing a more professional recording. Other students might want to develop a slide presentation to accompany the recording. Consider sharing the entire effort with other classes or perhaps at an all-school liturgy.

Playing with Sayings

Every generation—in fact, nearly every class that goes through a school—develops "in" sayings, code words, and so on. Many times these evolve from popular songs, TV commercials, and radio jingles. (Some examples from past years are "Today is the first day of the rest of your life," "Love means never having to say you're sorry," and "You only go around once.") This activity is designed to convey the similarities between the popular sayings the students use and the short sayings, or proverbs, found in the Gospels.

1. Begin with the students brainstorming as many currently popular sayings, statements, and proverbs as they can, and write these on the chalkboard. In case your students do not come up with many examples, have a collection of statements from popular posters or banners available as backups and let your students select favorites from among them. (For good ideas, see poster catalogs from Argus Communications, P.O. Box 6000, Allen, TX 75002-1304; phone 800-527-4748.)

At some point, make a comment along these lines:
- Notice what a large part of our language and communication these sayings are, even though when they are on their own, and taken out of context, they can be hard to understand, maybe even unintelligible. The same may be said about some of Jesus' short sayings and proverbs—though it must be admitted that the content and intent of his statements was definitely different than that of ours!

2. Have the class select six or seven sayings from the board that they feel have some real merit, some kernel of truth, some insight beyond just exclamation or humor.

3. Divide the class into six or seven groups and assign each group one of the selected sayings. Inform the groups that they are to create a skit that will show how their assigned saying might have originated as a logical punch line or moral to a certain situation or event. The skits can—and probably will—be humorous, which is fine. In all cases, the assigned saying should be the last line delivered. Give the groups 15 minutes to prepare, and then ask them to perform their skits. Encourage applause.

4. Close the activity with a comment such as the following:
- Though Jesus' short sayings were of a much more serious nature than the sayings we have talked about here, there is one basic similarity: Our sayings are products of our contemporary culture and of our particular community. Many of them can be understood only by those who share

the same experiences. Jesus' sayings grew out of the long history and complex culture of the Jews, and they carried a great deal of meaning that we might miss. If we recognize and try to understand Jesus' words in the context of the Jewish history and culture, we can learn of their significance for us as well.

Paraphrasing the Sermon on the Mount

As noted in the student text, the Sermon on the Mount (Matthew, chapters 5–7) is actually a literary device that Matthew used to present many of Jesus' popular sayings. This interesting exercise is designed to help the students think through the meaning this important Gospel sermon holds for their own life.

Handouts 7–A through 7–G

The exercise requires handouts 7–A through 7–G, "Paraphrasing the Sermon on the Mount." Each handout contains a passage from the Sermon on the Mount. However, key elements of the passage are omitted and replaced with blank spaces. The object is for the students, working first as individuals and then in small groups, to develop their own version of the assigned passage and then later to compare their version with the original.

1. Divide the class into seven groups and assign each group one of the seven passages covered by the handouts. Distribute a copy of the appropriate handout to each student in every group, plus an additional copy for the whole group to use later.

2. Instruct the individual students to fill in the blanks on their handout with words they feel make sense in the passage. Then they are to share these with the others in their group, and the group as a whole should work toward a mutually acceptable version of the passage to be printed on the remaining copy of the handout. (Some humor will no doubt be involved in this, and depending on the age and maturity of the class, some off-color remarks may be made. To limit this, make sure the students know they will be asked to share their group version with the class.) Allow 15 minutes or more for this part of the exercise.

3. Ask each group to share its version of its assigned passage with the class, going in order so that the progression parallels the order of the original sermon. Comment appropriately.

Close by having selected students read the original versions of the passages from the Sermon on the Mount. Compare the students' interpretations with Jesus' original intent.

Translating the Lord's Prayer

This exercise aims to help the students view the Lord's Prayer from a fresh perspective.

1. Begin with a short comment such as the following:
- As your textbook indicates, the Lord's Prayer is a summary of the entire Gospel message, and it is an example of Jesus' teachings that were meant to be instructions for his disciples. In this next activity, you will get a chance to translate the Lord's Prayer, which Jesus taught his disciples, into language you feel would make sense to people today.

2. Invite the students to recite the Lord's Prayer together. Remark that this familiar communal version is only one of many possible translations. Distribute as many different translations of the Christian Testament as you can find and ask several students to read aloud the versions of the prayer as it is offered in Matt. 6:9–13 and Luke 11:2–4. Without belaboring the point, indicate and discuss the wide variety of ways Christians can translate this one prayer.

3. Have the individual students spend 5 to 10 minutes rewriting the Lord's Prayer in their own words. To help, you might break the prayer down into separate phrases on the chalkboard, suggesting that the students take just one phrase at a time and try to express it in words that make the most sense to them.

4. Many students might be embarrassed if asked to share their final version of the prayer with the class. An alternative and less threatening approach would be to ask volunteers to share only a certain part of their paraphrased prayer (e.g., "Who will share their version of the opening phrase, 'Our Father, who art in heaven'?"). Get as many suggested paraphrases as possible for each part of the prayer, asking the class to then select the paraphrase that best captures the intended meaning. Record their selections on the board in order.

By the end of the exercise, you will have developed a class version of the Lord's Prayer. As a last step in the process, you may want to smooth out the language and provide a transitional word or two where needed. Type up the class version and reproduce it for distribution to all the students. Use the prayer occasionally as a communal prayer in class.

Concept C: A Closer Look at the Parables

Through parables, Jesus was able to connect his teaching with the everyday experiences of his listeners. (Pages 148–155 of the student text)

Review Questions: A Closer Look at the Parables

Question: Why did Jesus often conclude his parables with a surprise ending?

Answer: The surprise endings would keep Jesus' listeners alert, or catch them off-guard. The idea was to make people think, to stop them in their tracks and get them to reflect on the lessons he was trying to teach.

Question: List and describe the four main themes by which we can categorize Jesus' parables. What is the common thread that runs through all of these themes?

Answer: We can categorize Jesus' parables by these four themes:
1. *Descriptions of the King:* These parables deal primarily with God's nature, qualities, attitudes in dealing with people, and so on.
2. *"Kingdom" responses:* Parables in this category emphasize how we should act if we hope to "enter the Kingdom."
3. *Relationships with our neighbors:* Parables in this category address people's relationships with one another and the world at large.
4. *The fulfillment of the Kingdom:* These parables refer to the future coming of God's Kingdom in its fullness.

The common theme shared by the parables is that most of them are related in one way or another to Jesus' understanding of or preaching about the Kingdom of God.

Question: Why might a parable be used, or even modified, to teach different lessons in different Gospels?

Answer:

- It is quite possible that Jesus used the same story more than once to illustrate different points and that the Gospel authors simply differed in which version of the story they selected.
- An individual Gospel author may have changed the setting of the parable to better illustrate the point *he* wished to make to his readers.

Question: List three suggestions that can make the parables more enjoyable and enlightening for us.

Answer:

1. Look for the central messages of the parables.
2. Look for the questions posed in the parables, pause, and attempt to answer the questions ourselves.
3. Compare our answers with those recorded in the Gospels.

Text Activities: A Closer Look at the Parables

Activity 4

For each of these three areas—your daily life, your family life, and your culture—list five to ten elements that could serve as the basis for a modern parable.

Activity 5

Rewrite Luke's version of the parable of the lost sheep (15:4–7) to make it into a modern parable.

Activity 6

As you read, select one example from each of the four categories of parable themes and spell out, in your own words, the main point Jesus was trying to make.

Activity 7

Browse through any one of the synoptic Gospels and note all the occasions when Jesus asks a question. Write down each question (and its chapter and verse numbers) and try to answer it before reading the answer recorded in the Gospel. Write down the Gospel's answer if it is different from your own.

Additional Activities: A Closer Look at the Parables

Playing with the Parables

1. As a kind of brainstorming exercise, divide the class into seven groups and assign each group three of the twenty-two parables listed in the chart on

page 154 of the student text. Instruct the groups to quickly look up and read their assigned parables. (For parables with multiple versions listed, the groups need only look up one version.)

2. After reading the parables, the groups should jot down the answers to the following questions:
- What is the common life experience that each parable is built around?
- Can you determine why each parable might have surprised or caught the attention of Jesus' listeners?

3. Ask the students to report their answers. Record the list of life experiences on the chalkboard and briefly discuss the surprising elements in each parable.

The Parable

Although you may have seen the film *The Parable* (Rolf Forsberg, 1964) many times and may even have used it with any number of classes, it deserves consideration for use as part of your treatment of concept C. First of all, few if any films in religious education are as superbly produced and as rich in meaning as this one. That is the main reason it is so popular. Second, this film of only 22 minutes is so complex and intriguing that it almost demands multiple viewings. A third point to consider is that there is a good chance that your students have never seen the film, just because their previous teachers all assumed they had! And finally, the method suggested here for viewing the film will likely be a new one for you and your students.

The film or videotape is available through many diocesan media centers, or it can be rented for $25 from Mass Media Ministries, 2116 North Charles Street, Baltimore, MD 21218; phone 800-828-8825. Purchase of the videotape from Mass Media Ministries is $125.

1. Obtain the film *The Parable* and the sound track from the film *Godspell*. In this activity, side 2 of the *Godspell* sound track will be played simultaneously with the film. Practice the following procedure in advance of the class session:
- Allow the sound from *The Parable* itself to play until the point, early in the film, when Magnus the Great places his foot on the ground while getting out of bed. The credits on the screen at that point read "filmed with the cooperation of." Start side 2 of the *Godspell* sound track at that point and turn off the sound from *The Parable*. Once the *Godspell* sound track is playing, no further adjustments should be required. *The Parable* will conclude just before the final song on the *Godspell* sound track, which is "Day by Day." Turn off the *Godspell* sound track at that point.

2. *The Parable* will likely be accompanied by a discussion guide, but you could pursue the following questions instead:
- Who were the characters encountered by the clown, in their order of appearance, and how did each respond to him?
- Describe what happened to the clown while he was in the tent. What did he do (or have done to him) and why?
- Who responded positively to the clown? Why did they, and how did they demonstrate their response?
- Who responded negatively? Why did they, and how did they demonstrate that?
- What did the clown actually offer to each person he encountered?

- What did Magnus do at the end of the film, and what did it mean?
- Who did the clown represent, and what indicated this most clearly?
- Explain the title of the film in terms of our present chapter in this course. What qualifies the film to be called a parable?

To close the discussion, consider playing the song "Day by Day," from *Godspell*.

Variation: *The Parable* is also suggested for use with Thomas Zanzig's course *Understanding Catholic Christianity*. In that case, however, the use of the *Godspell* sound track is not suggested, and the discussion of the film centers around a very effective contest arrangement. Find out if that approach has been used with the students previously; if not consider it here. See *Teaching Manual for Understanding Catholic Christianity* (Winona, MN: Saint Mary's Press, 1989), page 172, for details.

A Short Story: "The Window"

1. Share these introductory remarks with your students:
- One of the difficulties we encounter in dealing with the Scriptures and, in particular, the parables of Jesus is that they were originally *oral* presentations. They were only eventually written down. Something gets lost in the tradition of storytelling when we move from oral to written transmission, especially the strong sense of personal interchange that exists when the stories are shared orally.

    Another related problem we face is that we have become "video people" in many respects, accustomed to passively viewing television rather than actively and imaginatively reading or listening as required if we are to fully understand the parables and other stories.

    In this session, we will try to get a sense of the active listening that should be an integral part of our understanding the parables.

2. Ask the students for quiet and encourage them to relax. When you believe you have their attention, read the short story "The Window," provided below.

Make sure you have practiced the reading and can do it well. In fact, it would be ideal if you could be so familiar with it that you could share it orally without having to read it. Either approach will work here, however.

- "The Window"

    There once were two men, Mr. Wilson and Mr. Thompson, both seriously ill in the same room of a great hospital. Quite a small room, just large enough for the pair of them. Two beds, two bedside lockers, a door opening on the hall, and one window looking out on the world.

    Mr. Wilson, as part of his treatment, was allowed to sit up in bed for an hour in the afternoon (something to do with draining the fluid from his lungs). His bed was next to the window. But Mr. Thompson had to spend all of his time flat on his back. Both of them had to be kept quiet and still, which was the reason they were in the small room by themselves. They were grateful for the peace and privacy, though. None of the bustle and clatter and prying eyes of the general ward for them. Of course, one of the disadvantages of their condition was that they weren't allowed to do much: no reading, no radio, certainly no television. They just had to keep quiet and still, just the two of them.

    Well, they used to talk for hours and hours. About their wives, their children, their homes, their jobs, their hobbies, their childhood, what they did during the war, where they'd been on vacations, all that sort of thing. Every afternoon, when Mr. Wilson, the man by the window, was propped up for his hour, he would pass the time by describing what he could see outside. And Mr. Thompson began to live for those hours.

The window apparently overlooked a park with a lake where there were ducks and swans, children throwing them bread and sailing model boats, and young lovers walking hand in hand beneath the trees. And there were flowers and stretches of grass, games of softball, people taking their ease in the sunshine; and right at the back, behind the fringe of trees, there was a fine view of the city skyline. Mr. Thompson would listen to all of this, enjoying every minute. How a child nearly fell into the lake, how beautiful the girls were in their summer dresses, then an exciting ball game, or a boy playing with his puppy. It got to the point that he could almost see what was happening outside.

Then one fine afternoon, when there was some sort of parade, the thought struck Mr. Thompson: Why should Wilson, next to the window, have all the pleasure of seeing what was going on? Why shouldn't *he* get the chance? He felt ashamed and tried not to think like that, but the more he tried, the worse he wanted a change. He would do anything for it! In a few days, he had turned sour. *He* should be by the window. He brooded. He couldn't sleep and grew even more seriously ill, which the doctors just couldn't understand.

One night as Mr. Thompson stared at the ceiling, Mr. Wilson suddenly woke up, coughing and choking, the fluid congesting in his lungs, his hands groping for the call button that would bring the night nurse running. But Mr. Thompson watched without moving. The coughing racked the darkness. On and on. He choked and then stopped. The sound of breathing stopped. Mr. Thompson continued to stare at the ceiling.

In the morning, the day nurse came in with water for their baths and found Mr. Wilson dead. They took his body away quietly, with no fuss.

As soon as it seemed decent, Mr. Thompson asked if he could be moved to the bed next to the window. So they moved him, tucked him in, made him quite comfortable, and left him alone to be quiet and still. The minute they'd gone, he propped himself up on one elbow, painfully and laboriously, and strained as he looked out the window.

It faced a blank wall.

3. The story is a touching one, and the surprise twist at the end is, of course, illustrative of the nature of Jesus' parables. Relay the latter point to the students. Say as well that a follow-up discussion was an important part of Jesus' parables, often initiated by his disciples' asking, "Lord, tell us, what does this mean?"

The following are some suggested questions for discussing the story "The Window":

- What was your initial reaction to the story? Why?
- Describe Mr. Wilson. What kind of man did he appear to be? Did you like or dislike him? Why?
- Describe Mr. Thompson. What was he like, and did you like or dislike him?
- What did Mr. Wilson do, and what do you think his motives were?
- Would you identify Mr. Wilson's "descriptions" of what was outside the window as lying? creativity? unselfish concern for another? cruelty? Why?

- Did Mr. Wilson do anything wrong?
- Why did Mr. Thompson's mood change from enjoyment to resentment? Do you think his feelings of resentment were justified? understandable?
- Did Mr. Thompson actually murder Mr. Wilson by not calling for help?
- Would both men have been better off if Mr. Wilson had never started his descriptions of life outside the window?
- Put yourself in Mr. Thompson's place. How would you have felt when you finally looked out that window and saw nothing but a blank wall? angry? resentful? guilty? disappointed? grateful? confused? shocked?
- If you had to think up a moral or, to use the language of your textbook, a "punch line" like those at the end of some of Jesus' stories, what would it be? What would you offer as a one-line summary of the chief lesson of this story? [This may require additional time for small-group work.]

(This activity is adapted from Wayne Rice, John Roberto, and Mike Yaconelli, eds., *Creative Learning Experiences,* pp. 96–98.)

The Labor Game

The Labor Game is based on the parable of the laborers in the vineyard (Matt. 20:1–16). This sometimes perplexing parable can be made more understandable by arranging for the students to experience the satisfaction and frustration of the laborers, who received an equal distribution of pay at the end of the day even though some did not work as long or as hard as others. The landowner was just and kept his promise, paying exactly what he said he would. This satisfied the laborers until greed crept in.

1. Before class, prepare several tables by placing a puzzle, brainteaser, or other task to do on each one. Some tasks should be very easy; others, impossible. Specify points for the successful completion of each task, depending on the difficulty. As the students enter the room, invite them to circulate and try the tasks. Each person is to keep track of his or her own score.

2. After 20 to 30 minutes, call a stop. Go to each student, ask how many points she or he has, then reach into a bag and give her or him a prize. The prizes can be small; just be sure that they are all identical.

As you continue to award prizes, what is happening will soon become obvious to everyone. No matter how high or low the score the students tell you, they are all receiving equal payment. Allow free talk as you distribute the prizes.

3. Follow the distribution of the prizes with a class discussion, prodding with questions such as the following:
- How do you honestly feel?
- What is your attitude toward me, the prize-giver?
- How do you feel toward the other people in the class?
- How do those of you who scored the highest and the lowest feel?

Then read the scriptural account of the parable and discuss greed, envy, lust, competition, and how these can foul up one's relationship with God.

(This simulation game is taken from Wayne Rice, John Roberto, and Mike Yaconelli, eds., *Creative Learning Experiences,* pp. 125–126.)

Note: With a bit of imagination and some practice, you can create other simulation games based on the parables. Begin by considering the chief lesson of a given parable. Try to create a situation that might lead to an awareness of that same theme or reality. Then after the simulation, during discussion, make the connection with the parable itself. For helpful information on simulation games and their design, see *Simulation Games for Religious Education,* by Richard Reichert (Winona, MN: Saint Mary's Press, 1975), especially pages 7–17.

Seeing Ourselves in the Parables

This activity is meant to demonstrate how the parables can be meaningful to modern readers. The student text suggests that we can help the parables speak to us by viewing ourselves as participants in the parables, that is, by seeing ourselves as the lost sheep, the prodigal son or daughter, and so on.

1. Turn to the list of parables on page 154 of the student text. Divide the class into groups of two to three students and assign each group a parable. Ask the groups to do two things:
    - Jot down the characters or elements that you believe Jesus is calling his listeners to identify with. Be sure to use your imagination here; there are more possibilities than may be readily apparent. For example, the parable of the sower offers multiple possibilities to choose from. Which of those elements apply most directly to young people today? Are young people like the hard ground? the rocky ground? Why?
    - For each character or element you have listed, state one direct implication or message for the lives of young people today. For example, with the parable of the prodigal son, what message is conveyed to young people when the parable is viewed from the perspective of the prodigal? What about when viewed from the perspective of his brother?

Give the groups about 15 minutes to complete these tasks.

2. When the students have finished working with their parable, ask the groups to read their parable to the class and share their responses to the above questions. Encourage brief comments or questions by the rest of the class after each group report.

Modern Skits of the Parables

1. Divide the class into four groups, and if the resulting groups have more than six members, divide the groups into smaller sections of three or four students. Assign each of the four groups one of the categories of parables discussed on pages 149–152 of the student text. Ask the groups or sections to select the one parable from their assigned category that most appeals to them. The groups can choose Gospel parables other than those given as examples in the student text, but they should make certain their selection fits within their assigned category.

2. Pass on the following instructions to the groups or sections:
    - Rewrite your chosen parable as if Jesus were telling it in our contemporary culture. Ask yourself, how would Jesus share the same lesson if he were to walk into our classroom today? Keep in mind that the original parables were constructed around common, everyday images and experiences.

- When you have completed your rewrite, develop a short skit (about three minutes long) of your parable. You will present your skit to the class without telling them what the original parable was.

Allow the students about 20 minutes to do their rewrite and develop their skit.

3. As the skits are presented, the class should attempt to identify the Gospel parable upon which each was based. After all the skits have been presented, discuss how each group or section attempted to capture the central meaning of its chosen parable.

Paraphrasing the Sermon on the Mount: The Beatitudes

Matthew 5:1–12, NRSV

When Jesus saw the crowds, he went up the mountain; and after he sat down, his disciples came to him. Then he began to speak, and taught them, saying:

"Blessed are the _____,

    for theirs is the kingdom of heaven.

"Blessed are those who mourn,

    for they will _____.

"Blessed are the meek,

    for they will _____.

"Blessed are those who hunger and thirst for _____,

    for they will be filled.

"Blessed are the merciful,

    for they will _____.

"Blessed are the pure in heart,

    for they will _____.

"Blessed are the _____,

    for they will be called _____.

"Blessed are those who are persecuted for _____,

    for theirs is _____.

"Blessed are you when people [insult] you and persecute you and utter all kinds of evil against you falsely on my account. Rejoice and be glad, for _____ _____."

Paraphrasing the Sermon on the Mount: Being Salt and Light

Matthew 5:13–16, NRSV

"You are the salt of the earth; but if salt has lost its taste, _____
_____?
It is no longer good for anything, but _____
_____.

   "You are the light _____.
A city built on a hill cannot be hid. No one after lighting a lamp puts
_____
_____.

In the same way, let your light _____,
so that _____
_____."

Paraphrasing the Sermon on the Mount: Loving Your Enemy

Matthew 5:43–48, NRSV

"You have heard that it was said, 'You shall love your neighbor and _____
_____.'
But I say to you, Love your enemies and _____
_____,
so that you may _____
_____;
for [the Father] makes [the] sun rise on the evil and on the good, and sends
_____.
For if you love those who love you, _____
_____?
Do not even the tax collectors do the same? And if you _____
_____,
what more are you doing than others? Do not even the _____
do the same? Be _____, therefore, as your _____
_____."

Paraphrasing the Sermon on the Mount: Not Being a Hypocrite

Matthew 6:1–4, NRSV

"Beware of _____
in order to _____;
for then you have no _____.
   "So whenever you give _____, do not _____
_____, as the hypocrites do in the _____
_____, so that they may be _____
_____.
Truly I tell you, they have _____.
But when you give alms, _____
_____;
and your Father who _____
will _____."

Paraphrasing the Sermon on the Mount: How to Pray

Matthew 6:5–8, NRSV

"And whenever you pray, do not be like _____;
for they love to _____
_____, so that
_____.

Truly I tell you, they have received _____.
But whenever you pray, go into _____
_____
and pray to your Father who _____; and your Father who
_____ will _____.

   "When you are praying, do not _____
_____;
for they think that they will be heard because _____.
Do not be like them, for your Father knows _____
_____."

Handout 7–E: Permission to reproduce this handout for classroom use is granted.

Paraphrasing the Sermon on the Mount: Not Judging Others

Matthew 7:1–5, NRSV

"Do not judge, so that you may not _____.

For with the judgment you make you will _____,

and the measure you give _____.

Why do you see _____,

but do not notice _____?

Or how can you say to your neighbor, '_____
_____,'

while the _____?

You hypocrite, first take _____,

and then you will see clearly _____
_____."

[Cartoon: Two men standing outdoors. An older man wearing glasses and a sweater-vest is pointing at a younger man wearing sunglasses, saying: "I WANT THAT EXHAUST PIPE FIXED ON THAT HEAP OF YOURS, SON! THAT THING PUTS OUT MORE POLLUTION THAN A FACTORY!!!" Smoke is billowing from the older man's pipe.]

Paraphrasing the Sermon on the Mount: Hearing and Acting on the Word of God

Matthew 7:21–27, NRSV

"Not everyone who says to me, '_____,' will enter the kingdom of heaven, but only the one who _____
_____.

On that day many will say to me, '_____
_____
_____?'

Then I will declare to them, '_____
_____.'

"Everyone then who hears these words of mine and acts on them will be like _____.
The rain fell, the floods came, and the winds blew and beat on that _____, but it did not fall, because it had been founded on _____.
And everyone who hears these words of mine and does not act on them will be like _____.
The rain fell, and the floods came, and the winds blew and beat against that _____, and it fell—and great was its fall!"

CHAPTER 8

Jesus Heals: Signs of the Kingdom

Major Concepts

A. **Jesus' Marvelous Deeds:** Jesus' actions, particularly his miracles, are important because they affirm the truth of his words.

B. **Why Are the Miracles So Challenging?** The Gospel accounts of Jesus' miracles challenge the modern reader in two main ways: (1) the contemporary Western worldview demands proof, evidence, and logical explanations for virtually everything, and (2) the Gospels themselves seem to disagree with one another about the same miracles. Jesus did work some wonders, but understanding them requires guidance.

C. **The Jews and Miracles:** The ancient Jews' worldview—particularly their understanding of God, suffering, and evil—provides much insight into the Gospel accounts of Jesus' miracles.

D. **Understanding Jesus' Miracles Today:** Like the parables, the miracles of Jesus are best understood in the context of Jesus' Dream of the Kingdom of God.

A Note to the Teacher: An Open Attitude on the Miracles

The miracles of Jesus represent one of the most perplexing areas of his life and ministry. A clear admission of this fact by you, as well as an honest and open attitude, will be important when discussing this material. Any defensiveness on this topic may quickly deteriorate into a fundamentalist stance, which has been carefully avoided throughout this course.

The difficulty in dealing with Jesus' miracles lies mainly in the fact that a lot of questions cannot be answered—questions about what actions Jesus actually performed, about the implications of various literary techniques employed in the development of the Gospels, about the true symbolic meaning of certain miracle stories, and so on. The author of this course has tried to walk a fine line on these matters in the student text, and you are encouraged to make that a goal in your teaching as well—to lead a balanced, faithful, honest, and relaxed discussion of this area of Christian faith.

Concept A: Jesus' Marvelous Deeds

Jesus' actions, particularly his miracles, are important because they affirm the truth of his words. (Pages 157–159 of the student text)

Review Questions: Jesus' Marvelous Deeds

Question: Identify and describe the kinds of miracles found in the Gospels.
Answer:
- *Healing miracles:* Jesus relieves people's physical suffering.
- *Exorcisms:* Jesus drives evil spirits or demons out of people.
- *Restorations of life:* On three occasions Jesus raises people from the dead.
- *Nature miracles:* Jesus demonstrates apparent control over the forces of nature by, for example, walking on water.

Question: Why are Jesus' miracles of special significance?
Answer: The miracles demonstrate that the power of God was truly manifested in Jesus. Without some concrete demonstration of Jesus' power over sin and evil, his words would lack credibility.

A Text Activity: Jesus' Marvelous Deeds

Activity 1

In a paragraph, react to this statement: *Jesus was one of three things: a lunatic, a con artist, or precisely who he claimed to be.*

Additional Activities: Jesus' Marvelous Deeds

Discussion Starters

Consider one or all of the following options to initiate discussion on concept A.

Option 1: Ask the students to discuss their personal encounters with religious fundamentalism and scientific skepticism. Share experiences of your own as well. Discuss the attitudes of people they have met who hold these positions.

This could be a delicate discussion because students in your class may hold the fundamentalist and skeptical positions. These positions should have surfaced earlier in the course, and you will no doubt already be sensitive to them. An interesting point to be aware of, however, is that some people who are apparently quite liberal and open-minded on many religious issues become defensive and more conservative regarding Jesus' miracles. If you notice this in your class discussion, *gently* raise your students' awareness of this fact and discuss possible reasons for it.

Option 2: Explain the following to the class:
- Central to our understanding of Jesus and his proclamation of the Kingdom is his commitment to freedom of the individual. Jesus never forced, coerced, or tried to overpower people into believing in him. The invitation to join the Kingdom was always precisely that—an invitation, not a threat or a bribe.

Then discuss this question:
- How is Jesus' commitment to freedom of the individual related to his use of miracles and to our understanding of them?

If the students have difficulty answering this question, tell them to reconsider the meaning of Jesus' rejecting the devil's temptation to throw himself off the tower of the Temple and have God catch him (see pp. 111–113 of the student text). Recall that in this incident, Jesus refuses to use a magical approach, which would almost force people to believe in him simply because of his wonder-working.

Option 3: Lead a class discussion using the following questions:
- Do you think it is ultimately of great importance that we determine which of Jesus' miracles, if any, occurred exactly as described in the Gospels?
- How central to your own acceptance of Jesus are his miraculous actions?
- If you were asked to list, in order of priority, all the reasons a person might have for believing in Jesus as the Christ, what—if anything—would be listed before his miracles?

A Reflection on "Miracle of Miracles"

Prepare copies of the lyrics to the song "Miracles of Miracles," from *Fiddler on the Roof*. Review the lyrics with the students and discuss the meaning. Then listen to the song and ask the students to identify the kinds of miracles that the song refers to.

Resurrection

The 1980 movie *Resurrection,* starring Ellen Burstyn, was nominated for an Academy Award for best picture and best actress. It is an intriguing story of a woman who experiences a close brush with death—if not an actual experience of it—in a car accident. She recovers from the accident with the apparent power to heal people.

An interesting ingredient in the movie is the fact that Burstyn's character refuses to credit God for her power (thereby alienating many of the fundamentalists in the story), but she also refuses to make money from the use of her power. It is a wonderful portrayal by Burstyn and a definite discussion starter for concept A. There is some adult language, making this perhaps more suitable for older students. The movie is available in many video rental stores.

Concept B: Why Are the Miracles So Challenging?

The Gospel accounts of Jesus' miracles challenge the modern reader in two main ways: (1) the contemporary Western worldview demands proof, evidence, and logical explanations for virtually everything, and (2) the Gospels themselves seem to disagree with one another about the same miracles. Jesus did work some wonders, but understanding them requires guidance. (Pages 160–163 of the student text)

Review Questions:
Why Are the Miracles So Challenging?

Question: What is the fundamentalist response to the Gospel miracles?
Answer: Fundamentalists simply accept all of the Gospel miracles at face value. And in doing so, they feel forced to reject many of our modern scientific and biblical findings.

Question: Why should Christians avoid extreme positions regarding the historical accuracy of the miracle accounts?
Answer: It is not right or necessary to lump all of the miracle accounts together and treat them the same way, giving one as much factual validity or significance as another. But if we get too bound up with whether an individual event occurred exactly the way the Gospels describe it, we risk completely missing the truth that the story can reveal to us.

Question: Briefly summarize the evidence given to uphold the conviction that Jesus did work some miracles.
Answer:
- Some non-Christian historians of ancient times referred to Jesus as a "wonder-worker."
- Even the Pharisees in the Gospels do not deny that Jesus worked many wonders.
- Many eyewitnesses to the works of Jesus believed so firmly in him and his message that they became committed followers, even to the point of death.

Question: What persistent problem regarding the miracles exists even for those who accept them all literally?

Answer: The Gospels themselves seem to disagree with one another about the same miracles.

Text Activities: Why Are the Miracles So Challenging?

Activity 2

Draw a horizontal line. At the far left end of the line write, "All of the Miracles Exactly as Described." At the far right end of the line, write, "None of the Miracles." Mark on the line where you think *most young people* stand in terms of believing in the Gospel miracles. Then mark where *you* stand. Follow up with a brief explanation of your responses.

Activity 3

Read any one of the miracle stories listed above. Write down any problems you can think of that would be associated with interpreting the story in a strictly literal way.

An Additional Activity: Why Are the Miracles So Challenging?

Interpreting the Miracle Stories

This exercise is intended to show the students the variety of ways that the miracle stories can be approached and interpreted. At the same time, it affirms the fact that regardless of the approach, these stories can offer us valuable insights and meaning.

1. Before class, prepare four large posters, with one of the following phrases printed on each in large letters:
- Historically true just as described
- Based on a historical incident that has been exaggerated
- Not historical at all—a totally symbolic story
- Not sure what to believe about this

Hang one of these posters in each corner of your room and, if possible, move the desks and chairs into circles under the signs.

2. From the chart on page 163 of the student text, select several miracle stories to read to the class, choosing whatever version you wish. Try to mix stories that would appear to have a stronger historical base with those that may be more symbolic (e.g., the healing of a paralytic and Jesus' walking on the water). For each miracle story, do the following:
a. Read the story aloud, asking the students to listen carefully to the details and to the lessons that might be learned from the story.
b. Give the students a moment to reflect on how they would judge the story according to the four options given on the posters. When they have made a decision, they should move to the appropriate corner of the room to join others who agree with their assessment of the story. (The number of students and the number of chairs in a given corner will seldom work out exactly, so extra students should either stand or sit on the floor if no seats are available for them.)

c. In their groups, the students should discuss and answer the following questions:
   • Why did you select this response to the miracle story? What evidence did you rely on to make your decision?
   • Would you acknowledge that those in the other groups might have had equally sound reasons for judging the miracle as they did? Why or why not?
   • What is the chief lesson that can be learned from this story, regardless of whether it is historically based or symbolic in nature?
d. Ask for representatives of the groups to share their answers with the class. Discuss their answers if you believe it would be profitable. Key in on the lessons that can be gleaned from the story, particularly noting if two or more groups gain the same lesson despite their differing viewpoints.

Read as many miracle stories, and thus repeat the exercise, as you like or believe will be effective.

Concept C: The Jews and Miracles

The ancient Jews' worldview—particularly their understanding of God, suffering, and evil—provides much insight into the Gospel accounts of Jesus' miracles. (Pages 164–167 of the student text)

Review Questions: The Jews and Miracles

Question: How do the differences between the modern Western worldview and that of the ancient Jews help to explain the ancient Jews' understanding of miracles?

Answer: People in our modern Western culture tend to view everything from a scientific perspective. They also tend to view God as remote and not particularly involved in the day-to-day happenings of life. The Jews of Jesus' day, however, viewed the world primarily from the perspective of their faith in Yahweh. To them, miracles were evidence of the presence and power of God. Though the Jews were naturally awed by works of wonder, they were not terribly surprised by them. They expected God to work that way.

Question: Why would the ancient Jews have viewed any cure of illness as an exorcism?

Answer: In the ancient Jewish view, everything was an expression of either God's creative power or the power of evil in the world. All illness was the result of evil. Any cure, therefore, was an exorcism, because it "cast out," or conquered, evil.

Question: Why should we hesitate to condemn the ancient Jews for their treatment of physically and mentally ill people?

Answer: We must remember *why* the Jews treated physically and mentally ill people the way they did. All sickness, insanity, and disease was seen as the direct manifestation of the power of evil. Sheer terror, not cruelty, motivated people to reject and banish those who were in need.

Question: What did the Gospel writers try to say about Jesus through the miracle stories?

Answer: The Gospel writers sought to address the belief that the Reign of God would not be truly present until all the manifestations of evil were overcome.
- Through Jesus, God was destroying evil in all its forms and manifestations and expressions.
- Because God was using Jesus in this way, Jesus was truly the Messiah, the One sent by God to establish the new Kingdom that the Jews had been waiting for.

Text Activities: The Jews and Miracles

Activity 4

List at least ten of your everyday experiences that the Jews of Jesus' day might have considered miracles.

Activity 5

Write either a pro or a con reaction to this statement: *It is much more difficult to believe in God today than it was during Jesus' time.*

Activity 6

Major catastrophes—earthquakes, tornadoes, floods, and even diseases like AIDS—are viewed by some as being directly caused by God for a specific reason, such as punishment of the victims. Write a short response to this view.

Additional Activities: The Jews and Miracles

Discussion Starters

Consider one or both of the following options to initiate discussion on concept C.

Option 1: Have the students reflect on and discuss the following:
- It has been said that we have experienced a radical change in our perception of our world because of the wonders of space travel, space photography, and so on, which have allowed us to gain a profoundly new perspective on who we are as people. For example, the photos of earth taken from space, such as the one on page 98 of your textbook, have led to the common notion now of the earth as a "global village," a relatively small planet on which we all must recognize our interdependence if we hope to survive.

    To gain a clearer sense of the worldview of the ancient Jews, we must recognize how phenomenally different our understanding of the world is. From your knowledge of history and science, what radical changes in perspective between the days of Jesus and our own can you identify (for instance, the discoveries of Columbus, Galileo, Newton, Einstein, and Darwin)?

Wonderful resources on humankind's evolving understanding of the world are available, especially the PBS television series, and subsequent books, titled "Cosmos," with Carl Sagan, and "The Ascent of Man," with Jacob Bronowski. Both books are available in school and city libraries. Also, consider inviting a teacher from your history or science department to offer a presentation on this theme. If such a presentation is not possible, he or she may at least be able to recommend some helpful films or other resources for this purpose.

Option 2: To approach the difference between the world of the ancient Jews and our contemporary world, lead a "time machine" discussion with the class. Ask the students to imagine that a person from the days of Jesus has been brought forward in time, directly into the present. Ask them to imagine that person from the past just roaming through today's world, marveling at and asking questions about anything strange or unknown to him or her. (You might play the role of the ancient Jew yourself.)

Have the students list all the things, events, and so on, that would have to be explained. Obviously, the list could become interminable, but that fact in itself will drive home the point here—that the world experienced by the Jews of Jesus' day and, therefore, by Jesus himself was radically different from our own.

A Presentation on the Ancient Jewish Worldview

Present the class with the following material on the ancient Jewish concept of the world and the mentality that grew out of that concept.

- In reading any book of the Bible, it is extremely important to discover the actual message intended by the writing. This means that we must discover *what a given narrative means* rather than merely take at face value the *story* through which the author has conveyed the meaning. Also, we need to realize that the Scriptures are a collection of various kinds of stories. The temptation for many people is to conclude that the Bible is simply a collection of fairy tales and, thus, that it is useless for the contemporary person who relies on precise scientific explanations of all phenomena. This conclusion is not only poor judgment, but it is, in fact, an unfair criticism. The Scriptures reveal their life-giving message through and within the context of given styles of writing used by given authors who had particular cultural backgrounds and lived at given points in time. All of these elements—the authors, their cultures, their styles of writing, and the times in which they wrote—*all of these* must be considered if we hope to arrive at the real kernels of truth that the scriptural authors wished to convey.

  The accounts of the Creation found in the first two chapters of Genesis are excellent examples of different literary forms, or styles of writing, used by different authors to convey essentially the same message—the revelation of a loving God from whom all creation emanates, a God who provides a world that is good and is to be enjoyed and cared for by those "made in God's image," or people. The first account of the Creation [Gen. 1:1—2:4*a*] is set within the framework of a seven-day week, ending with an allusion to the Sabbath day of rest. The theology in the narrative reflects the work of one well-versed in numerous religious beliefs and liturgical ideas. These characteristics lead scholars to refer to this as "the priestly account of the Creation."

  The author of this Creation account obviously relied on a primitive scientific understanding of the world. To him, the world was a flat disk or platform (remember, it took quite a while to discover that it wasn't!).

This disk was held up by pillars or columns sunk into a deep abyss. The earth, in the priestly account, was originally totally surrounded by water (a symbol of chaos), so one of God's first acts was to construct a bowl-like vault, or firmament, over the earth to separate the water from the land. On this dome God placed the sun, the moon, and the stars, "the greater light to govern the day, the smaller light to govern the night." From this point on, everything was simple and *sensible* to the ancient Jew. Whenever it rained, God had simply opened a kind of trapdoor and allowed the waters above the earth to pour through until enough rain had fallen. Rivers and lakes were formed when God opened holes in the earth and let the waters below it flood in. The wind was easily explained as the breath of God moving over the earth.

The image of the world on page 204 of your textbook goes a long way toward explaining the ancient Jews' apparently incredible awareness of the presence of God. Every time even the most basic event occurred in nature, the Jews "saw" and felt God actively present. It is unfortunate that our contemporary Western culture has lost that sense of wonder.

It was with that view of the world, a very reasonable view for the ancient Jew, that the author of the first Creation account expressed the real message of the narrative—that there exists one loving God who brings forth all creation and who shares the responsibility for its care with men and women, who are "made in God's image." There is no conflict here between science and theology; a scientific account of the Creation was far from the author's intention. The theological insights of the author, the actual meaning of the account, remain forever valid as the basis for a true understanding of our God and of our role as people in a world made good and sacred.

The second account of the Creation [Gen. 2:4*b*–25] is a completely different analysis of the origins of the world. (If scientific truth were the intent of the authors of the Scriptures, would they have kept two accounts of the Creation?) The second account is less complex than the first, yet it offers, in a sense, a more intriguing and beautiful image of the world and the relationship between God and people. The world is depicted as a paradise, a Shangri-la of shaded garden paths lined with breathtaking foliage and trees heavy with succulent fruits. Man is formed from the clay of the ground and brought to life with the breath of God. God makes woman from the rib of man to be a suitable partner for him. In the garden, man and woman live in perfect harmony with their God.

Essentially the author's message is the same as that of the author of the first account: Our God is a loving Creator who shares with the most glorious creation—people—not only the goodness of the earth but indeed God's very life. Again, we see different literary forms with essentially the same intent.

In conjunction with your presentation of these ideas, you might want to have the students refer to the two accounts of the Creation in Genesis and perhaps to several psalms that express the Hebrews' incredible sense of God's presence in nature (e.g., Psalms 8, 29, and 104). Also, suggest that the students turn to the illustration of the ancient Jewish worldview on page 204 of the student text. Follow the presentation with a discussion on the connection between that worldview and the Jewish sense of miracles as discussed in the student text.

A Note to the Teacher: Films on the Wonder of Creation

Many films can help us gain a deeper appreciation of the miraculous, which can be found around us all the time if we only, in the words of Jesus, "have the eyes to see." Films that offer a microscopic view of our everyday world, as well as those that explore the incredible immensity of the universe, are particularly effective for this purpose. Check with your diocesan resource center or public library for possibilities.

Concept D: Understanding Jesus' Miracles Today

Like the parables, the miracles of Jesus are best understood in the context of Jesus' Dream of the Kingdom of God. (Pages 168–173 of the student text)

Review Questions: Understanding Jesus' Miracles Today

Question: Why can the meaning of the miracles be answered only from a faith perspective?
Answer: The real significance of the miracles is their religious meaning, which is recognized and accepted in light of faith in Jesus.

Question: What is the key to understanding the miracles of Jesus? What realities are at the core of the miracles?
Answer: The key to understanding the miracles of Jesus is grasping their relationship to his proclamation of the Kingdom of God. At the core of that proclamation—and therefore at the core of the miracles—are these realities:
- God's promise of unconditional love
- God's commitment to the poor and outcasts of society
- God's complete control over the power of sin and evil
- God's offer of complete reconciliation

Question: Name two things that motivated Jesus to perform miracles.
Answer: Love and the intention to show God's power over all creation, especially over the forces of sin and evil

Question: What happens once people have faith in Jesus and his message? Give an example to illustrate your answer.
Answer: Once people have faith in Jesus and his message, a real miracle has already begun in their heart. The physical cure they experience becomes an expression of an interior reality, a conversion, a change of heart. [Any of the following examples from the student text would be appropriate.]
- They are liberated not only from lameness but also from legalism.
- They are liberated not only from a crippling deformity but also from a closed mind.
- They are liberated not only from physical blindness but also from the inability to recognize the needs of their neighbors.

Text Activities: Understanding Jesus' Miracles Today

Activity 7

Write a response to this opinion: *Miracles that take place in people's hearts are as significant as dramatic, physical cures.*

Activity 8

Read another miracle story listed in the shaded box "Jesus' Miracles in the Synoptic Gospels," on page 163. Using the list of Kingdom realities above as a guide, write an essay on the connections between the miracle story and Jesus' proclamation of the Kingdom of God.

Activity 9

Write about an incident in your life (or in the life of someone you know) that could be considered a modern miracle, a sign of God's loving power.

Activity 10

Write a short essay comparing what you thought about Jesus' miracles before you studied this chapter with what you understand about them now.

Additional Activities: Understanding Jesus' Miracles Today

Seeing God in Everyday Life

This activity is meant to help the students see how the Evangelists wrote their stories of the miracles.

1. Divide the class into three groups, assigning each group one of the three "modern miracles" described in the feature boxes in chapter 8 of the student text (pp. 165, 169, and 172–173). Instruct each group to rewrite its assigned story as it might have been written by a writer of the Gospel miracles who was telling the story to a community of believers. Offer the following hints for this task:
   - The revised version of the story should be condensed, or shortened, to simplify it and increase the impact of the details.
   - The details can be exaggerated to make a point.
   - The names of characters and situations can be changed to sound more "biblical."
   - The story might conclude with a "punch line" to increase its teaching power.

2. Ask the groups to either read their version of the story to the class or role-play it. Follow each presentation or performance with a class discussion on whether the retold story has taken on greater meaning than the original, whether it could be considered true in its revised form, and so on.

After the revised stories have been shared, point out how the various literary techniques the groups used were also used by the Evangelists in their miracle stories.

Human Limitations and the Freeing Power of God

Use the following simulation activity to help the students get a sense of what people in the Gospels experienced when Jesus performed a miracle for them.

1. During the class session before the one you have set aside for the simulation, tell the students that in the next session you will be leading an exercise that they must cooperate fully with if they are to get the greatest benefits from it. This comment will probably pique their interest and motivate their cooperation.

Ask one or two students to assist with the simulation rather than actually experience it.

2. On the day of the simulation, meet the students at the door of the room as they arrive for class. Before they enter the room, tell them to maintain absolute silence until they are told that they may speak. Then bind their wrists together with a piece of cloth and blindfold them. Have one of your assistants lead each student to a chair. This should not be the student's usual chair. (To intensify the experience, before class turn all the chairs in various directions, thus giving a greater sense of disorder and chaos.)

After all the students have been seated, give them these instructions:
- Please remain perfectly silent and still. Try to identify and become conscious of all the various feelings and emotions you experience.
- After a few moments, I will slowly move around the room. As I do this, I will stop and untie the bindings on your wrists. When this happens, you can move your arms and hands to loosen them up if you wish, *but you will remain blindfolded and are to keep perfectly silent.*
- Later I will return to remove the blindfold from your eyes. When this happens, you can look around to satisfy your curiosity about what is happening, *but you cannot speak to anyone or make any other sounds.*
- Finally, when everyone's blindfold has been removed, I will tell you that you can speak and move around.

Make sure that everyone understands these instructions; repeat them if necessary.

3. Before beginning to untie any of the bindings on the students' wrists, pause quietly and give them time to experience some of the tension and strange feelings generated by the situation. Perhaps even leave the room for a few minutes at this point. Then begin slowly and quietly to walk around, untying the bindings on someone in one corner of the room, then moving to a different area before untying another student's bindings, and so on, until all the bindings have been untied. The students will have a sense of your presence or absence most of the time, and you may even want to shuffle your feet past some students without untying their bindings, just to increase their sense of confusion and frustration. The intent is to generate such feelings, along with anxiety, perhaps anger, and so on.

4. After all the students have had their wrists freed, begin to remove blindfolds in the same fashion, that is, while quietly moving from one part of the room to another. When all the students have had their blindfold removed, tell them they can now talk and can move the chairs back to their proper order.

5. Discussion of the exercise is, of course, the critical factor in all of this. Ask the students to share reflections upon the following questions:
- What feelings did you experience throughout the exercise, and what caused them? [Go through the exercise from beginning to end to find out how the feelings progressed and changed.]

- What was the most frustrating part of the exercise? the most anxiety-causing? Did you get angry during any part of the exercise?
- How did you feel when your wrists were released? Why?
- How did you feel when your blindfold was removed? Were you surprised by anything? How did it feel to be freed from the blindness? What was your feeling toward those who were still blind? Why?
- Can you make a connection between this experience and the various aspects of Jesus' miracles that we have been discussing? [Go through this connection in as much detail as possible. This exercise has great application beyond the experience of physical limitation. It also offers richness in terms of the experience of emotional limitation, the sense of isolation and possibly even community within this experience of emotional limitation, the wondrous sense of freedom at the end, the relationship between your role as leader and the role of Jesus as the One who frees, etc.]

6. Close with appropriate comments and perhaps a prayer.

CHAPTER 9

The Cross: The End or a Beginning?

Major Concepts

A. **The Road to the Cross:** Jesus was clearly a man of peace, love, and compassion. Yet many people, especially those with religious and political power, saw his words and behavior as threatening. That fact brought Jesus to his death on the cross—the most extensively discussed event in the Gospel story.

B. **Jesus' Final Days:** Even though Jesus could see that his enemies were closing in on him, he refused to run away from his commitment to proclaiming the Kingdom of God. Jesus' free acceptance of his death is central to all of Christian theology.

C. **Jesus' Final Hours:** In a rapid series of events, Jesus was condemned by the Jewish leadership for blasphemy and by the Roman authorities for inciting a revolt. His scourging and execution by crucifixion brought his earthly life to an end.

D. **Understanding the Cross:** No single interpretation of the cross can fully express its meaning.

Concept A: The Road to the Cross

Jesus was clearly a man of peace, love, and compassion. Yet many people, especially those with religious and political power, saw his words and behavior as threatening. That fact brought Jesus to his death on the cross—the most extensively discussed event in the Gospel story. (Pages 175–177 of the student text)

Review Questions: The Road to the Cross

Question: Why is the image of Jesus as a man of peace, love, and compassion not a complete one?
Answer: We must remember as well that Jesus seemed to cause conflict and tension wherever he went. His words were often challenging, even threatening, to his listeners. His behavior ran contrary to many of the accepted practices of the time. He was a very real threat to religious tradition and political stability.

Question: What are the literary characteristics of the Passion accounts in the Gospels?
Answer: The arrest, trial, and crucifixion of Jesus are the most extensively reported events in the Gospels. The Gospels seem keyed to these events, as if everything in the Gospels is intended to prepare the reader for Jesus' execution. Even the writing style of the Passion accounts is much different from that of the Gospels' typical stories and short sayings.

Question: Why did the Evangelists use a style different from their typical stories and sayings to tell the story of Jesus' death?
Answer:
- The death and resurrection of Jesus are at the heart of the Christian story. His crucifixion had to be very carefully explained to the early community of faith.
- What happened to Jesus was totally contrary to what the people had been expecting for their Messiah. Their desire for information about these events would have been natural and intense.
- The Evangelists were writing to and for the early followers of the Risen Jesus. These followers themselves would confront almost immediate persecution for their faith in him. The reminder that Jesus had suffered persecution and death would be a constant consolation to them.

Text Activities: The Road to the Cross

Activity 1

Write a short piece about a time in your life (or in the life of someone you know) when doing good became a source of conflict and tension.

Activity 2

Draw four columns and label each one with the name of one of the Gospels. As you read the four accounts of the Passion, take brief notes on the progress of events and compare accounts.

Additional Activities: The Road to the Cross

Comparing the Passion Narratives

Break the class into the four groups that were assigned to read a Gospel from beginning to end in "A Special Reading Assignment," on pages 63–64 of this manual. Have the groups spend time in class becoming familiar with the Passion narrative of their respective Gospels. Instruct them to develop a brief but complete outline of the passages. For example, the group assigned Matthew's Gospel might begin its outline as follows:

> Matt. 26:1–5: The plot to arrest Jesus
> Matt. 26:6–13: The anointing at Bethany
> Matt. 26:14–16: Judas's betrayal of Jesus

Some versions of the Bible, such as the New American Bible, basically provide such outlines by way of boldfaced headings that appear throughout the narratives. Depending on the time available and the ability of your class, you may or may not want the students to have this type of help.

When all the groups have finished working, make four columns on the board and ask students to report the outlines, recording these on the board. In doing so, you will be sure that all the students have examined the material, that they have some sense of the similarities and differences between the Passion accounts, and that they are therefore ready for detailed discussion on the Passion.

A Dramatic Reading of a Passion Narrative

Consider involving the class in a dramatic reading of one of the Passion narratives (preferably the one in Luke, chapters 22–23). This would require competent readers and a cooperative attitude on the part of the entire class. You could assign particular roles to individual students and ask them to practice their parts in advance, or you could simply rotate the responsibility for reading throughout the class, without concern for assigning roles. The first approach ensures better reading, while the second involves more students. The primary purpose of this activity is to ensure that all the students are fully familiar with the Passion story before discussing it. If done well, however, a dramatic reading can also greatly enhance the students' interest in the topic.

Reflections on Martyrdom

Jesus practically invited his own death through the force of the message he proclaimed and his absolute refusal to compromise his beliefs and principles. As Gethsemane testifies, he certainly did not *seek* death. However, he did not run from the threat of it either. The following are ways to help the students explore this kind of heroic commitment to one's values.

Option 1: View and discuss the film *Dr. Martin Luther King: An Amazing Grace*. (The producers of this film, McGraw-Hill—CRM Films, have discontinued distribution of it, but it can still be found in local and diocesan libraries and resource centers.) Focus on how Dr. King, like Jesus, was a source of conflict because of his commitment to equality. Place emphasis on the question, What things in life are worth dying for?

Option 2: In recent years, a number of Christians have given their life rather than shirk what they believed were their Christian responsibilities. Some of these people were Archbishop Oscar Romero; several North American women missionaries, six Jesuit priests, their cook, and her daughter in El Salvador; missionaries in Nicaragua; and Christian Brother James Miller in Guatemala. The students should be made conscious of these remarkable examples of Christian principles lived out to the extreme.

The story of Archbishop Romero is told in the powerful, award-winning movie *Romero*. The videotape is available in many video rental stores, or it can be purchased for $29.95 from Paulist Press, 997 MacArthur Boulevard, Mahwah, NJ 07430; phone 201-825-7300.

Option 3: Invite guest speakers from the Maryknoll missionaries, the Ursuline Sisters, the Jesuits, or the Christian Brothers—religious orders directly touched by the lives and deaths of the martyred witnesses mentioned in option 2. Ask the speakers to discuss the impact these martyrs had and continue to have on those who knew them. The intent of this in terms of concept A is to help the students reflect on the death of Jesus in human terms—as a commitment to die for one's principles—rather than only as a theological reality that can seem removed from us.

Concept B: Jesus' Final Days

Even though Jesus could see that his enemies were closing in on him, he refused to run away from his commitment to proclaiming the Kingdom of God. Jesus' free acceptance of his death is central to all of Christian theology. (Pages 178–183 of the student text)

Review Questions: Jesus' Final Days

Question: With what historical Jewish event is the Last Supper linked? What two main points do the synoptic Gospels make about Jesus' words and actions at the Last Supper?
Answer: The Last Supper is linked with Yahweh's delivering the Israelites from slavery in Egypt and the Israelites' pledge of loyalty to Yahweh in the Sinai covenant.

The synoptic Gospels suggest these two main points about Jesus' words and actions at the Last Supper:
- Jesus had his approaching death in mind as he gathered his disciples for that meal.
- He made a real connection between the meal itself and his death on the cross.

Question: What is the Roman Catholic conviction regarding the presence of Jesus in the Eucharist?
Answer: Roman Catholics are firm in their conviction that the Risen Jesus is truly and fully present in the consecrated bread and wine of the Eucharist.

Question: Explain the meaning of this statement: *Jesus could read the signs of the times regarding his death.*
Answer: Jesus could look at what was happening around him and put all the pieces together. He was aware, for instance, of the building hostility toward him, the tension in Jerusalem resulting from his presence there, and the way his people had treated their prophets throughout history.

Question: Why is Jesus' free acceptance of his death central to all of Christian theology?

Answer: The Good News crumbles if Jesus is seen as a dreamer who was somehow fooled by circumstances; or as someone who would have sacrificed his convictions by running away, had he known what was coming; or even as someone who knew with absolute certainty that he would be raised from the dead in three days.

Text Activities: Jesus' Final Days

Activity 3

Using an encyclopedia or other sources, write a short essay on the origins and major characteristics of the Passover meal.

Activity 4

Compose a personal letter to Jesus as you imagine him facing his last days. Base your words on your own experiences of loneliness and fear.

Additional Activities: Jesus' Final Days

Reflections on Loneliness

As a class, brainstorm all the ways in which people experience loneliness (e.g., when they are rejected, confused, or isolated from loved ones; when no one seems to understand; when a friend or loved one dies). Ask the students to give examples to illustrate each idea. Then try to identify similar situations in Jesus' life. Finally, discuss the following questions:
- Explain why Jesus' experience at Gethsemane can be considered his ultimate experience of loneliness.
- Does the knowledge of Jesus' pain in that situation in any way help us to bear pain in our own lives? Why or why not?

Discussion on the Song "Gethsemane"

The lyrics of the song "Gethsemane," from *Jesus Christ Superstar,* are powerful and haunting. Working with the lyrics in this exercise will enable the students to better appreciate Jesus' struggle in the garden. Get ahold of the recording and transcribe the lyrics before having the students work with the song, so that you are familiar with the words.

1. Have the students listen to the song "Gethsemane," perhaps several times, working as a class to transcribe the lyrics. Then divide the class into four groups, assigning one group to each of four different sections from the lyrics.

2. Ask the groups to discuss their section of the lyrics, arriving at what they think the lyricist was trying to express about Jesus' attitude. Then, with the whole class, discuss the following questions:
- Do you agree with the lyricist's interpretation of what Jesus is experiencing within himself? Why or why not?

- These lyrics seem to imply that Jesus is blaming his Father for the position he is in. From your reading of the passages about Jesus in the garden, as well as from your understanding of the religious and political opposition confronting him, do you agree with this interpretation of God's role in the death of Jesus?
- Does any part of the song adequately express the Gospel verse in which Jesus says, "'yet, not what I want, but what you want'" [Mark 14:36]? If you were to paraphrase those important words, how would you do it?

A Creative Writing Project on the Cross

In one stage production of the Gospel story, *The Son of Man,* Jesus is depicted during his ministry standing next to one of the permanent upright beams used for crucifixion. As a carpenter, he does a soliloquy reflecting his sense of God's purpose for such good wood and how people have defiled it by using it for a hideous purpose.

If the students have shown a reasonable openness to and ability for literary expression, assign as a homework project the development of a similar soliloquy. The students could express any aspect of Jesus' crucifixion and death through poetry, as a prayer uttered by Jesus to his Father, or in whatever other format they prefer. After collecting and reviewing their work, select the most thought-provoking and insightful pieces, share these with the class, and discuss them.

The Seder Meal

The Seder meal is the highlight of the Jewish Passover celebration, and tradition links the meal closely to our Christian Eucharist. Some parishes and schools share an abbreviated Seder as part of their Easter season festivities, many times on Holy Thursday. Doing this would be a prayerful way to get at the heart of concept B, and it would likely prove memorable for your students. Many resources are available to help you explain and actually plan and share such a meal.

One useful set of resources is *The Passover Celebration,* by Rabbi Leon Klenicki, which is a participation book for the Seder meal, along with the audiocassette *Songs for the Seder Meal.* These are available from Liturgy Training Publications, 1800 North Hermitage Avenue, Chicago, IL 60622-1101; phone 800-933-1800. The book costs $2.25, and the audiocassette costs $5.95.

Here are some other suggestions for teaching the students about the Seder:
1. Prepare your own presentation on the Seder, using the resources available. Consult your diocesan resource center for possible films.
2. Have the students study and report on the history and meaning of the Seder and then discuss its relationship to the Eucharist.
3. Invite a rabbi to give an "insider's" understanding of the Seder. Then perhaps follow that presentation with one by a priest or another Christian who would discuss the Seder's connection with the Eucharist.

In Remembrance

In Remembrance is a marvelous, thought-provoking film. It is 57 minutes long and is of high technical quality. The film presents imaginary interviews with five of the disciples who were at the Last Supper, who recount the experience and its meaning for them in light of the death of Jesus. As each disciple tells his story, viewers see flashbacks to the meal, providing a sensitive portrayal of what it may have been like. The disciples' comments are instructive and stimulating.

To purchase or rent *In Remembrance,* contact the film's producer, Evangelical Films (also known as Grace Products), 1761 International Parkway, Richardson, TX 75081; phone 214-437-6575 or toll free 800-527-4014. You can purchase the videotape for $49 or rent the 16mm film for $69. Or check with your diocesan library or resource center to see if the film is available.

A Eucharistic Celebration

Celebrating the Eucharist may be an obvious activity for concept B, but keep in mind the need to connect this liturgy with its roots in Jesus' time. To enhance the students' experience of the celebration, have them do prior study on the origins of the Eucharist and the Eucharist's relation to the Passover. Consider making "covenant" the theme of the celebration and choosing readings and music accordingly. If possible, try to create an atmosphere that would suggest the Last Supper, perhaps celebrating in a room with low lighting, with the students seated on the floor in groups of twelve, and so on. A sensitivity to such dimensions, along with the leadership of a celebrant who is in touch with the students' needs and attitudes, could make this a powerful experience of the realities reflected in concept B.

Concept C: Jesus' Final Hours

In a rapid series of events, Jesus was condemned by the Jewish leadership for blasphemy and by the Roman authorities for inciting a revolt. His scourging and execution by crucifixion brought his earthly life to an end. (Pages 184–189 of the student text)

Review Questions: Jesus' Final Hours

Question: The high priest Caiaphas asked Jesus if he was the Messiah. What was significant about Jesus' answer?
Answer: Jesus not only accepted the title *Messiah* but even expanded that to say he was uniquely in touch with God. Jesus' response drew an immediate charge of blasphemy. In other words, by responding as he did, Jesus had gone too far. He had taken the final step toward virtually guaranteeing that he would be executed.

Question: Why did the Jewish leaders bring their charges against Jesus to the Romans?
Answer: To carry out the death penalty against Jesus, the Jewish leaders needed the help of the Romans.

Question: Why did Pontius Pilate not accept the Jews' first charge against Jesus?
Answer: Blasphemy was a religious offense, not a political one that in any way threatened the Roman state.

Question: Why do scholars debate the meaning of Jesus' utterance on the cross, "My God, my God, why have you forsaken me?"

Answer: If the words reflect a sense of deep despair, this in turn would seem to suggest that Jesus had a certain lack of faith in his Father's love for him.

Text Activities: Jesus' Final Hours

Activity 5

Imagine yourself as the prosecuting attorney at the trial of Jesus. Write a brief summary of the charges you would bring against him to prove he deserved execution.

Activity 6

In writing, briefly express the degree to which you think each of the following were responsible for Jesus' death: *Judas, the Jewish leaders, Caiaphas, Pontius Pilate.* Give reasons for your answers.

Activity 7

Create a prayerful meditation on the scourging and crucifixion of Jesus and the meaning of those events for you.

Activity 8

Which quotation of Jesus' last words impresses you most—the one provided by John or the one provided by Luke? Explain your choice in a paragraph.

Additional Activities: Jesus' Final Hours

Discussion Starters

Consider one or all of the following options to initiate discussion on concept C.

Option 1: Share the following insights with your students:
- Some scholars dispute that Jesus ever claimed divinity as blatantly as his claim is recorded in the accounts of his exchange with Caiaphas. Among other arguments, the scholars cite that Jesus, given the limitations he experienced in his humanity, would not have been able to comprehend such an identity for himself. As a deeply devout and loyal Jew, he would have found such an identity impossible to accept or comprehend. Also, as noted earlier, what we have in the Gospel accounts is the *early followers'* post-Resurrection testimony about what *they* discovered Jesus to be—namely, divine.

Ask for the students' reactions to these comments. Use the following questions to elicit their responses:
- Is it essential to your Christian belief that Jesus consciously acknowledged his divinity? Why or why not?
- Is his acknowledgment of that identity necessary in order to explain the Jews' and Romans' desire to execute him, or would all his other teachings and actions have given them sufficient cause?

Option 2: Discuss the following questions on Pontius Pilate:
- How would you characterize Pontius Pilate, given the information in this chapter?
- What were his apparent strengths and weaknesses?

To provide your students with more information on Pilate, see John L. McKenzie's *Dictionary of the Bible,* under "Pilate," and *The New Jerome Biblical Commentary,* page 1249. Also, note that one tradition—the Ethiopian Coptic church—has even venerated Pilate as a saint, and discuss with your students how this might be explained.

Option 3: Have the students search the Scriptures for all the words Jesus spoke on the cross, perhaps dividing them again into the four groups that were assigned to read a Gospel from beginning to end in "A Special Reading Assignment," on pages 63–64 of this manual. Record the students' discoveries on the chalkboard, compare, and discuss.

Jesus on Trial

This exercise assumes that the students have read, studied, and discussed all the material in chapter 9 of the student text up to page 187. It serves as an effective means of summing up the arrest and trial of Jesus.

    1. Divide the class into three groups that will take the following roles:
- Group 1 is to be the prosecution in the trial of Jesus, developing as tight a case as it can against Jesus by using all the material available in the Gospels and in the student text.
- Group 2 is to serve as the defense, using the Gospels and the student text to demonstrate that Jesus does not deserve to die.
- Group 3 is to serve as the jury and must base its decision as much as possible on the strength of the arguments offered by the prosecution and the defense.

Though not required, one student could be elected to play the role of Jesus during the trial, or perhaps you could assume that role more effectively.

    2. Give the prosecution and the defense sufficient class time to build their cases. Explain that the actual trial will be conducted in a fishbowl discussion manner, with both sides initially electing four representatives to present their arguments. However, all students for the prosecution and the defense will have their say, if they wish, by changing places with one of their representatives.

While the prosecution and the defense are working on their arguments, ask the jury to determine rules of order and general procedures, to review their understanding of standard courtroom procedures, to list the points that they will definitely demand each side speak to, and so on.

Be flexible about the time allowed for all this preparation, giving more time if the groups either need it or are using it creatively. If possible, arrange for the groups to work in separate rooms so that they can practice oral presentations, and so on.

    3. In conducting the trial, be prepared to interrupt occasionally to point out comments of particular interest, to ask for clarification, or perhaps to indicate major inaccuracies offered by one side or the other (though it should generally be the responsibility of the opposition to catch these mistakes). Remark that the jury in this trial should function more like a supreme court or the Great Sanhedrin than like a jury in the normal sense. In other words, the jury members can speak, ask questions, and so on.

4. At the end of the individual presentations by the prosecution and the defense, allow for counterarguments. Eventually call the jury to deliberate and make a decision.

TV Interviews with Witnesses to the Passion Events

A takeoff on a TV news program was suggested for use with chapter 5 (see p. 105 of this manual). Consider having the class prepare a similar "Special Report" here, featuring interviews with people who attended the Last Supper or witnessed Jesus' trial and crucifixion. Do not be concerned about repeating the news program idea.

Stations of the Cross

Several options are available for the stations of the cross, from simply praying the stations in a way you think will be effective with your students to having the students design their own approach. If you opt for the latter, do as follows:

1. Have students study the origins of this devotion, learn the meaning of the fourteen stations, and review available versions of the prayers that have been created for it through the years.

2. Direct the class in determining some basic guidelines for developing their own approach to the stations: how much time should be spent in praying or reflecting on individual stations, whether recorded music should be used, what part must involve original prayers, and so on.

3. Divide the class into fourteen groups (fifteen if, like some, you prefer to add another station for the Resurrection) and assign each group the responsibility of preparing a prayerful reflection on one station, according to the guidelines determined previously. Give a specified amount of time for this part of the exercise. Be sure to circulate among the students during this time in order to answer questions and perhaps occasionally check the quality of work to ensure a good experience later.

4. The class should experience the stations of the cross in an appropriate setting. Consider closing the experience with refreshments, both as a sign of appreciation for the students' efforts and to affirm the spirit of community that may have developed during the exercise and actual prayer.

Option: If the stations designed by the groups are particularly well done, consider arranging for the class to either lead other classes in the devotion or offer this as a service to local grade schools.

Concept D: Understanding the Cross

No single interpretation of the cross can fully express its meaning. (Pages 190–191 of the student text)

Review Questions: Understanding the Cross

Question: Why would it be dangerous to settle on only one expression for the meaning of the cross?
Answer: We would risk seriously misinterpreting the cross's complex meaning.

Question: The statement that Jesus died for our sins is important, but what confusion can it lead to?
Answer: It can convey an image of God that is far removed from the one Jesus revealed to the world. It can give a sense, for instance, that Jesus had to die in our place in order to satisfy an angry God who was demanding "a pound of flesh" in payment for past offenses.

A Text Activity: Understanding the Cross

Activity 9

From the three common expressions for the meaning of Jesus' death on the cross, choose the one that has the most meaning for you and write a brief essay explaining why. Or if you wish, write about your own, more personal, interpretation of the cross's meaning.

Additional Activities: Understanding the Cross

Research on the Cross

Give a presentation, or have the students research and prepare reports, on the evolution of the cross or crucifix as a major Christian symbol. (Technically, a crucifix differs from a cross in that it bears the likeness of the corpus of Jesus.) This might involve studying works of art as they have changed through the years, each change representing, to a certain extent, a shift in theology. Also, see *The New Encyclopaedia Britannica,* Micropaedia, 15th edition, under "Cross," for a brief summary of the cross as a religious symbol. Then follow with the further resources suggested in that article.

Reflection on Christian Liturgical Music

This exercise helps the students see liturgical music as a marvelous expression of the church's growing and changing understanding of Jesus' death.

1. With the students, review the most common theological images that the church uses for Jesus' death.

2. Distribute various hymnals representing the broadest range of liturgical music. (Most parishes have more than one hymnal these days, using both traditional and contemporary music. You may be able to borrow hymnals for this exercise.)

3. Divide your class into as many groups as there are images from step 1 that you wish to discuss. Assign an image to each group and instruct the group members to go through their hymnals and do the following:
- Find lyrics that refer directly to your group's assigned theological image of Jesus' death. Either write down those lyrics or list page references that will help you locate them later.
- If possible, find the date and nationality of origin for the lyrics you find. This information is normally found in small print near the title of the hymn.

4. Have the groups share the results of their research. Then discuss the following questions:
- During what ages were most of the hymns written?
- Was one image of Jesus "in vogue" during certain periods of history?
- Can you identify what might have been going on in the church during those times to explain this?
- What major changes, if any, can you identify when you compare the approach to Jesus' death in traditional or ancient hymns with the approach to Jesus' death in contemporary hymns?

Teacher Background:
The Justification Theory of the Cross

If your students are somewhat advanced, consider preparing a brief presentation on the impact that Saint Anselm of Canterbury's theory of justification has had as an explanation for Jesus' death on the cross. Though never officially defined as doctrine, this theory gained such popularity in the church that many people accept it as authoritative church teaching. The brief summary offered here can be supplemented by reviewing material in many encyclopedias, in Richard P. McBrien's *Catholicism,* and in other resources.

Saint Anselm lived from 1033 to 1109. His theory of justification was based on his experience of medieval society. In that society, any person committing a crime or another offense was required to make up for the crime done to the one offended *according to the status of the person offended.* Therefore, a crime committed against a king required more satisfaction than the same crime committed against a lord or a peasant.

Anselm believed that humanity, through the sin of Adam, had committed a crime against the infinite God, and because of humanity's finitude, or limited, imperfect condition, we could never adequately compensate or make satisfaction to God. We were therefore doomed to eternal death. The instrument of our salvation, however, was Jesus. Because he himself was divine, he merited the forgiveness of God by offering an infinite level of satisfaction—that is, by offering himself in death to God on our behalf.

It was out of Anselm's theory that we evolved our common notion of Jesus as our "substitute" in offering a perfect sacrifice to God. It was also in part because of this theory that we developed a false understanding of the ransom image in the Scriptures, viewing the death of Jesus as a kind of price, or "pound of flesh," demanded by an angry God before we could be freed from the power of sin.

The purpose of treating this theory is to lead the students away from their possibly simplistic notions of the meaning of Jesus' death and to encourage them to see his death primarily as an act of incredible love—not only an expression of Jesus' love for us but a revelation of God's infinite love for us as well. This will help dispel the notion some students, and certainly many parents, have of a God who somehow was able to demand the brutal sacrifice of his own Son. This image of God is so strong that it threatens, if not works against, our recognition of the image of God offered to us by Jesus, the image of one we dare to call "Abba, Father."

CHAPTER 10

The Resurrection: God Is Victorious! Jesus Is Lord!

Major Concepts

A. **The Resurrection of Jesus:** Neither the Gospels nor Christianity itself would exist were it not for the resurrection of Jesus. Even though significant evidence supports the historical reality of the Resurrection, it can really be understood only in the light of faith.

B. **What Does the Resurrection Mean?** The Resurrection stands as an affirmation that everything Jesus said and did is worthy of our trust. Jesus is, Christians believe, the Christ, the One who transforms all of life.

C. **Recognizing the Risen Jesus Today:** Christians today can encounter the Risen Jesus in the Eucharist, in the community of believers, and in remembering and living out the Dream of Jesus, the Kingdom of God.

D. **The Ascension of Jesus:** The most important point that the scriptural authors wished to teach by describing the Ascension was this: Following his resurrection, Jesus passed totally into the presence of God, who is always and everywhere with us in the world. Thus, Jesus can now be more truly present to us than he could possibly have been as he walked the earth.

E. **Pentecost:** With the gift of the Holy Spirit at Pentecost, Jesus' disciples came to the full realization that the Jesus of History is the Christ of Faith, the Son of God, and our Lord. Pentecost marks the birthday of the church.

Concept A: The Resurrection of Jesus

Neither the Gospels nor Christianity itself would exist were it not for the resurrection of Jesus. Even though significant evidence supports the historical reality of the Resurrection, it can really be understood only in the light of faith. (Pages 193–197 of the student text)

Review Questions: The Resurrection of Jesus

Question: According to Matthew's Gospel, why did Pontius Pilate assign Roman soldiers to guard the tomb of Jesus?
Answer: To prevent Jesus' disciples from stealing the body and then claiming that Jesus had risen from the dead

Question: Summarize the common points in the Gospel accounts of Jesus' resurrection.
Answer:
- Jesus is buried in a tomb by a wealthy disciple named Joseph of Arimathea.
- Various people go to the tomb and discover that the body of Jesus is no longer there.
- The people who go to the tomb find out that Jesus is no longer dead but alive, and that he will reveal himself to them again soon.
- The witnesses' initial reactions are shock and then fear. But soon they experience Jesus among them.

Question: List and summarize the four pieces of evidence given to support the reality of Jesus' resurrection.
Answer:
- *A consistent belief in the early church:* The Resurrection was a consistent belief in the early church. The letters of Saint Paul, the Acts of the Apostles, and all four Gospels mention it.
- *The empty tomb:* All the accounts of the Resurrection agree that the tomb was empty on the morning that the women went to prepare Jesus' body for burial. Surely the Romans would have produced Jesus' corpse if they could have, to destroy any stories of his resurrection that might have been falsely created by his disciples. And the disciples themselves would eventually choose to die rather than deny their faith in a resurrected Jesus. Would they have freely died for a hoax? Moreover, if the authors of the accounts had been seeking to convince an audience of something untrue, they would never have chosen women, who were not perceived as credible, as primary witnesses to the empty tomb.
- *Jesus' post-resurrection appearances:* Many people claimed to have experienced the Risen Jesus, and the appearances follow a common pattern.
- *A courageous community:* A thoroughly shattered group of Jesus' followers was transformed into a community of courageous witnesses after the Resurrection. The total conviction with which the disciples proclaimed the Risen Jesus as a sign of joy and hope is undeniable.

Question: Why was the resurrection of Jesus not a historical event in the usual sense?
Answer: Jesus' *death* was historical in that even nonbelievers would have been able to see Jesus crucified. But only people of faith experienced Jesus after his resurrection. The Risen Jesus could not have been scientifically proven to exist. The Resurrection, in other words, goes beyond history as we know it.

Text Activities: The Resurrection of Jesus

Activity 1

In writing, give any ideas you have in response to the four questions listed above. Write down any questions you have that are not listed on this page.

Activity 2

Imagine yourself as one of the disciples, first hearing the news of Jesus' resurrection. In writing, briefly describe how you, as a disciple, might react to this news.

Activity 3

Write your own evaluation of the four pieces of evidence given on pages 194–197 to support the reality of the Resurrection.

Additional Activities: The Resurrection of Jesus

Comparing the Resurrection Accounts

Divide the class into the four groups that were assigned to read a Gospel from beginning to end in "A Special Reading Assignment," on pages 63–64 of this manual, and have the students read their respective accounts of the Resurrection as those accounts are cited on page 193 of the student text. Instruct the students to do a brief but complete outline of the accounts, like that suggested earlier for the Passion accounts (see "Comparing the Passion Narratives, on page 168 of this manual). Again, the outlines can be recorded on the chalkboard. Compare the accounts for both similarities and differences. The differences are rather glaring. (See John L. McKenzie's *Dictionary of the Bible*, point 2 under "Resurrection," for a summary of the differences.)

By doing this comparison early in your coverage of concept A, the students will be better prepared for any related activities and discussions that follow. Make sure that they are also aware of the fact that these accounts are not attempts at historical reporting but are faith testimonies.

Headlines from Palestine on the Resurrection of Jesus

Chapter 4 of this manual, on daily life in Jesus' time, suggested that the students "publish" newspapers from Jesus' time (see pp. 91–92). If you used that activity, do not worry about repetition here; the earlier experience should only help to make this activity more effective.

The task, for each of several small groups, is to create an issue of a newspaper as it might appear on the Monday following Easter weekend. (The activity can be restricted to a front page only, depending on the amount of time available.) The procedure suggested here is more ambitious than that suggested in chapter 4. It requires at least two class sessions and perhaps some homework as well.

1. Bring several recent newspapers to class. Announce the task of creating an imaginary newspaper from Jesus' time, as it might look on the Monday following all the events of Holy Week—the Last Supper, the trial and execution of Jesus, and just yesterday, the rumors of his rising from the dead.

Distribute the recent newspapers and have the students browse through them, determining all the features they could include in their papers. List all these options on the chalkboard. Possibilities include the following:
- a lead story and other feature articles
- interviews with key persons—the disciples, a Roman soldier who was at the cross, those who gambled for Jesus' cloak, Pontius Pilate, and so on
- editorials by both Jews and Romans, offering their varying perspectives on the events of the weekend
- miscellaneous items such as weather reports, want ads, artwork, photos, and political cartoons

After listing several possibilities, ask the students to vote on which features should be included in their papers.

2. Divide the class into groups of a size equaling the number of newspaper features you have determined. (For example, a class of thirty that has chosen five features would be divided into six groups of five students.)

Give each group the following items: one or more sheets of poster paper (depending on how many pages the newspaper is to have), scissors, glue and tape, crayons or felt-tip markers, a ruler, and many strips of paper of such a width that six of them side-by-side will cover the width of the poster paper. The strips of paper will function as the columns for the newspaper.

3. Each small group should organize itself in terms of who will be responsible for the features of its newspaper. Every student in the group should receive a specific assignment and must get involved in the project. Determine an appropriate amount of time for the group work and announce the time limit to the groups. Then let them begin.

4. After all of the features are completed, the members of each group are to work together as an editorial team to decide where each feature should go on the page, where they would like to add "photos" or other artwork, and so on. They will also need to choose a name for their paper.

5. Conclude the exercise with group presentations of the projects. The group members should explain with reasonable detail the contents of each column or article, but not actually read the material. Encourage applause after each presentation. Announce that the projects will be displayed on the walls of the room for several days so that all can look at them closely.

A TV News Special on the Events of Holy Week

A takeoff on a TV news program was suggested for use with chapter 5 (see p. 105 of this manual). As in the case of the repeated newspaper idea above, do not be concerned that repetition of the news program idea will decrease the effectiveness of the exercise. The concepts considered in chapter 5 and here are so dissimilar that this will be a unique experience regardless of what took place earlier.

1. Begin the exercise by informing the class of the following:
- Today you are going to be asked to do a thirty-minute special report for a "major TV network" in ancient Palestine. The report will interrupt the normal viewing of the gladiator games on a very special Sunday—the first Easter—with news of strange and perhaps significant happenings in Jerusalem. The report should be based on the information already discussed in this course rather than be a totally fictionalized account.

2. Depending on the size of the class, only one report may need to be created, with groups of students either assigned to or volunteering for the following or similar suggested features of the report:
- an "update on the news" report by two or more reporters who summarize the events from Thursday through Sunday morning
- "reporter on the street" interviews with representatives of all the major groups discussed earlier in this course: the Great Sanhedrin, the Apostles, the Pharisees, the Zealots, the Romans, and so on
- in-depth stories of Jesus' background in Galilee, his ministry, the message that got him into trouble, and so on
- editorial comments by one or more famous newspersons
- interviews with Joseph of Arimathea, the witnesses to the empty tomb, the witnesses to the apparitions, and so on

Determine in advance how much time to allow for the preparation, and announce this limit. Your class will probably need one full session for preparation, and each group will need 5 minutes to present its feature to the rest of the class.

3. When the students present the news program, be prepared to play the role of director, making sure things keep moving smoothly. Overall, though, allow the students to present the program without interruption, and jot down questions and issues to discuss later. After the presentation, lead a discussion centering on interesting insights that were expressed during the program.

On the Road to Emmaus

The feature box on page 196 of the student text recounts the story of the disciples on the road to Emmaus. Consider discussing the story and the feature box in class. Begin by reading the story with the students. Then ask them for their insights and discuss the story along the following lines:
- What do you think prevented the disciples from recognizing Jesus right away? Your textbook says that they were too wrapped up in their grief, but can you think of other possible explanations?
- Is it significant that Jesus would "play dumb" and let the disciples talk about their own convictions and feelings first? What does this show us about Jesus? What might it suggest to us about our own relationships with others?
- Jesus reviewed the history of the Jews with the two disciples, showing how the Hebrew Scriptures had been fulfilled in him. The reading mentions only that he started with Moses. What other persons and incidents from Jewish history do you think he might have talked about in that conversation?
- The reading does not say directly what the disciples' response was to all that Jesus said. Rather, it subtly says that they pressed him to stay with them. Why was their desire for Jesus to remain with them so strong? What needs of theirs was he apparently responding to?
- Can you explain through examples from your own life what the reading means when it says that the disciples' eyes were opened and they recognized Jesus in the breaking of the bread? Have you ever had a "real eye-opener" about Jesus and his message, a time in your life when "the lights went on" and you discovered him present?
- Try to describe the feeling of having one's heart burn within. Is this a standard form of heartburn or something else?
- Why is the word *recognize* significant in connection with the story?

Concept B: What Does the Resurrection Mean?

The Resurrection stands as an affirmation that everything Jesus said and did is worthy of our trust. Jesus is, Christians believe, the Christ, the One who transforms all of life. (Pages 198–200 of the student text)

Review Questions: What Does the Resurrection Mean?

Question: What fact about the Resurrection is of most significance to the Christian faith?
Answer: The Resurrection demonstrates the truth of Jesus' claims and teachings about God. It affirms that in everything Jesus said, he spoke the truth.

Question: Why is viewing Jesus as just an extraordinary man rather than the Christ an unacceptable position for Christians?
Answer: The church has a constant commitment to belief in the Resurrection as *the* central characteristic of Christian faith. As stated earlier, Jesus was one of three things: a lunatic, a con artist, or exactly who he professed to be—the Christ.

Question: What is the origin and meaning of the term *paschal mystery?*
Answer: The term *paschal mystery* builds upon the theme of the slaughter of the paschal lambs as part of the Passover celebration, and it refers to the profound meaning that Jesus' death and resurrection can hold for many aspects of human life. The redemptive meaning of the paschal mystery is reflected in the recurring pattern of dying and rising found in many areas of life, including nature and our pain experiences.

Text Activities: What Does the Resurrection Mean?

Activity 4

Copy and complete this statement: *In my own life, I see the paschal mystery most clearly reflected in _____ because _____.*

Activity 5

Look back at the four reasons that the Resurrection is of critical importance to Christian faith. Choose the reason most significant to you and explain your choice in a paragraph.

Additional Activities: What Does the Resurrection Mean?

What Does It All Mean?

The student text identifies these four major implications of the Resurrection:
- It affirms Jesus' teachings.
- It verifies Jesus as the Messiah.
- It transforms our understanding of human life.
- It reveals the presence of the paschal mystery in all of life.

In this activity, the students will examine these implications more closely.

Divide the class into four groups. Assign each group one of the four implications of the Resurrection and instruct them to do the following:
- Determine three insights not already mentioned in the textbook that can be drawn from that implication if it is true.
- Determine if a particular age-group would be most affected by, and therefore most concerned with, the implication.
- Identify what is most important about this implication for the lives of young people today.

Give the students 20 minutes or more to discuss. Then call for brief summaries of their discussions and comment appropriately.

A Field Trip to a Cemetery

Arrange for the class to visit a cemetery. Mention beforehand that there may be a tendency on their part to fool around a bit, primarily as a cover-up for the discomfort felt when confronted with the reality of death. Encourage them to cooperate and take the exercise seriously.

1. While at the cemetery, the students should spend their time quietly walking about, reading headstones, and trying to imagine the life story of the person buried in each plot.

2. After returning from the trip, spend a class session discussing the students' thoughts, feelings, questions, and insights.

As part of the process, consider having the students construct their own "headstones" using poster paper or cardboard and felt-tip markers or crayons. On one side of the headstone, they should print their name and an epitaph they feel would be appropriate if they were to die tomorrow. On the other side, they should print an epitaph they think might suit them if they live to age seventy. The results could be shared with the class and displayed on the walls.

Questions for discussion include these:
- What would you do tonight if you knew you were going to die tomorrow. Why?
- Have you considered the question of life after death? Do you believe in life after death? Why or why not?
- If we took the possibility of eternal life with God seriously, how would it affect the way we live today?
- Have you experienced the death of a loved one or someone you knew quite well? If so, would you be willing to share the experience and what you learned from it? [On this point, be sensitive to the students' feelings and their right to refuse to share such information. Generally, however, young people are willing to share this information with remarkable openness.]

Recognizing the Paschal Mystery

Chapter 10 of the student text includes two illustrations that try to capture and express the reality of the paschal mystery (see pp. 198–199). Consider using the illustrations in these ways:
1. Divide the class into small groups and ask each group to interpret the illustrations for the class.

2. Similarly, but as a homework assignment, ask the individual students to write a reflection on the meaning of the illustrations. Then share the best efforts with the class.
3. Based on the text's examples, ask the students to find in nature and other areas of life further symbols of the presence of the paschal mystery.

Concept C: Recognizing the Risen Jesus Today

Christians today can encounter the Risen Jesus in the Eucharist, in the community of believers, and in remembering and living out the Dream of Jesus, the Kingdom of God. (Pages 201–202 of the student text)

Review Questions: Recognizing the Risen Jesus Today

Question: Why do some Christians have difficulty experiencing Jesus as present in the Eucharist?
Answer: Those who make little or no attempt to recall and live out Jesus' message have a difficult time fully experiencing Jesus as present in the Eucharist. The Eucharist is not magical. Only "those with the eyes to see" will see.

Question: In what sense can a memory be "alive and present"?
Answer: A fragrance or a popular song first experienced several years ago can create within us today the emotions associated with the original experience. And even more so, we never truly forget good friends or relatives who died when we were much younger. They continue to live within us, sometimes in very real and powerful ways.

Question: What is the key criterion for judging if someone is a Christian?
Answer: Whether the person is willing to let his or her life be shaped and led by the power of Jesus' life and message

Text Activities: Recognizing the Risen Jesus Today

Activity 6

Read the story of Doubting Thomas in John 20:24–29. Then imagine yourself as Thomas and write a letter to another disciple who has asked for help in dealing with doubts about Jesus.

Activity 7

In writing, describe an incident from your life that stands out as an encounter with the Risen Jesus.

Additional Activities: Recognizing the Risen Jesus Today

Developing "the Eyes to See"

This activity explores the falsity of the notion that it was easier for people to believe in Jesus when he walked among them in ancient Palestine

1. Begin the activity with a summary and comment on the point made at the beginning of the student text section "If Only We Could See Him Too" (p. 201). Include especially the following comments:
   - People today often hold the illusion that it was easier for people in Jesus' time to believe in him, because he walked among them. The fact is, however, that faith in Jesus was demanding and difficult then, and it continues to take effort today.
   - As your textbook suggests, today's Christians can encounter Jesus in three main ways: in the Eucharist, in the community of believers, and in remembering and living out Jesus' Dream of the Kingdom of God. Let's take a closer look at these suggestions.

2. Divide the class into three groups, one for each of the three ways of encountering Jesus suggested in the student text. If the class is rather large, break each group into smaller sections. Then assign these tasks:
   - For your assigned way of encountering Jesus, identify five reasons that it often *fails* to lead to a true or satisfying encounter with the Risen Jesus. What keeps the encounter from happening, or at least from happening in a way that satisfies your needs?
   - Then, for each of the five reasons for failure, identify at least one way in which that obstacle could be overcome *by and for young people*.

   The three groups will have varying levels of difficulty with their assignment. The students who are assigned the Eucharist, for example, may finish their work rather quickly (at least the part in which they have to identify the problems with the liturgy!). The most difficult of the three assignments is the third one, focused on remembering and living out Jesus' Dream. If one group seems to lag significantly behind the others in completing its assignment, reduce the number of answers that group has to identify from five to, say, three.

3. Ask for group reports, invite further comments on each report from the class, and comment appropriately.

Encountering Jesus in Prayer

This exercise explores a fourth way Christians can encounter the Risen Jesus (in addition to the three ways discussed on pp. 201–202 of the student text). That is, the exercise explores private prayer. Here you will use a fantasy prayer, or guided imagery experience, an approach most young people find helpful and enjoyable. It would be best to find an atmosphere more conducive to prayer than the classroom, but the exercise normally works regardless of where it is conducted.

1. Begin the activity with a comment such as this:
   - Another way Christians can encounter the Risen Jesus, besides the three ways mentioned in your textbook, is in private prayer. Many people have difficulty with prayer because their understanding of it is too narrow, too restricted. Today I want to share with you a different kind of prayer that involves your entire person, especially your imagination.

This experience is meant to help you get in touch with the presence of Jesus in a more personal way. Your cooperation will help us all have a good experience.

2. Ask the students to begin by relaxing as much as possible. If they are restricted to their chairs, this may be a bit difficult but not impossible. Adjust the following instructions to fit the environment.
- Close your eyes and try to imagine yourself alone in the room. [Pause.]
- Take several deep but quiet breaths, allowing your breathing to become deep and steady rather than shallow and hurried. [Pause.]
- Now imagine that your body, from your feet gradually up to your head, is growing more and more relaxed, free of tension, at ease, comfortable. [If time permits, you can slowly move the relaxation from one part of the body to another, asking the students to concentrate briefly on each part and then allow it to relax and be free of tension.]

3. When students are relaxed yet attentive, ask them to go along on the following fantasy. As you speak, pause for a moment at the ellipses (. . .).
- A sculptor has been engaged to make a statue of you. The statue is ready and you go to his studio to have a look at it before it appears in public. He gives you the key to the room where your statue is so that you can see it for yourself and take all the time you want to examine it alone.

    You open the door. The room is dark. There, in the middle of the room is your statue, covered with a cloth . . . You walk up to the statue and slowly take the cloth off . . .

    Then you step back and look at your statue. What is your first impression? . . . Are you pleased or dissatisfied? . . . Notice all the details in your statue . . . How big it is . . . what material it is made of . . . Walk around it . . . see it from different angles . . . Look at it from far, then come closer and look at the details . . . Touch the statue . . . notice whether it is rough or smooth . . . cold or warm to the touch. What parts of the statue do you like? . . . What parts of the statue do you dislike? . . .

    Say something to your statue . . . What does the statue reply? . . . What do you say in return? . . . Keep on speaking as long as you or the statue have something to say . . .

    Now become the statue . . . What does it feel like to be your statue? . . . What kind of existence do you have as the statue? . . . .

    I want you to imagine now that, while you are your statue, Jesus walks into the room . . . How does he look at you? . . . What do you feel while he looks at you? . . . What does he say to you? . . . What do you reply? . . . Continue the dialogue as long as either Jesus or you have something to say . . .

    After a while Jesus goes away . . . Now return to yourself and look at the statue again . . . Is there any change in the statue? . . . Is there any change in you or in your feelings? . . .

    Now say good-bye to your statue . . . Take a minute or so to do this and then open your eyes. [Anthony de Mello, *Sadhana: A Way to God*, pp. 87–88]

4. When the students have all "returned" from their fantasy, discuss the *experience* of the exercise with them, without asking them to reveal the contents of their individual fantasy. For example:
- Did you enjoy it?
- How do you feel now compared with when the exercise began?
- Would you say you learned something about yourself during this exercise? Did you learn something about Jesus?

The reason for discussing the experience rather than the content of the prayer is to respect the students' privacy. This particular fantasy can be extremely personal, involving reflection on one's self-image, body, and so on. On the other hand, a marvelous discussion on the details of this experience can be had when some trust in the group has been established and the students are engaged voluntarily. Consider *inviting* the students to share insights gained from the experience, but do not pressure them to do so.

5. Close the discussion along these lines:
- Though this may come as a surprise to you, what you have experienced today was actually prayer in its fullest sense. Prayer is really a dialog with the ever-present God. Experienced in this way, prayer can be refreshing, moving, and deeply satisfying. Jesus is always and everywhere present to us. In prayer we strive to make ourselves present to him!

Note: Anthony de Mello's *Sadhana: A Way to God* has numerous other prayer exercises that could be used or adapted in other situations.

Concept D: The Ascension of Jesus

The most important point that the scriptural authors wished to teach by describing the Ascension was this: Following his resurrection, Jesus passed totally into the presence of God, who is always and everywhere with us in the world. Thus, Jesus can now be more truly present to us than he could possibly have been as he walked the earth. (Pages 203–205 of the student text)

Review Questions: The Ascension of Jesus

Question: What human limitation makes it difficult to understand the Ascension?
Answer: We cannot escape images of space and time in our speaking, writing, and even thinking.

Question: What was the main lesson that the scriptural authors wished to teach by describing the Ascension?
Answer: That following his resurrection, Jesus passed totally into the presence of God

Text Activities: The Ascension of Jesus

Activity 8

Write a description of what you hope heaven will be like.

Activity 9

List at least five implications that the following statement has for the lives of young people: *God is not "out there" but rather "right here."*

Additional Activities: The Ascension of Jesus

Heaven on Earth

Assign text activity 8 as homework. Collect and evaluate the responses and then select particularly creative ones to share with the class. Consider using the students' work as the focus of a class discussion along the following lines:

   1. Ask the students to privately reread their description of heaven and to try to identify, with only one or two words, each major characteristic of their vision of heaven. Use these questions to help them:
- What does heaven look like?
- Who is there?
- What are they doing there?
- What feelings do you identify with heaven?
- How do people relate to one another in heaven, if at all?

   2. Make five vertical columns on the chalkboard and label them "Me," "People," "God," "Nature," and "Misc."

   After the students have had a few minutes to review their descriptions of heaven, ask them to call out all the key words or phrases they came up with. As they call these out, ask if the things or realities named have to do directly with any of the columns on the board. Write the items in the appropriate columns. For example, if someone says that heaven means "I'm rich," put that under "Me." If they say, "Good relationships," write that under "People." And so on. Try to avoid putting items in the "Misc." column, but do so for any item that just does not fit anywhere else.

   3. Comment on any unusual or striking insights that are triggered by the activity. Then ask the students to recall their work with chapter 6 and Jesus' proclamation of the Kingdom of God. Remind them that Jesus' vision of the Kingdom of God is his Dream, and ask them to consider and discuss the following question:
- What connections do you see between Jesus' Dream of the Kingdom of God and your idea of what heaven might be like? For example, could it be said that if people lived and acted out of the vision of the Kingdom proclaimed by Jesus, we would almost literally have "heaven on earth"?

   4. Close with a comment such as the following:
- Many people live with their heart and hope focused so much on getting to heaven after death that they forget to truly live while they are here. We can gain a sense of what heaven will be like by living out Jesus' vision and values as fully as possible today. And by doing that, we can experience the reality that the Risen Jesus is "right here and right now," not "out there."

Where Is Heaven?

Remind the students of their discussion of the ancient Jewish worldview, from chapter 8. Take some time to look over the illustration of the worldview of the first-century Jews (and Gentiles) on page 204 of the student text and connect that worldview with the Gospels' description of Jesus' ascension "into heaven."

Concept E: Pentecost

With the gift of the Holy Spirit at Pentecost, Jesus' disciples came to the full realization that the Jesus of History is the Christ of Faith, the Son of God, and our Lord. Pentecost marks the birthday of the church. (Pages 206–209 of the student text)

Review Questions: Pentecost

Question: Why was the first Pentecost a significant happening in the life of the early church? What is the message of the Pentecost story?
Answer: The first Pentecost was significant in the life of the early church because it was then that the disciples began a whole new way of living in communion with one another. Pentecost is often referred to as "the birthday of the church."
The message of the Pentecost story is that when a disheartened and frightened people encounter the spirit of the Risen Jesus, they are transformed by the experience.

Question: What three titles for Jesus reflect the early Christian community's post-Resurrection, post-Pentecost understanding of him?
Answer: The Christ, the Son of God, and *our Lord*

Question: Define the doctrine of the Trinity.
Answer: The church's formal proclamation that Jesus is one of three divine persons—Father, Son, and Holy Spirit—in the one God

Question: Why was referring to Jesus as "the Lord" or "our Lord" a radical step for early Christians?
Answer: The Christians were proclaiming a divine identity for Jesus, a unity with Yahweh that was absolutely beyond understanding.

A Text Activity: Pentecost

Activity 10

List at least five titles or names for Jesus that reflect the meaning he holds for you, or list at least five titles or names for Jesus that might appeal to young people in general.

Additional Activities: Pentecost

The Disciples' Dilemma

This exercise is intended to help the students identify with the disciples in the choices the disciples had to make immediately after the Resurrection.

Handout 10–A

1. Distribute handout 10–A, "The Disciples' Dilemma," to everyone and ask them to complete it individually according to the instructions at the top of the handout.

2. When all have finished the handout, divide the students into groups *according to their choice on the handout.* That is, call for all those who opted for number 1 to raise their hand, and then organize them into a group. Do the same for each option. (If any one group turns out to be quite large, divide it into smaller groups to facilitate the next part of the exercise.) Students who opted to develop a response under number 8 on the handout will have to remain alone.

3. In the small groups, the students should develop an argument supporting the decision they made. Why is their decision an appropriate response to the Resurrection? As an added touch, the groups could develop a slogan to explain the option they chose. For instance, those who chose number 1 might develop the slogan "Spread the Word." Those who chose number 2 might say, "Live the Good News now."

4. Give each group 5 minutes to "evangelize" the class by explaining its chosen course of action and trying to convince others to join the group. Finally, state that all students must make a final decision on which group to join, given the presentations. Students who actually decide to switch groups should explain what convinced them to do so.

5. Close the exercise by noting that this dilemma was essentially what confronted the disciples, and the attempt to resolve this dilemma eventually led to the development of the early community of faith, which is now called the church.

Handout 10–B

Reflecting on the Titles for Jesus

Distribute handout 10–B, "The Titles for Jesus," and have the students follow the directions at the top of the page. When everyone is done, develop two lists on the chalkboard, based on the handout column titled "Humanity or Divinity?" In other words, one list is to reflect titles that emphasize Jesus' humanity; the other is to reflect titles that emphasize his divinity. Rely on a vote to determine which titles from the handout belong on which list. When you come across significant disagreement or a title with many question marks, discuss the title until some consensus is reached.

Then consider the students' answers from the handout column titled "Before or After Death?" Most likely the students tended to name titles that emphasize Jesus' humanity as those given him *before* his death and resurrection, and titles emphasizing Jesus' divinity as given him *after* his death and resurrection. Remark on this tendency.

The Disciples' Dilemma

Imagine that you are one of the disciples who lived and worked with Jesus during his ministry in Palestine. You have just experienced the Last Supper, the trial and execution of Jesus, and now his resurrection from the dead. The question you face is, What do I do now? Below are some options that you have. Circle the number of the one that you feel is right for you and most in line with Jesus' message.

1. Go out into the streets and the synagogues to announce that Jesus is the Christ and that the people are to repent and believe in him.
2. Seek out the poor and oppressed people and search for ways to serve them.
3. Organize people who feel like you do into social-action groups.
4. Go off alone to pray and reflect on the meaning of the incredible events.
5. Organize classes to inform people about Jesus and the lessons you learned from him.
6. Begin work on a written record of what you have experienced, while the thoughts and feelings are still fresh in your memory.
7. Wait until someone tells you what to do.
8. Can you think of any other option? If so, write it down here.

_____

_____

The Titles for Jesus

Listed at the right are many of the titles given to Jesus in the Christian Scriptures. You are asked to do the following:

- In the column titled "Humanity or Divinity?" print an *H* next to each title that you think emphasizes Jesus' **humanity**. Print a *D* next to each title that you think emphasizes his **divinity** as God. Put a question mark next to any title you are unsure about.
- In the column titled "Before or After Death?" print a *B* next to each title that you think may have been given to Jesus **before** his death and resurrection. Print an *A* next to each title that you think he received only **after** his death and resurrection. Put a question mark next to any title you are unsure about.

Humanity or Divinity?   **Before or After Death?**

1. Lord
2. Servant of God
3. Holy One
4. Prince of Life
5. Messiah
6. Nazarene
7. Prophet
8. Judge of the living and the dead
9. Redeemer
10. Son of God
11. Savior
12. Master
13. Rabbi
14. Son of David
15. Son of Man
16. Bread of Life
17. Teacher
18. Christ
19. Good Shepherd
20. Son of Abraham
21. The new Adam
22. Firstborn of all creation
23. The Way, the Truth, and the Life
24. Image of God
25. God
26. The Anointed One
27. Son of Joseph
28. Lamb of God
29. Carpenter's son
30. Emmanuel
31. High Priest
32. Word of God

Handout 10–B: Permission to reproduce this handout for classroom use is granted

CHAPTER 11

Paul: Apostle to the Gentiles

Major Concepts

A. **A Brief Review:** All of the Christian Testament was written from a post-Resurrection faith perspective. But whereas the Gospels focus on the Jesus of History, who walked and preached in first-century Palestine, the remaining books—especially the epistles of Paul—focus on the risen Christ of Faith and the concerns of the early church.

B. **Getting to Know Paul:** Without Paul, early Christianity might have remained little more than a small Jewish sect, and over the course of time, it might well have died away. Paul's history uniquely prepared him for his special ministry to the Gentile world.

C. **The Damascus Experience:** Paul's encounter with the Risen Jesus on the road to Damascus was an experience of both conversion and vocation.

D. **Paul's Missionary Work:** Paul's missionary work included three main journeys to cities throughout the northern and eastern Mediterranean region of the Roman Empire. Paul founded Christian communities in many of the cities he visited. Over the course of his missionary activity, he wrote his epistles to these communities.

A Note to the Teacher: Additional Activities in This Chapter

The primary purpose of this chapter is to provide a context for understanding the theology of Paul, which is described in chapter 12. Also, the content of this chapter does not lend itself readily to experiential learning activities like those suggested for the preceding chapters in this course. The activities that are suggested here are essentially optional approaches to group reflection and discussion. You may choose to just focus on the review questions and activities provided in the student text, making sure that the students comprehend the material and moving through the chapter rather quickly.

Concept A: A Brief Review

All of the Christian Testament was written from a post-Resurrection faith perspective. But whereas the Gospels focus on the Jesus of History, who walked and preached in first-century Palestine, the remaining books—especially the epistles of Paul—focus on the risen Christ of Faith and the concerns of the early church. (Pages 211–216 of the student text)

Review Questions: A Brief Review

Question: How did the ancient Jews view death by crucifixion?
Answer: As a certain sign that the one crucified had been cursed by God

Question: Which writings of the Christian Testament were produced first?
Answer: Letters that Paul wrote to various church communities

Question: In what ways do the Epistles differ from the Gospels?
Answer: The Gospels were a special literary form that emerged to preserve the story of Jesus and his message, but epistles, or letters, were a common means of communication of the day. And like the other non-Gospel books of the Christian Testament, the Epistles virtually leave out the language and images for Jesus that dominate the Gospel portrait. Rather, these books focus on the attempts by the early church to come to terms with the *meaning* of Jesus. The Epistles, for example, offer little about the actual words and actions of Jesus while he walked the roads of Palestine.

Question: Why would Paul not have expected his letters to be preserved?
Answer: He accepted the widespread conviction that the Risen Jesus would soon return in glory "to judge the living and the dead," and that the world as the people knew it would then end.

A Text Activity: A Brief Review

Activity 1

Looking at the diagram above, list the understandings of Jesus held by the church, in the order in which those understandings developed. Next, match the following persons with the understanding of Jesus they would most likely hold: *a fifth grader, a senior-high student, an atheist, a non-Christian Jew of Jesus' day, the pope, yourself.*

Additional Activities: A Brief Review

Putting Things in Order

This activity is designed to reinforce the students' understanding of the church's evolving sense of Jesus' identity, as that evolving sense is summarized by the diagram on page 214 of the student text. Simply put, the students are to take a scrambled list of the seven understandings of Jesus (Jesus of Nazareth, Special Teacher, Prophet, etc.) and organize them in the proper sequence. They are to do this *without* referring to the text. You can choose to direct the activity in one of three ways:

Option 1: Create a master sheet of the understandings of Jesus by dividing an 8½-by-11-inch piece of paper into seven equal sections, one section for each of the seven understandings, and labeling each section appropriately. Then make enough photocopies of the master for everyone in your class. Cut the copies into strips, creating one set of understandings for each student, and distribute the sets to the class. Ask the students to individually do the activity at their desk, while you circulate and comment as needed. This approach best ensures that all the students grasp the material.

Option 2: Ask the students to do the activity in small groups, each group using a set of seven cards that you provide.

Option 3: Create one set of large cards (e.g., 8½ by 11 inches) with a piece of double-faced tape on the back of each card. Ask the students as individuals or perhaps in pairs to come forward and organize the understandings by sticking them in the proper sequence on the chalkboard. This approach can be repeated profitably only a few times, so it limits the number of students involved but reduces the time required for the activity.

In the Eyes of Young People

Text activity 1 can be adapted as an additional activity. For example, assign the text activity as homework. Then, in class, write the understandings of Jesus down the chalkboard in the proper sequence. Ask the students, perhaps in small groups, to come to some consensus on what percentage of young people their age would choose each of the seven understandings of Jesus as reflecting their primary image of him. The total of the seven percentages must equal 100. Discuss why the various understandings have greater or lesser appeal to young people. Consider asking the students to repeat the exercise for other age-groups. For example, how might their parents respond to the understandings and why? What might be the implications if the difference between the young people's majority understanding and their parents' majority understanding is significant?

Reading and Discussion on the First Letter to the Thessalonians

The feature box on pages 212–213 of the student text describes the nature of letters in Paul's day. In class, have the students read the feature box and comment on any points they find particularly interesting. Then note that the First Letter to the Thessalonians was the first of Paul's letters, written from Corinth around 51 C.E. As a relatively short epistle, it can serve as a basic model of Paul's letters.

Divide the class into two groups. Then direct a class reading of the First Letter to the Thessalonians, asking members from each group to alternate reading the paragraphs. After a member from one group reads a paragraph, ask the other group to comment on how that passage fits in the organization of Paul's letters as outlined in the feature box (i.e., is the passage part of the greeting, the body, the final instructions?). Also ask if the paragraph reflects any interesting insights into Paul himself. This exercise will relay the flavor of Paul's early writing as well as the nature of the Epistles.

Concept B: Getting to Know Paul

Without Paul, early Christianity might have remained little more than a small Jewish sect, and over the course of time, it might well have died away. Paul's history uniquely prepared him for his special ministry to the Gentile world. (Pages 217–221 of the student text)

Review Questions: Getting to Know Paul

Question: Briefly describe Paul's significance in the development of the Christian church.
Answer: Without Paul, early Christianity might have remained little more than a small Jewish sect, and over the course of time, it might well have died away. It was Paul who spread the early Gospel proclamation beyond the limits of Judaism and into the Gentile world.

Question: Why would Paul have felt at home among both Jews and Gentiles? Why does he have two names in the Christian Testament?
Answer: Paul was born a Jew, but his family had been granted the rare privilege of Roman citizenship. This combination of Jewish faith and Roman citizenship accounts for his two names—*Saul* being his Jewish name and *Paul* being his name in Roman or Greek circles.

Question: What connection can be made between Paul and the Diaspora?
Answer: Paul was raised in a Jewish colony in Tarsus that was part of the Diaspora. In his later missionary work, he would encounter and frequently experience conflicts with such colonies throughout the Roman Empire.

Question: Describe Paul's initial relationship with the Christian church.
Answer: As a Pharisee, Paul initially persecuted Christians. He was fanatical in his desire to destroy the early church.

A Text Activity: Getting to Know Paul

Activity 2

Before reading further in this book, read any one of Paul's epistles. Based solely on that epistle, jot down your impressions of who Paul was and what kind of person he was. Then compare your impressions with what is said about him in this course, briefly noting any similarities and differences.

Additional Activities: Getting to Know Paul

Further Reflection and Discussion

Concept B does not require extensive treatment. If you care to expand the discussion prompted by the review questions and the text activity, consider the following options:

Option 1: Divide the class into two groups. Assign one group the pro position and the other group the con position regarding the following statement: *Because Paul was a good, faithful Jew, his hatred for and persecution of the Christians was reasonable and justified.*

Option 2: Reinforce how uniquely qualified Paul was to serve the role that he did. Write the following list of Paul's characteristics on the chalkboard:
- a faithful Jew
- a Roman citizen
- a small, physically weak person
- one who never knew Jesus
- a student of Greek philosophy
- a child of the Diaspora
- a persecutor of Christians
- a Pharisee
- a laborer (tent maker)

Then, in open conversation with the class, discuss why and how Paul's ministry would have been affected if any of the characteristics had *not* been true of Paul.

Concept C: The Damascus Experience

Paul's encounter with the Risen Jesus on the road to Damascus was an experience of both conversion and vocation. (Pages 222–224 of the student text)

Review Questions: The Damascus Experience

Question: What criterion was required for recognition as an Apostle in the early church? On what grounds did Paul claim to meet that requirement?
Answer: To be recognized as an Apostle in the early church, one had to have a personal relationship with Jesus. On the basis of his encounter with the Risen Jesus on the road to Damascus, Paul claimed to meet that requirement.

Question: What can be said with certainty regarding Paul's experience on the road to Damascus?
Answer: Whatever happened to Paul on that road was such a profound encounter with the Risen Christ that it radically changed his life.

Question: Define the terms *conversion* and *vocation* and explain their relevance to Paul's Damascus experience.
Answer: Conversion can be used to describe a radical change in, or deepening of, one's attitude toward God and religion. *Vocation* is based on a Latin word meaning "call." Paul's Damascus experience was one of both conversion

and vocation: conversion from persecutor of Christians to believer in Jesus, and vocation in the call to be a missionary to the Gentile world.

A Text Activity: The Damascus Experience

Activity 3

In a short paper, compare and contrast Luke's description of Paul's Damascus experience (Acts 9:1–22) with Paul's own description of the event (Galatians 1:15–24; 2:1).

Additional Activities: The Damascus Experience

Dramatic Readings or Skits on the Damascus Experience

Ask the students, in groups of four or five, to prepare either a dramatic reading or a skit based on Acts 9:1–22. You may choose one or the other approach based on the students' abilities or assign the reading approach to some groups and the skit approach to others. In the case of skits, state that girls can take the roles of the male characters, including Paul himself. Encourage the students to interpret the scene as they wish. Discuss their presentations.

Through the Eyes of Ananias

Chapter 5 of this manual recommended William J. Bausch's book *Storytelling: Imagination and Faith* (Mystic, CT: Twenty-third Publications, 1984) as a fine source of stories that can enliven this course on Jesus. In his book, Bausch retells the story of Paul's Damascus experience—or more specifically, Paul's recovery from that event—from the perspective of Ananias, "'a simple cobbler,'" the one called by God to heal Paul of his blindness. It is an engaging and touching tale of a simple person called to great things by God.

In Bausch's story, Ananias, at the end of his life, has no idea what ever became of the man on whom he laid his hands years earlier. But God tells Ananias as he lies dying, "'Don't worry, Ananias, about how much you have done—or how little. You were there when I wanted you to be there. And that, "my little shoemaker of a saint, is all that really matters"'" (p. 193).

A well-delivered reading of the story will engage your students' imagination and "humanize" a story that, in its biblical presentation, may appear to skeptical students as too fantastic to be taken seriously.

Playing Scholar

The student text states on page 223 that scholars argue about the nature of Paul's Damascus experience. Suggest to the students that three basic options are available for interpreting the event:
- It may have been a historical incident that took place just as described in the Scriptures.
- It may have been strictly an interior experience of Paul's, around which an imaginative story eventually developed.

- Or what we find in the Scriptures may be a combination of those two extremes, that is, a historical event that took on some imaginative characteristics in the recounting of the story over time.

Ask the students to choose their personal preference from these three options. You may want to do this as a "forced choice activity," creating three signs representing the options, placing them in different corners of the room, and asking the students to congregate under their preference. Or assign each of the options to different rows of desks or chairs, asking the students to take a seat according to their preference. In either case, invite representatives of each of the three options to explain why they chose as they did. Close the discussion by asking if the *significance or meaning* of Paul's Damascus experience is altered in any way if one of the options is in fact true. In other words, is the event in any way less significant if it was "only" an interior experience of Paul's?

Concept D: Paul's Missionary Work

Paul's missionary work included three main journeys to cities throughout the northern and eastern Mediterranean region of the Roman Empire. Paul founded Christian communities in many of the cities he visited. Over the course of his missionary activity, he wrote his epistles to these communities. (Pages 225–233 of the student text)

Review Questions: Paul's Missionary Work

Question: Summarize the controversy regarding the entry of Gentiles into the early church. What decision was made at the Jerusalem Council?
Answer: The controversy was whether Gentiles had to become Jews before they could be baptized into Christianity. At the Jerusalem Council, it was decided that the mission to the Gentile community could continue without demanding that the Gentiles become Jews before being accepted into the church.

Question: Why is Paul's letter to the Romans considered his masterpiece? From where was it written? Where does it appear in the Christian Testament and why?
Answer: Paul's letter to the Romans is considered his masterpiece because it reflects his lengthy missionary experience, his maturity as an Apostle, and his insightful understanding of the meaning of Christian faith. It contains his strongest statements regarding the relationship between the Jewish Law and the faith of Christians. Paul wrote the letter from Corinth. It appears before all his other letters in the Christian Testament because of its length.

Question: What false accusation against Paul led to a riot and his arrest in Jerusalem? On what basis did Paul request to be tried in Rome?
Answer: Paul was mistakenly accused of bringing a Gentile convert into one of the inner courts of the Temple, beyond the barrier that excluded non-Jews. When Paul was to be tried in Jerusalem, he resisted this and, based on his Roman citizenship, appealed to the tribunal of Caesar in Rome.

Question: When, where, and how was Paul executed?
Answer: According to tradition, Paul was executed sometime around 67 C.E. in Rome. As a Roman citizen, he would have been beheaded.

Text Activities: Paul's Missionary Work

Activity 4

Using an encyclopedia or other sources, write a short paper on any one of the cities in which Paul established a Christian community. (See the map on page 226 for city names.)

Activity 5

Rewrite Paul's famous description of love (1 Corinthians 13:1–13) in language that would appeal to young people today. Use as few of Paul's original words as possible.

Additional Activities: Paul's Missionary Work

Map Readings

For each of Paul's journeys described on pages 227–230 of the student text, go over the locations that Paul visited, shown on the map on page 226.

Reflecting on the Letter to the Romans

The student text identifies the Letter to the Romans as Paul's masterpiece. It was written about eight years after the First Letter to the Thessalonians. The Letter to the Romans is long and complex, so it is not recommended that the students read this epistle in a way similar to that suggested earlier for the letter to the Thessalonians. However, to illustrate Paul's growth as a thinker and writer, ask several volunteers to randomly select a few paragraphs from Romans and read them to the class. Then invite comments from the class regarding the content of the passages, what the passages reflect about the development of Paul's thought over eight years, how the passages might have been received by Paul's readers, and so on. Remark that the meaning of some of Paul's complex writing will become clearer in the next chapter of the course.

An Epitaph for Paul

Remind the students of Paul's death by beheading in Rome. Then have them, either as individuals or in small groups, create a fitting epitaph for Paul, one that captures in a few words his significance in the history of the church. (Suggestion: Tell the students that they cannot simply say, "Paul lost his head over the church"!) You may wish to have the students use poster paper to actually create an imaginary headstone for Paul's grave, acknowledging that this was not the custom in his day but that creating a headstone for an epitaph is an interesting exercise for us. Have the students share the results of their work and, if headstones are made, post the most creative ones.

Reflecting on the Book of Revelation

Many students have a high interest in the Book of Revelation, often because of the emphasis placed on the book by fundamentalists. Have the students read and then discuss the feature box about this fascinating book, on pages 232–233 of the student text. Does the feature box support or contradict any of their past impressions of the book? In what ways? You may choose to illustrate the basic points raised in the feature box by calling on students to randomly select a passage from Revelation, read it, and comment on it in light of the feature box information. What point raised in the feature box is illustrated by the passage?

CHAPTER 12

The Letters of Paul: Proclaiming Christ Crucified and Risen

Major Concepts

A. **An Introductory Overview of Paul's Epistles:** When reading Paul's epistles, we must remember that they are directed to small Christian communities in particular places, times, and cultures. The letters are responses to issues in those communities, and they reflect the lessons Paul learned from his Damascus experience.

B. **Salvation Through Christ Crucified:** The Jewish concept of sin as the breaking of relationships underlies Paul's notion of salvation in and through Christ. Paul realized that the people could not earn salvation by following the letter of the Law. Love, not the Law, was the goal. This understanding by Paul reflected Jesus' teaching that the person who fully loves fulfills everything written in the Law.

C. **Salvation and Contemporary Culture:** An awareness of the pervasiveness of sin in the world and in our personal life is essential to understanding Paul's writings on salvation. One manifestation of sin in the lives of modern Western people is the hunger for a sense of meaning and purpose. Only Jesus and his message can fully satisfy that hunger.

D. **The Church as the Body of Christ:** Paul's Damascus experience awakened him to the reality that Christ is encountered in other people and, in a special way, in the community of believers, the church. Paul expressed this awareness in his writings on the church as "the body of Christ."

Concept A:
An Introductory Overview of Paul's Epistles

When reading Paul's epistles, we must remember that they are directed to small Christian communities in particular places, times, and cultures. The letters are responses to issues in those communities, and they reflect the lessons Paul learned from his Damascus experience. (Pages 235–239 of the student text)

Review Questions:
An Introductory Overview of Paul's Epistles

Question: In what sense are Paul's letters only one side of a two-sided conversation?
Answer: Several of Paul's letters were written as *responses* to issues that had emerged within the early Christian communities.

Question: What issues are most often the main focus of Paul's epistles?
Answer: Conflicts within the early Christian communities and matters involving personal morality and spirituality among the believers

Question: What are the two main themes of Paul's letters? What experience forms the background for these two themes?
Answer: The two main themes are the following:
- Salvation is found in and through Jesus the Christ.
- The church is "the body of Christ."

Paul's experience of the Risen Jesus on the road to Damascus forms the background for these two themes.

Question: List the various expressions Paul uses for the activity of God in the lives of people.
Answer: Salvation, redemption, righteousness, justification, reconciliation

Text Activities:
An Introductory Overview of Paul's Epistles

Activity 1

Write a paragraph on what being saved by Jesus means to you, based on your current understanding of Jesus' message.

Activity 2

Paul's writings indicate that a personal encounter with God is possible. In a paragraph, tell about someone—perhaps yourself—who believes he or she has had such an encounter with God.

Additional Activities:
An Introductory Overview of Paul's Epistles

Finish the Story

As either a homework assignment or a small-group activity during class, ask the students to write a one-page essay or create a skit spinning off from one of the three modern-day scenes described on page 235 of the student text. Each scene raises a question about what it means to be saved by Jesus.

You can leave the assignment rather open-ended, allowing the students' imagination to run freely. Or you may require that the essays or skits make a certain point. For example, you might tell the students to include a statement that represents their own understanding of what it means to be saved by Jesus. Or consider asking them to imagine themselves as the main character in one of the text situations. How would *they* respond if they were that person?

If some students write essays, select the most creative essays and share them with the class. If some small groups create skits, arrange for them to perform the skits, and then invite comments by the class on each group's interpretation of its chosen situation.

What's Missing?

Bring a personal letter of your own to class, either one you have received or a copy of one you have written to someone else. Select a letter that refers to many people and events that are familiar to you but will not be familiar to the students. Also, of course, make sure the letter does not reveal information you wish to keep private.

Ask the students to find a piece of scrap paper for taking notes. Tell them that you are going to slowly read a letter to them. Their task is to jot down any questions that come to mind as they listen. No question they have is too obvious or unimportant to be included.

After you read the letter, ask the students to call out any questions they jotted down. You may want to list these on the chalkboard. Then make the point that any personal letter is always, in a sense, one side of a two-sided conversation. Your letter makes sense to you only because you already know the person who sent or received it, you are familiar with the people and events the letter refers to, and so on. For the students to understand the letter, you would have to give them some of that background.

The connection between the activity and the student text's discussion of Paul's letters is clear: If we are to understand Paul's epistles, we must remember that they too are only one side of a two-sided conversation. To understand them, we must discover as much as we can about the people to whom he was writing, the issues they were struggling with, and so on.

Something Old, Something New

The student text (p. 237) quotes a sentence from Paul's second letter to the Corinthians: "So if anyone is in Christ, there is a new creation: everything old has passed away; see, everything has become new" (5:17). As a way to reflect on the quotation, this activity invites the students to think of what difference the life and message of Jesus might mean in a person's life.

Refer the students to the quotation in their text and read it with them. Request interpretations of what the statement means. Ask if anyone might be able to rephrase the statement in a way that makes better sense to them. Explain that the statement suggests that any real encounter with Christ somehow radically changes a person. Then put the following on the chalkboard:

Old Creation J **New Creation**
                    E
                    S
                    U
                    S

Challenge the students to come up with pairs of words or phrases that might describe a person before and then after an encounter with the Risen Jesus. Write the words or phrases in the appropriate columns. Some relatively simple terms will probably be suggested first (e.g., sad/happy; lonely/among friends; afraid/courageous). If such basic parallels are all the students can come up with, that is fine. If, however, you think that your students are capable of deeper reflection on this theme, continue to challenge them. For instance, make a connection between this activity and the question raised on pages 235–236 of the student text: What does it mean to be "saved by Jesus"? Suggest to the students that another way of thinking of "the old creation" would be to identify what people might want to be "saved from." Again, then, what would parallel those ideas for the "new creation" side?

When the students have completed their brainstorming, sum up the two columns by saying this:
- According to the members of this class, a person living under the old creation is [add description]. Someone living under the new creation brought about by Jesus is [add description].

Regardless of the depth of reflection achieved by the students, this activity will help prepare them for further discussion of Paul's understanding of Jesus. Throughout your work with the chapter, be alert for opportunities to remind the students of this activity and compare their descriptions of the old and new creations with Paul's descriptions.

Concept B: Salvation Through Christ Crucified

The Jewish concept of sin as the breaking of relationships underlies Paul's notion of salvation in and through Christ. Paul realized that the people could not earn salvation by following the letter of the Law. Love, not the Law, was the goal. This understanding by Paul reflected Jesus' teaching that the person who fully loves fulfills everything written in the Law. (Pages 240–243 of the student text)

Review Questions: Salvation Through Christ Crucified

Question: Define the Jewish understanding of sin and briefly summarize its origins.

Answer: The Jewish understanding of sin was connected with the Jews' intimate and deeply personal relationship with their God, Yahweh. Sin was not a breaking of rigid rules. Sin was a rupturing of relationships, first between the

Jews and Yahweh and then inevitably among the people themselves. This understanding had its origins in the story of Adam and Eve, in the accounts of God's constant attempt to bring reconciliation throughout the Jews' history, and in the Law.

Question: What false understanding of the Law emerged over time among some Jews, and which Jewish group most strongly held this understanding?

Answer: Over time, some Jews started to believe that they could win God's favor by following every letter of the Law rigidly. They started to think that a person could *earn* the favor of God, that people were in control of their own salvation in some way. Such notions about the Law were held especially by the Pharisees.

Question: Summarize Paul's new understanding of the Law in light of his faith in Jesus.

Answer: Paul saw that the Law had its limits. Laws can provide order in a society, but they cannot meet deeper human needs. Only love can do that. Paul taught that when people truly love, they begin to live in such a way that they achieve the Law's intentions without even really thinking about it.

Text Activities: Salvation Through Christ Crucified

Activity 3

Without reviewing what was said about sin earlier, write a brief definition of sin as you currently understand it. Then, using your definition of sin, explain what it means to be saved from sin.

Activity 4

Write a pro or con response to the following statement: *Most people who follow religious laws do so either to win God's favor or to avoid God's anger. That is, they act religiously out of greed or fear.*

Activity 5

List the qualities a person needs to possess before she or he can live a good moral life without worrying about laws.

Additional Activities: Salvation Through Christ Crucified

Art for Theology's Sake

This activity challenges the students to symbolically represent the complex ideas treated under concept B. The students, working in small groups, must in some way represent the interrelationship between God, humanity, sin, the Law, and Jesus Christ. Two approaches are suggested below, but other possibilities might be triggered by these.

Option 1: Prior to class, prepare the following materials, one set for every three or four students: a sheet of poster paper, 18 by 24 inches or larger; a box of crayons; several pencils; and at least one ruler. The students will likely already have some of the materials.

Also provide each small group with a slip of paper that gives the following instructions:
- As a group, you are to graphically depict the interrelationships between the following: *God, humanity, sin, the Law,* and *Jesus Christ.* You must include all five of these concepts on one poster, and you must show how they fit together. You will be expected to present and explain your poster to the class.

Specify a time limit for the exercise, with a minimum of 30 minutes. You may choose to give the students an entire class period to prepare their posters, followed by another class period for presentations and discussion.

The students may hesitate at the activity, claiming that it is too difficult. Assure them that not only are they capable of accomplishing the task, but they can gain wonderful insights while doing so. To further encourage them, give them this hint: Suggest that they consider some item from their common experience that can serve as a basic symbol for the entire exercise, with a part of that item symbolizing each of the five concepts in the assignment. For example, how might a stereo system, a television, a desk lamp, a computer, or a car engine serve as a basic symbol for the exercise? In each case, the students must show how the symbol *reasonably* demonstrates the relationships between God, humanity, sin, the Law, and Jesus Christ.

When the allotted time is up, collect all the materials except the posters. Then ask each group to present its creation, and invite questions or observations from the class. Hold your own comments and insights until all the groups have completed their presentations.

Option 2: This approach has essentially the same goal as the first one, but in this case the students are to create a sculpture rather than a poster. Provide each small group with the following items and others of your choosing: modeling clay or Play-Doh (about the size of a tennis ball), five to ten pipe cleaners, ten sturdy round toothpicks, and small paper or plastic cups.

Depending on the size of the class, it may be more difficult for the students to present their sculptures than it would be for them to present posters. However, this approach will force the students to stretch their imagination even further. Consider using this approach with students of more advanced ability.

Experiencing the Nature and Effects of Sin

Note: This activity is a variation on the activity "Human Limitations and the Freeing Power of God," suggested for use with chapter 8. If you used that activity with chapter 8, you will probably not want to use this similar activity now.

The activity works best in an area that is carpeted and relatively free of furniture and other obstructions. Perhaps your school has such a space available—for example, a chapel. The exercise, when properly conducted, is so effective that it is worth making special arrangements. Also, breaking from the normal setting of the classroom for such a special activity can provide a helpful spark to the course.

Gather the students in your selected space. Ask them to stand in a large circle around you. Then tell them that you are going to ask them to do four things in order, and they must listen carefully or they might ruin the exercise. Then provide the following overview of the process they will be following:
- I will ask you to fold your arms in front of you, to close your eyes and keep them closed, and then to walk around the room for a minute or two.

- When I tell you to, you are to sit down where you are, keeping your eyes closed, and you are to get into as tight a position as possible. [This should not only be clearly stated but also demonstrated so that students get the idea. Sit on the floor, draw your knees up to your chest, and clasp your arms around them, pulling in as tightly as possible.]
- You are to remain in that tight position until I tap you on the shoulder. At that time, you can stand up where you are, but you must remain silent and keep your eyes closed.
- When I tap you on the shoulder a second time, you can open your eyes, but you must remain perfectly quiet until everyone has been tapped a second time.

Repeat these instructions until everyone understands them. (You won't be able to talk once the exercise begins.) *Stress that throughout this exercise the students are to be aware of how they feel.* Then begin the activity as described.

After the students are all in their tight position, move as silently as possible (perhaps take off your shoes) and quietly tap some students who are on one side of the room. Then move to another part of the room and tap some students, move back again, and so on. Occasionally shuffle your feet next to an individual and then move silently away without tapping her or him, thus increasing her or his sense of frustration or even anger. Complete the first round of tapping the students (and therefore have them all standing but their eyes still closed) before beginning the second round, in which they are allowed to open their eyes but must remain silent. For the second round, face the students when tapping them, so that when they open their eyes you can gesture that they are to remain silent.

The exercise should be done slowly to heighten the initial feelings of uptightness and therefore to increase the sense of relief that will follow. With a group of twenty-five students, for example, the exercise from the end of giving the instructions to the end of the second round of tapping should take about 20 minutes.

When all the students are standing with their eyes open, ask them to sit down for discussion. First, ask for their initial impressions of the exercise.

- What feelings did you experience while you were in a tight ball?
- Have you ever had those same kinds of feelings in other situations? Can you give any examples?
- How did it feel to be tapped the first time? the second time?
- Did it seem like a long time before you were tapped? Were you getting anxious, angry, frustrated?
- When were you the most uncomfortable?

Flowing from this discussion and as a conclusion to it, make the following comments:

- During this activity, you experienced being uptight in a physical sense and perhaps in an emotional sense as well. All of us in our life have been uptight in an emotional sense. We have all experienced fear, anxiety, loneliness, frustration. [Give examples from your own life or refer to the examples the students volunteered in response to the related question listed above.]

    These feelings are the effects of something we tend not to talk about but that is at the heart of the messages of both Jesus and Paul. That "something" is sin. Sin is not just a breaking of rules or an offense against God. Sin involves the corruption or breaking of *relationships*. Whenever people fail to love—that is, whenever they are cold, indifferent, or apathetic toward others—they cause loneliness, fear, frustration, and anxiety in the lives of those they meet and live with. That's what sin is all about.

If we really want to overcome this sin dimension of our life, if we really want to care for and love others, we need the help of others. We need people who can help free us from our own uptightness, the effects of our sins and the sins of others in our life. In other words, we need someone to "tap us on the shoulder," to free us to be the kind of person we want to be. If we are lucky, some people have already entered our life and "touched us" in this special way. But no one person can ever free us completely. Only God can do that.

Christians believe that is precisely what Jesus was all about. He was a human being so completely one with God and so totally free of the effects of sin in his own life that he could touch people and free them from all that oppressed them. That is what Paul is talking about when he speaks of salvation through Jesus. The salvation offered by Jesus is not just the forgiveness of our past sins, as wonderful as that is. Rather, "being saved," according to Paul, also means being liberated from the crippling effects of fear, loneliness, and anxiety. No law, says Paul, can bring about such liberation. Only the love of God that is revealed in and through Jesus can.

The Ten Commandments: A Gift from God

Have the students call out the Ten Commandments while you list them on the chalkboard in an abbreviated fashion. The students may have a difficult time doing this (as would many adults!), but do not overreact to their haziness. Just give them occasional hints and ask them to get all ten in proper order and stated accurately.

After all ten are listed, challenge the class to identify any one commandment that Jesus or Paul could have comfortably ignored or acted against. That is, could Jesus or Paul have broken any commandment and still have been considered a faithful Jew?

Then broaden the discussion to include the Christian community, the church, which has inherited the Ten Commandments from the Jews. Pose the question this way:
- Could individual Christians consistently break or ignore any commandment without harming the life of the Christian community?

You may wish to have the students discuss this question in small groups before sharing their reactions with the class.

The discussion will likely surface the notion that the Commandments are not just arbitrary religious laws but, rather, a commonsense code of behavior that grew out of human experience. Point this out to the students and then comment along the following lines:
- The Ten Commandments grew out of the Jewish community's attempt to deal with the real world in terms of the people's relationship with their God and the implications of that bond for them as they related to one another and to nature. Through years of experiencing and reflecting on the revelation of God, the Jews realized that certain laws were necessary if they were to have any kind of order in their society and any kind of longevity as a people dedicated to one God. If they allowed stealing, then trust would break down and the community would fall apart. If the members of the community did not hold Yahweh's name sacred and worship Yahweh regularly, then the foundation of their existence as a people would break down. If children did not look up to, admire, and respect their parents, then the basic unit of Jewish society—the family—would disintegrate.

So the Ten Commandments were not simply imposed upon the people. On the contrary, these laws were tested long and hard against human experience and human needs. That's why the Jews could view the Law as a great gift from God, so much so that they repeated over and over the marvelous story about God's giving the Law to Moses on Mount Sinai.

Given that the Law was seen by the Jews as a great gift from God, it is important to recognize that neither Jesus nor Paul *rejected* the Law. Rather, they both recognized that the Law *alone* could not fully save people. Despite the necessity of laws for the preservation of order in society, laws are limited in their capacity to meet deeper human needs, such as the needs for companionship, meaning, and happiness. Only love can meet such needs. This is the point that Paul preached about so forcefully.

Concept C: Salvation and Contemporary Culture

An awareness of the pervasiveness of sin in the world and in our personal life is essential to understanding Paul's writings on salvation. One manifestation of sin in the lives of modern Western people is the hunger for a sense of meaning and purpose. Only Jesus and his message can fully satisfy that hunger. (Pages 244–251 of the student text)

Review Questions: Salvation and Contemporary Culture

Question: List some ways in which we experience the effects of sin, both on a social and on a personal level.
Answer: On a social level, we encounter war, poverty, sexism, and racism. On a personal level, we often experience deep loneliness, a lack of hope, or a desperate yearning for meaning.

Question: What is the basic meaning of the term *righteousness?*
Answer: Being right with God

Question: What does Jesus save us from? What does he save us for? How is salvation an act of grace?
Answer: In his life, death, and resurrection, Jesus saves us from all the false values and misleading messages of contemporary society. Jesus saves us from society's distorted claims about what it means to be fully human, and he frees us to be fully human in the way God intends us to be—as persons who have God at the center of our life and who love our neighbors as ourselves. Jesus saves us *from* sin and frees us *for* life.

Salvation is an act of grace in that it is God's work, not the result of human effort. We cannot *earn* salvation; we can only receive it as a gift from God.

Question: In what sense is loving action a response?
Answer: Loving action is the response that flows from God's gift of grace.

Question: What is the source of the power to love in accordance with Jesus' Dream?
Answer: Our dependence upon God through faith in Jesus

Text Activities: Salvation and Contemporary Culture

Activity 6

List the names of the four young people just described. Next to each name, put a check mark for every person you can think of who has a similar difficulty.

Activity 7

Write a pro or con response to this statement: *If it were not for the bad influences of society and culture, most people would naturally do what is right and good for themselves and others.*

Activity 8

Jot down your reflections on Paul's message to the Corinthians about the foolishness of the cross.

Activity 9

In a paragraph, explain the meaning of this statement: *Salvation is as much about being freed for life as it is about being saved from sin.*

Additional Activities: Salvation and Contemporary Culture

The Social Effects of Sin

Note: This activity can be enhanced by having done the simulation exercise "Experiencing the Nature and Effects of Sin," recommended under concept B. If you did not use that exercise at that time, consider using it as part of your work with this major concept. The connection between the exercise and the theme of the need for salvation in contemporary culture is strong.

Divide the class into small groups. Give each group the following sentence stems to complete:
- Four ways that we cause loneliness, fear, anxiety, or frustration in the lives of our parents are . . .
- Four ways that we cause loneliness, fear, anxiety, or frustration in the lives of our friends are . . .
- Four ways that we cause loneliness, fear, anxiety, or frustration in the lives of persons of the other sex are . . .

Instruct each group to appoint a recorder to take notes on the group's responses. Give the groups 15 minutes to complete the sentence stems, telling them that they should view this more as a brainstorming activity than as an in-depth discussion.

When time is up, gather the groups together for a whole-class discussion. Given the number of topics that might be raised, you will likely have to choose the areas that will be most worthwhile for your class to focus on. Consider having all the groups simply state their completion of the first sentence stem and listing the answers on the chalkboard to see if patterns emerge. Choose one or two of those answers for further discussion for a limited period of time. Then move on to the next sentence stem. Continue until you have discussed the completion of all three sentence stems.

Playing Ann Landers

Divide the class into four groups. Assign to each group one of the four vignettes on pages 244–245 of the student text, the situations of Nina, Justin, Geralyn, and Chad. Tell the groups to imagine that they are advice columnists for the local newspaper and that their assigned situation has been described to them in a letter. Their task is to respond, providing brief advice to the young person in the situation. The groups have just 10 minutes.

Have each group appoint a recorder to take notes on the discussion and compose the group's response. Or consider appointing the four recorders yourself, choosing students who have demonstrated an ability to handle the task.

When time is up, ask each group to identify the situation they were assigned and then to read their response. Invite reactions from the class. When possible, connect the discussion with the theme of the need for salvation in contemporary culture, repeatedly pointing out that salvation has to do with the *real* world and with *real* life experiences, not just with "religious stuff."

Negative Cultural Values: Learning to Fight Back

Our contemporary culture is deeply influenced by a variety of negative values. These are so pervasive that we all have a difficult time avoiding their impact. Four such values seem particularly influential and bear discussion within the context of concept C:

- *Excessive consumerism:* Excessive consumerism is the cultural drive to acquire more and more goods, many of which are totally unnecessary, while much of the world goes without the necessities. While we eat tons of junk food, millions go hungry; while we buy the latest fashion craze and then quickly discard it, many go without clothing.
- *Extreme individualism:* Extreme individualism is individuality (which can be good) stressed to the point that we lose all sense of responsibility to others. Service to others is replaced with the belief that "I must take care of myself first." The sense of the common good is lost.
- *Immediate gratification:* Immediate gratification is the basis for the conviction "If it feels good, do it." We want and expect all of our needs to be met right now, not tomorrow, and certainly not in a few years. Many people even view as friends only those people who can make them feel good; when the friendship becomes more demanding, the relationship ends.
- *Sexual permissiveness:* Sexual permissiveness is difficult to even talk about for fear of being labeled a prude. It is the approach to sexuality that results from the other negative cultural values defined above. In sexual permissiveness, people are viewed as products to be consumed, the desire for individual freedom leads to the inability to make a commitment, and the desire for immediate gratification leads to the inability to wait for sexual fulfillment until a person is in a commited, lasting relationship.

Make large posters naming each of these four cultural values and place the posters on the wall in four different parts of the room. Move from poster to poster and comment on each cultural value, defining it to the degree you feel is necessary to give your students a clear sense of its meaning.

Divide the class into four groups, assigning each group to one of the four posters and asking the group members to gather near it. Then tell the groups that they have just 5 minutes to brainstorm three ways that people their age can fight against the negative cultural value specified on their poster. When time is up, tell the groups to rotate to the next poster. Repeat the procedure until all four groups have spent 5 minutes brainstorming on each of the four values.

Then gather the groups together for a general discussion on the four values, summarizing all the ideas generated by the groups. (You might want to emphasize, during the discussion on extreme individualism, the Christian conviction that we can never save ourselves by ourselves but must rely on both God and others.) Consider concluding the discussion with an adaptation of the ideas in the student text section titled "Asking the Right Questions" (p. 249). That is, create a *question* for each of the four cultural values to reflect society's perception (e.g., for the value immediate gratification, "How can I get my own needs met right now?"). Then suggest the question that Jesus might ask (e.g., "What larger Dream will give me the strength to endure suffering today?").

Something Old, Something New

This activity, dealing with Paul's concept of the "new creation" available in and through Jesus, is described under concept A. If you did not use the activity in your work with that concept, consider using it here.

Concept D: The Church as the Body of Christ

Paul's Damascus experience awakened him to the reality that Christ is encountered in other people and, in a special way, in the community of believers, the church. Paul expressed this awareness in his writings on the church as "the body of Christ." (Pages 252–257 of the student text)

Review Questions: The Church as the Body of Christ

Question: Complete this sentence: *Just as Jesus on earth was the visible manifestation of God, so the church is _____.*
Answer: The visible presence of the Risen Jesus

Question: With what imagery does Paul explain the value of each member of the church? Illustrate your answer with an example.
Answer: Paul uses the imagery of the human body to explain the value of each member of the church. [The following are examples from the student text.]
- Just as the body needs both hands and eyes, so the church needs people with different talents and gifts.
- Jesus is the head of the body.
- Whenever members of the church community are in pain, the body of Christ is in pain.
- Whenever members of the church community work and pray together as one, the body of Christ is strong and healthy.

Question: What does Paul mean when he describes Jesus as the head of the body?

Answer: Jesus is the one "in charge," the one whose vision and message must guide the workings of the body.

Question: What is the basic principle behind Paul's understanding of Christian morality?

Answer: Christians live out their relationship with Jesus by living well in community with one another.

Text Activities: The Church as the Body of Christ

Activity 10

List other images that express the same reality about the church that Paul's image of the human body does. Pick your favorite image from your list and expand on why you think it works.

Activity 11

Paul's letter to the Romans describes several requirements for Christians. Select the ten behaviors or attitudes that you feel are most important. In a short essay, explain your selections, using language that your friends could relate to.

Additional Activities: The Church as the Body of Christ

Images of the Church

This activity can serve as either an elaboration of text activity 10 or an alternative to it. If you decide to assign the text activity, build off of the results when using this activity. If you do not use the text activity, follow these instructions.

At the top of the chalkboard, write the phrase "The church is → the body of Christ." Then repeat the arrow about five to ten times under the arrow in the phrase at the top, as follows:

The church is → the body of Christ.
→
→
→
→
→

Next, invite the students to offer other images of the church, and write those in the spaces under the words "the body of Christ." Encourage the students to come up with concrete images that have some symbolic potential. Examples: The church is the *school* of Christ, the *home* of Christ, the *nation* of Christ, the *communication system* of Christ. You may choose to provide such images rather than elicit them from the students.

Then divide the class into small groups, one group for each image of the church that has just been generated. Assign each group one of the images and ask them to rewrite 1 Cor. 12:14–27, as quoted on pages 252–253 of the student text, in light of that image. Each group should elect a recorder. Emphasize that they should strive to make the image "work" rather than simply replace words in the original passage with random words associated with the new image. Allow about 10 minutes and then call for the groups to share the results.

A Discussion: Feeling Like Part of the Body

Introduce this discussion on the students' sense of participation in the church with comments similar to these:
- Each of us is a member of many groups or communities. Each of those groups helps us define ourselves, our goals, and how we are going to achieve them. We as individuals are like the hub of a wheel, attached to the world by many "spokes" or groups.

At this point, draw on the chalkboard a wheel-like diagram with about ten spokes. Have the students name groups they are a part of. Fill in the wheel with these group names, and if necessary, add more spokes. Groups could include the following: *family, friends, school, neighborhood, city, state, nation, world, athletic team, school organization, this class, parish group, the parish as a whole, the church.* Continue with these words:
- All of these groups keep us in touch with others. In each case people are drawn together to achieve a certain goal—whether it be physical and emotional security [family], education [school], or winning a game [athletic team]. The degree to which we feel like part of a group, and therefore the degree to which we are willing to sacrifice our own needs and desires for the sake of the group and its goals, is a measure of how important that community is to us.

    The church is a community gathered together to achieve certain goals. [At this point, ask the students to identify the church's goals, and list these on the board. The church's primary goal, of course, is to further Jesus' Dream of the Kingdom through loving service to others, but students will likely suggest other goals before or instead of this one. If some of the goals are questionable in your mind, raise them for broader discussion by the class.]

    Like other communities, the church can achieve its goals only if it nurtures a sense of belonging among its members and, therefore, their sense of ownership of and commitment to its goals. [Pause to discuss what the church could do to deepen the sense of belonging and commitment among its members, initially speaking of this issue in broad, not age-specific, terms. Then, after the general discussion, focus on the sense of belonging and commitment specifically among *young* members of the church. Pose questions like the ones below.]
- What can the church do to nurture a sense of belonging and commitment among its young members?
- Is it reasonable, given the abilities and concerns of young people, to seek or expect such commitment? Why or why not?
- If you as a class were the council of a parish that was just being founded—that is, one with no past to worry about—what would you do to engage and hold the interest of young people?

Close the discussion by stating that the church will truly be "the body of Christ" only if its members can grow in their understanding of Jesus' vision of the Kingdom and in their willingness to work to make it real in the world.

Wouldn't It Be Great If . . .

The student text (pp. 254–255) quotes Paul's idealized description of life in the community of faith, from his letter to the Romans, chapter 12. In this activity, the students are challenged to rewrite the passage in language that will speak to people their age.

Note: A similar, though less demanding, use of this passage is suggested in text activity 11.

Handout 12–A

Handout 12–A, "The Ideal Church: Romans, Chapter 12," divides the passage into individual phrases. There are twenty-six phrases in all, so if your class is larger than that, one or more students will have to share phrases. If your class is smaller than twenty-six, you might choose to simply eliminate some of the phrases.

Make one copy of the handout and cut it along the dotted lines. Put the resulting strips in a bag or box. You will also need four pieces of poster paper about 22 by 24 inches in size. Cut the poster paper into strips 3 inches high by the width of the paper. This will give you eight strips per sheet of poster paper—one strip for each of the twenty-six phrases from the handout plus some extra strips, which you will likely need. Also, have available either felt-tip markers or crayons. (Avoid light colors that will not be readable from a distance.) You may want to have two or more dictionaries available for the students' reference during the activity. Finally, have a tape dispenser handy for the final part of the activity.

As you introduce the activity, either read or ask one of the students to read the student text's quotation of the passage from Romans. Remark that many of the phrases, though poetic and uplifting, are difficult to understand in our day. In this activity, the class will translate the passage, trying to make it understandable for today's Christians.

Distribute to each student one strip of poster paper and a marker or crayon. Then show the class the bag or box in which you have the slips of paper with the phrases on them. Walk through the class, allowing each student to randomly choose one of the slips. When all have a slip, indicate that each slip has a number to the left of the phrase. The students are to write that number lightly in pencil in a corner of their strip of poster paper.

Give the students just 5 minutes to reflect on their selected phrase and to rewrite it on their strip of poster paper in words that retain the meaning of the original phrase but make it more understandable today. They may need to use the dictionary to look up some words. Also, you may choose to let them talk to one another while they do the activity, sharing ideas on the best way to restate their assigned phrase.

When all the students are done, ask them to come one at a time to the front of the room, in the order of the numbers penciled in on their strips of poster paper. They are to quickly read the original phrase and then read their revised version of it. You or a student volunteer can then tape each strip of poster paper on the chalkboard in the appropriate sequence. When all the strips are on the board, read through the revised passage from beginning to end, commenting as appropriate.

Naturally, some students will have intentionally written a humorous or even off-color version of their assigned phrase. Or some students may simply have had difficulty finding optional ways of stating their assigned phrase. Avoid overreacting in either case and use such situations as opportunities for further discussion or comment.

Variation: The activity can be carried out in a variety of other ways. For example, it can be adapted as a homework assignment in which the students are asked to rewrite all or part of the passage. You might evaluate the results and then share the best efforts with the class. This approach involves a little less preparation on your part but also less class participation by the students and more "homework" by you.

The Ideal Church: Romans, Chapter 12

1 Let love be genuine
2 hate what is evil
3 hold fast to what is good
4 love one another with mutual affection
5 outdo one another in showing honor
6 Do not lag in zeal
7 be ardent in spirit
8 serve the Lord
9 Rejoice in hope
10 be patient in suffering
11 persevere in prayer
12 Contribute to the needs of the saints
13 extend hospitality to strangers
14 Bless those who persecute you; bless and do not curse them
15 Rejoice with those who rejoice
16 weep with those who weep
17 Live in harmony with one another
18 do not be haughty, but associate with the lowly
19 do not claim to be wiser than you are
20 Do not repay anyone evil for evil
21 . . . take thought for what is noble in the sight of all
22 If it is possible, . . . live peaceably with all
23 . . . Never avenge yourselves
24 . . . "if your enemies are hungry, feed them"
25 "if [your enemies] are thirsty, give them something to drink"
26 Do not be overcome by evil, but overcome evil with good

CHAPTER 13

Good News from Age to Age: The Church's Understanding of Jesus Christ

Major Concepts

A. **The Church's History:** The church's structure and the way it presents its message about Jesus are inevitably affected by the cultures and times in which the church finds itself. Under the guidance of the Spirit, the church has constantly struggled to retain a balance in its understanding of Jesus.

B. **Understanding Jesus in the Early Centuries:** As the church moved into the second century, it encountered and became dominated by the Greek way of thinking. One consequence of the shift to a Greek philosophical view and the debates that followed was the emergence of three major false teachings about Jesus. The three Great Christological Councils were convened to settle the matters, and they produced creedal statements about Jesus.

C. **Understanding Jesus in the Middle Ages:** In the Middle Ages, Scholastic philosophy became the basis for the thinking and teaching employed by the church. Its sometimes extreme emphasis on order and rationality spawned among the common people a movement to a more personal and emotional response to Jesus. Both Scholasticism and the popular movement had their problems, however. Toward the end of the Middle Ages, poor leadership and corruption in the church led to the Protestant Reformation. Overall, the conflict between the Roman Catholic church and the Protestant churches focused more on the nature of the church than on Jesus.

D. **Understanding Jesus in the Modern Age:** The Age of Enlightenment produced the claim that religion was obsolete and atheism was a reasonable option for people. The Catholic church responded to the attack by closing itself off from the new thinking and scientific advances that were part of the Enlightenment. With Vatican Council II, the church re-evaluated its view of the modern world, supported advances in scriptural study, and encouraged Catholics to read the Scriptures. This has impacted the church's teachings about Jesus, which in turn has sparked tremendous renewal as well as many challenges in the life of the church.

E. **The Journey of Faith in Jesus:** Finding an answer to Jesus' question, "Who do you say that I am?" is an intensely personal journey that is best made in the company of a faith community.

A Note to the Teacher: The Broad Nature of Chapter 13

It becomes evident just by perusing chapter 13 of the student text that the material there is somewhat different from that in the rest of the book. The twenty-one pages in chapter 13 summarize the development of the church's understanding of Jesus over nearly two thousand years of complex history. In order to summarize so concisely, the chapter necessarily offers broad generalizations about many theological developments. This has the great advantage of giving the students a bird's-eye view of the history of the Christian community, a faithful church trying in every age to come to grips with the meaning of Jesus and his message.

The disadvantage of this chapter—if it can be called a disadvantage—is having to deal with this breadth of information in a teaching situation. In order to effectively work with this material, therefore, keep the following in mind:

1. Though a major concept may comprise only about five pages of the student text, those few pages may summarize hundreds of years of history and a great many theological developments. Arranging the material in this fashion, it is hoped, will enable you to provide the students with the broadest sense of the church's evolving understanding of Jesus—precisely the intent of the chapter.
2. The material in this chapter does not always lend itself to experiential teaching methods like those that have been preferred throughout this course. In some cases, you may want to rely more heavily than you have in past chapters on assigned reading, classroom discussion, and quizzing. Because of this, look to the review questions and text activities available throughout this chapter as handy and effective discussion tools. In other words, in teaching this chapter, you may wish to move your students rather quickly through the material, leading discussions and providing quizzes to gauge and deepen their understanding, and avoiding additional input or activities.

Concept A: The Church's History

The church's structure and the way it presents its message about Jesus are inevitably affected by the cultures and times in which the church finds itself. Under the guidance of the Spirit, the church has constantly struggled to retain a balance in its understanding of Jesus. (Pages 259–263 of the student text)

Review Questions: The Church's History

Question: Briefly, how did the early church form?
Answer: Individuals, moved and transformed by their experience of Jesus, gathered with others to share and celebrate and deepen their awareness of Jesus' message. They expressed themselves as a community by recalling their past experiences of Jesus and the Apostles' teachings about him, committing themselves to care for one another, and celebrating Jesus' risen and living presence among them through signs and symbols such as the breaking of the bread.

Question: What do Christians believe has been the guiding force behind the church's journey through history?

Answer: The presence of God's Spirit

Question: What importance does the question of whether Jesus intended to found a church have for individual Christians? Briefly summarize the evidence supporting the claim that Jesus intended to found some kind of continuing community.

Answer: If Jesus did intend to found a church, then it would seem that he wanted his followers to discover him and preserve his teaching in union with one another. If Jesus did not intend to found a church, then it would seem that individuals have a perfect right to "do their own thing" in response to Jesus.

The evidence supporting the claim that Jesus intended to found a church can be summarized as follows:

- Many Gospel images imply that Jesus' followers shared some kind of communal experience. Parables like those of the shepherd and his flock and the vine and the branches reinforce the imagery of a community nurtured by Jesus. The Gospels' many sayings about the Kingdom convey a similar picture.
- The moral teachings of Jesus also show a real concern for the communal nature of our actions.
- Jesus' relationship and training of the Apostles seems to indicate an ongoing role for them as the foundation of some sort of gathering for those who believed in and followed Jesus.

Question: Name the persistent tensions in the church's historical struggle to understand Jesus and his message.

Answer:
- Jesus' humanity and divinity
- The intellectual and the emotional approaches to understanding Jesus

Text Activities: The Church's History

Activity 1

Respond in writing to this opinion: *Belonging to the church was important when Christians were threatened by their society. But today Christians can stay faithful to Jesus even without the church.*

Activity 2

In a paragraph, describe some area of your life in which you have had to struggle for balance—for instance, in working out the tension between your schoolwork and your involvement in other activities. What helped you find the right balance?

Additional Activities: The Church's History

Reflections on the Early Church: Starting Over

This exercise enables the students to look backward at the early church in order to look forward to the future church. It begins with a guided meditation.

You obviously have to set the mood for, as well as practice your part in, the guided meditation. It can be far more elaborate than what is offered here, perhaps by mentioning the sights, sounds, and odors of the streets of ancient Palestine; describing the occupations your students might imagine having there; and so on. However, the brief meditation offered below, properly shared, should be adequate as an introduction to the group work that follows the meditation.

Handout 13–A

In preparation for the group work, make one or two copies of handout 13–A, "Helping the Church of Today and Tomorrow" (one copy if you have a class of twenty-four or fewer, two copies if you have a class of more than twenty-four). Cut along the dotted lines to make separate assignment slips.

1. Invite the students to get in a relaxed position, close their eyes, and remain silent and peaceful for a few moments. Then ask them to try to place themselves emotionally, mentally, and—in their imagination—even physically back at the time of Jesus. Have them imagine, perhaps based on movies they have seen depicting this period, a small village at the time of Jesus. They are residents of this village. Have them call to mind Jesus' entry into the town one day. Ask them to imagine sitting at his feet during the Sermon on the Mount, feeling the power of his words burning in their heart. Tell them to imagine following Jesus, physically, from town to town—touching him, hearing his words, eating with him, gathering with him around campfires at night and listening to his wise and wonderful parables, and asking him the parables' meaning. They find themselves coming to deeply love this man.

But then, tell them to imagine Gethsemane, the kiss of Judas, the trial, the scourging, and finally, Jesus' brutal death on the cross.

Ask them, "Is this the end of the Dream?" The answer, of course, is no! Have them focus on the incredible experience of Jesus' resurrection. "He lives! He is among us!" "I believe, my God, I believe!" Continue the reflection with a similar recounting of the apparitions and, finally, the Ascension.

2. After the meditation, ask the students to listen carefully while you read Acts 2:1–25,37–47.

Option: If your class really seems to have been with you during the meditation, you may want to leave them in their relaxed position for this reading. Also, you may choose to read the entire passage of Acts 2:1–47.

Tell the students that this passage records the earliest days of the church. Some say that the modern church has lost touch with the sense of Jesus' presence that was apparently so real to those who walked with him, watched him die and rise, and believed fully that he continued to live among them. Tell the students that you now want them to see themselves as carrying that early sense of Christian community to the future church. Tell them they will be reflecting on what it would be like to help the church of today and tomorrow return to the sense of community experienced by the early Christians.

3. Divide the class into groups of no more than eight students each. Give each group one assignment slip from handout 13–A and tell them that they have 20 minutes to brainstorm—not to discuss in great depth—their assigned topic. They should appoint a recorder to take notes. The groups can then share the results of their discussion, and the class can have the opportunity to react, ask questions, and so on.

Searching the Scriptures for the Origins of the Church

Divide the class into the four groups that were assigned to read a Gospel from beginning to end in "A Special Reading Assignment," on pages 63–64 of this manual. Have the groups search their respective Gospels for all incidents, teachings of Jesus, parables, and comments by Jesus or the Evangelists that indicate the need for a community or fellowship of believers. The groups can use the information offered on pages 261–262 of the student text, in the section titled "Did Jesus Intend to Found a Church?" for some helpful hints on what to look for, but they should not be restricted by this. Invite the groups to share the results of their search.

   Note: The question of Jesus' intentions regarding the establishment of a church is not as easy to answer as one might think. Several Gospel references seem to indicate that he did intend such a community. The most obvious reference is Matt. 16:18–20, in which Jesus says to Peter, "'You are Peter, and on this rock I will build my church, and the gates of Hades will not prevail against it. I will give you the keys of the kingdom of heaven, and whatever you bind on earth will be bound in heaven, and whatever you loose on earth will be loosed in heaven.'" And in a later comment on the need for people to correct the wrong behavior of others, Jesus says, "'If the [offender] refuses to listen to [his or her fellow Christians], tell it to the church; and if the offender refuses to listen even to the church, let such a one be to you as a Gentile and a tax collector'" (18:17). One difficulty with these statements, however, is that scholars think they may have been added by Matthew himself as he tried to give direction to the community for which he was writing his Gospel.

Contemporary Commercials for the Church

The early believers were in the position of having to "sell" their convictions about Jesus, his message, and the community of faith. Christians are in the same position today, but the available means of "selling" are considerably different than those in the early church. Have the students, in groups of eight or fewer, develop skits that represent TV commercials for the church. They can either adapt commercials that are already on the air or create entirely new ones. Their commercials should be no longer than 1 minute. Give the groups time to practice, access to props if possible, and so on. Then invite the groups to perform their commercials. After all of the performances, lead a discussion as follows:
- Is it possible to "advertise" the church and its message in this way? Are there problems with the whole concept and methods of commercial advertising that work against presenting the Christian faith this way? Explain.
- What do you think about the so-called electronic evangelists, the TV ministers who use highly polished programs to promote the faith? How do you think Jesus would react if he were to sit down and watch these programs? Support your feelings with information from the Gospels.
- How did the members of the early church "sell" their faith to nonbelievers? What does this tell us about the way contemporary Christians must ultimately evangelize the world?

The Disciples' Dilemma

"The Disciples' Dilemma" was suggested in chapter 10 of this manual (see pp. 191–192). If you did not use it at that time, consider using it here as an effective approach to teaching concept A.

Concept B:
Understanding Jesus in the Early Centuries

As the church moved into the second century, it encountered and became dominated by the Greek way of thinking. One consequence of the shift to a Greek philosophical view and the debates that followed was the emergence of three major false teachings about Jesus. The three Great Christological Councils were convened to settle the matters, and they produced creedal statements about Jesus. (Pages 264–268 of the student text)

Review Questions:
Understanding Jesus in the Early Centuries

Question: What significant things were happening in the early church about the time it began searching for a full understanding of Jesus?
Answer:
- The early Christians believed the Risen Jesus would come again soon.
- The four Gospels were written to preserve and pass on the story and message of Jesus.
- Tensions increased between Christians and Jews.
- The canon of the Hebrew Scriptures was set.

Question: What role did the Fathers of the church play?
Answer: The Fathers of the church were second-century church leaders trained in the Greek philosophy of the time. They tried to translate the experiences of the Apostles and earliest Christian communities into a language and mind-set that made sense to themselves and suited their audiences.

Question: Identify the three Great Christological Councils and briefly explain what each council decided about Jesus' identity.
Answer:
- *The Council of Nicaea* defended Jesus' divinity as the Christ.
- *The Council of Ephesus* defended Jesus' unity as both God and man.
- *The Council of Chalcedon* defended Jesus' full humanity.

Question: Why did the church officially name Mary as "Mother of God"?
Answer: To affirm its belief in Jesus' humanity and divinity

Text Activities:
Understanding Jesus in the Early Centuries

Activity 3

List what you think are the dangers or implications of viewing Jesus and his message as a mystery to be explained rather than as a relationship and vision to be lived.

Activity 4

Which, if any, of the three christological heresies dealt with by the early church do you think might still exist today? Write a comment expressing your thoughts.

Additional Activities:
Understanding Jesus in the Early Centuries

Heroes or Heretics?

This activity is designed to clarify for the students the issues and outcomes of the Great Christological Councils.

1. Divide the class into three groups. Assign each group one of the three heresies mentioned in the student text on pages 265–268. The groups are to research their assigned heresy. (You should provide or advise them on resources for this—for instance, suggest good encyclopedias.) However, within each group, the students are to divide into two sections, taking either a pro or a con position on the heresy. In other words, while doing the research, one section is to concentrate on understanding the position of the person or group that initiated the false teaching, while the other section is to concentrate on the church's argument against the false teaching.

2. If you have a class of thirty or fewer, invite all the students in a group to come to the front of the room, with the pro and con sections facing each other. Give the "heretics" 5 minutes to state their case, followed by the "church leaders" presenting their reactions and arguments in 5 minutes. Then open the case to discussion by the class at large, perhaps ending with a vote on which is the "winning" side. This method works because it reduces the pressure that may be placed on individuals in a more conventional debate format. If you have a class of more than thirty students, you may want to use a fishbowl technique to limit the number of students speaking at any one time. (See p. 34 of this manual for information on running a fishbowl.)

The Nicene Creed Today

Note: This activity was initially created for the *Teaching Manual for Understanding Catholic Christianity* (Winona, MN: Saint Mary's Press, 1989), pages 235–236. If your school offers the course *Understanding Catholic Christianity,* check to see if the activity has already been used with your students.

This exercise encourages serious reflection on the Nicene Creed and, it is hoped, recognition of the creed as a personal and rich expression of faith.

Handout 13–B

1. Distribute handout 13–B, "The Nicene Creed Today," and assign it as homework. Instruct the students to paraphrase the Nicene Creed by rewriting each phrase in the "Personal" column in words that make sense to them. The students can be as creative as they like, but their version must reflect what they believe to be the essential truth stated in the original creed.

2. In the next class session, divide the students into groups of no more than five. The group members are to share their personal versions of the creed with one another *one phrase at a time* and, for each phrase, compare their various versions and make some decision on which best expresses the central truth of the original. The group's decisions should be printed in the "Group" column *by each member* on his or her own handout.

3. When the groups are done with their work, ask them to share their final and complete version of the creed with the class. If you care to take the exercise one step further, work toward a version of the creed that the majority of the class can accept as representative of their beliefs and convictions.

Option: Consider using the small groups' creeds for either opening or closing prayers during the remainder of the course. Each creed should be read by the *entire group* that created it (hence the reason for *all* members recording their group's creed in step 2). In this way, the Nicene Creed is reinforced as a communal rather than strictly personal statement of faith.

Concept C: Understanding Jesus in the Middle Ages

In the Middle Ages, Scholastic philosophy became the basis for the thinking and teaching employed by the church. Its sometimes extreme emphasis on order and rationality spawned among the common people a movement to a more personal and emotional response to Jesus. Both Scholasticism and the popular movement had their problems, however. Toward the end of the Middle Ages, poor leadership and corruption in the church led to the Protestant Reformation. Overall, the conflict between the Roman Catholic church and the Protestant churches focused more on the nature of the church than on Jesus. (Pages 269–272 of the student text)

Review Questions:
Understanding Jesus in the Middle Ages

Question: Define *Scholasticism*. What can happen to the discussion of Jesus and his message when the Scholastic approach is taken to an extreme?

Answer: Scholasticism is a form of philosophy based heavily on the concepts of the Greek philosopher Aristotle, and it relies to a great extent on order and logic. When the Scholastic approach is taken to an extreme, Jesus and his message seem like cold and impersonal realities, more like problems to be solved than the Good News of a loving God. An emphasis on an intellectual response to Jesus can come at the expense of a more personal, emotional response.

Question: What popular response did the extreme use of Scholasticism evoke during the Middle Ages? What were the dangers of the new movement?

Answer: The extreme use of Scholasticism led to a strong reaction by "the common folk" against the image of Jesus presented by the philosophers. There emerged a popular movement based on imitating the Jesus of the Gospels and performing other acts of piety. The danger then shifted from overcomplicating to *oversimplifying* the person of Jesus and his message. The new movement was also open to superstition, distortion, and even magical understandings of Jesus.

Question: What factors led Catholics such as Martin Luther to yearn for a renewal of the church?

Answer: Toward the end of the Middle Ages, the church became increasingly concerned about itself—its own identity, purpose, and role in the world. New teachings and ideas challenged the church's accepted traditions, and scandalous behavior among the clergy became commonplace. These factors, combined with a rise in an awareness of the Scriptures and a heightened personal spirituality among some members of the church, led many people to yearn for a renewal of the church.

Question: What was the central conflict of the Reformation? What was in danger of being lost because of the conflict?

Answer: The central conflict of the Reformation was over the nature of the church—the Roman understanding of the church, the papacy, questionable practices by church leaders, proper forms of church government, the number and nature of the sacraments, and so on. The church was dangerously close to losing touch with the Jesus of the Gospels.

Text Activities: Understanding Jesus in the Middle Ages

Activity 5

Ask an adult Catholic fifty years old or older to describe her or his religious education. Write a report on your interview and note any connections with the material discussed on pages 271–277.

Activity 6

Using an encyclopedia or other sources, write a brief report on one of the following leaders of the Reformation: Martin Luther, Huldrych Zwingli, John Calvin. Include a discussion of the main denomination and its major characteristics that grew out of the efforts of the person you choose.

Additional Activities: Understanding Jesus in the Middle Ages

Optional Homework and Discussion Activities

Option 1: Assign a two-page report on Saint Thomas Aquinas—his background and his major contributions to the church.

Option 2: Review with the students the dangers of losing balance regarding the intellectual and the emotional dimensions of faith. Give current examples of both extremes. Then, given the class discussion, work with the students to develop a list titled "Ten Characteristics of the Balanced Christian."

Option 3: In light of the student text's discussion of Easter and Christmas as central church feasts, engage the students in more reflection on these feasts. Have different groups research and prepare written or oral presentations on the history of these feasts and the traditions that surround them. Or challenge the students to develop a list of guidelines or principles to govern the celebration of Christmas. The goal of the exercise would be to make Christmas a balanced and truly religious feast rather than the commercial or theologically confused experience it is for many people.

The Students' Evaluation of Their Religious Education

This exercise will help the students grasp a central point of concept C while possibly giving you new insights into both their past religious education and the educational approaches they will need in future religion courses.

1. Remind the students of the lesson learned from the church's experience of Scholasticism and the popular religious movement that reacted to it—that as a faith community, the church must always seek a balanced approach to understanding and celebrating its faith. Note to the students that this need is as strong today as it has been at any other time in history. The question is, Is the church meeting this need?

2. To help the students get in touch with their past religious education, have them separate into three groups (four groups if your students are juniors or seniors). Give the groups the following instructions:
- Group 1, try to recall as much as possible about your religious education through the third grade. Try to remember teachers, which will normally help you to remember certain classes, religious experiences, and so on. Did you enjoy your religious education then? Why or why not?
- Group 2, do the same assignment, but for grades four through six.
- Group 3, do the same assignment, but for grades seven through nine.
- Group 4 [if one is needed], do the same assignment, but for grades ten and up.

This part of the exercise should be done in brainstorming fashion, with one student in each group taking notes. It should last no longer than 10 minutes.

3. Have the groups share the results of their brainstorming in brief reports.

4. Conclude with questions such as these:
- How would you rate your religious education in terms of its balance between meeting your intellectual needs and meeting your more personal, emotional, and spiritual needs? What have been the strengths of your religious education in light of this? What have been its weaknesses?
- What would you now say are your greatest faith needs as a young person? Define them as specifically as you can.
- Finally, given your past religious education and your present needs, what kind of religion curriculum or program would you devise for your remaining years in high school? Be as specific as possible on this. [Consider inviting other staff members—the religion department chairperson, campus minister, school chaplain, and so on—to sit in on and participate in this discussion.]

Ecumenical Activities

The chief point to make about the relationship between the Catholic Tradition and the traditions of the Protestant churches in terms of Christology is

that to a great extent, the Christian churches are all far more unified in their shared convictions about Jesus than divided by differing church structures and religious practices. The possibilities for encouraging greater understanding and communication between our churches are almost unlimited. Among the possibilities for your class are these:
- Invite local ministers or other representatives of Protestant churches to present brief sketches of their historical origins and their major convictions about Jesus Christ.
- Present a lecture on the Catholic church's current stand on and efforts toward ecumenism, including reference to the "Decree on Ecumenism," from Vatican Council II.
- Organize an ecumenical prayer service for the students from your school and young people from a local Protestant church. Focus your service on a topic of shared concern (e.g., the environment, hunger).
- Organize field trips to various Protestant churches to gain a sense of their liturgical expressions, community activities, congregational organization, and so on.

Concept D: Understanding Jesus in the Modern Age

The Age of Enlightenment produced the claim that religion was obsolete and atheism was a reasonable option for people. The Catholic church responded to the attack by closing itself off from the new thinking and scientific advances that were part of the Enlightenment. With Vatican Council II, the church re-evaluated its view of the modern world, supported advances in scriptural study, and encouraged Catholics to read the Scriptures. This has impacted the church's teachings about Jesus, which in turn has sparked tremendous renewal as well as many challenges in the life of the church. (Pages 273–277 of the student text)

Review Questions: Understanding Jesus in the Modern Age

Question: Define *Age of Enlightenment* and describe its attitude toward religion. How did the church respond to the Age of Enlightenment?

Answer: The Age of Enlightenment was an explosion of growth in the study and development of science and technology in the eighteenth and nineteenth centuries. During this period, religious beliefs and practices began to be looked down on as "unenlightened" and obsolete. Some people tried to prove that Jesus had never even existed, and God was explained as "a projection of people's minds," a kind of psychological "father figure" created by people through the years to explain the mysteries of the world. The church reacted to the Enlightenment with increased defensiveness. Christian education, for example, became recognized as the process of preparing Catholics to become "soldiers of Christ," ready to stand in defense of the faith. For that role, students were expected to memorize answers to basic questions about Catholic belief.

Question: In the early part of the twentieth century, how did many average Catholics view Jesus?

Answer: From an intellectual approach of knowing correct answers rather than from an approach of developing a love relationship with Jesus

Question: Name three significant changes resulting from the Second Vatican Council that have had great impact on current Catholic understandings about Jesus.

Answer:
- A renewal in the church's interest in and study of the Scriptures
- A different understanding of the church—a movement away from the sense of it as a defensive protector of the faith and toward an image of it as a faith-filled "People of God"
- A decreased tension between religion and science

Question: Briefly compare the major characteristics of an approach to Jesus "from above" with an approach "from below"—including the benefits and limitations of both.

Answer: In an approach to Jesus "from above," Christians begin their understanding of Jesus with a recognition of his special relationship with God. Great weight is given to the Incarnation, and Jesus' divinity is stressed. The limitation of this approach is that it can give the sense that the Jesus of the Gospels is more a superman than a human like us. He can seem removed from our human experience.

In an approach to Jesus "from below," Christians begin not with Jesus' divinity but with his humanity. They gradually come to terms with his message about the kingdom of God and its implications. They see Jesus as truly sharing in their humanity. It is in his resurrection from the dead, then, that such Christians, like the early disciples, recognize the divinity of Jesus. The limitation of this approach is that it can lead to an image of the church as a kind of "self-help group," with an image of Jesus as just a particularly good man who was its founder and model.

Text Activities: Understanding Jesus in the Modern Age

Activity 7

Over the ages, the church has withstood periods of severe attack and ridicule. Today, many people simply ignore the church. Which do you think is the greater threat to the church and why?

Activity 8

Write down your reflections on this statement: *Some young people my age claim they do not believe in God. But I think their problem is with religion, not God.*

Activity 9

Using resources suggested by your school librarian and teacher, write a report on the Second Vatican Council. Why was it convened? In what ways did it change life in the church? What impact does it have on the church today?

Activity 10

Respond in writing to this statement: *"Christology from above" and "Christology from below" are simply two different paths to the same truth.*

Additional Activities: Understanding Jesus in the Modern Age

A Panel Discussion: "The Good Old Days"?

Invite to your class a panel of parents, grandparents, and other adults who were raised as Catholics before the changes brought about by Vatican Council II had an impact. Invite the panel members to share reflections on their upbringing as Catholics. Have them illustrate "the way it was" in terms of education, the Mass, confession, basic approaches to morality, and so on. They should also offer observations on what the changes of Vatican Council II meant for them personally in terms of adjustment, renewal, questioning, freedom, and so on. Encourage discussion with the students.

Option: You may want students to prepare an agenda or questions for the panel ahead of time, both to help prepare the adults as well as to focus the thoughts and questions of the students.

A Presentation on Models of Christology

If your students are interested in and capable of dealing with a deeper discussion of the shift in our understanding of Jesus in recent decades, offer a presentation based on this manual's essay "The Theology of the Course," on pages 13–20. Perhaps even photocopy and distribute the summary chart of the two christological perspectives offered on page 19.

Variation: This would also make a marvelous parent session some evening, perhaps followed in class with a discussion between the parents and the students like that suggested in the preceding activity, "A Panel Discussion: 'The Good Old Days'?"

Looking Below the Surface

This activity invites the students, in a creative, imaginative way, to explore and express their understanding of the church in light of the history in this chapter. It can be implemented as either a written exercise or a topic of classroom discussion, or some combination of the two.

Ask the students to reflect closely, even meditatively, on the photograph of the sea that opens this chapter in the student text (see p. 258). Why, do they think, did the publishers of the text choose that photo to open a chapter on the history of the church's understanding of Jesus? What does the photo suggest about the church's deepening insights into Jesus? Where in the photo are the church and its teaching best symbolized? in the rocks? in the water? in the crashing wave? If any one of those elements represents the church and its teaching, what do the *other* elements in the photo represent? For example, if the rocks symbolize the church and its teaching, what does the water symbolize?

"The Sermon of the Mouse"

This activity is intended to motivate the students to reflect on the nature of the church and its role in the world.

Handout 13–C

1. Distribute handout 13-C, "The Sermon of the Mouse." As a homework assignment, instruct your students to read the handout and to reflect on Mickey Mouse's four suggestions for making the church "as successful as Disneyland."

2. In class, divide the students into four numbered groups, giving each group one of the following sets of questions about the four suggestions made by Mickey Mouse. Allow at least 10 minutes for group discussion.

Group 1
- Mickey says the church should give the illusion of great risk but make sure everything is perfectly safe. What are the risks involved in being a Christian today?
- Can you think of examples of the church creating illusions of risk?
- How, if at all, does the church make people feel safe?

Group 2
- Mickey says the church should entertain people. How does the church entertain people, if at all? Should the church be entertaining?
- Respond to this statement: *The church is competing for people's time and attention and must give people something to make them want to come to church. After they get there, the church can slip in the message of Jesus somehow.*

Group 3
- Mickey says the church should make everything look religious. Define what *religious* means in this context.
- What do you think true religion consists of?

Group 4
- Mickey says the church should pretend that there are no problems. Do you think the church should admit to having problems of its own?
- If the church wants Christianity to appear true, shouldn't it avoid or hide problems that raise doubts in the minds of people who are searching for answers?

Concept E: The Journey of Faith in Jesus

Finding an answer to Jesus' question, "Who do you say that I am?" is an intensely personal journey that is best made in the company of a faith community. (Pages 278–279 of the student text)

A Review Question: The Journey of Faith in Jesus

Question: Why is it important for a person to be in community with other believers as he or she seeks to make a personal decision about Jesus?

Answer: The history of the church has demonstrated that one's personal search for a response to Jesus seems to take place best in communion with other believers, who can share that search.

A Text Activity: The Journey of Faith in Jesus

Activity 11

Write an honest evaluation of this course and your experience of it. What were its strengths and weaknesses? What would you change about the course? What would you tell another student who is about to begin taking the course?

An Additional Activity: The Journey of Faith in Jesus

An End-of-Course Celebration

If you made it to this point, you and the students deserve a party!

Helping the Church of Today and Tomorrow

Spreading the Word

You are members of the church who are in charge of sharing Jesus' message with young people who do not know about him yet. Remember, you were there in the beginning; you saw Jesus and loved him and watched him die. You have faith in him, but some young people have never experienced him. Develop three means of letting them know about Jesus.

Worshiping

You as a group are responsible for the sacramental life of the church. Jesus left several signs of his presence to help the church carry on in memory of him and his message. How would you make the following experiences real and meaningful to other young people?

a. *Baptism:* How should young people be initiated into the church? Who should be initiated? What kind of preparation should they go through?

b. *The Eucharist:* When should the Eucharist be available? How often should we gather for it? How old should one be to participate?

c. *Orders:* Do we need priests? If so, how should we determine who is qualified for the priesthood? And what should a priest's responsibilities be?

d. *Penance:* Does the community need to recognize sin and evil and to be reconciled? If so, in what way?

Responding

The church is called by Jesus to be a witness to his values, particularly regarding poor and oppressed people. How should Christians respond in the following areas?

a. *War:* Should the church publicly oppose all war?

b. *Poverty:* Should wealthy nations share with nations less fortunate than they are, and if so, how? For example, should all members of the church in wealthy nations be required to give to a fund for the poor?

c. *Current social issues:* Should the church make a public stand on issues such as abortion, pornography, and the environment?

The Nicene Creed Today

Original	Personal	Group
We believe in one God, the Father, the Almighty,		
maker of heaven and earth, of all that is seen and unseen.		
We believe in one Lord, Jesus Christ, the only Son of God, eternally begotten of the Father,		
God from God, Light from Light, true God from true God, begotten, not made, one in Being with the Father. Through him all things were made.		
For us men and for our salvation he came down from heaven: by the power of the Holy Spirit he was born of the Virgin Mary, and became man.		
For our sake he was crucified under Pontius Pilate; he suffered, died, and was buried.		

Original	Personal	Group
On the third day he rose again in fulfillment of the Scriptures;		
he ascended into heaven and is seated at the right hand of the Father.		
He will come again in glory to judge the living and the dead, and his kingdom will have no end.		
We believe in the Holy Spirit, the Lord, the giver of life, who proceeds from the Father and the Son.		
With the Father and the Son he is worshiped and glorified. He has spoken through the Prophets.		
We believe in one holy catholic and apostolic Church. We acknowledge one baptism for the forgiveness of sins.		
We look for the resurrection of the dead, and the life of the world to come. Amen.		

The Sermon of the Mouse

The day had finally arrived. Everyone in the congregation was waiting expectantly. The negotiations had taken months, but finally everything had been worked out. It wasn't every congregation in the country that could have an opportunity like this. It was a rare visit from a very well-known celebrity.

The pastor and his guest mounted the platform. The first hymn was sung. Then the pastor rose. "I'm sure everyone is aware of who our guest speaker is this morning," he said.

Aware? How could anyone help being aware? There were posters all over town. There was a big yellow and black banner stretched across the entry to the parking lot. Seating in the sanctuary had been assigned on a reservation basis with preferential treatment given to members in good standing. An overflow crowd was watching the service on closed-circuit television. Everybody knew about it.

"It isn't often," said the pastor, "that we have an opportunity to meet someone who has become a legend in his own time. Starting back in the bleak years of the depression, with a shoestring budget and a very simple plan, our guest, with hard work and contagious enthusiasm, built an empire for himself that rivals that of Howard Hughes. His name is a household word; he is admired by young and old alike; and he has even survived his mentor. He reigns over a multimillion-dollar business venture that was so successful in southern California that he established an even more spectacular venture in Florida. By now, I'm sure you know who I am talking about. We are so honored to have Mickey Mouse with us today to share with us the secrets of Disneyland's success. We hope that our church will be stimulated and helped by his story."

A hush came over the congregation as this famous mouse rose to his feet, cleared his throat, and began his sermon.

"Thank you for inviting me to come to your church. I must admit that at first I was surprised that a church would ask me to give a sermon. Oh, I have been invited to religion classes where they give each person a Mickey Mouse hat and expect me to shake hands with everyone and act funny, but a sermon is something new.

"But after I thought about it, I realized that maybe Disneyland and the church did have a lot in common. As I began to organize my thoughts, I saw how ingenious it was to invite me to share. I really believe that if your church were to apply our principles you could become as successful as Disneyland.

"First, make sure your enterprise seems exciting, even dangerous; but be quick to let your people know that there really is no danger involved. *Give the illusion of great risk,* but make sure everything is perfectly safe.

"Second, admit that you are in the entertainment business. People won't care what you say as long as they're entertained. Keep your people happy. Don't tell them anything negative. And don't make demands on them. Just keep them diverted from the ugly reality of today's world, and they will keep coming back for more.

"Third, make everything look religious. Make the religious experience so elaborate, so intricate, so complex that only the professionals can pull it off and all the laypeople can do is stand around with their mouths open and watch. People would rather watch an imitation mechanical bird sing than a real bird, anyway. They would rather watch worship than do it.

"Fourth and finally, pretend that there are no problems. At Disneyland we dress up our security guards as smiling rabbits or friendly bears because we don't want anyone's experience at Disneyland to be ruined by the sight of law enforcement personnel. Disguise your problems and failures behind a warm smile and a firm handshake. Leave them at home, and let the church be a happy place where there aren't any ugly problems.

"People today want good, clean entertainment. They want an environment that is safe for children, and they want a place that is safe for their family and friends. I am so glad to see that the church is moving in this direction. Thank you, and God bless you."

Reprinted from Wayne Rice, John Roberto, and Mike Yaconelli, editors, *Creative Learning Experiences* (Winona, MN: Saint Mary's Press, 1981), pages 77–80.

Appendices

APPENDIX 1

Sample Test Questions

Chapter 1: The Search for Jesus

Multiple Choice

b 1. The most important faith statement about Jesus is that he is
   a. the one who performs good works
   b. the crucified one who has been raised by God and is now alive
   c. the conquering king
   d. the child of Bethlehem
   [pp. 8, 12]

a 2. This course invites you to
   a. learn why Jesus came to be recognized as the Christ of Faith
   b. learn why we go to Mass on Sunday
   c. make a definite decision to believe in Jesus by the end of the year
   d. memorize the books of the Scriptures
   [pp. 11, 12]

c 3. The historical sources of information about Jesus are valuable because they
   a. prove that Jesus is God
   b. are the source of our faith
   c. support the historical reality of Jesus
   d. are written in an old language
   [pp. 15, 17]

b 4. Our truest and best foundation for learning about Jesus is
   a. magicians and soothsayers
   b. the Christian Scriptures
   c. theologians and biblical scholars
   d. Catholic bookstores
   [p. 14]

a 5. The Christian Scriptures include
   a. the Hebrew Scriptures and the Christian Testament
   b. the writings of Tacitus and Pliny the Younger
   c. Greek and Roman myths
   d. the thoughts of theologians and biblical scholars
   [pp. 14, 15]

a 6. If we are searching for stories about Jesus' life, death, and resurrection, we will find them in
   a. the Gospels
   b. the Epistles
   c. the writings of Suetonius
   d. the Book of Revelation
   [p. 19]

<u>d</u> 7. If we want to know about the life of the first Christians, we can learn about it in
   a. the Gospels
   b. the writings of Suetonius
   c. the Book of Revelation
   d. the letters of Saint Paul
   [p. 19]

<u>c</u> 8. The books of the Christian Testament developed over the course of about
   a. four centuries
   b. thirty-three years
   c. fifty years
   d. fifty days
   [p. 18]

<u>a</u> 9. The twenty-seven books of the Christian Testament, which the church regards as the authoritative Christian writings, are often called "the Christian canon." The word *canon* comes from the Greek word for
   a. "standard" or "rule"
   b. "military armament"
   c. "collection of stories"
   d. "theological works"
   [p. 19]

<u>d</u> 10. The constant concern in this course will be
   a. memorizing the names of the books of the Christian Testament
   b. exploring the writings of historians
   c. becoming biblical scholars
   d. learning who Jesus is and what the meaning of his life is
   [p. 21]

True or False
Put a *t* in the blank next to each true statement and an *f* in the blank next to each false statement. Turn each false statement into a true statement by drawing a line through the incorrect wording and writing in the correct wording.

Note: In no case is it necessary to rewrite an entire false statement in order to make it true.

<u>f</u> 1. The *Acts of the Apostles tells* [*Gospels tell*] about the life, death, and resurrection of Jesus [p. 19].
<u>t</u> 2. The Acts of the Apostles tells about the early days of the Christian community [p. 19].
<u>f</u> 3. The epistles attributed to Peter, James, John, and Jude are referred to as "catholic," which means *"Roman Catholic"* [*"universal" or "general"*] [p. 20].
<u>f</u> 4. The Gospels are attributed to Matthew, Mark, *James* [*Luke*], and John [pp. 14, 19].
<u>t</u> 5. Most of the Epistles are attributed to Saint Paul [p. 19].
<u>t</u> 6. The Book of Revelation was written to encourage early Christians who were suffering persecution for their beliefs [p. 20].

Essay

1. Briefly describe each of these collections of writings: *Christian Scriptures, Hebrew Scriptures, Christian Testament* [pp. 14, 15].
2. Write a paragraph explaining why the Gospels are so important to the church's teaching about Jesus. Why are they more important than other writings, such as the Acts of the Apostles or the Epistles? [pp. 14, 18]

Extra Credit

1. Imagine that you have to tell someone about Jesus. Draw on your own knowledge and write down three things you know about him. Then write down three questions *you* have about him as you begin this course.
2. Write a paragraph about someone or something that has helped you grow in your understanding of Jesus: for example, a parent or another family member, a friend, an adult you admire, your own prayer, or the story of another person. (This can be an influence from some earlier point in your life. It need not be influential in your life right now.)
3. Think of the many titles given to Jesus. Here are a few: *Lord, Savior, Redeemer, Teacher, Messiah, Friend, Companion, Good Shepherd*. Of all the titles or descriptions you have heard, which one is the most appealing to you? Why?

Chapter 2: The Gospels

Multiple Choice

<u>a</u> 1. In general, which of the following sources will give you the most objective facts?
   a. high-tech measuring and recording systems
   b. people on the street
   c. books of poetry
   d. comic books
   [p. 23]

<u>d</u> 2. Historical information is
   a. purely objective
   b. transmitted by robots that do not interpret data
   c. mostly untrustworthy propaganda
   d. a combination of fact and interpretation
   [p. 23]

<u>d</u> 3. Religious truth is concerned with
   a. proving the facts beyond a shadow of a doubt
   b. memorizing information in a religion class
   c. facts that the majority of theologians agree on
   d. the deeper meaning that God intends to reveal through historical events
   [p. 25]

<u>c</u> 4. The Gospel writers set out to
   a. record objective facts about Jesus
   b. record their private feelings about Jesus
   c. interpret events in light of their faith or that of their community
   d. interpret events in light of the teachings of popes and scholars
   [p. 25]

<u>b</u> 5. Biblical literature primarily discloses
   a. objective truth
   b. religious truth
   c. historical truth
   d. scientific truth
   [p. 25]

__b__ 6. The followers of Jesus began recording the Good News out of an attitude of
   a. vengeance
   b. faith
   c. doubt
   d. fear
   [p. 29]

__a__ 7. Which of the following is the least reliable source of growth for our understanding of the Scriptures?
   a. the personal opinions of a self-assured speaker
   b. our personal and prayerful use of the Scriptures
   c. respected biblical scholars and theologians
   d. official teachings of the Roman Catholic church
   [p. 26]

__c__ 8. The pivotal event of Christian faith is
   a. the birth of Jesus
   b. Jesus' choice of Peter as the leader of the church
   c. the resurrection of Jesus
   d. the Last Supper
   [p. 29]

__a__ 9. As the disciples preached the Good News throughout the Roman Empire, they gradually
   a. preserved the parts of his life story and teachings that carried great meaning and value
   b. began to keep a record of every detail of Jesus' life
   c. became interested in charming stories of Jesus' childhood
   d. lined up proof of Jesus' existence
   [p. 32]

__c__ 10. The Gospels were eventually written because of a need to
   a. provide precise scientific data to explain Jesus' miracles
   b. preserve the riches of the Hebrew language
   c. preserve Jesus' message and instruct and inspire his followers
   d. have a history of Jewish life from 3 B.C.E. to 100 C.E.
   [p. 34]

__a__ 11. In writing the Gospels, the Evangelists generally paid close attention to
   a. gathering the oral tradition and addressing it to the understanding and situation of their communities of faith
   b. picking and choosing those stories from the oral tradition that were comforting and pleasant
   c. lining up logical proof of Jesus' existence
   d. providing timeless documents equal to the great literature of the world
   [pp. 34, 35]

True or False

__f__ 1. In a given situation, usually one person possesses the truth and the others have a distorted view [pp. 23, 24].
__f__ 2. The Gospels are biographies of Jesus [p. 24].
__f__ 3. Christians read the Gospels because they wish to find the historical facts about Jesus [p. 24].
__f__ 4. The Gospels' main purpose is to explain the Resurrection [p. 24].
__t__ 5. The Gospels are testimonies of faith [p. 24].
__t__ 6. The Gospels proclaim a message of faith in Jesus [p. 24].
__t__ 7. For Christians, the Jesus of History is also the Christ of Faith [p. 30].

<u>t</u> 8. The early Christians' oral tradition was the basis for the written Gospels [p. 32].
<u>f</u> 9. Each of the four Gospels was written by a single author who wrote in isolation [p. 35].

Fact or Interpretation

Each numbered item below is a type of newspaper article. Write an *f* in the blank if the article reflects objective facts. Write an *i* in the blank if the article is concerned with the meaning, value, or importance of an event. [p. 23]

<u>f</u> 1. A report of the Friday-night football scores
<u>i</u> 2. An article on the relationship between football and academic standing
<u>f</u> 3. A map showing the temperatures of major cities around the world
<u>f</u> 4. A recipe for pizza
<u>f</u> 5. A list of drunk driving arrests that were made in the state during a weekend in October
<u>i</u> 6. An editorial on a couple whose daughter was killed by a drunk driver

Matching

<u>b</u> 1. The meaning of the name *Jesus* [p. 30]   **a.** good news
<u>d</u> 2. The meaning of the word *Christ* [p. 30]   **b.** Yahweh saves
<u>e</u> 3. The meaning of the word *Gentile* [p. 37]   **c.** to see together
<u>c</u> 4. The meaning of the word *synoptic* [p. 40]   **d.** anointed one
<u>a</u> 5. The meaning of the word *gospel* [p. 24]   **e.** non-Jewish person

Fill in the Blank

Fill in each blank with the name of one of the Gospels: *Matthew, Mark, Luke* or *John*.

1. <u>Mark</u> was written first [p. 36].
2. <u>John</u> was written last [p. 41].
3. <u>Mark</u> was written for Christians facing severe suffering and trials [p. 37].
4. <u>Matthew</u>, <u>Mark</u>, and <u>Luke</u> are synoptic Gospels [p. 40].
5. <u>John</u> is not a synoptic Gospel [p. 40].
6. <u>Matthew</u> and <u>Luke</u> drew from Mark as a source [pp. 38, 39].
7. <u>Mark</u> concentrates on the humanity of Jesus [p. 37].
8. <u>Mark</u> and <u>Luke</u> were written for Gentiles [pp. 37, 38].
9. <u>Luke</u> offers a portrait of a compassionate Jesus [p. 39].
10. <u>Matthew</u> emphasizes the relationship between Jesus and the Messiah who is promised in the Hebrew Scriptures [pp. 39–40].
11. <u>John</u> is filled with symbolic language [p. 40].
12. <u>Matthew</u> seems concerned about the early Christians as a community or church [p. 40].
13. <u>John</u> focuses on Jesus as the divine Son of God [p. 42].
14. <u>Luke</u> seems to have been written for both Gentiles and well-to-do Christians [p. 38].
15. <u>Matthew</u> portrays Jesus as a teacher [p. 40].

Essay

1. Recall a personal experience that meant a great deal to you. List the facts about the event—what happened, where, when, and how—as accurately as you can. Next, write about your *interpretation* of the event, the meaning it held for you. Discuss the relationship between the facts and your interpretation. If you tell someone about the personal experience, which do you want them to remember most clearly—the facts or your interpretation? Why? [p. 24]

2. List the people to whom you communicated the personal experience discussed in the first essay question. Then explain how you could have, or did, record the experience so that you would always remember it.

    Compare your three-step process of experiencing, talking about, and recording with that same three-step process in the development of the Gospels. That is, what did Jesus' followers experience? Who did they tell? How did they record the story in order to have a permanent record? [pp. 28–34]
3. Write either a pro or a con response to this statement: *People who actually experienced Jesus during his earthly life in Palestine had a much easier time understanding and accepting him than people do today* [p. 43].
4. Explain the difference between the Roman Catholic church's approach to the Scriptures and the approach used by many Protestant churches. Use the term *Tradition* in your explanation, and explain why Roman Catholics view Tradition as authoritative. [p. 27]

Extra Credit

Drawing on your knowledge of the Gospels, which one Gospel would you choose as a guide and help to you? Why does that Gospel attract you at this stage of your life?

Chapter 3: The World of Jesus

Matching

Note: Some of the letters from the right-hand column will be used more than once.

_h_	1. I was the child of Isaac and Rebekah, and later I was the father of twelve sons [p. 47].	a. Abraham
_a_	2. I was the first to enter into a covenant with a loving and personal God [p. 47].	b. Abram
_k_	3. I was a brutal and brilliant leader who ruled Israel when Jesus was born [p. 65].	c. Alexander
_t_	4. I was the first king of Israel. I was a good warrior, and I did not like the young David [p. 53].	d. David
_l_	5. Abraham, Jacob, and I are called "the patriarchs" [p. 48].	e. Diaspora
_o_	6. After a deep religious experience of God, I led my people out of slavery [p. 48].	f. Essenes
_d_	7. I ruled over a peaceful and strong kingdom, and even to this day I am recognized as the greatest king Israel ever had [p. 53].	g. Galileans
_u_	8. I built the Temple in Jerusalem [p. 54].	h. Jacob
_j_	9. Though I was sold into slavery in Egypt, I prospered there and made a place for my family, where they eventually grew and prospered too [p. 48].	i. Jesus

Right column continued: j. Joseph, k. Herod, l. Isaac, m. Isaiah, n. Maccabeus, o. Moses, p. Pharisees, q. Romans, r. Sadducees, s. Samaritans, t. Saul, u. Solomon, v. Zealots

_h_ 10. God gave me the name *Israel* [p. 47].
_b_ 11. God gave me the name *Abraham* [p. 47].
_o_ 12. God's name *Yahweh* was revealed to me, and that is how I realized that God intended to care for and rule me and my people [pp. 48, 50].
_n_ 13. I was a leader in the Jewish overthrow of the Syrian Greeks [p. 60].
_m_ 14. I and others like me spoke forcefully to the people, trying to call them back to their covenant with Yahweh. I spoke of a good and strong person from the line of David who would bring peace. [p. 54]
_e_ 15. We were among the Israelites who were not exiled in Babylon. We moved away from Judah after Jerusalem was destroyed. [p. 54]
_c_ 16. I am called "the Great." I established Greek influence and domination throughout the Mediterranean world. [p. 58]
_o_ 17. On Mount Sinai, I received the covenant that made the Israelites God's beloved people [p. 52].
_s_ 18. We were descendants of the old northern tribes of Israel, who had not been sent into exile in Babylon. Our religious practices differed from those of the rest of Israel. The remnant did not like us at all. [pp. 62, 64]
_r_ 19. We were the priestly class, and we tried to get along with the Jewish political leaders [p. 61].
_q_ 20. We were only too glad to "help" rule the Jews, who did not seem able to rule themselves [p. 64].
_f_ 21. We are not mentioned in the Bible, but we were important. We withdrew from Jewish society entirely and strictly followed our traditions. [p. 61]
_p_ 22. We had a reputation for strict faithfulness to the covenant and, as a result, were respected by and influential among the common people [pp. 61–62].
_g_ 23. Of all the people in Palestine, we were the least respected, but Jesus was born in our area [p. 64].
_v_ 24. We were a revolutionary group who were interested in overthrowing the Romans [p. 67].
_i_ 25. I am from the line of David. I was a Galilean carpenter and a teacher. The story of Israel is my family story.

Essay

1. Explain why understanding the history of Israel is important to understanding Jesus [pp. 45–46].
2. What does God's name *Yahweh* mean? What was significant about God's revealing that name to the Israelites? [pp. 48, 50]
3. Briefly explain the origin and meaning of the term *Passover* [pp. 51–52].
4. Why was the covenant of Sinai so important? Discuss its meaning to the people of Israel, how it differed from the covenant God had made with Abraham, and how it helped the people understand themselves and their relationship to Yahweh. [p. 52]
5. Identify the various religious and political groups that existed in Israel during Jesus' public ministry. Explain why their expectations of and belief in a Messiah did not prepare them to accept Jesus as the Messiah. [pp. 61–62, 64, 68–69]

Extra Credit

1. Make a timeline using these dates: 1900 B.C.E., 1250 B.C.E., 1200 B.C.E., 1000 B.C.E., 598 B.C.E., 539 B.C.E. Label the dates with these events: *the Babylonian Exile, the Exodus and the Sinai covenant, Israel united under David, return from the Exile, the time of Abraham, settlement in the Promised Land.* [p. 56]
2. Make a timeline using these dates: 323 B.C.E., 164 B.C.E., 142 B.C.E., 63 B.C.E., 5 B.C.E., 70 C.E. Label the dates with these events: *birth of Jesus, beginning of Roman rule in Palestine, Israel's independence, beginning of Egyptian Greek and Syrian Greek rule, the Maccabean Revolt, destruction of the Temple by the Romans.* [p. 66]
3. Write a paragraph explaining the differences between these titles for God's people: *Hebrews, Israelites, Jews* [pp. 47, 48, 57].

Chapter 4: Daily Life in Jesus' Time

Multiple Choice

<u>b</u> 1. When Jesus spoke of himself as "living water," his listeners understood his meaning, because in Palestine water was
   a. plentiful and always present
   b. precious and life-giving
   c. contained only in the salty Mediterranean Sea
   d. found only in the Jordan River
   [p. 74]

<u>a</u> 2. In Jesus' time, bread was
   a. an essential, nourishing food
   b. rare because of the lack of yeast
   c. available only to the rich
   d. served only on feast days
   [p. 76]

<u>d</u> 3. For Jesus and his people, sharing a meal was
   a. an inconvenience
   b. a formal, solemn affair
   c. confined to the kitchen
   d. a sacred act
   [p. 78]

__b__ 4. Which animals were not common in Jesus' hometown?
   a. cows and sheep
   b. camels and horses
   c. donkeys and oxen
   d. geese and chickens
   [p. 76]

__d__ 5. When Jesus visited poor people, he would not have been surprised to see that they shared their homes with
   a. dignitaries from the Temple
   b. visitors from Rome
   c. their family cats
   d. their domestic animals
   [p. 80]

__d__ 6. For a special holiday meal, Jesus would have
   a. used a knife, fork, and spoon
   b. sat on a chair and eaten at a table
   c. gone to the best hotel in town
   d. eaten meat, such as lamb
   [pp. 78–79]

__a__ 7. Most of the men Jesus met as he walked about his country would have had jobs as
   a. farmers, fishers, or tradesmen
   b. teachers or writers
   c. workers in the oil fields
   d. scientists
   [pp. 81–82]

__b__ 8. It is believed that Jesus' trade was
   a. tent making
   b. carpentry
   c. farming
   d. botany
   [p. 82]

__a__ 9. Which of the following statements is *not* true about the Jewish marriage traditions of Jesus' time?
   a. Young men and women dated and chose their own spouses.
   b. Parents arranged their children's marriages.
   c. Many young men and women married in their teens.
   d. The time of formal engagement was about one year.
   [p. 83]

__d__ 10. If a woman was caught in adultery, she was
   a. forgiven by her husband
   b. brought before the Roman authorities
   c. exiled to the Dead Sea area
   d. stoned to death
   [p. 83]

__b__ 11. The Jewish laws regarding adultery were an attempt to
   a. control the society in the Mediterranean world
   b. protect family life
   c. limit legal problems
   d. make life hard for women
   [p. 83]

_d_ 12. Which of the following situations is evidence that Jesus' society did not view women as equal to men?
   a. Women served meals to men but did not sit and eat with them.
   b. Women were excluded from certain areas of the Temple.
   c. In public, women were expected to keep a certain distance from men.
   d. All of the above
   [p. 84]

_a_ 13. Jesus' treatment of women was noticeable because he
   a. treated them with respect and dignity
   b. treated them worse than the rest of the men did
   c. treated them like servants
   d. expected them to wait on him
   [pp. 84, 86]

_b_ 14. Jesus was most interested in
   a. starting a revolution to gain equal rights
   b. proclaiming freedom for all people
   c. being accepted by the rich and powerful
   d. learning and following all the rules of society
   [p. 86]

_c_ 15. According to Jesus, the Temple was meant to be
   a. a museum
   b. a center of trading and money changing
   c. the center of Israel's religious life
   d. equal to the synagogue in importance
   [p. 89]

_b_ 16. The great prayer of Israel is
   a. the Lord's Prayer
   b. the Shema
   c. the rosary
   d. Psalm 23
   [p. 89]

_a_ 17. The holiest day of the Jewish week is
   a. the Sabbath
   b. Good Friday
   c. the Feast of Tabernacles
   d. Pentecost
   [p. 90]

_d_ 18. The greatest feast of the Jewish year is
   a. Pentecost
   b. the Day of Atonement
   c. New Year's Day
   d. Passover
   [p. 92]

_b_ 19. The Jewish Sabbath begins on
   a. Saturday at sunrise
   b. Friday at sunset
   c. Sunday morning
   d. Sunday evening
   [p. 90]

__a__ 20. Synagogues are places of
   a. prayer and study
   b. sacrifice and offering
   c. retail and wholesale
   d. fasting and abstinence
   [p. 89]

True or False

__f__ 1. Because of the large size of Palestine, the people of Jesus' time tended to stay close to home [p. 73].
__t__ 2. The land of Palestine was geographically diverse [pp. 73–74].
__t__ 3. When Jesus spoke of fields and plants and animals, he spoke from firsthand experience of them [p. 71].
__t__ 4. The people of Palestine knew their country "by heart" [p. 73].
__f__ 5. The weather in Palestine was predictable and dull [p. 74].
__f__ 6. Water was plentiful in Palestine [p. 74].
__t__ 7. Most of the people Jesus met were poor working people [p. 85].
__f__ 8. Equality of the sexes was a matter of fact in Jesus' time [pp. 83–84, 86].
__t__ 9. Compared with other societies of Jesus' time, the Jewish society was relatively just [p. 84].
__t__ 10. Jesus' treatment of women is marked with respect for them as equals [pp. 84, 86].
__t__ 11. Observance of the Jewish Law was a subject of great debate during Jesus' time [pp. 91, 93–94].

Matching 1: Key Religious-Political Groups and Persons

Note: Some of the letters from the right-hand column will be used more than once.

__i__ 1. According to the Jewish Law, these people were to be freed after seven years [p. 86].
__c__ 2. "Unclean" people, the extremely poor, the sick, and women belonged to this group [p. 86].
__b__ 3. This man was the head of the priestly caste [p. 92].
__g__ 4. They were part of the Jewish upper class and possessed a lot of political power [p. 93].
__e__ 5. They offered sacrifices in the Temple, acting as intermediaries between the people and God [p. 92].
__a__ 6. This was the official governing body of the Jews [p. 94].
__b__ 7. Caiaphas served in this role during Jesus' trial [p. 93].
__a__ 8. Elders, members of priestly families, and scribes belonged to this assembly [p. 94].
__g__ 9. Members of this group were very conservative in religion, accepting only the first five books of the Hebrew Scriptures as the Law [p. 93].
__d__ 10. This group was open to new developments in Jewish thought [p. 93].

a. Great Sanhedrin
b. high priest
c. outcasts
d. Pharisees
e. priests
f. rabbi
g. Sadducees
h. scribes
i. slaves
j. tax collectors
k. Zealots

g 11. This group was committed to the purity of sacrifice and worship in the Temple [p. 93].
j 12. They were accused of "pocketing" the money of the Jewish citizens [pp. 94–95].
a 13. In Jesus' trial, this group acted like a kind of supreme court [p. 94].
k 14. This group worked and fought for Jewish independence [p. 94].
h 15. This group originated during the Babylonian Exile [p. 95].
j 16. They were also called "publicans" [p. 95].
h 17. The title *doctor of the Law* was given to the most respected members of this group [p. 95].
f 18. This man's title meant "master" or "teacher" [p. 95].
e 19. They became an exclusive class, often resented by the common people [p. 92].
g 20. This group died out after the destruction of the Temple in 70 C.E. [p. 93].

Matching 2: Holy Days and Holidays

Note: Some of the letters from the right-hand column will be used more than once.

d 1. It begins at sunset on Friday and ends at sunset on Saturday [p. 90].
c 2. It was originally a celebration of the harvest [p. 92].
b 3. A special meal shared on this day recalls one that was eaten by the Israelites before their escape from Egypt [p. 92].
c 4. It is also called the Feast of Weeks, and it commemorates Yahweh's giving the Law to Moses [p. 91].
d 5. It commemorates the Creation, the Sinai covenant, and the Exodus [p. 90].
b 6. It is the holiest and greatest celebration of the Jewish people [p. 92].
a 7. It is a day for repentance of sins [p. 92].

a. Day of Atonement
b. Passover
c. Pentecost
d. Sabbath

Essay

1. Explain the steps that went into making bread during Jesus' time. What place did bread have in the lives of poor people? [pp. 76, 77, 78]
2. Make up a menu of a meal Jesus might have shared with his friends on an ordinary day. Then make up a menu of a meal that he might have shared with his friends on a special Jewish feast day. [pp. 78–79]
3. Describe the setting and utensils of an everyday meal that Jesus might have shared with his friends [pp. 78–79].
4. Describe (or draw and label) a typical family home of Jesus' day. Tell how it differed from the home of a rich person of that time. [pp. 80–81]
5. Describe the role and responsibilities of a married woman in Palestine during Jesus' time, or describe the role and responsibilities of a married man in Palestine during Jesus' time [pp. 83–84].

6. Explain Jesus' views in one of the following areas: respecting women, respecting and including every person, or valuing persons above laws. Tell what group or groups of people Jesus would have angered or upset because of his attitude and actions. [pp. 84, 86, 91, 92–95]

Chapter 5: The Mission Begins

Multiple Choice

<u>a</u> 1. The Gospels provide Christians with
   a. the meaning and significance of Jesus' life
   b. a historical record of Jesus' life
   c. a biography of Jesus
   d. stories of Jesus' life that make them feel comfortable and peaceful
   [p. 101]

<u>d</u> 2. Matthew wrote his infancy narrative to show his Jewish readers that Jesus was
   a. accepted by Eastern scholars
   b. born to punish them for their sins
   c. a military leader like David
   d. the promised Messiah
   [p. 103]

<u>b</u> 3. In Matthew's Gospel, the Holy Family is called out of Egypt to Israel after Herod's death. This would have reminded Matthew's readers of
   a. David's conquest of Egypt
   b. the Exodus
   c. Abraham and Sarah's journey
   d. Anwar Sadat and the peace accords
   [p. 103]

<u>c</u> 4. To show that Jesus' message is addressed to all people, Luke begins Jesus' genealogy with
   a. the Magi
   b. Abraham
   c. Adam
   d. Mary
   [p. 103]

<u>a</u> 5. Luke included shepherds in his story of the birth of Christ because
   a. Luke wanted to indicate that poor people would be the first to recognize and respond to Jesus
   b. Luke wanted to address his Gospel to rich people only
   c. Luke himself was a shepherd
   d. records showed that shepherds had been present
   [p. 103]

<u>d</u> 6. The story of Mary and Joseph taking Jesus to the Temple shows us that they
   a. were overly religious
   b. were afraid to break any laws
   c. were aware that Jesus was God
   d. lived out the traditions of their religion
   [pp. 100, 106, 108]

__a__ 7. Jesus' strong Jewish faith had its source in
   a. his family life
   b. the attitudes and choices of his friends
   c. the rules of the Roman soldiers who were always around
   d. Greek and Persian scholarship
   [p. 108]

__b__ 8. John the Baptist's task was to
   a. gain as much personal power as possible
   b. prepare the way for Jesus' ministry
   c. avoid attracting the attention of the Roman soldiers
   d. upset the peaceful lives of the Pharisees
   [p. 109]

__b__ 9. Baptism by John the Baptist was a sign of
   a. unity with all people
   b. spiritual purification
   c. John's intolerance of dirt
   d. solidarity with those who were sinful
   [p. 109]

__c__ 10. According to Matthew's Gospel, Jesus accepted baptism as a sign of his willingness to
   a. go with the flow
   b. spare John any embarrassment
   c. be one with the people and live as they lived
   d. follow the rules set down by the Sadducees
   [p. 111]

__b__ 11. At his baptism, Jesus understood that he
   a. had to play out a role he had known about since his birth
   b. would be given the power to fulfill his mission through the Spirit of God
   c. would have an interesting, easy life
   d. all of the above
   [p. 111]

__a__ 12. For the people of Israel, the desert was
   a. the place that had tested their ancestors' faithfulness to Yahweh
   b. a warm, inviting place to rest
   c. an interesting part of Israel's geography
   d. a place to bury the Dead Sea Scrolls
   [p. 112]

__a__ 13. Jesus refused to turn stones into bread, because he
   a. had come to satisfy the people's spiritual hunger, not their material needs
   b. was holding out for a better offer
   c. knew that bread alone was not appetizing
   d. did not believe that the one who tempted him really existed
   [p. 112]

__b__ 14. Jesus refused to prove his relationship with God by throwing himself off the Temple and surviving, because he
   a. was not sure God was with him
   b. did not want people to put their faith in magic
   c. preferred an easier way to prove the relationship
   d. was afraid of heights
   [p. 112]

__a__ 15. Jesus rejected the temptation to worship the devil and control all the kingdoms of the world, because doing so would have
   a. meant relying on political power as a way to accomplish his Dream
   b. aligned Jesus with the Romans
   c. made Jesus unpopular with the Jews
   d. meant Jesus had to train soldiers
   [p. 113]

__c__ 16. Jesus' manner of teaching was new and surprising because he relied on
   a. the authority of other scriptural scholars
   b. the authority of those who held the weapons
   c. his own authority
   d. the authority of Herod the Great
   [p. 114]

__c__ 17. Jesus' claiming himself as the sole judge of the truth of what he taught
   a. made people dismiss him as irrelevant
   b. made the Pharisees admire him
   c. both impressed and alienated his listeners
   d. both humored and entertained his listeners
   [p. 114]

__a__ 18. The pattern of discipleship among Jesus' first followers continues today. Christians are still called to
   a. develop a relationship with Jesus and share his mission
   b. develop a "Jesus and me" relationship
   c. do good works and trust that their personal relationship with Jesus will take care of itself
   d. obey the rules of discipleship as those rules are stated in the Acts of the Apostles
   [p. 116]

__d__ 19. The Apostles were
   a. ordinary people with an extraordinary mission
   b. commissioned to carry forth the Good News of the Kingdom of God
   c. twelve in number
   d. all of the above
   [pp. 116–117]

__b__ 20. The Apostle Peter
   a. was flawless in his following of Jesus
   b. took on the leadership role in the early community
   c. was calm and coolheaded
   d. was the oldest Apostle
   [p. 115]

True or False

__f__ 1. The infancy narratives in the Gospels of Matthew and Luke offer the very same information [p. 99].

__t__ 2. The infancy narratives tell us as much, if not more, about the Christ of Faith as they do about the Jesus of History [p. 103].

__f__ 3. We can learn a great deal about Jesus' childhood and early schooling by reading the infancy narratives [p. 105].

__f__ 4. The term *hidden years* refers to the time when Jesus had to keep a low profile in order to escape the wrath of Herod the Great [p. 105].

__t__ 5. Jesus was a human being like us, with all the needs each of us has [p. 106].

_t_ 6. The Holy Family followed the Jewish Law [p. 108].
_f_ 7. The prologue to John's Gospel proclaims Jesus as a perfect human being but does not hint at his divinity [p. 98].
_t_ 8. The Magi represent all Gentiles who accepted Jesus [p. 103].
_f_ 9. The names of the Magi are found in John's Gospel [p. 102].
_t_ 10. The Gospels' portrait of Peter shows us that ordinary people committed to Christ are capable of extraordinary things [p. 115].

Fill in the Blank

Fill in each blank with the name of one of the Gospels: *Matthew, Mark, Luke,* or *John.*

1. <u>Matthew</u> and <u>Luke</u> contain infancy narratives [p. 97].
2. <u>John</u> begins with a prologue referring to Jesus' origins [p. 98].
3. <u>Matthew</u> tells the story of the Magi, or Wise Men [p. 99].
4. <u>Luke</u> is the only Gospel that describes Jesus being laid in a manger after his birth [p. 100].
5. <u>Matthew</u> traces Jesus' family tree back to Abraham [p. 97].
6. <u>Luke</u> traces Jesus' family tree back to Adam [p. 103].
7. <u>Luke</u> contains Mary's Magnificat [p. 99].
8. <u>Mark</u> and <u>John</u> do not describe Jesus' birth and childhood [p. 97].
9. <u>Luke</u> is the only Gospel that offers the story of the boy Jesus lost in the Temple [p. 100].
10. <u>Luke</u> tells the story of Elizabeth and Zechariah, the parents of John the Baptist [p. 99].
11. <u>John</u> does not describe Jesus' baptism [p. 109].
12. <u>Mark</u> was the first Gospel written [p. 101].
13. <u>Matthew</u> was directed to devout Jews [p. 101].
14. <u>Luke</u> was directed to Gentiles [p. 101].
15. <u>John</u> portrays Jesus as the divine Son of God [p. 101].

Essay

1. Explain the main intentions of each writer of the infancy narratives. Give an example of how each intention is reflected in the writer's narrative. [p. 103]
2. Identify and discuss the religious influences on Jesus as he grew up in Galilee [pp. 106–108].
3. How was Jesus like the rabbis of his time? How was he different from them? [p. 114]
4. How did Jesus' relationship with his disciples differ from the rabbi-disciple relationship commonly accepted in Israel [p. 116]?

Chapter 6: The Kingdom of God

Multiple Choice

_a_ 1. The term that refers to Jesus' vision, or Dream, is
   a. Kingdom of God
   b. Promised Land
   c. Temple of Jerusalem
   d. Time of Promise
   [p. 119]

__a__ 2. Jesus' miracles were expressions of God's ushering in the
   a. Kingdom of God
   b. Century of Peace
   c. Reign of Light
   d. Promised Land
   [p. 119]

__c__ 3. Jesus rooted his Dream in
   a. his family's inheritance
   b. Joseph's construction business
   c. his own history, life experiences, and hopes
   d. his easy way with people of power
   [p. 120]

__a__ 4. A good substitution for the word *kingdom* in the term *Kingdom of God* is
   a. reign
   b. beatitude
   c. church
   d. nation
   [p. 122]

__d__ 5. The only Gospel that does not mention the theme of the Kingdom of God is the Gospel of
   a. Matthew
   b. Mark
   c. Luke
   d. John
   [p. 122]

__b__ 6. The Jews saw God's kingship revealed in
   a. a heavenly military force
   b. natural wonders and the Law
   c. the Roman control of Jerusalem
   d. democratic governments
   [p. 122]

__a__ 7. Expectations of the Messiah as a warrior or military leader were rooted in the Jews' memory of
   a. David
   b. Moses
   c. Adam
   d. none of the above
   [p. 123]

__c__ 8. The word *Abba,* used by Jesus, was a term
   a. of fear and reverence
   b. often used by Jews of his time to refer to God
   c. of intimacy and familiarity
   d. used when addressing kings and lords
   [p. 124]

__a__ 9. In Matthew's Gospel, the Kingdom of God is called the
   a. kingdom of heaven
   b. Holy of Holies
   c. kingdom of David
   d. nation of Israel
   [p. 126]

__b__ 10. Jesus taught us about a God whose love is
   a. dependent on our goodness
   b. unconditional
   c. ruled by strict justice
   d. fickle
   [p. 126]

__c__ 11. Our participation in the Kingdom of God requires
   a. obedience to the Law of Moses
   b. the ability to pass religion tests
   c. conversion
   d. sinlessness
   [p. 127]

__c__ 12. Jesus' idea of love for others was
   a. totally new
   b. borrowed from the Romans
   c. an expansion of a Jewish notion
   d. his idea of common sense
   [p. 127]

__d__ 13. Jesus' insistence on universal love conflicted with the Jews' tendencies toward
   a. rest and relaxation
   b. athletic and scholastic competition
   c. trade and commerce
   d. nationalism and legalism
   [pp. 127–128]

__b__ 14. Jesus' insistence on universal love
   a. is a nice but ineffective idea
   b. includes love of enemies
   c. is too difficult to carry out
   d. is to be interpreted loosely
   [p. 128]

__c__ 15. Jesus wanted people to act out their love by
   a. obeying the rules exactly
   b. having faith that everything would turn out all right
   c. serving and forgiving others
   d. being nice and polite
   [pp. 128–129]

__a__ 16. The story of Adam and Eve's temptation helps us understand that sin is the result of
   a. human choice
   b. God's anger
   c. the devil's trickery
   d. pollution
   [p. 131]

__b__ 17. The rupture between God and people in the story of Adam and Eve is called
   a. injustice
   b. original sin
   c. actual sin
   d. a sad fact of life
   [p. 131]

c 18. The conflict between good and evil
   a. happened once and for all in the Book of Genesis
   b. is too scary to think about
   c. takes place in the hearts of individuals and in their relationships
   d. took place only in the garden of Eden and during Jesus' agony in the garden
   [p. 132]

a 19. The Resurrection is
   a. God's triumph over evil
   b. God's way of showing us that life does not have to be difficult
   c. evidence of the power of sin
   d. a minor event in church history
   [p. 132]

b 20. Jesus' followers fully recognized the Kingdom of God
   a. during their time with Jesus in his ministry
   b. after Jesus' death and resurrection and the sending of the Holy Spirit
   c. when God's voice from heaven alerted them
   d. only after it was too late
   [p. 133]

b 21. The full expression of the Kingdom of God through Jesus' life, death, and resurrection
   a. is too good to be true
   b. shapes the Gospels
   c. shapes the Hebrew Scriptures
   d. cannot be proven
   [p. 133]

True or False

t 1. Many psalms celebrate God's kingship [p. 122].
f 2. The Psalms are religious hymns that were written by early Christians [p. 122].
t 3. In Jesus' time, many Jews expected the Messiah to be a military leader [p. 123].
f 4. Though Jesus rejected the idea of being a "warrior" type of messiah, he accepted the idea of being a political leader [p. 123].
f 5. The Kingdom of which Jesus spoke was confined within the boundaries of the land of Israel [p. 123].
t 6. Jesus' vision of the Kingdom of God was closely tied to his understanding of God as Father [p. 124].
f 7. Participation in the Kingdom of God is strictly a private agreement between "God and me" [p. 127].
f 8. Jesus believed that the Jewish Law was bad and had to be discarded [p. 130].
t 9. Sin is both a communal and a personal evil [p. 132].
f 10. Disasters that bring tragedy to individuals and communities are punishments for human sin [p. 132].

Essay

1. Explain how a Dream affects the choices a person makes [p. 120].
2. Describe Jesus' Dream of the Kingdom of God and give three examples of how and when that Dream is made real in today's world [pp. 124, 126–130, 133–134].

3. Define sin, both personal and communal [p. 132].
4. Give a real-life example to show that the Kingdom is "right now." Explain how that incident manifested, or brought forth, the Kingdom of God. [pp. 133–134]
5. Choose one of the following and explain how it helps us understand the Kingdom of God: *the Gospel parable of the mustard seed, the Gospel parable of the weeds among the wheat, the Gospel parable of the hidden treasure and the pearls, the textbook "parable" of the Kingdom of God as a great party* [p. 121].
6. Suppose someone told you that the Kingdom of God and the Roman Catholic church are the same. How would you respond? What evidence can you offer to support your view? [p. 130]

Extra Credit

1. Identify a Dream for yourself and tell how it affects or will affect the choices you make [p. 120].
2. Define *legalism* and *nationalism*. Discuss how these tendencies are active in our world today. [pp. 127–128]

Chapter 7: Jesus Speaks

Multiple Choice

b 1. Jesus' thoughts and ideas as found in the Gospels
    a. were accurately recorded by his secretary, John
    b. are expressed through the words of those who followed him
    c. were transmitted by the miracle of technology
    d. have become hopelessly confused over the centuries
    [p. 138]

a 2. The speaking style of the Jews of Jesus' time was
    a. poetic and filled with imagery
    b. logical and orderly
    c. filled with contradictions
    d. dominated by Greek and Roman thought
    [pp. 139–140]

a 3. Jesus' teaching drew on
    a. imagery from the Hebrew Scriptures
    b. the profound thoughts of Aristotle
    c. the local newspapers
    d. the current jargon imposed by Rome
    [p. 140]

d 4. Jesus' pronouncements were set in stories
    a. prepared ahead of time by John the Baptist
    b. approved by Jesus, so that nothing would go wrong
    c. controlled by the Pharisees
    d. composed by the Evangelists to meet the needs of their readers
    [p. 141]

__a__ 5. A classic example of the use of Jesus' short sayings is the
   a. Sermon on the Mount
   b. Ten Commandments
   c. Seven Last Words
   d. Bill of Rights
   [p. 143]

__b__ 6. A Gospel style of teaching that sometimes incorporates other styles of Gospel teaching is
   a. a proverb
   b. an instruction
   c. a pronouncement
   d. a parable
   [p. 146]

__a__ 7. Jesus' parables are noted for their
   a. surprising twists
   b. length
   c. similarity to Persian myths
   d. rhyming quality
   [p. 148]

__d__ 8. The parable of the wedding banquet primarily tells us about
   a. God's nature
   b. how "Kingdom people" act
   c. how we should treat our neighbors
   d. the fulfillment of the Kingdom
   [p. 151]

__b__ 9. The parable of the Pharisee and the tax collector and the parable of the rich fool primarily tell us about
   a. God's nature
   b. how "Kingdom people" act
   c. how we should treat our neighbors
   d. the fulfillment of the Kingdom
   [p. 150]

__c__ 10. The parable of the good Samaritan primarily tells us about
   a. God's nature
   b. how "Kingdom people" act
   c. how we should treat our neighbors
   d. the fulfillment of the Kingdom
   [p. 151]

__a__ 11. The parable of the lost sheep and the parable of the prodigal son primarily tell us about
   a. God's nature
   b. how "Kingdom people" act
   c. how we should treat our neighbors
   d. the fulfillment of the Kingdom
   [pp. 148–150]

__b__ 12. Minor differences in how Jesus' parables are used in the Gospels
   a. cause many problems
   b. demonstrate how rich the parables really are
   c. show that the Evangelists had faulty memory
   d. present a great challenge for scriptural scholars
   [p. 152]

True or False

Put a *t* in the blank next to each true statement and an *f* in the blank next to each false statement. Turn each false statement into a true statement by drawing a line through the incorrect wording and writing in the correct wording.

Note: In no case is it necessary to rewrite an entire false statement in order to make it true.

_t_ 1. Jesus is called "Master," "Rabbi," and "Teacher" almost interchangeably in the Gospels [p. 137].

_f_ 2. Jesus' reference to God as "Abba" was a reference *frequently* [*never*] used in the writings of the rabbis [p. 138].

_t_ 3. Jesus' saying "Amen" at the beginning of a teaching was a manner of giving weight to his words [p. 139].

_t_ 4. Jesus' use of the word "Amen" was unique to him and his message [pp. 138–139].

_t_ 5. The Holy Spirit guided the Gospel writers to convey the truths Jesus taught to his earliest followers [p. 139].

_f_ 6. Jesus' thought and speech patterns were thoroughly *Greek* [*Jewish*] [p. 139].

_f_ 7. Perhaps the most significant of Jesus' teachings came in the form of *proverbs* [*parables*] [p. 141].

_t_ 8. In ancient cultures, pronouncement stories were frequently used to demonstrate famous teachers' wisdom and insight [p. 141].

_t_ 9. Pronouncements are like punch lines [p. 141].

_f_ 10. The Lord's Prayer is an example of *a proverb* [*an instruction for disciples*] [p. 146].

_t_ 11. Proverbs are wise, insightful sayings that can stand alone [p. 142].

_f_ 12. The word *pronouncement* [*parable*] comes from a Greek word meaning "comparison" [p. 146].

_f_ 13. Jesus probably *never* [*sometimes*] repeated himself [p. 152].

_t_ 14. The Evangelists may have placed Jesus' parables in differing settings [p. 152].

_f_ 15. John's Gospel offers extended presentations by Jesus called *parables* [*discourses*] [p. 147].

_t_ 16. The "I am" sayings attributed to Jesus are unique to John's Gospel [p. 147].

Essay

1. Identify the four most common styles of speech used by Jesus in the Gospels and give an example of each [pp. 141–147].
2. List and describe the four main themes by which we can categorize Jesus' parables. What is the common thread that runs through all these themes? [pp. 149–152]
3. List three suggestions that can make the parables more enjoyable and enlightening for us [p. 153].
4. List the three main lessons conveyed in both Matthew's and Luke's versions of the Beatitudes [p. 143].
5. Write a response to the person who says, "I don't trust the Gospels. They don't even have the Lord's Prayer straight. There are two versions!" [pp. 144–145].

Extra Credit

Rewrite one of Jesus' parables in modern-day language.

Chapter 8: Jesus Heals

Multiple Choice

b 1. Which of the following does *not* support belief in Jesus as a miracle worker?
   a. nonscriptural written history
   b. twentieth-century scientists' acceptance of Jesus as a miracle worker
   c. the Pharisees' acceptance of Jesus as a miracle worker
   d. eyewitnesses' acceptance of Jesus as a miracle worker
   [p. 161]

a 2. The task of Christians is to
   a. seek to understand the meaning of Jesus' miracles
   b. seek to establish proof of the reality of Jesus' miracles
   c. find ways to explain away Jesus' miracles
   d. swallow any doubts and believe in the Gospel miracles because a lot of other people do
   [pp. 158, 168]

c 3. The Jews of Jesus' time viewed the world from the perspective of their faith in Yahweh, so miracles were
   a. doubted and generally ignored
   b. condemned by the Roman government
   c. seen as evidence of God's presence and power
   d. viewed as boring occurrences that happened frequently
   [p. 164]

c 4. For the people of Jesus' time, illness was an evil to be "cast out" by
   a. liquids and aspirin
   b. good medical practice
   c. exorcism
   d. none of the above
   [p. 164]

a 5. A commitment to a scientific worldview
   a. provides an opportunity to discover glimpses of the meaning and value of miracles
   b. means that one cannot believe in miracles
   c. means that one will always have to be nostalgic for the good old days
   d. inevitably makes Christian faith impossible
   [p. 166]

b 6. Christians who seek to understand the meaning of Jesus' miracles must be guided by
   a. the hope that they will not be betrayed
   b. a faith that frees and opens them
   c. fear of discovering something they cannot handle
   d. a need to discover clear answers as soon as possible
   [p. 168]

__b__ 7. In exploring Jesus' miracles, the most important question we can ask is
   a. "Can the miracles be proved?"
   b. "What do the miracles mean?"
   c. "How will this improve my attitude?"
   d. "Why isn't this easier?"
   [p. 168]

__d__ 8. Jesus' miracles were recorded as signs of
   a. Jesus' almost magical abilities
   b. the nearness of the end of the world
   c. Jesus' insight into science
   d. God's power over creation and over evil
   [p. 170]

__a__ 9. The nature miracles reveal God's reign over
   a. all creation
   b. the natural world only
   c. human beings only
   d. none of the above
   [p. 170]

__b__ 10. Jesus' nature miracles connect very closely with
   a. yet-to-be-proven scientific theories
   b. occurrences in the Hebrew Scriptures
   c. miracles in Babylon and Persia
   d. the prophecies in the infancy narratives
   [pp. 170–171]

__b__ 11. Jesus' miracles give us a glimpse into
   a. Jesus' belief in the power of magic
   b. Jesus' intense compassion
   c. Jesus' longing to show people his power
   d. all of the above
   [p. 169]

__c__ 12. The seven miracle accounts in John's Gospel focus on the
   a. spectacular impact of Jesus' presence
   b. irritation of the scribes and Pharisees
   c. symbolic meaning of Jesus' miracles
   d. threat that Jesus' miracles bring to Israel
   [p. 159]

True or False

__t__ 1. Those who accept all of the Gospel miracles at face value are often called "fundamentalists" [p. 160].
__f__ 2. We have to choose between accepting all of the Gospel miracles at face value or rejecting all of them [p. 160].
__t__ 3. The tendency to view everything from a scientific perspective leads people in our modern Western culture to doubt whatever does not fit into our explanation of the laws of nature [p. 164].
__f__ 4. In order to believe in miracles today, we have to hold the worldview that the Jews held in Jesus' time [p. 164].
__t__ 5. Jesus' compassionate love led him to work miracles [p. 169].
__t__ 6. In the synoptic Gospels, the most common word used for Jesus' miracles is *power* [p. 170].

 _f_   7. Jesus' message would have been sufficient to convince his listeners of who he was, and his miracles have proven to be an embarrassment to Christians [p. 157].

 _t_   8. Miracle workers were commonly found in the Jewish and Greek cultures of Jesus' time [p. 164].

 _f_   9. The fact that Jesus worked miracles was surprising and embarrassing for the Jews of Jesus' time [p. 164].

 _t_ 10. Christians have a solid tradition of believing in Jesus' miracles [p. 168].

Essay

1. Identify and describe the kinds of miracles found in the Gospels [p. 157].
2. Identify two of Jesus' motives for performing miracles [pp. 169–170].
3. Select one of Jesus' healing miracles that appeals to you. Imagine that you are in the Gospel story of the miracle. Focus on the openness and trust that faith brings and write about your experience of seeing the miracle or of being the person healed. [p. 170]
4. Tell of a time when you or someone you knew moved from spiritual blindness to spiritual insight. Use the Gospel story of the man born blind, who moved from physical blindness to spiritual insight, as a model. [p. 159]

Extra Credit

1. Write a letter to Jesus as he is described in this quote: "Jesus was a man so charged with God's own compassion and love that any cry of pain or confusion drew from him an instant response of healing and restoration" (Donald Senior, *Jesus: A Gospel Portrait* [Dayton, OH: Pflaum Publishing, 1975], page 131) [p. 171].
2. Recall your experience of a transformation or event that changed or surprised you. Tell how that experience was similar to the experience of a miracle. [pp. 165, 169, 172–173]

Chapter 9: The Cross

Multiple Choice

 _a_   1. Jesus disagreed with authority because
       a. his choice was to be faithful to his Father and to value his Dream
       b. he valued the role of a reactionary
       c. his greatest goal was to topple the Romans
       d. he would do almost anything to be popular
       [pp. 175–176]

 _a_   2. The accounts of Jesus' passion
       a. were probably among the first stories about Jesus to take on a consistent form
       b. were consistently avoided in the early church because they were upsetting to readers
       c. were hidden in the Dead Sea Scrolls
       d. were first recorded by Roman soldiers
       [p. 177]

_b_ 3. Knowledge of Jesus' suffering and death
   a. was an embarrassment to the Romans, who thought of themselves as gentle people
   b. was a comfort to early Christians who, as believers, risked martyrdom
   c. was spread solely as part of the gossip passed on in the marketplace
   d. was uncommon among the early followers of Jesus
   [p. 177]

_d_ 4. The "new covenant" spoken of by Jesus linked the Last Supper with
   a. Hanukkah
   b. Solomon's construction of the Temple
   c. the Magna Charta
   d. Israel's deliverance from slavery
   [p. 178]

_c_ 5. At the Last Supper, the bread broken and the cup of wine poured out were signs of
   a. Jesus' good manners
   b. Jesus' knowledge of Temple sacrifice
   c. Jesus' death
   d. a special code intended for Peter
   [p. 178]

_a_ 6. While Jesus prayed in the garden of Gethsemane, he experienced
   a. terror and darkness
   b. fear and dread only for appearance's sake
   c. sure knowledge that he was God
   d. profound relief from real pain
   [p. 181]

_a_ 7. Because Jesus was aware of Israel's history and the times in which he lived, he expected to
   a. face opposition and even death
   b. escape into Damascus
   c. be defended by the Roman armies
   d. be saved by angels
   [pp. 181–182]

_b_ 8. Jesus was most likely aware that his life was threatened, but he
   a. was not concerned
   b. drew strength from his faith in God's love
   c. knew the Roman army was strong enough to overthrow the Pharisees and the scribes
   d. knew he could draw on the Zealots' tactics to deliver himself
   [p. 182]

_b_ 9. Jesus stayed and faced his death because he
   a. had a death wish
   b. was committed to doing God's will
   c. had no escape route
   d. knew he would rise from the dead
   [pp. 182–183]

_c_ 10. Caiaphas condemned Jesus for claiming equality with
   a. a Greek god
   b. the Roman emperor
   c. the God of Israel
   d. the queen of Sheba
   [p. 184]

c 11. Because Pontius Pilate was unimpressed with the Jewish leaders' case against Jesus, he
    a. planned Jesus' escape route to Egypt
    b. decided to become a Christian
    c. sought to turn Jesus over to the leader of Galilee
    d. sought to free Jesus by appealing to the Roman emperor
    [p. 185]

a 12. The official charge brought against Jesus by the Romans was that he had
    a. incited a revolt among the Jews
    b. blasphemed against the Jewish God
    c. sided with the Zealots
    d. cursed Caesar
    [p. 185]

d 13. The sign placed above Jesus' head on the cross
    a. stated his crime
    b. gave a statement of faith
    c. announced his intentions
    d. gave a mocking title for him
    [p. 186]

d 14. Crucifixion was designed to
    a. humiliate Greeks
    b. cause a quick and merciful death
    c. scare the Roman citizens
    d. bring on a slow and painful death
    [p. 186]

a 15. The Jewish people wanted Jesus to be removed from the cross because
    a. it was against the Jewish laws to have a body on a cross during the Sabbath
    b. it was an embarrassment to have crucified a Galilean
    c. they did not want visitors to think they were vengeful
    d. reminders of executions are distasteful
    [p. 186]

b 16. In Luke's Gospel, Jesus' last words express
    a. despair and loneliness
    b. acceptance and self-surrender
    c. vengeance and defiance
    d. exhaustion and futility
    [p. 187]

a 17. In the Roman world, a ransom was
    a. a price paid to release a slave
    b. a payment for one's child
    c. a kind of fungus
    d. an act of vengeance
    [p. 191]

True or False

Put a *t* in the blank next to each true statement and an *f* in the blank next to each false statement. Turn each false statement into a true statement by drawing a line through the incorrect wording and writing in the correct wording.

Note: In no case is it necessary to rewrite an entire false statement in order to make it true.

- _t_ 1. Jesus' opinion often conflicted with the opinion of the people in positions of power [p. 175].
- _f_ 2. Jesus made the *scribes and Pharisees* [*outcasts of society*] the cornerstone of his message about God's Kingdom [p. 176].
- _t_ 3. Jesus posed a religious and political threat to the way things were in his society [p. 176].
- _f_ 4. The *birth and childhood* [*arrest, trial, and crucifixion*] of Jesus are the most extensively reported events in the Gospels [p. 176].
- _f_ 5. The earliest recorded account of the institution of the Eucharist is found in *the Gospel of John* [*Paul's first letter to the Corinthians*] [p. 178].
- _t_ 6. The Eucharist was instituted at the Last Supper [pp. 178–179].
- _f_ 7. At Gethsemane, Jesus found *an escape from* [*courage to accept*] his coming suffering [pp. 181, 182–183].
- _f_ 8. The Great Sanhedrin had no authority to condemn Jesus to death, because it was a *Greek* [*Jewish*] body under Roman control [p. 184].
- _t_ 9. Caiaphas was the high priest at the time Jesus appeared before the Great Sanhedrin [p. 184].
- _f_ 10. *Barabbas* [*Pontius Pilate*] thought Jesus was innocent [p. 185].

Essay

1. Explain why the Gospels detail Jesus' suffering and death [pp. 176–177].
2. When Jesus went to Jerusalem during Passover, what signs of the times could he read that would tell him his life was in danger [pp. 181–182]?
3. Explain why Jesus' free acceptance of his death is central to Christian faith [pp. 182–183].
4. Discuss the problems that can arise in identifying Jesus' death on the cross solely as an act of dying for our sins [p. 190].
5. Discuss the role of Judas in Jesus' death [p. 182].

Extra Credit

1. Create a map tracing the "path" of Jesus' trial. Name the people he faced and what happened in each situation. [pp. 184–185]
2. Read Psalm 22:1–5,28–31. Discuss how the psalm expresses Jesus' emotions during his suffering and death. [p. 187]
3. What does the expression "Jesus conquered death" mean to you [p. 190]?
4. What is the significance of Jesus' washing the feet of his disciples at the Last Supper? Explain the relationship between this action and the eucharistic action of taking, blessing, breaking, and sharing bread. [p. 180]

Chapter 10: The Resurrection

Multiple Choice

<u>c</u> 1. The initial reactions of those who saw the empty tomb were
   a. joy followed by shouting
   b. doubt followed by disillusionment
   c. shock followed by fear
   d. confusion followed by more confusion
   [p. 194]

<u>a</u> 2. In the Acts of the Apostles, experiencing the Risen Jesus is
   a. a key qualification for being accepted as one of the Apostles
   b. not important enough to be debated
   c. something of an embarrassment to Peter
   d. all of the above
   [p. 195]

<u>d</u> 3. Ultimately, recognizing the Risen Christ is
   a. a matter of proof
   b. a thing you have to do to get along
   c. an unimportant decision as long as you are kind
   d. a matter of faith
   [pp. 194–195, 197]

<u>b</u> 4. The Gospel accounts of Jesus' resurrection are all
   a. detailed explanations
   b. proclamations of faith
   c. attempts to document the details as history
   d. folktales
   [p. 197]

<u>a</u> 5. Because of the Resurrection, Christians can see that
   a. happiness and fullness of life come from God
   b. self-fulfillment is the be-all and end-all of life
   c. self-giving means death
   d. a happy life can be accomplished through careful obedience to laws
   [p. 199]

<u>a</u> 6. The term *paschal mystery* refers to Jesus' death and resurrection as a "new Passover" for
   a. all humanity
   b. Christians only
   c. Jews only
   d. Pharisees only
   [p. 199]

<u>b</u> 7. People can be
   a. compelled to accept Jesus as their Redeemer
   b. invited to accept Jesus as their Redeemer
   c. persuaded to accept Jesus as their Redeemer
   d. none of the above
   [p. 201]

<u>a</u> 8. The celebration of the Eucharist reminds Christians that the Risen Jesus is with them
   a. constantly
   b. only on Sunday
   c. when they deserve it
   d. when they are aware of his presence
   [p. 201]

<u>b</u> 9. Jesus said that wherever two or three are gathered in his name, he is there among them. He was referring to
   a. his presence during the Easter vigil
   b. his presence within the community of believers
   c. his preference for small groups
   d. none of the above
   [p. 202]

<u>c</u> 10. The key criterion for judging whether someone is a Christian is their willingness to
   a. follow rules
   b. try to get along with everyone
   c. let their life be shaped by Jesus' life and message
   d. suffer and experience pain
   [p. 202]

<u>d</u> 11. The description of Jesus' ascension into the presence of God teaches us about Jesus'
   a. spiritual qualities
   b. distance from us
   c. life as an angel
   d. unlimited presence among us
   [p. 205]

<u>b</u> 12. To call Jesus "the Christ" recalls the Jewish expectation of
   a. a prophet
   b. the Messiah
   c. the new Moses
   d. a new salesman
   [p. 208]

<u>b</u> 13. The doctrine of the Trinity refers to
   a. God, self, and others
   b. Father, Son, and Holy Spirit
   c. mother, father, and child
   d. life, death, and resurrection
   [p. 208]

True or False

<u>t</u> 1. The Resurrection gave Jesus' life and death full meaning [p. 193].
<u>f</u> 2. After Jesus died, his body was claimed by the Pharisee named Nicodemus [p. 193].
<u>f</u> 3. The differences among the Gospel accounts of the Resurrection are so significant that they indicate that the writers were trying to deceive people [p. 194].
<u>t</u> 4. If the Evangelists were concerned with proving Jesus' resurrection, they would have left out the women as primary witnesses [p. 195].
<u>f</u> 5. Only John witnessed a post-Resurrection appearance [p. 195].
<u>f</u> 6. The knowledge of Jesus Risen was intended to be a private revelation [p. 195].

| t | 7. In his resurrection, Jesus was transformed and experienced a new kind of existence [p. 197].
| f | 8. If we try hard, we can explain what resurrected life is like [p. 197].
| f | 9. We must seek pain and suffering in order to be like Jesus, who died on the cross for us [p. 200].
| t | 10. Only Luke's Gospel and the Acts of the Apostles specifically describe Jesus' ascension [p. 203].
| t | 11. In the Ascension, Jesus passed totally into God's presence [p. 205].
| t | 12. The gift of the Holy Spirit was given to the disciples at the first Pentecost [p. 206].
| f | 13. Shortly after the Resurrection, the church formally proclaimed Jesus as one of three divine persons in the one God [p. 208].
| t | 14. By giving Jesus the title *Lord*, the early Christians proclaimed a divine identity for him [p. 208].

Essay

1. Summarize the common points in the Gospel accounts of Jesus' resurrection [pp. 193–194].
2. List the evidence that supports the Christian conviction of the Resurrection [pp. 194–195, 197].
3. Summarize the common points in the Gospel accounts of Jesus' appearances after his resurrection [p. 195].
4. Why was Jesus' resurrection not a historical event in the same sense that his crucifixion was [p. 197]?
5. What is the origin and meaning of the term *paschal mystery* [p. 199]?
6. In what sense can a memory be "alive and present"? Give examples from your own experience. [p. 202]
7. What was the main lesson that the scriptural authors wished to teach by describing the Ascension [p. 205]?
8. What is the significance of Pentecost in the life of the church [p. 207]?

Extra Credit

1. Drawing on your own experience, show how one or more of these truths affirmed by Jesus' triumph in the Resurrection apply to your own life:
   a. Jesus' claim about God's unconditional love for us
   b. Jesus' promise that we can find fulfillment in loving God and one another
   c. Jesus' commitment to a prayerful and personal relationship with God
   d. Jesus' conviction that forgiveness is more life-giving than revenge
   e. Jesus' teaching that rich people must share with poor people
   f. Jesus' refusal to accept anything that would separate one person from another
   [p. 198]
2. What occurrences in nature reflect the cycle of death leading to new life [pp. 199–200]?
3. Discuss a personal experience (or an experience of someone you know) in which a type of death led to new life [p. 200].

Chapter 11: Paul

Multiple Choice

<u>a</u> 1. All we know about Paul can be found in
   a. the Acts of the Apostles and Paul's letters
   b. the Gospel of Luke
   c. the Book of Revelation
   d. Paul's travel guide
   [pp. 217–218]

<u>b</u> 2. Because Paul was a Roman citizen who understood Greek culture, he was
   a. able to play one nation against the other
   b. able to move freely and confidently among Gentiles
   c. resented by the Jews, who were jealous of him
   d. able to dine with Nero when he was in Rome
   [p. 219]

<u>c</u> 3. Paul's writings reflect his
   a. knowledge of English and French philosophy
   b. care not to offend or challenge anyone
   c. knowledge of the Jewish Law and Greek philosophy
   d. poor grasp of spelling and grammar
   [p. 219]

<u>b</u> 4. Paul did not expect his letters to be preserved, because
   a. he was a poor writer
   b. he expected the Risen Lord to come and the world to end
   c. the papyrus used at the time deteriorated rapidly
   d. he was disorganized and lost things easily
   [p. 216]

<u>a</u> 5. It is important to note that Paul
   a. never met the historical Jesus face-to-face
   b. never heard of Jesus
   c. met Jesus in the last year of his preaching
   d. was interested in advancing his preaching career
   [p. 220]

<u>c</u> 6. Luke's and Paul's accounts of Paul's conversion
   a. are completely contradictory
   b. give exactly the same version of the event
   c. differ in some details
   d. indicate that Luke copied Paul's account
   [pp. 218, 222]

<u>b</u> 7. Paul's conversion experience was so
   a. shocking that it scared his horse
   b. profound that it changed his life
   c. stunning that he was permanently disabled
   d. magical that he became bewildered
   [p. 223]

<u>a</u> 8. Paul discovered that his vocation was to
   a. be a missionary to the Gentile world
   b. convince his Jewish friends of Jesus' lordship
   c. convert Nero and the Roman army
   d. argue Jesus' case with the Greek philosophers
   [p. 224]

<u>c</u> 9. Paul's meeting with the Apostles Peter and James was significant because it
   a. was the first summit meeting
   b. was the first council of the church
   c. established that Paul could be recognized as an Apostle
   d. none of the above
   [p. 225]

<u>a</u> 10. The debate over whether Gentiles had to become Jews before being accepted into the Christian church was resolved at the
   a. Jerusalem Council
   b. Second Vatican Council
   c. United Nations Assembly
   d. Council of Athens
   [p. 227]

<u>d</u> 11. Paul established his most famous church in
   a. Athens
   b. Rome
   c. Paris
   d. Corinth
   [p. 227]

<u>b</u> 12. Paul's letter to the Romans reflects his
   a. need to write a letter to the center of prestige and power in the Roman world
   b. maturity as an Apostle and insight into the meaning of Christian faith
   c. amazing grasp of Greek language and ideas
   d. ability to explain the difference between faith and reason
   [p. 229]

<u>a</u> 13. Scholars commonly hold that Paul
   a. was beheaded in Rome
   b. died of old age in Barcelona, Spain
   c. was crucified in Jerusalem
   d. died embittered in his hometown of Tarsus
   [p. 231]

True or False

<u>f</u> 1. Paul expected his letters to be preserved for all time [p. 216].
<u>f</u> 2. In Paul's time, it was unusual to communicate by letter [p. 216].
<u>t</u> 3. In the Christian Testament, Paul emerges as second only to Jesus in importance [p. 217].
<u>t</u> 4. Paul's Jewish name was *Saul* [p. 219].
<u>f</u> 5. Paul was a committed Zealot [p. 219].
<u>f</u> 6. Paul was a lawyer [p. 219].
<u>t</u> 7. Paul approved of the stoning of Stephen at the time it happened [pp. 220–221].
<u>t</u> 8. The Acts of the Apostles tells the story of Paul's conversion three times [p. 222].

_f_ 9. We can assume that Paul's conversion experience was an identity crisis [p. 223].
_t_ 10. Paul failed to establish a church in Athens [p. 227].

Gospels or Epistles

Each numbered item below applies to either the Gospels or the Epistles. Write a *G* in the blank if the item applies to the Gospels. Write an *E* in the blank if the item applies to the Epistles.

_E_ 1. Are letters [p. 216]
_G_ 2. Are primarily concerned with the Jesus of History [pp. 211–212]
_E_ 3. Are primarily concerned with the Christ of Faith [pp. 214–215]
_E_ 4. Were among the first written documents of the Christian Testament [p. 216]
_G_ 5. Were written relatively later [pp. 215–216]
_G_ 6. Focus on Jesus' divinity [p. 216]
_E_ 7. Seek to come to terms with the meaning of Jesus [p. 216]
_E_ 8. Presume that the readers know about the life of Jesus [p. 216]
_E_ 9. Deal with the growth of the early church [p. 215]
_E_ 10. Deal with the personal spirituality of the early Christians [p. 215]

Essay

1. Put the following titles in order to show the development of the disciples' and the early church's understanding of Jesus' identity: *Risen Lord, Jesus of Nazareth, Messiah or Christ, Special Teacher, Son of God, Prophet.* Then choose two titles and for each one give an example of an event that led Jesus' followers to give Jesus that title. [p. 214]
2. Identify and give the characteristics of each of the three non-Gospel parts of the Christian Testament [pp. 214–215, 218, 223, 232–233].
3. What is the connection between Paul and the Diaspora? What advantages and disadvantages for his mission of spreading the Gospel can you imagine this connection gave him? [p. 219]
4. Describe Paul's initial relationship with the early church and give reasons for his views and actions [pp. 218–221].
5. Define the terms *conversion* and *vocation* and explain their relevance to Paul's Damascus experience [p. 224].
6. Identify the two sides of the debate about accepting Gentile converts into the Christian church. Explain why Paul's argument is significant for you and for the future of the church in general. [pp. 225, 227]
7. Briefly describe what is included in each of the two parts of the Acts of the Apostles [p. 215].

Extra Credit

1. Drawing on the Acts of the Apostles, Paul's letters (especially 2 Corinthians 10:9–10), and your own study, write a description of Paul as a person and as a missionary [pp. 216, 217–231, 233].
2. Explain why Paul could not simply "dash off a letter" [pp. 212–213].
3. Name the following epistles:
   a. the seven epistles credited to Paul and actually written by him
   b. the three pastoral epistles, which are attributed to Paul but now believed not to have been written by him
   c. the three other epistles credited to Paul but not written by him
   d. the seven catholic epistles
   e. the epistle of unknown authorship
   [pp. 218, 223]

4. Explain the reason scholars suggest for why the Book of Revelation was written. How are its images to be interpreted? [pp. 232–233]

Chapter 12: The Letters of Paul

Multiple Choice

_b_ 1. Paul's teaching and writing were anchored in his
   a. experience as a Pharisee
   b. conversion on the road to Damascus
   c. knowledge of Roman law
   d. tricky personality
   [p. 237]

_b_ 2. Paul's letters convey
   a. brutal honesty and logical activity
   b. a sincere love for people and an unshakable faith in Jesus
   c. ready obedience and rigorous discipline
   d. a wild disregard for his health and a distrust of health remedies
   [p. 237]

_d_ 3. Paul's letters are generally concerned with
   a. conflicts within the communities of believers
   b. the spirituality of the believers
   c. the believers' personal morality
   d. all of the above
   [p. 237]

_c_ 4. Sin can best be described as
   a. breaking laws and rules
   b. criticizing church and national rulers
   c. rupturing relationships with God and one another
   d. questioning authorities
   [p. 241]

_b_ 5. Paul understood that the spirit of the Law was based on
   a. fear
   b. love
   c. justice
   d. slavery
   [pp. 242–243]

_a_ 6. According to Paul, righteousness, or being right with God, is brought about by
   a. the death and resurrection of Jesus
   b. strict obedience to the Law of Moses
   c. unyielding attempts to succeed alone
   d. giving up and trusting God
   [p. 247]

__b__ 7. Christian life can be characterized as
   a. an interdependence among weak people
   b. an acceptance of God's grace
   c. a solitary climb toward heaven
   d. a free ride, with no effort required
   [pp. 250–251]

__a__ 8. God's offer of grace requires
   a. our acceptance and cooperation
   b. our awareness of the offer's presence
   c. a sense that if the offer is too good to be true, it is not true
   d. a willingness to work to deserve God's grace
   [pp. 250–251]

__d__ 9. The church is called to be
   a. an institution of immense strength and authority
   b. a democratic organization run by the will of the people
   c. a gathering of soldiers of Christ
   d. the visible presence of the Risen Jesus
   [p. 252]

__a__ 10. Paul compared the church to
   a. the human body
   b. a container
   c. a boat filled with passengers
   d. an army of soldiers
   [pp. 252–254]

__d__ 11. According to Paul, Christian morality rests on the principle that Christians live out their relationship with Jesus by
   a. keeping track of their sins and successes
   b. avoiding occasions of near sin
   c. going it alone
   d. living well in community with one another
   [p. 254]

True or False
Put a *t* in the blank next to each true statement and an *f* in the blank next to each false statement. Turn each false statement into a true statement by drawing a line through the incorrect wording and writing in the correct wording.

Note: In no case is it necessary to rewrite an entire false statement in order to make it true.

__f__ 1. Paul was a *quiet, mild-mannered* [*passionate* or *fiery*] Apostle [p. 237].
__f__ 2. The story of Adam and Eve teaches us that the presence of evil is a result of *God's will* [*the free actions of men and women*] [p. 240].
__t__ 3. In the Hebrew Scriptures, Yahweh always reaches out to call the people to be reconciled with their Creator [pp. 240–241].
__t__ 4. Paul taught that through Jesus, God is calling all people to reconciliation [p. 241].
__f__ 5. Paul called Jesus "the new *Moses* [*Adam*]" [p. 241].
__t__ 6. The error of equating salvation with obedience to laws was taught by the Pharisees of Paul's time [pp. 241–242].
__f__ 7. Paul understood that slavish adherence to the Law was a *connecting bridge* [*barrier*] between his people and God [p. 243].
__t__ 8. People today are as much in need of salvation as people were in Jesus' and Paul's day [p. 246].

_t_ 9. Grace is the totally free gift of God's unconditional love [p. 250].

_t_ 10. If a person accepts God's grace, he or she will respond in a loving manner [p. 251].

Essay

1. Explain why it is helpful to learn about the people Paul wrote to and the purpose of his letters to them [p. 236].
2. Identify the two main themes of Paul's writing [p. 237].
3. Discuss the ways in which Jesus can be called "the new Adam." Compare and contrast the first Adam and the Creation with the new Adam (Jesus) and the new creation in him. [pp. 246–248, 251]
4. What does Jesus save us from? What does he save us for? [p. 248]
5. Discuss the advantages and disadvantages of viewing the church as a perfect body [pp. 256–257].

Extra Credit

1. List a number of false or shallow expectations that your culture asks you to fulfill. How do these hold up against the questions that Jesus might ask of you today—questions that express his values? [p. 249]
2. Tell about your experience (or another person's experience) of the church functioning as a perfect body, manifesting Christ's presence in the world [pp. 256–257].
3. Discuss your experience (or another person's experience) of the church as a broken body. Explore the attitudes you (or the other person) will need as you deal with this broken body. [pp. 256–257]

Chapter 13: Good News from Age to Age

Multiple Choice

_b_ 1. The survival of the church over the centuries is a result of the presence of the guiding Spirit and the
   a. willingness of the church to compromise
   b. faith of the church's members
   c. church's wise investments
   d. church's use of communication systems
   [p. 260]

_c_ 2. Throughout time, in order to be true to their Christian identity, the church's members must constantly seek ways to
   a. win converts to Catholicism
   b. establish institutions and take care of them
   c. more fully attune themselves to the Jesus of the Gospels
   d. seek ways to win arguments with atheists
   [p. 261]

_c_ 3. Parables such as the one about the vine and the branches provide images of
   a. rugged individualism
   b. the monastic life
   c. a community nurtured by Jesus
   d. an army
   [p. 262]

_d_ 4. A marked and dramatic change in the relationship between Judaism and Christianity occurred when the church decided to
   a. become a state religion that excluded Jews
   b. expand beyond Israel
   c. ignore Jewish scholars
   d. admit Gentiles without their first being converted to Judaism
   [p. 264]

_a_ 5. The establishment of the canon of the Hebrew Scriptures around 90 C.E. had the effect of
   a. further defining Judaism and Christianity as distinct religions
   b. making Christians angry and frustrated
   c. protecting Greeks from being overly confused
   d. preserving Hebrew as a language
   [p. 264]

_b_ 6. The church's move toward Greek thought and interpretation aided the
   a. confidence of those who spoke Latin
   b. spread of the church beyond Palestine
   c. growth of schools teaching Greek
   d. frequent use of concrete, poetic language
   [p. 265]

_a_ 7. In the second century, words such as *substance, person,* and *nature* described Jesus in terms of
   a. abstractions
   b. poetic images
   c. Gospel understandings
   d. popular culture
   [p. 265]

_d_ 8. The Great Christological Councils were called to
   a. seek a democratic vote on belief
   b. raise money for missionary work
   c. combat Latin interpretations of church doctrines
   d. clarify the church's statement of who Jesus is
   [p. 265]

_a_ 9. Arius taught that Jesus was
   a. less than divine
   b. merely human
   c. at the same level as God
   d. truly God and truly human
   [pp. 265–266]

_d_ 10. The creed that explicitly articulates the church's belief about Jesus as both human and divine is the
   a. Hippocratic Creed
   b. Apostles' Creed
   c. Creed of Rome
   d. Nicene Creed
   [p. 266]

_a_ 11. In giving Mary the title *Mother of God,* the Council of Ephesus declared that Jesus is
   a. truly God and truly human
   b. a human being
   c. like a Greek god
   d. unrelated to the Jewish people
   [p. 268]

_a_ 12. The Council of Chalcedon held that Jesus is
   a. not only divine but also fully human
   b. the son of Mary and Joseph
   c. God disguised as a human being
   d. largely a figment of the imagination
   [p. 268]

_b_ 13. Scholasticism is a
   a. disordered mix of prayer and visionary experience
   b. logical and orderly approach to the study of God and religion
   c. "new age" style of thinking that is only barely understood at this time
   d. way of thinking that led to the Third Vatican Council
   [p. 269]

_c_ 14. A problem with Scholasticism is that
   a. it is a disordered mix of prayer and visionary experience
   b. it relies too much on feelings and emotions
   c. its logic and orderliness can make God and Jesus seem like distant, cold realities
   d. it is too difficult for people in the twentieth century to understand
   [pp. 269–270]

_c_ 15. A reaction against Scholasticism led to
   a. an overly intellectual approach to Jesus
   b. a reliance on Greek philosophy
   c. oversimplified and superstitious understandings of Jesus
   d. a sophisticated understanding of Jesus
   [p. 270]

_c_ 16. The Reformation was rooted in a desire to
   a. express adolescent rebellion
   b. make the church more democratic
   c. renew the church's faith and practice
   d. win a battle at any cost
   [p. 271]

True or False

_f_ 1. Because of the influence of God's Spirit, the church's journey through history has been easy and flawless [p. 260].

_t_ 2. Sometimes it becomes necessary for the church to restore a sense of integrity, stability, and cohesiveness as a community of believers [pp. 260–261].

_f_ 3. Jesus' moral teachings address the necessity to act in isolation to save your soul [p. 262].

_f_ 4. The church's task is to present Jesus' message and to avoid being affected by the culture in which it finds itself [p. 262].

_t_ 5. The Gospels were written to preserve and pass on the story and message of Jesus [p. 264].

t   6. The Epistles are proclamations of the Good News [p. 264].

t   7. The Fathers of the church fostered a Greek philosophical understanding of the Christian Testament [pp. 264–265].

f   8. Church councils are gatherings of laypeople [p. 265].

t   9. Thomas Aquinas is likely the most influential theologian in the church's history [p. 269].

f 10. The struggle to balance our understanding of the Jesus of History and the Christ of Faith was settled once and for all at the Council of Ephesus [pp. 270–271].

Essay

1. List the four ways that the early church expressed itself as a community. Select one of those expressions and tell how it continues in the church today. [p. 259]
2. Briefly summarize the evidence supporting the claim that Jesus intended to found some kind of continuing community [pp. 261–262].
3. Name the three Great Christological Councils and explain what each stated about Jesus' identity [p. 268].

Extra Credit

1. Give an example of the hazards of overemphasizing the Jesus of History [p. 277].
2. Give an example of the hazards of overemphasizing the Christ of Faith [pp. 275, 277].

APPENDIX 2

The Learning Process and This Course

Jesus of History, Christ of Faith employs a learning process modeled after one described in Richard Reichert's *A Learning Process for Religious Education* (Dayton, OH: Pflaum Publishing, 1975). It is student-centered, combines a concern for formation with a concern for information, offers students opportunities for self-examination and reflection, and seeks to move them along in their personal faith development. The process can be divided into four interrelated moments:
- the starting point
- the significant experience
- reflection
- assimilation

The Starting Point

The *starting point* in any learning process is basically the sum total of all that the learner has learned up to that point. In this sense, the starting point involves the learner's present value system, her or his conscious behavior patterns, the principles she or he uses in making decisions, and so on. A teacher needs to consider the backgrounds, values, concerns, and life experiences of the students in order to accurately assess their starting point.

To a certain extent, each student comes to class proclaiming, "This is what I am"—not always with words, certainly, but with attitudes, behavior patterns, values, and more. The teacher must be alert to such unarticulated information about the student's starting point. To further complicate matters, each student reflects, to a greater or lesser degree, a starting point that is different from that of his or her classmates. This implies that an important task of the teacher is to remain flexible and adaptable while an understanding of the group's *communal* starting point gradually evolves and comes into focus.

The starting point in the learning process simply verifies a commonsense reality about the teaching enterprise: the effective teacher must begin as much as possible where the students are and must act as a midwife, helping the students give birth to new personal insight and perspectives. This course offers various ways of helping the students draw out a sense of their own starting point regarding each topic covered. It then builds on this to nudge the students along in the learning process. What actually accounts for such nudging is the significant experience, the second component in the learning process.

The Significant Experience

The *significant experience* is an internal or external event that leads to movement beyond the starting point. Something motivates the learner to reflect upon or become uncomfortable with her or his starting point. The event is

called "significant" because it invites a meaningful change in the person. It often involves the *whole person*—emotions, values, behavior, and intellectual awareness. Significant experiences related to this course might be the following:
- receiving new information from the student text or the teacher
- challenging previously held attitudes or positions
- examining a fresh perspective on oneself or one's world
- simulating or trying on new behaviors
- experiencing prayer or a deeper sense of prayer
- questioning personal values
- developing new relationships, seeing old relationships in a new light

Of course, some of the most significant experiences in a student's process of change will happen outside the classroom. A family crisis, a loss of a relationship, or exposure to people from a different culture is loaded with potential for moving a student to a different starting point. A course like *Jesus of History, Christ of Faith* enhances the moving power of such an experience by giving the student an opportunity to reflect on it and by throwing a new light on it. In this respect, even the student text itself (in addition to the activities led by the teacher) can become a significant experience.

This teaching manual offers numerous strategies—group exercises, games, discussion starters, and more—for helping the students move from one point in their understanding of Jesus to another. All of the suggested strategies are designed to prompt the students to get in touch with their starting point—where they are, who they are, and what they believe—regarding the concept at hand.

Given the variable starting points of the individual students, not every lesson or activity will be significant for *all* of the students. This does not mean that the course or the teacher has failed. Rather, such situations simply urge the teacher to seek other experiences that will be significant, for the failure to do so will interrupt, if not abort, the hoped-for learning process. This search for the magic keys that will open the students' minds to new growth and insight is precisely what makes the art of teaching so challenging and exciting.

Once the teacher has discovered the keys that can engage the students' interest and focus their attention on the topic at hand, the next phase of the learning process, reflection, comes into play.

Reflection

When a person asks, What does this experience mean? he or she is engaging in the *reflection* stage of the learning process. This stage often involves solitary thinking, sorting things out in writing, intense discussions with others, even prayer. Reflection can be described as a slowing down after the speeding up associated with the significant experience. It is not inaction or passivity but *creative quietude*. Reflection activities allow students an opportunity to think through the growth to which they are invited.

Reflection activities for this course include the many activities located at the bottom of the pages of the student text. These can be used as homework assignments, classroom activities or discussion starters, or prompts for private reflection. Also, for each of the additional activities, or significant experiences, offered in this manual, various means of reflection are provided.

The process of reflection eventually results in a decision by the student. That decision may be either conscious and deliberate or spontaneous and intuitive. It is essentially a response to this question: Do I want to accept this new information as part of my worldview? Implicit in this question is a more fundamental one that is at the center of all real learning: Am I willing to change who I am? The resolution of these questions directly affects the fourth and final phase of the learning process: assimilation.

Assimilation

Education seeks to change a person. *Assimilation* refers to a change integrated into the life of the student—a changed perspective, understanding, value, or attitude. If a change is integrated into the student's life, then changed behavior occurs. Real values, in other words, are lived values.

Jesus of History, Christ of Faith offers many opportunities for truly significant change—that is, for real learning—on the part of the students. It is *not* the goal or expectation of this course that the students come to a firm sense of commitment to Jesus Christ or Catholic Christianity. Such a decision is more appropriate at a later age, perhaps during young adulthood. However, the course *is* intended to guide the students to a deliberate and conscious reassessment of their understanding of and attitudes about faith and religion in general and about Jesus in particular. The course intends to challenge and, yes, change the negativity and apathy toward things religious that is normal and even necessary at the students' stage of development. Students who successfully complete the course may leave it with a new interest in and openness to further exploration of the religion they have inherited from others. This is the stuff of profound learning—and of gratifying teaching.

A Note on the Learning Process

The four steps of the learning process often occur naturally. The purpose of dividing the unified process into four separate parts is to assist the teacher in making directed, conscious, and purposeful contributions to the students' learning. While planning lessons for this course and considering the suggestions offered in this manual, it is beneficial to refer to the four elements of the learning process.

During your lesson planning, ask yourself, Does this lesson reflect consideration of each of the four elements of the learning process? An exciting, meaningful activity can provide a significant experience, but unless it also offers an opportunity for reflection, the activity may not result in the growth described as assimilation. Likewise, if a number of students harbor strong negative feelings toward a topic, a well-planned presentation on the topic will be ineffective unless the students' starting point is addressed.

Because the starting point of your students may differ from that of other groups of students, you will need to select activities appropriate for your students' particular situation. Also, consider your own starting point. One teacher might be comfortable with quiet reflection, silent prayer, and journal keeping, while another is more at home with lively discussion, movement, and activity. Be sensitive to your own starting point but also be open to the significant experience of trying new approaches.

Something worth remembering about the learning process for this course is that it is a shared process. No one is a Christian apart from community; Christian education occurs in a community context. Awareness of other students' starting points can be, in itself, a significant experience for a student. Experiencing community, sharing reflection, deciding on group goals, and performing group tasks all enhance and reinforce the learning process. They also more clearly distinguish Christian education as the activity it is meant to be—education of the Christian community.

What the Teacher Offers

What role does the teacher play in aiding the adolescent's faith journey in relation to this course? Primarily, the teacher should assist and direct the journey of the student and also join in the journey. The student text and this teaching manual provide numerous suggestions to help you in assisting the student's learning process. However, for personal faith development to occur, your joining in the process is all-important. An atmosphere of mutual learning and journeying reflects the spirit of the course. You can help create such an atmosphere by communicating two things to the students:
1. that it is a good thing for them to look inquiringly and wonderingly on their world and their religion
2. that you are also on a faith journey—inquiring, wondering, and seeking new meaning

In this way, the activity of personal reflection is encouraged, and the risk of responding in faith to God's presence is supported. The atmosphere is one of trusting that our God is a living God who can be found in the midst of our world. It is the atmosphere appropriate for the Christian community as well as for Christian education.

One writer describes the role of the teacher as follows: "The role of the catechist is to journey with students and to enable them to keep growing in their relationship with the Lord. Their role is not to 'sell' adolescents the faith, but rather to share, listen, challenge, and affirm" (Michael Carotta, "We're All on the Journey," *Religion Teacher's Journal* [October 1983]: 29). *Sharing the Light of Faith: National Catechetical Directory for Catholics of the United States* (Washington, DC: United States Catholic Conference, 1979) affirms this spirit of mutual journeying when it states, "Catechists not only instruct young adults but learn from them; they will be heard by young adults only if they listen to them" (no. 227).

The teacher who offers new information on faith and provides an atmosphere where significant experiences, personal reflection, and assimilation can occur sets in motion the spirit of community itself. When the learning leads to action, the students will more readily recognize the presence of God in their life and will accept that their own life is sacred.

Finally, a special note intended to alleviate the guilt and frustration so often associated with the teaching of religion: *The responsibility for learning is always that of the learner.* We cannot learn *for* our students. In terms of the learning process presented here, the teacher has a responsibility to remain attuned to the students' starting point, to provide significant experiences that are responsive to who the students are (or to help the students become aware of their own significant experiences), and then to facilitate the students' reflection upon those experiences. However, whether an individual student actually chooses to accept and assimilate the new information is entirely the student's responsibility. We can provide an environment in which such acceptance is encouraged, but we cannot force it. This can be expressed more creatively, perhaps, with a twist on an old saying: We can lead a horse to water, but we can't make it drink. With a little salt, however, we *can* make the horse thirsty!

Jesus of History, Christ of Faith will, it is hoped, create in the young people a thirst for a greater understanding of the faith that is their heritage. The role of the teacher in this effort is so pivotal that it warrants further consideration. Appendix 3, "The Teacher as a Witness of Faith," takes up this consideration.

APPENDIX 3

The Teacher as a Witness of Faith

A Relational Approach

A central focus of *Jesus of History, Christ of Faith* is the conviction that Christian faith is not just an intellectual assent to a body of doctrines and dogmas—an academic matter. Rather, Christian faith is essentially a believer's gradual response in love to the unconditional love of God revealed in Jesus—a relational concern. The implications of this relatively recent way of thinking about faith are truly extensive. It affects those of us involved in the educational ministry of the church on all levels:

1. A relational rather than academic approach to faith dramatically affects the way we view the student. If faith is viewed as agreement with a body of truths, the student is simply called upon to memorize those truths, in the hope that she or he will make some intellectual commitment to them. If faith is viewed as primarily relational, the student is seen as a unique individual who can enter freely into a growing, changing relationship with God.
2. A relational approach to faith affects the content of religion courses in many ways, but it affects the pedagogical approach to that content even more. The content must be in touch with the lived experience of the student. Anything less than this makes real learning (as distinct from the simple accumulation of knowledge) impossible. Educational methodologies must be inclusive, not exclusive. Faith as a system of truths can be taught from the basis of intellectual inquiry; faith as a personal relationship must involve the whole person—intellectually, emotionally, spiritually, even physically.
3. An academic approach to faith necessarily emphasizes the academic qualifications of the teacher. With such an approach, the "good" teacher is one who (*a*) knows theology and (*b*) has the skills required to share that knowledge. In the case of a relational concept of faith, the preferred teacher is one who (*a*) knows theology, (*b*) is personally involved in the development of his or her own faith, and (*c*) makes a commitment to grow in faith along with the student.

The academic and relational approaches are delineated here for the sake of clarity, but in reality, a marriage of the two approaches—a healthy blending of academic knowledge with the relational sharing of faith—is possible. Such a blending is precisely what this course seeks to provide. Nevertheless, it should be clearly stated here that the relational approach to faith is the primary approach used in this course. Academic knowledge is necessary to shed light on the personal experience of faith, but without that foundation of personal faith, academic knowledge is unappealing, if not groundless.

Witness of Faith

So faith is more than an intellectual commitment to a set of beliefs, doctrines, or religious practices. It is a developing response in love to the love of God. In the same sense, we must recognize that we are called to be more than teachers of religion, if by "teachers of religion" we mean teachers of creeds, moral codes, and religious traditions. We are ultimately called to be sharers of faith as well, and the implications of this are far-reaching.

Religion can be taught. It has been said—and perceptively so—that *faith* is caught, not taught. The seed of faith is a gift from God planted in the hearts of people, but that seed must be nourished and nurtured if it is to grow. Parents have the most responsibility to provide such care and encouragement. And the environment of the Catholic school offers a tremendous support to parents who conscientiously seek the faith growth of their children. But the teacher of religion courses, as a formal representative of the faith, is in a particularly strong position to influence the faith development of the students. This is even more true when the students are adolescents, who are often reacting against their past in an attempt to establish a personal identity. At this age, the students may look to the teacher for help in making the transition from childhood to adulthood.

Recognizing the religion teacher as a witness of faith poses some obvious and perhaps disconcerting questions for the conscientious teacher:
- How can I best present myself as a person of faith?
- To what degree can I share my own religious doubts and questions with the students?
- Am I primarily a representative of the Catholic Tradition or a witness to my own personal faith convictions—and what do I do if the two roles do not agree?

These are terribly difficult—and extremely important—questions.

Pursuing answers to such questions is usually not a purpose of a teaching manual. However, for this course, it is important to clearly state the following principles or realities that should be remembered as a teacher of religion strives to be a witness of faith:

1. If faith involves a developing love relationship between an individual person and God, it is clear that the experience of the relationship will be unique to each person. Though we can say that all Christians share the same faith in the sense of a mutual commitment to Jesus and his message, it is also true that each of us experiences the reality and implications of that commitment in personal ways.
2. Because of our unique experiences, it can be rightly said that each of us, as an individual Christian, reflects in a special way the creative power and wisdom of our God. You do this differently than anyone else does, and you reveal a facet of God that no other person in the history of the world or in its future will be able to reveal. This is the foundation for the sense of human dignity that is so much a part of Jesus' message.
3. One of the chief functions of a church is to facilitate the sharing of personal faith among the members and to provide opportunities to celebrate such personal experiences communally. If the church is to fulfill its purpose and its promise, therefore, it can do so only to the degree that individual Christians can openly and honestly share their own faith stories, their special and personal experiences of the revelation of God in and through their life.
4. The only way our young people will comprehend the relational dimension of Christian faith is by witnessing it in the lives of adult Christians. Young people need to see the faith lived and proclaimed in a personal way in the witness of parents and teachers and in the communal expressions of the faith community.

To clarify the importance of sharing your faith experience, recall, if you can, teachers who have particularly impressed you, who have made a real impact on your life. Recall as well effective public speakers you have heard—the kind of speakers who can capture the attention of a large audience. Pay close attention to those moments in a formal talk or presentation when the audience became particularly quiet and attentive. Most important of all, recall your own most fulfilling and exciting moments as a teacher. In all these cases, it is likely that there was a personal sharing between the teacher and the students or between the speaker and the audience. As soon as it is clear that a person is sharing more than facts and figures and more than book knowledge, as soon as it is clear that one is sharing one's self rather than simply one's ideas, the entire relationship takes on a different tone, and effective communication becomes possible. The good teacher is, above all, a master communicator, and what she or he communicates most is a person—herself or himself. "What you are speaks so loudly that I cannot hear what you are saying."

Suggestions for Effective Storytelling

Although our religious education is obviously based on revealed truths, the faith that we attempt to share can be conveyed only through our own convictions, our own personality, our own life. No teacher of religion will be effective until he or she can somehow share personal faith stories, about how he or she has come to terms with faith. The following suggestions are intended to help you effectively share a life experience—a story from your faith journey—in the context of a relatively formal educational setting (e.g., a religion class, retreat, or discussion group).

1. Your story must have clear purpose. In planning a lesson, always start from your intended conclusion—the point you want to teach—and then back up from there. What have you personally experienced that relates to that point?
2. Generally, the tone of the story should fit the lesson to be taught and should create the attitude you need for whatever will follow. For example, you will generally not want to tell a humorous story before prayer.
3. In preparing to tell a story from your life, you must get so in touch with your own experience that others will be able to "touch" it. Your story must flow from your life honestly, sincerely. Any phoniness will be rejected. God speaks in your real, everyday life, not in artificiality. Implied in this is the idea that good storytellers are persons of prayer, sensitive to the ongoing revelation of God in their personal life.
4. Practice your story! Good stories can be told a hundred times—and should be. Usually if a story does not go over well, it just needs better telling. Try different approaches, expressions, and so on. This is not a threat to spontaneity but a courtesy to your listeners.
5. Lead up to your story logically and make it fit in with the rest of your plan for the class. If it is presented out of context, it will lose impact.
6. As you begin to tell your story, relate the experience to the students' lives and concerns. This need not be done elaborately and will normally happen naturally, but it is important.
7. Give your story time to develop. The details are vital! Be sure to describe the atmosphere, the location, the people you were with—all the things that made the happening important to you in the first place.
8. At the conclusion of your story, clearly state the lesson to be learned, unless it is so evident that such an explanation is unnecessary. With young people, however, it is better not to assume that they get the point.

9. You may have discovered that your own personal stories are the most difficult for you to share, but these same stories may be the most important and compelling—the stories that you need to share. This is not to suggest that you should pour out your deepest secrets to your students, but you can hope to freely share some elements of your life journey.

APPENDIX 4

Suggestions for Effective Teaching

The teaching strategies in part 2 of this manual rely rather heavily on the experiential techniques used in contemporary education and on the discussion that such techniques are intended to generate. This does not negate the importance of the academic content of the course. Indeed, the student text itself has an abundance of cognitive and conceptual material, all of which will be covered more or less directly during the course. But techniques such as games, group exercises, and films can contribute dramatically to teaching effectiveness. This manual suggests a wide variety of these activities.

If the techniques in this manual are to be beneficial and effective, it is essential that you develop an ability to use them easily. A sensitivity to detail, a clear perception of intent, and an awareness of the need for good timing are all necessary elements in the effective use of group exercises. Skill in leading discussions is also crucial. Without effective discussion, many group exercises can degenerate into party games with no purpose or benefit. With effective discussion, the exercises can become enjoyable activities that lead to a deepening awareness of a particular topic.

Of course, most teachers already have a firm background in these pedagogical techniques. The points that follow here are merely reminders of general guidelines for conducting group exercises and discussions. Even the experienced teacher will occasionally forget the basics, and it is often this oversight that makes the difference between success and failure in the classroom.

General Principles for Conducting Class Sessions

1. **Be sure that the students understand the student text after they have read a section of it.** Ask if anyone has questions about what the author was explaining, whether any words or definitions were not clear, and so on. Obviously, for meaningful discussion to take place, the basic content of the student text must be grasped by the class. For that reason, another and perhaps more effective approach to assuring comprehension is to begin the session by asking some questions on the main points of the section. Review questions of this kind are found at the end of each section in the student text.

In some situations, a quiz can provide an incentive to both read and understand the material. While this practice does not reflect the pedagogical ideal of self-motivation, it may be a prudent measure. Questions for quizzes are provided in appendix 1 of this manual, "Sample Test Questions."

2. **Spend time determining in what areas and to what extent students disagree with the student text. Remember that voicing such disagreement should not only be allowed but also be encouraged.** As the teacher, you must discover where problems lie and which topics need greater attention. Once the students are convinced that constructive disagreement with the content is allowed, they usually will express it freely.

3. Discussion between peers plays a particularly important role. Studies show that peer interaction, especially when one group disagrees with another, does more to alter or to shape students' views than similar interaction with authority figures such as parents or teachers. For that reason, encourage debates whenever significant differences of opinion are involved. The teacher can both guide and participate in, but should never dominate, such debates.

4. It is always beneficial to keep the focus on the students' real world. Theorizing on issues that the students seldom if ever face will cause them to lose interest quickly. However, it is important to distinguish between theorizing on those issues and teaching the facts about them. As the facts are studied, most students come to discover how all of us are part of social, moral, and religious issues—a discovery that can motivate them to want to learn more and to see how they can be part of a solution.

5. On sensitive issues, no student should be forced to speak if she or he prefers not to. The teacher should not hesitate to invite and encourage the students to probe more deeply. However, it should be understood by the teacher and the class that students can simply say that they prefer not to comment at the time.

6. Class discussion will raise some issues that are not addressed in the student text. It is important that issues raised by the students be dealt with properly. One approach would be to treat each of these issues as it comes up. This can be unwieldy, though. A more orderly approach (and often more effective to any discussion of these topics) might be to recognize the issues when they are raised and then design a later class session to deal with them. This allows you and the students to do some thinking in preparation for discussing the issues.

7. Discussion of an issue should not be put off if the majority of the students show a keen interest or if it is relevant to the situations they face. Usually until an especially timely topic has been satisfactorily discussed, the students will show little interest in whatever else is pursued. If a real concern is expressed by only one or two students, you can perhaps arrange to discuss it with them privately outside of class.

8. Begin each class session with time for review and reports. Also, try to include prayer, however brief, in each session.

9. Finally, keep in mind that this course is meant to be only one more step in the students' faith journey. Your task is not to lead your students to a profound sense of commitment to Jesus. Rather, the intent of the course is that they become familiar with and reflect on the basics of Christology with an honest sense of searching that is appropriate to young adolescents. If you have achieved that, you have succeeded in teaching the course. The rest is up to God and to the individual student.

Effective Use of Group Exercises

1. Make sure that you understand thoroughly the purpose of each exercise. Any exercise could be used to bring out a number of points; be sure that you know precisely where you want to go with the experience.

2. Complete the exercise yourself before conducting it with the class. At times this may be difficult, as in the case of an exercise that requires group involvement. However, you can still experience it, with some imagination and effort. In cases where a handout will be used, go through each part of the handout completely, reacting not only as an individual but as you imagine the students themselves will react.

3. Have all the materials required for the exercise available and ready for use. Do not let some minor problem, such as an inadequate number of copies of a handout, ruin the entire experience.

4. Try to set the appropriate mood in the class before introducing the exercise. For example, if the exercise is going to be loose and intentionally humorous, set the proper tone with a joke or a casual welcoming. If silence during the exercise will be critical, begin setting a quiet tone even before conducting the exercise.

5. Explain the directions and then ask for feedback. Students can be staring right at you, apparently attentive, and yet be miles away in their thoughts. When you get the feeling that they are distant from you, say something like, "Does everyone know what I mean? Dave, do you know? How about you, Beth?" Then, if indicated by a student's response, re-explain the directions. More exercises are wasted because of a lack of attention and understanding than for any other reason.

6. Despite the need for clear directions, do not get trapped by over-explaining. Too many details can so influence the students' response that nothing will be gained by the exercise.

7. Always stress the need for cooperation. Emphasize that nothing will be gained, nor will the students have any fun, if they fail to go along with the exercise. Normally students will become progressively more cooperative during the course, as they realize how enjoyable exercises can be when they work together. At the beginning of the course, however, you might have to stress the importance of cooperating.

8. When the purpose of the exercise is to create certain emotions in the students, time the exercise in such a way that these emotions are heightened as the exercise progresses. The key is to do the exercise yourself, when possible, to get a feel for this.

9. Go immediately into discussion at the close of the exercise. If you wait too long or allow other conversations to start, you might lose the attention of the group.

10. Be patient with yourself. You will learn a great deal from your first experience with an exercise; by the time you have conducted it several times, you will have mastered it and will have adjusted the details to fit your personality, the environment in the room, and so on. Each time, you will be more relaxed, you will enjoy the exercise more, and your students will gain more from the experience.

Leading Discussions

Discussion, as a learning technique, may refer to a teacher-centered discussion involving an entire class or to the placement of students into small groups ranging in number from pairs to eights. Naturally, guidelines for effective discussion vary, depending on the size of the group.

The following are general guidelines applicable to both large- and small-group discussions:

1. Do not expect discussion to do what it cannot do or is not intended to do. Discussion must be seen as one part of a much larger learning experience or process.

2. Discussion is primarily a reaction to a stimulus. The students need something real and tangible to discuss. This course is designed so that discussions are normally introduced by a group exercise, a reflection activity, an assigned reading, a handout, or some other input. The discussion will only be as effective as the activity that motivates it.

3. Discussion works only if the students are interested in, excited about, and knowledgeable about what is to be discussed. You cannot expect ninth graders, for example, to have a good discussion on the commitment required in marriage. Their level of knowledge and experience might only allow a discussion on relating with the other sex.

4. Specific questions are more effective than vague ones in stimulating discussion. For example, rather than asking, "What do you think of the film we just viewed?" a teacher could say, "What three important points did this film make?"

5. Discussions should have a definite time limit. Be stingy—let the students ask for more time if they want or need it.

6. Let each student have a chance to talk. Remember, though, that putting undue pressure on those who are shy will only make them more reluctant to participate.

7. Do not mistake silence for disinterest. At times, students will have nothing to say, simply because they are thinking through the question at hand. Though silence can be frustrating and can cause tension, it is often this very tension that will spark a response later.

8. If the students seem particularly mature or demonstrate a genuine attitude of cooperation, it is often helpful to let them choose their own discussion groups. In this way, initial nervousness or discomfort in the groups is dispelled, and the group members can get right into the matter at hand. If the class is not cooperative, the students may have to be assigned to groups, although discussion—almost by definition—will not work well when an uncooperative attitude persists. Some other form of sharing (e.g., a project to work on) might be necessary in such a situation.

9. Usually each small group should appoint a student recorder to take notes and report to the class.

10. The teacher should participate directly only at the end of the discussion. The teacher's role until that time is to stimulate interest and ask questions. At the end of the discussion, the teacher's own ideas and attitudes can be offered by way of summary. If the teacher gives direct input too readily, he or she can become the focus of the discussion, someone to whom the students are always looking for information.

11. Always close a discussion with a summary of the points raised, in order to highlight them.

APPENDIX 5

An Annotated Bibliography on Christology

In teaching *Jesus of History, Christ of Faith,* you may occasionally want to deepen your understanding of some of the theology incorporated into the course, or you may want to respond to new issues that emerge from your work with the material. Briefly described here are the resources that I, the author, have found particularly helpful in my work on this course.

It is common in teaching manuals for the author to provide a bibliography of resources. The problem with most such lists, I believe, is that they are *so* comprehensive that they are either overwhelming in length or impossible to interpret. I want to avoid such problems here, but I am also well aware that the publication of exciting material on Christology has virtually exploded in recent years. Even as I write this, reviews of impressive new works on Christology lay on my desk. I cannot help but wonder if this course would have been in some way affected by the books if only I had been able to read them. I guess that in itself explains why periodic revisions of texts are needed.

The fact is, at some point both the author and the teacher have to say, "This is the best and most helpful material I have available now, and I'll trust that it is sufficient." Therefore, the list of books you find here does not pretend to be exhaustive, and it may fail to include one or more of your favorite resources. Yet it is the best I can do, and I trust it will more than meet the needs of most teachers.

I have rather arbitrarily divided this bibliography into categories. (Some of the books listed may well fit into two or more of the categories.) I have also attempted to order the books in each category in terms of relevance to this course as well as according to relative difficulty. So as you move through the list for each category, the books will tend to become more challenging. In no case, however, is any book in this bibliography beyond the ability of the average high school teacher. I tend to distrust books that are so esoteric that multiple readings are required before one can even guess the author's intent, let alone comprehend it!

Developing *Jesus of History, Christ of Faith* has been extremely enriching and gratifying for me, in large part because it has motivated me to diligently read and study the kind of material recommended here. The Jews have long recognized study as an integral part of their spirituality, viewing it as not only a necessary companion of prayer but as a form of prayer in and of itself. I encourage you to pick up some of these books, to read them both for their benefit to you as a teacher and for the source of enjoyment and prayer they can be to you as an adult Christian. Be prepared, however, to change in some way, large or small, since every new insight into Jesus inevitably calls us to growth.

The Scriptures and Theology in General

Brown, Raymond E., Joseph A. Fitzmyer, and Roland E. Murphy, eds. *The New Jerome Biblical Commentary.* Englewood Cliffs, NJ: Prentice Hall, 1990. Respected as perhaps the most ambitious and accurate commentary on the entire Bible by Catholic scriptural scholars. Virtually verse-by-verse commentary on each book of the Bible, complemented by superb essays on the greater areas of interest. Whenever I encountered a point of theology on which scholars considerably disagree—and in Christology, that is a frequent occurrence!—I relied upon *The New Jerome Biblical Commentary* for the final word.

Senior, Donald, ed. *The Catholic Study Bible.* New York: Oxford University Press, 1990. Contains the entire New American Bible (the preferred translation for Catholic liturgy) along with extensive study materials written by highly regarded Catholic scholars. Included among its helpful resources are an outline of biblical history, reading guides for every book of the Bible, and clearly written articles.

McKenzie, John L. *Dictionary of the Bible.* New York: Macmillan Publishing, 1965. A classic reference work. Though published more than twenty-five years ago, it is still mentioned in virtually every scholar's list of "must have" resources. You will find brief articles on every biblical topic you are likely to encounter in your work with this course.

McBrien, Richard P. *Catholicism.* Vol. 1. Minneapolis: Winston Press, 1980. A major scholarly achievement when first published, it is still an invaluable reference work for any teacher of Catholic theology. Written with excellent clarity, theological balance, and solid scholarship. Of particular interest for teachers of this course is part 3, "Jesus Christ," and more specifically, chapter 15, "Special Questions in Christology." The superb index allows one to locate a brief, clear presentation on nearly any topic in Catholic theology. I would not attempt to develop or teach a religion course without this book.

Christ in the New Testament

Senior, Donald. *Jesus: A Gospel Portrait.* Dayton, OH: Pflaum Publishing, 1975. Beautifully written and summarizes the best in a scripturally rooted Christology. You may now have to look in a library rather than a bookstore to find this resource, but it was so influential and helpful in my writing of the first edition of the student text that I could not resist including it here. I would particularly recommend this book for novices in the challenging area of Christology.

Perkins, Pheme. *Reading the New Testament: An Introduction.* Rev. ed. New York: Paulist Press, 1988. A very accessible introduction to the Christian Testament, including helpful background on the world and life of Jesus and a thorough index of themes for easy reference. A popular text for undergraduate college courses.

Neyrey, Jerome H. *Christ Is Community: The Christologies of the New Testament.* Wilmington, DE: Michael Glazier, 1985. A biblical study of the various understandings of Jesus presented in the Christian Testament.

Richard, Earl. *Jesus: One and Many.* Wilmington, DE: Michael Glazier, 1988. Subtitled "The Christological Concept of New Testament Authors," this book is similar in intent to Neyrey's *Christ Is Community* but considerably more comprehensive and at times more challenging. This is not particularly easy reading, yet I was often struck by Richard's fine writing ability—not a common trait among scholars!

Contemporary Issues in Christology

Johnson, Elizabeth A. *Consider Jesus: Waves of Renewal in Christology.* New York: Crossroad, 1990. I was impressed with this little book as a highly readable yet well-grounded presentation of major trends in contemporary Christology. Its chapters deal with current theological positions on such issues as the humanity of Jesus, his self-knowledge, liberation and feminist Christologies, and so on. If I had to recommend just one book for someone wanting to know where the church currently stands in its understanding of Jesus, this would be the one.

Two highly regarded Catholic biblical scholars have written concise question-and-answer books—almost pamphlets—on current issues in scriptural study and Christology. Along with McBrien's section "Special Questions in Christology," in *Catholicism,* volume 1, these books will equip you to respond effectively to almost any theological questions on Christology that might arise in this course:

Brown, Raymond E. *Responses to 101 Questions on the Bible.* New York: Paulist Press, 1990. Brown, a popular scholar, has lectured on the Bible to literally thousands of audiences all over the world. In many of those presentations, he has held a question-and-answer period. This small book collects his responses to the most common questions about the Bible that have been raised by his audiences.

Fitzmyer, Joseph A. *A Christological Catechism: New Testament Answers.* New York: Paulist Press, 1982. Fitzmyer, an eminent scholar and one of the editors of *The New Jerome Biblical Commentary,* gives succinct answers to twenty major questions asked about the scriptural understanding of Jesus. For example: How much can we claim to know about the historical Jesus? How do contemporary scholars interpret the miracle stories? This book also contains the text of the very important document "Instruction on the Historical Truth of the Gospels," issued by the Pontifical Biblical Commission in 1964 (see the reference to this document on p. 16 of this manual, in my essay on Christology).

Paul: His Letters and Theology

Plevnik, Joseph. *What Are They Saying About Paul?* New York: Paulist Press, 1986. Part of a popular series of short works on contemporary theology, this small book summarizes current theological positions on themes such as Paul's Damascus experience, Paul's theology of justification by faith, and so on.

The following three books attempt to achieve essentially the same goals as one another with, naturally, different perspectives and writing styles. Each author claims to be presenting an introduction to Paul's letters and theology. Each also provides background on Paul's life and ministry and then a commentary on each of his letters. As mentioned earlier, I have listed the books in order of depth and difficulty, beginning with the easiest and recognizing that this is a subjective judgment. I personally found Marrow's book to be written in the most engaging style.

Soards, Marion L. *The Apostle Paul: An Introduction to his Writings and Teaching.* New York: Paulist Press, 1987.

Flanagan, Neal. *Friend Paul: His Letters, Theology and Humanity.* Wilmington, DE: Michael Glazier, 1986.

Marrow, Stanley B. *Paul: His Letters and His Theology.* New York: Paulist Press, 1986.

APPENDIX 6

A Pretest: "The Good News: Did We Hear It?"

This is a pretest on the content of the Gospels, particularly the synoptic Gospels. It is intended to serve several functions:
1. to raise the students' consciousness of all they know—and all they have yet to learn—about Jesus as he is presented in the Gospels
2. to introduce and outline the Gospels' (particularly the synoptics') portrait of Jesus as it is presented in *Jesus of History, Christ of Faith*
3. to provide a tool for measuring the effectiveness of the course

The pretest asks a combination of true-or-false, fill-in-the-blank, and multiple-choice questions, all generally organized in the sequence of the student text material. The correct answers are given here, so you will need to type up the pretest without answers and duplicate it as a student handout. The students are to complete the test individually first, and then the class can correct it as a means of promoting discussion. Afterward, you should collect and save all the test papers. By repeating the test at the end of the course, both you and the students will have a solid measure of how much they have learned.

Another approach to this pretest, which would not require handing out individual test papers, would be to ask the questions of the class orally, giving the students a chance to see how much they as a class know about Jesus.

The Good News: Did We Hear It?

Part A: True or False

- _f_ 1. There are 365 Gospels, one for each day of the year.
- _f_ 2. The Gospels are biographies, or life stories, of Jesus.
- _t_ 3. The word *gospel* comes from a word meaning "good news."
- _f_ 4. All of the Gospels were written within twenty-five years of Jesus' death.
- _t_ 5. The Gospels are not as concerned with historical facts as they are with the meaning behind certain events.
- _f_ 6. Abraham, Isaac, and Jacob lived about 150 years before Jesus.
- _t_ 7. In Jewish history, the special bond or relationship between God and the people is known as a covenant.
- _f_ 8. The Ten Commandments were given to the Israelites as a punishment for their sinfulness.
- _f_ 9. Prophets get their title from their ability to make wise investments.
- _f_ 10. God gave the name *Jew* to the Israelites when they were given the Ten Commandments.
- _t_ 11. The Temple of Jerusalem was so large that it could hold thousands of priests and tens of thousands of believers at once.
- _f_ 12. The Jewish priests of Jesus' time were popular and respected by the common people.

_f_ 13. The most important Jewish feast is Christmas.
_t_ 14. The Jewish Sabbath is observed from Friday evening through the daylight hours of Saturday.
_t_ 15. Both Christian and Jews have a feast called "Pentecost."
_f_ 16. The favorite beverage of the ancient Jewish people was a hearty variety of beer.
_f_ 17. The Jewish people ate their meals at precisely the same times each day, in keeping with their strict religious laws.
_t_ 18. Jewish girls most often married at about age thirteen.
_f_ 19. One of the great features of the ancient Jewish society was equality between men and women.
_t_ 20. One of the main reasons that Jesus' society rejected him was that he challenged and condemned many of its values and practices.
_f_ 21. The fact that Jesus was raised in Galilee made his fellow Jews respect him.
_t_ 22. When Jesus told the story of the good Samaritan, many people were shocked and offended.
_t_ 23. The Sadducees were powerful members of the Jewish aristocracy.
_t_ 24. Many ancient Jews expected the Messiah to be a warrior who would overthrow the Romans by military means.
_f_ 25. All of the Gospels tell the story of Jesus' birth.
_f_ 26. From historical records, we can determine the exact date of Jesus' birth.
_f_ 27. The Gospels often mention Jesus' love for the Pharisees.
_f_ 28. Jesus probably demonstrated magical powers even as a child.
_t_ 29. The story of Jesus' temptation in the desert illustrates his human struggle to decide on the values that would guide his life.
_f_ 30. Nearly all of the Apostles were educated men, respected for their knowledge of the Jewish Law.
_t_ 31. Jesus revealed a new understanding of God, referring to God with the equivalent of our word *Daddy*.
_f_ 32. The Gospels record Jesus' words just as he spoke them nearly two thousand years ago.
_t_ 33. Jesus' parables often had a surprise ending, which would catch his listeners off-guard.
_f_ 34. The parables, though they taught helpful lessons in Jesus' day, do not have much to offer modern readers.
_t_ 35. Some of Jesus' miracles may be explained today through our understanding of science and psychology.
_t_ 36. Jesus' miracles make sense only if we understand his vision of the Kingdom of God.
_f_ 37. Jesus performed miracles primarily to prove to nonbelievers that he was God.
_f_ 38. The Jewish and Roman leaders had no logical reasons for wanting to execute Jesus.
_t_ 39. At the Last Supper, Jesus made a connection between his death on the cross and the ritual of sharing a meal.
_t_ 40. Judas may not have been such an evil person after all.
_f_ 41. Jesus only pretended to be afraid of his death, because he knew all along that his Father would save him.
_t_ 42. Jesus was condemned to death for the political offense of inciting a revolt and the religious offense of blasphemy.
_f_ 43. In the Gospels we find detailed historical accounts of Jesus' resurrection.
_f_ 44. The disciples knew that when Jesus died he would come back to life, so they were not afraid.

__t__ 45. If the Resurrection had not happened, the Gospels would not have been written.
__f__ 46. Jesus is in heaven now, but someday he will be present among us again.
__t__ 47. Jesus did not organize the church or even imagine it as it is today.
__f__ 48. The most popular title for Jesus in his day was *Son of God*.
__f__ 49. The Nicene Creed, often recited at Mass, was written about 150 years ago.
__f__ 50. Catholics differ from Protestants primarily in their understanding of and teaching about Jesus.

Part B: Fill in the Blank

1. The editors or authors of the Gospels, who are commonly referred to by name, are also known as <u>the Evangelists</u>.
2. The Acts of the Apostles is actually a sequel to or second part of the Gospel written by <u>Luke</u>.
3. In terms of religion, Jesus was a faithful <u>Jew</u>.
4. Jewish history began nearly two thousand years before Jesus, with a man named <u>Abraham</u>.
5. <u>Moses</u> led the Israelites out of slavery in Egypt.
6. The greatest king in Jewish history was <u>David</u>.
7. <u>Jerusalem</u> was the holiest city in ancient Palestine.
8. In Jesus' time and today, a local house of prayer and study of the Jewish Scriptures has been called <u>a synagogue</u>.
9. Jesus learned and practiced the trade of <u>carpentry</u>.
10. Jesus was born in the town of <u>Bethlehem</u> and raised in the village of <u>Nazareth</u>.
11. Another word for "Jewish teacher" is <u>rabbi</u>.
12. The Greek term for the Hebrew word *Messiah* is <u>the Christ</u>.
13. The common religious ritual of bathing in water is called <u>baptism</u>.
14. The unifying theme in all of Jesus' teaching is his vision of <u>the Kingdom of God</u>.
15. The special stories Jesus used in teaching are called <u>parables</u>.
16. The "casting out" of a demon from a possessed person is called <u>an exorcism</u>.
17. The religious ritual based on the Last Supper is referred to today as <u>the Eucharist</u> or <u>the Mass</u>.
18. The Roman official who was most involved in the trial and execution of Jesus was <u>Pontius Pilate</u>.
19. The event in which Jesus passed totally into the presence of God is called <u>the Ascension</u>.
20. The event often referred to as the birthday of the church, when the gift of the Holy Spirit was poured out upon the first Christians, is called <u>Pentecost</u>.

Part C: Multiple Choice
In the spaces provided, check the proper answer or answers for each question.

1. Which of the following men are called "patriarchs"?
   - ✓ Jacob
   - ___ King David
   - ___ Isaiah
   - ✓ Abraham
   - ___ Adam
   - ✓ Isaac

2. The Hebrew name for God was
   - ___ Elijah
   - ___ Allah
   - ✓ Yahweh
   - ___ the Trinity

3. The land of Jesus, called Palestine, was roughly the size of
   - ___ California
   - ___ Canada
   - ✓ Massachusetts
   - ___ Australia

4. What are the names of the Gospels?
   - ✓ Luke
   - ___ Paul
   - ✓ Matthew
   - ✓ John
   - ___ Peter
   - ✓ Mark
   - ___ Timothy

5. Check all of the following that are acceptable definitions of sin:
   - ✓ freely chosen, personal actions that hurt us and others
   - ✓ social evils that affect all people
   - ___ physical pain and suffering

Handout Masters

List of Photocopy Masters

Lesson Planning Chart

Handouts

- 1–A To Know Another

- 2–A A Reference Guide to the Gospel Story

- 3–A The Samaritan Woman at the Well

- 4–A Searching the Scriptures for the World of Jesus

- 5–A Jesus' Priorities

- 6–A Who Is Your God?
- 6–B The Consequences of Moral Decisions

- 7–A Paraphrasing the Sermon on the Mount: The Beatitudes
- 7–B Paraphrasing the Sermon on the Mount: Being Salt and Light
- 7–C Paraphrasing the Sermon on the Mount: Loving Your Enemy
- 7–D Paraphrasing the Sermon on the Mount: Not Being a Hypocrite
- 7–E Paraphrasing the Sermon on the Mount: How to Pray
- 7–F Paraphrasing the Sermon on the Mount: Not Judging Others
- 7–G Paraphrasing the Sermon on the Mount: Hearing and Acting on the Word of God

- 10–A The Disciples' Dilemma
- 10–B The Titles for Jesus

- 12–A The Ideal Church: Romans, Chapter 12

- 13–A Helping the Church of Today and Tomorrow
- 13–B The Nicene Creed Today
- 13–C The Sermon of the Mouse

Lesson Planning Chart

Date, Class	Major Concept	Text Pages	Activities	Homework Assignment	Evaluation

To Know Another

Listed below are twenty-eight items of information that we might be able to discover about another person. In column A, rank the items in terms of how important it would be to discover each of them if you wanted to develop a deep friendship with someone. Use **1** for the most important item to discover, **2** for the second most important, and so on. Then your teacher will tell you what to do with columns B and C.

A	Item	B	C
_____	1. The amount of money they have	_____	_____
_____	2. Their favorite sport	_____	_____
_____	3. How they feel in a large group	_____	_____
_____	4. Their favorite color	_____	_____
_____	5. What they like most about themselves	_____	_____
_____	6. What grade school they attended	_____	_____
_____	7. What makes them cry	_____	_____
_____	8. Where they were born	_____	_____
_____	9. Who their best friend is	_____	_____
_____	10. What makes them feel secure	_____	_____
_____	11. Their favorite subject in school	_____	_____
_____	12. What they are afraid of	_____	_____
_____	13. What they would like to change about themselves	_____	_____
_____	14. Their favorite food	_____	_____
_____	15. How many brothers and sisters they have	_____	_____
_____	16. What makes them angry	_____	_____
_____	17. Whether they like little kids	_____	_____
_____	18. How they get along with their parents	_____	_____
_____	19. Their height, weight, and hair color	_____	_____
_____	20. Whether they believe in God	_____	_____
_____	21. Their birth date	_____	_____
_____	22. What makes them laugh	_____	_____
_____	23. What makes them feel lonely	_____	_____
_____	24. What they value most in life	_____	_____
_____	25. Their favorite time of day	_____	_____
_____	26. What makes them feel loved	_____	_____
_____	27. Their favorite TV program	_____	_____
_____	28. Their favorite hobby	_____	_____

A Reference Guide to the Gospel Story

A Partial Listing of Jesus' Miracles

Cleansing a leper (Matthew 8:1–4)

Healing a centurion's servant (Luke 7:1–10)

Calming a storm (Matthew 8:23–27)

Healing a paralytic (Mark 2:1–12)

Restoring life to Jairus's daughter (Luke 8:40–56)

Healing two blind men (Matthew 9:27–31)

Multiplying loaves (Mark 6:30–44)

Walking on water (Mark 6:45–52)

Healing a deaf man (Mark 7:31–37)

Healing the blind man of Bethsaida (Mark 8:22–26)

Healing a boy with a demon (Luke 9:37–42)

Cleansing ten lepers (Luke 17:11–19)

Cursing a barren fig tree (Matthew 21:18–22)

Changing water to wine at Cana (John 2:1–12)

Raising Lazarus (John 11:1–44)

A Partial Listing of Jesus' Parables

The sower (Matthew 13:1–23)

The weeds among the wheat (Matthew 13:24–30)

The wedding banquet (Matthew 22:1–14)

The faithful servant (Matthew 24:45–51)

The ten bridesmaids (Matthew 25:1–13)

The talents, or sums of money (Matthew 25:14–30)

The great feast (Luke 14:15–24)

The wicked tenants (Mark 12:1–12)

The mustard seed (Mark 4:30–32)

The good Samaritan (Luke 10:25–37)

The house built on rock (Matthew 7:24–27)

The rich man and Lazarus (Luke 16:19–31)

The rich fool (Luke 12:16–21)

The lost sheep (Matthew 18:12–14)

The prodigal son (Luke 15:11–32)

The unjust servant (Luke 16:1–13)

The laborers in the vineyard (Matthew 20:1–16)

The Pharisee and the tax collector (Luke 18:9–14)

Some of Jesus' Most Significant Teachings

The Beatitudes (Matthew 5:3–12)

Salt of the earth (Matthew 5:13)

Attitude toward sinners (Luke 15:1–32)

God and money (Matthew 6:19–34)

The vine and the branches (John 15:1–8)

The greatest commandment (Matthew 22:34–40)

The true disciple (Matthew 19:16–22)

Forgiveness of injuries (Matthew 18:21–22)

Finding life by losing it (Matthew 16:24–26)

God revealed in the simplicity of children (Mark 10:13–16)

Not judging others (Luke 7:36–50)

How to pray (Matthew 6:5–13)

The Last Judgment (Matthew 25:31–46)

Trust in God (Luke 12:22–31)

The gift of the Spirit (John 16:5–14)

Some Important Gospel Events

Jesus' birth in Bethlehem (Luke 2:1–20)

The boy Jesus lost in the Temple (Luke 2:41–50)

Jesus' baptism (Matthew 3:13–17)

The temptation in the desert (Luke 4:1–13)

The calling of the Apostles (Matthew 4:18–22)

Picking corn on the Sabbath (Matthew 12:1–8)

Dinner at Simon's house (Luke 7:36–50)

Jesus' conversation with the Samaritan woman at the well (John 4:4–30)

Jesus' conflicts with the Pharisees (Matthew 23:1–39)

The rejection of Jesus at Nazareth (Matthew 13:54–58)

The cleansing of the Temple (John 2:13–17)

Peter's confession of faith (Matthew 16:13–20)

The Transfiguration (Matthew 17:1–9)

The entry into Jerusalem (Mark 11:1–10)

The Last Supper (Luke 22:7–38)

The agony in the garden (Mark 14:32–42)

The arrest and trial of Jesus (Mark 14:43–65; 15:1–15)

The Crucifixion (Matthew 27:32–56)

The Resurrection (Matthew 28:1–10)

The post-Resurrection appearances (Luke 24:13–49)

The Ascension (Luke 24:50–53)

The Samaritan Woman at the Well

Characters: Narrator, Jesus, Woman, Disciple

Narrator: Jesus was journeying northward from Judaea to Galilee, and he had to pass through Samaria on the way. Samaria was near the village of Sychar on the piece of property that Jacob had given to his son Joseph. Tired from the long walk in the hot sun, Jesus sat down beside a well while his disciples went into the village to buy food. A Samaritan woman came to the well to draw water.

Jesus: Would you give me a drink of water?

Woman: You are a Jew, and I am a Samaritan. How can you ask me for a drink?

Narrator: The Jews usually would not even speak to Samaritans, much less drink from the same cup.

Jesus: If you only knew what wonderful gift God could give you and who I am, you would ask me for some living water.

Woman: But you don't even have a bucket, and this is a deep well. Where would you get living water? Besides, you surely are not greater than our ancestor Jacob. How can you offer better water than this which he and his family and his cattle drank?

Jesus: Everyone who drinks the water from this well will become thirsty again, but whoever drinks the water I will give him will never be thirsty again. For my gift will become a spring within him, which will provide him with living water and give him eternal life.

Woman: Please, sir, give me some of that water! Then I'll never be thirsty again and won't have to make this long trip out here to draw water.

Jesus: Go, get your husband, then come back here.

Woman: But I'm not married.

Jesus: You are telling the truth when you say you are not married. You have been married to five men, and the man you are living with now is not really your husband.

Woman: You must be a prophet, sir! But if I may ask a question, why do you Jews insist that Jerusalem is the only place of worship? We Samaritans, meanwhile, claim that where our ancestors worshiped—here at Mount Gerizim—is a fitting place.

Jesus: Believe me, ma'am, the time is coming when we will no longer be concerned about the *place* to worship the Father! For it's not where we worship that's important but how we worship. Worship must be spiritual and real, for God is Spirit and we must have his Spirit's help to worship as we should. The Father wants this kind of worship. But you Samaritans know so little about him, worshiping with yours eyes shut, so to speak. We Jews know all about him, for salvation comes to mankind through the Jewish race.

Woman: Well, at least I know that the Messiah will come—you know, the one they call the Christ—and when he does, he will make everything plain to us.

Jesus: I am the Messiah!

Narrator: Then the woman left her water pot beside the well, went back to the village, and excitedly told everyone about Jesus. Soon the people came streaming from the village to see him. In the meantime, the disciples had returned to Jesus. They had seen him talking to the Samaritan woman and were astonished, but they did not ask Jesus why nor ask him what he had said to the woman. Instead they urged Jesus to eat.

Disciple: Teacher, eat some of the food we bought.

Jesus: No. I have some food you don't know about.

Disciple [*to other disciples*]: Did someone else bring him food?

Jesus: My nourishment comes from doing the will of God, who sent me, and from finishing his work. Do you think the work of harvesting will not begin until the summer ends—four months from now? Open your eyes and look around you! Fields of human souls are ripening all around us, and they are ready for harvesting. The reaper of the harvest is being paid *now,* and he gathers the crops for eternal life; the planter and the reaper will be glad together, for in this harvest the old saying comes true: "One man plants and another reaps." I have sent you to harvest a crop in a field where you did not labor; others labored there, and you profit from their work.

Narrator: Many of the Samaritans in that town believed in Jesus because the woman had told them of his ability to know all things. So when the Samaritans came to him they begged him to stay with them, and Jesus stayed there two days. Many more believed because of Jesus' own words, and the villagers told the woman: "We believe now, not because of what you said but because we have heard him with our own ears and we know that he is the Savior of the world."

Reprinted from "Jesus Met a Woman (John 4)" in Wayne Rice, John Roberto, and Mike Yaconelli, editors, *Creative Learning Experiences* (Winona, MN: Saint Mary's Press, 1981), pages 104–106

Searching the Scriptures for the World of Jesus

Cut this handout along the dotted lines to form five slips of paper.

Geography and Climate

Go through your assigned Gospel and note all the occasions when the geography or climate of Palestine enters directly into the teachings of Jesus (that is, any time he refers to images of the land and its weather to make a point or teach a lesson). Record the chapter and verse references and brief descriptions of the occasions. You have 40 minutes.

Food and the Sharing of Meals

Go through your assigned Gospel and note all the occasions when Jesus refers to food or the sharing of meals in his teachings, and all the occasions when a meal is actually shared. Record the chapter and verse references and brief descriptions of the occasions. You have 40 minutes.

Family Life and Its Traditions

Go through your assigned Gospel and note all the occasions when Jesus refers to family life and its traditions (for example, marriage, child-rearing) in his teachings. Record the chapter and verse references and brief descriptions of the occasions. You have 40 minutes.

Housing and Occupations

Go through your assigned Gospel and note all the occasions when Jesus refers to the housing and various occupations of his people. Record the chapter and verse references and brief descriptions of the occasions. You have 40 minutes.

Social Classes

Go through your assigned Gospel and note all the occasions when Jesus refers to social classes—rich and poor people, slaves and free people, people in power and people without power—in his teachings. Record the chapter and verse references and brief descriptions of the occasions. You have 40 minutes.

Jesus' Priorities

For each value listed below, circle a number to indicate how much priority Jesus gave it in his ministry, from no priority at all to high priority. Your teacher will tell you what to do next.

No Priority High Priority	Value	Passage
0 1 2 3 4 5 6 7 8 9 10	**a.** Elimination of all laws	_____
0 1 2 3 4 5 6 7 8 9 10	**b.** Accumulation of material goods	_____
0 1 2 3 4 5 6 7 8 9 10	**c.** Public approval of one's faith	_____
0 1 2 3 4 5 6 7 8 9 10	**d.** Fair punishment for all offenses	_____
0 1 2 3 4 5 6 7 8 9 10	**e.** Avoidance of bad company	_____
0 1 2 3 4 5 6 7 8 9 10	**f.** Recognition for good deeds	_____
0 1 2 3 4 5 6 7 8 9 10	**g.** Speaking openly about one's convictions	_____
0 1 2 3 4 5 6 7 8 9 10	**h.** Intellectual ability	_____
0 1 2 3 4 5 6 7 8 9 10	**i.** Self-preservation	_____
0 1 2 3 4 5 6 7 8 9 10	**j.** Power over others	_____

Scriptural Passages

1. Matthew 5:11–12
2. Matthew 20:25–28
3. Matthew 9:10–13
4. Matthew 6:19–21
5. Matthew 10:26–31
6. Matthew 11:25–26
7. Matthew 16:24–26
8. Matthew 5:17–19
9. Matthew 5:38–42
10. Matthew 6:1–4

Who Is Your God?

Listed below are twenty-four possible understandings of God. Some of them you may have already heard, and some of them may be new to you. Put a check mark in the blank next to each understanding that you agree with. Then your teacher will give you further directions.

___ 1. The only one who loves me for myself

___ 2. The computer that programmed the universe

___ 3. A puppeteer who manipulates people as if they were toys

___ 4. An energy that is hinted at when a baby is born or when we fall in love

___ 5. A "world soul" that we are all a part of

___ 6. A creator who believes that all of creation is good

___ 7. A force that became inert sometime between when the world was created and today

___ 8. A parent who loves his or her children selflessly

___ 9. Someone who forgives my mistakes

___ 10. A being so beyond me that I cannot describe it

___ 11. Someone who loves us enough to die for us

___ 12. An eccentric being who created this world and then forgot all about it

___ 13. Someone who dares to let me be free

___ 14. A being who gave me life

___ 15. A lawgiver whose commands urge me to do right rather than wrong

___ 16. The future, the end of all human striving

___ 17. The type of being that humans will evolve into

___ 18. A ruler whose power is freedom and love rather than force

___ 19. A lover who urges me to come to the heavenly marriage feast

___ 20. An idea created by past generations to explain the world

___ 21. The peace that will reign when all persons are brothers and sisters

___ 22. The perfect one, who says that I am sinful and makes me feel guilty

___ 23. The one who wants me to be me

___ 24. A clown who created laughter by making human beings free

The Consequences of Moral Decisions

Our actions, decisions, and attitudes that are **loving** or **morally right** produce all or some of the following results in us or those we affect:

1. an increased ability to trust others
2. greater honesty in relationships
3. a lessened sense of separation from others; a breaking down of barriers
4. an increased attitude of cooperation
5. greater self-respect; the ability to look in the mirror and feel genuinely happy with oneself
6. a better attitude toward people in general; more confidence in the idea that people are really good
7. a feeling of peace and joy; a sense of doing what one is called to do and making the most of life

Our actions, decisions, and attitudes that are **selfish** or **morally wrong** produce all or some of the following results in us or those we affect:

1. a decreased ability to trust others; suspicion
2. phoniness in relationships; being two-faced
3. a sense of separation from others; a feeling of isolation
4. a decreased attitude of cooperation; trouble getting along with others
5. less self-respect; more guilt or embarrassment
6. difficulty in accepting others; a feeling that people are concerned only about themselves
7. a feeling that life is meaningless or hopeless

Two factors are closely related to the above sets of consequences and affect them in an important way:

First, when we talk about the breaking down of barriers between people (number 3), this means less separation and more unity between individuals. But this is also true of relationships between those individuals and others in the world around them. For example, a boy and a girl can be so "together" that they have no room for anyone else.

Second, in everything we do or decide, we have to be concerned not just with right now but also with what the long-range effects are going to be on ourselves and others. Each of us must ask, How will this affect me and others later on?

Paraphrasing the Sermon on the Mount: The Beatitudes

Matthew 5:1–12, NRSV

When Jesus saw the crowds, he went up the mountain; and after he sat down, his disciples came to him. Then he began to speak, and taught them, saying:

"Blessed are the _____,

   for theirs is the kingdom of heaven.

"Blessed are those who mourn,

   for they will _____.

"Blessed are the meek,

   for they will _____.

"Blessed are those who hunger and thirst for _____,

   for they will be filled.

"Blessed are the merciful,

   for they will _____.

"Blessed are the pure in heart,

   for they will _____.

"Blessed are the _____,

   for they will be called _____.

"Blessed are those who are persecuted for _____,

   for theirs is _____.

"Blessed are you when people [insult] you and persecute you and utter all kinds of evil against you falsely on my account. Rejoice and be glad, for

_____

_____."

Paraphrasing the Sermon on the Mount: Being Salt and Light

Matthew 5:13–16, NRSV

"You are the salt of the earth; but if salt has lost its taste, _____
_____?
It is no longer good for anything, but _____
_____.

"You are the light _____.
A city built on a hill cannot be hid. No one after lighting a lamp puts
_____
_____.

In the same way, let your light _____,
so that _____
_____."

Paraphrasing the Sermon on the Mount: Loving Your Enemy

Matthew 5:43–48, NRSV

"You have heard that it was said, 'You shall love your neighbor and _____
_____.'

But I say to you, Love your enemies and _____
_____,

so that you may _____
_____;

for [the Father] makes [the] sun rise on the evil and on the good, and sends
_____.

For if you love those who love you, _____
_____?

Do not even the tax collectors do the same? And if you _____
_____,

what more are you doing than others? Do not even the _____
do the same? Be _____, therefore, as your _____
_____."

Paraphrasing the Sermon on the Mount: Not Being a Hypocrite

Matthew 6:1–4, NRSV

"Beware of _____

in order to _____;

for then you have no _____.

   "So whenever you give _____, do not _____

_____, as the hypocrites do in the _____

_____, so that they may be _____

_____.

Truly I tell you, they have _____.

But when you give alms, _____

_____;

and your Father who _____

will _____."

Paraphrasing the Sermon on the Mount: How to Pray

Matthew 6:5–8, NRSV

"And whenever you pray, do not be like _____;
for they love to _____
_____, so that
_____.

Truly I tell you, they have received _____.
But whenever you pray, go into _____
_____
and pray to your Father who _____; and your Father who
_____ will _____.

"When you are praying, do not _____
_____;
for they think that they will be heard because _____.
Do not be like them, for your Father knows _____
_____."

Paraphrasing the Sermon on the Mount: Not Judging Others

Matthew 7:1–5, NRSV

"Do not judge, so that you may not _____.

For with the judgment you make you will _____,

and the measure you give _____.

Why do you see _____,

but do not notice _____?

Or how can you say to your neighbor, '_____
_____,'

while the _____?

You hypocrite, first take _____,

and then you will see clearly _____
_____."

> I WANT THAT EXHAUST PIPE FIXED ON THAT HEAP OF YOURS, SON! THAT THING PUTS OUT MORE POLLUTION THAN A FACTORY!!!

Paraphrasing the Sermon on the Mount: Hearing and Acting on the Word of God

Matthew 7:21–27, NRSV

"Not everyone who says to me, '_____,' will enter the kingdom of heaven, but only the one who _____ _____.

On that day many will say to me, '_____ _____ _____?'

Then I will declare to them, '_____ _____.'

   "Everyone then who hears these words of mine and acts on them will be like _____.
The rain fell, the floods came, and the winds blew and beat on that _____, but it did not fall, because it had been founded on _____.
And everyone who hears these words of mine and does not act on them will be like _____.
The rain fell, and the floods came, and the winds blew and beat against that _____, and it fell—and great was its fall!"

The Disciples' Dilemma

Imagine that you are one of the disciples who lived and worked with Jesus during his ministry in Palestine. You have just experienced the Last Supper, the trial and execution of Jesus, and now his resurrection from the dead. The question you face is, What do I do now? Below are some options that you have. Circle the number of the one that you feel is right for you and most in line with Jesus' message.

1. Go out into the streets and the synagogues to announce that Jesus is the Christ and that the people are to repent and believe in him.

2. Seek out the poor and oppressed people and search for ways to serve them.

3. Organize people who feel like you do into social-action groups.

4. Go off alone to pray and reflect on the meaning of the incredible events.

5. Organize classes to inform people about Jesus and the lessons you learned from him.

6. Begin work on a written record of what you have experienced, while the thoughts and feelings are still fresh in your memory.

7. Wait until someone tells you what to do.

8. Can you think of any other option? If so, write it down here.

_____

_____

The Titles for Jesus

Listed at the right are many of the titles given to Jesus in the Christian Scriptures. You are asked to do the following:

- In the column titled "Humanity or Divinity?" print an *H* next to each title that you think emphasizes Jesus' **humanity**. Print a *D* next to each title that you think emphasizes his **divinity** as God. Put a question mark next to any title you are unsure about.
- In the column titled "Before or After Death?" print a *B* next to each title that you think may have been given to Jesus **before** his death and resurrection. Print an *A* next to each title that you think he received only **after** his death and resurrection. Put a question mark next to any title you are unsure about.

Humanity or Divinity? — **Before or After Death?**

1. Lord
2. Servant of God
3. Holy One
4. Prince of Life
5. Messiah
6. Nazarene
7. Prophet
8. Judge of the living and the dead
9. Redeemer
10. Son of God
11. Savior
12. Master
13. Rabbi
14. Son of David
15. Son of Man
16. Bread of Life
17. Teacher
18. Christ
19. Good Shepherd
20. Son of Abraham
21. The new Adam
22. Firstborn of all creation
23. The Way, the Truth, and the Life
24. Image of God
25. God
26. The Anointed One
27. Son of Joseph
28. Lamb of God
29. Carpenter's son
30. Emmanuel
31. High Priest
32. Word of God

The Ideal Church: Romans, Chapter 12

1. Let love be genuine
2. hate what is evil
3. hold fast to what is good
4. love one another with mutual affection
5. outdo one another in showing honor
6. Do not lag in zeal
7. be ardent in spirit
8. serve the Lord
9. Rejoice in hope
10. be patient in suffering
11. persevere in prayer
12. Contribute to the needs of the saints
13. extend hospitality to strangers
14. Bless those who persecute you; bless and do not curse them
15. Rejoice with those who rejoice
16. weep with those who weep
17. Live in harmony with one another
18. do not be haughty, but associate with the lowly
19. do not claim to be wiser than you are
20. Do not repay anyone evil for evil
21. . . . take thought for what is noble in the sight of all
22. If it is possible, . . . live peaceably with all
23. . . . Never avenge yourselves
24. . . . "if your enemies are hungry, feed them"
25. "if [your enemies] are thirsty, give them something to drink"
26. Do not be overcome by evil, but overcome evil with good

Helping the Church of Today and Tomorrow

Spreading the Word

You are members of the church who are in charge of sharing Jesus' message with young people who do not know about him yet. Remember, you were there in the beginning; you saw Jesus and loved him and watched him die. You have faith in him, but some young people have never experienced him. Develop three means of letting them know about Jesus.

Worshiping

You as a group are responsible for the sacramental life of the church. Jesus left several signs of his presence to help the church carry on in memory of him and his message. How would you make the following experiences real and meaningful to other young people?

a. *Baptism:* How should young people be initiated into the church? Who should be initiated? What kind of preparation should they go through?

b. *The Eucharist:* When should the Eucharist be available? How often should we gather for it? How old should one be to participate?

c. *Orders:* Do we need priests? If so, how should we determine who is qualified for the priesthood? And what should a priest's responsibilities be?

d. *Penance:* Does the community need to recognize sin and evil and to be reconciled? If so, in what way?

Responding

The church is called by Jesus to be a witness to his values, particularly regarding poor and oppressed people. How should Christians respond in the following areas?

a. *War:* Should the church publicly oppose all war?

b. *Poverty:* Should wealthy nations share with nations less fortunate than they are, and if so, how? For example, should all members of the church in wealthy nations be required to give to a fund for the poor?

c. *Current social issues:* Should the church make a public stand on issues such as abortion, pornography, and the environment?

The Nicene Creed Today

Original	Personal	Group
We believe in one God, the Father, the Almighty,		
maker of heaven and earth, of all that is seen and unseen.		
We believe in one Lord, Jesus Christ, the only Son of God, eternally begotten of the Father,		
God from God, Light from Light, true God from true God, begotten, not made, one in Being with the Father. Through him all things were made.		
For us men and for our salvation he came down from heaven: by the power of the Holy Spirit he was born of the Virgin Mary, and became man.		
For our sake he was crucified under Pontius Pilate; he suffered, died, and was buried.		

Original	Personal	Group
On the third day he rose again in fulfillment of the Scriptures;		
he ascended into heaven and is seated at the right hand of the Father.		
He will come again in glory to judge the living and the dead, and his kingdom will have no end.		
We believe in the Holy Spirit, the Lord, the giver of life, who proceeds from the Father and the Son.		
With the Father and the Son he is worshiped and glorified. He has spoken through the Prophets.		
We believe in one holy catholic and apostolic Church. We acknowledge one baptism for the forgiveness of sins.		
We look for the resurrection of the dead, and the life of the world to come. Amen.		

The Sermon of the Mouse

The day had finally arrived. Everyone in the congregation was waiting expectantly. The negotiations had taken months, but finally everything had been worked out. It wasn't every congregation in the country that could have an opportunity like this. It was a rare visit from a very well-known celebrity.

The pastor and his guest mounted the platform. The first hymn was sung. Then the pastor rose. "I'm sure everyone is aware of who our guest speaker is this morning," he said.

Aware? How could anyone help being aware? There were posters all over town. There was a big yellow and black banner stretched across the entry to the parking lot. Seating in the sanctuary had been assigned on a reservation basis with preferential treatment given to members in good standing. An overflow crowd was watching the service on closed-circuit television. Everybody knew about it.

"It isn't often," said the pastor, "that we have an opportunity to meet someone who has become a legend in his own time. Starting back in the bleak years of the depression, with a shoestring budget and a very simple plan, our guest, with hard work and contagious enthusiasm, built an empire for himself that rivals that of Howard Hughes. His name is a household word; he is admired by young and old alike; and he has even survived his mentor. He reigns over a multimillion-dollar business venture that was so successful in southern California that he established an even more spectacular venture in Florida. By now, I'm sure you know who I am talking about. We are so honored to have Mickey Mouse with us today to share with us the secrets of Disneyland's success. We hope that our church will be stimulated and helped by his story."

A hush came over the congregation as this famous mouse rose to his feet, cleared his throat, and began his sermon.

"Thank you for inviting me to come to your church. I must admit that at first I was surprised that a church would ask me to give a sermon. Oh, I have been invited to religion classes where they give each person a Mickey Mouse hat and expect me to shake hands with everyone and act funny, but a sermon is something new.

"But after I thought about it, I realized that maybe Disneyland and the church did have a lot in common. As I began to organize my thoughts, I saw how ingenious it was to invite me to share. I really believe that if your church were to apply our principles you could become as successful as Disneyland.

"First, make sure your enterprise seems exciting, even dangerous; but be quick to let your people know that there really is no danger involved. *Give the illusion of great risk,* but make sure everything is perfectly safe.

"Second, admit that you are in the entertainment business. People won't care what you say as long as they're entertained. Keep your people happy. Don't tell them anything negative. And don't make demands on them. Just keep them diverted from the ugly reality of today's world, and they will keep coming back for more.

"Third, make everything look religious. Make the religious experience so elaborate, so intricate, so complex that only the professionals can pull it off and all the laypeople can do is stand around with their mouths open and watch. People would rather watch an imitation mechanical bird sing than a real bird, anyway. They would rather watch worship than do it.

"Fourth and finally, pretend that there are no problems. At Disneyland we dress up our security guards as smiling rabbits or friendly bears because we don't want anyone's experience at Disneyland to be ruined by the sight of law enforcement personnel. Disguise your problems and failures behind a warm smile and a firm handshake. Leave them at home, and let the church be a happy place where there aren't any ugly problems.

"People today want good, clean entertainment. They want an environment that is safe for children, and they want a place that is safe for their family and friends. I am so glad to see that the church is moving in this direction. Thank you, and God bless you."

Reprinted from Wayne Rice, John Roberto, and Mike Yaconelli, editors, *Creative Learning Experiences* (Winona, MN: Saint Mary's Press, 1981), pages 77–80